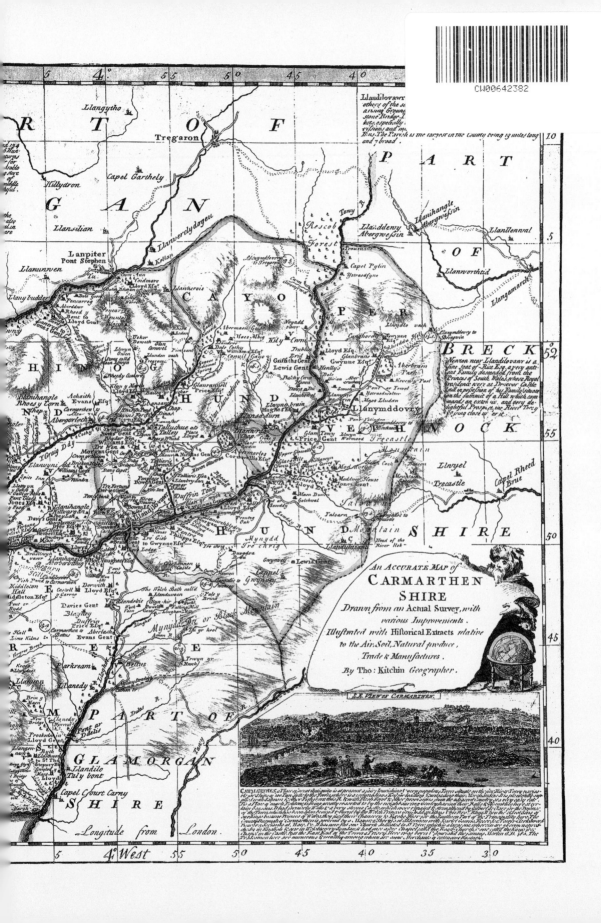

THE FRANCIS JONES TREASURY
OF
HISTORIC CARMARTHENSHIRE

Dedicated to the memory of Francis and Ethel Jones

The couple outside their Carmarthen home where they lived happy and productive lives from 1958 until their deaths.

Francis Jones used the following quotation to sum up his philosophy:

> *'Tis enough for me to have broken the ice; and I have gained my ends if I have set others about the same work, whether to write more or to amend what I have written.*
>
> Camden's *Britannia*

Major Francis Jones and his wife Ethel making final adjustments to Wales Herald's uniform. The regalia includes a silver collar of SS's, a jewel of office, and ivory baton. The Welsh people paid for the tabard by public subscription. It took the Royal College of Needlework a year-and-a-half to make.

THE FRANCIS JONES
Wales Herald at Arms 1963-1993

TREASURY
OF HISTORIC
CARMARTHENSHIRE

By MAJOR FRANCIS JONES,
C.V.O., T.D., D.L., F.S.A., M.A., K.St.J.
Late Wales Herald Extraordinary
1908 - 1993

Editor
CAROLINE CHARLES-JONES

Additional Material and Compilation
HUGH CHARLES-JONES

Published by
BRAWDY BOOKS, PEMBROKESHIRE
2002

Published by
Brawdy Books, Plas yr Wregin, Dinas, Newport
Pembrokeshire, SA42 0YH
Telephone: 01348 811450
www.brawdybooks.com
Email: *Plaswregin@aol.com*
info@brawdybooks.com

ISBN 0-9528344-64

Illustrations
Sylvia Gainsford
Leon Olin
Thomas Lloyd
Grenville Barrett, L.R.P.S.
National Library of Wales
Francis Jones Archives

Book Jacket Design
Hugh Charles-Jones

Design and Make-up
ARTdesigns
Meiros Hill, Felingwm Uchaf
Carmarthen SA32 7BB
Telephone 01267 290670
www.artdesigns.i12.com
artdesigns@hotmail.com

Printed and Bound by
Bath Press
Midsomer Norton

CONTENTS

PUBLISHER'S FOREWORD

THIS IS THE SIXTH BOOK my wife and I have published of my father's works. Yet this is less than a hundredth part of his massive archives. Nearly ten years after his death my awe of his achievements still grows. Even allowing a natural bias to a loved and admired parent, he still emerges as the Titan of Welsh historians. How did he accomplish this?

The Welsh oral tradition had much to do with it; combined with his God-given prodigious memory and his early ease with both the Welsh and English languages. His parents came of ancient families, rich with inherited family histories, genealogy and heraldry. His innate imagination seized upon this legacy, which, in turn, fired his curiosity, turning it into a lifelong passion. In his early teens he wrote and illustrated his local parish history during school holidays. His career had begun. With it came the knack of being in the right place at the right time, sometimes by luck, but mostly by design.

Whilst living near Haverfordwest castle in the late 1920s he rescued county records mouldering in a damp cell. Quite unaided he preserved and catalogued them, and so founded today's Public Record Office. Later he joined the National Library of Wales as a junior researcher. In later life he returned there as a Governor.

After active war service he went to the War Office in London to write a section of the Official War History. During fourteen years he also catalogued all Welsh MSS in the College of Arms. His researches took him to the Public Record Office, British Library, the records of the Hon. Society of the Cymmrodorion , and the Society of Antiquarians. All these places were within walking distance of his home. Not only was he an enthusiastic walker, but also he needed little sleep. He wrote in the early mornings, and often, into the small hours at night. His extraordinary time management became legendary.

He delved with the tenacity of a diamond prospector in many mines of recorded history. And all this apart from fieldwork in Wales tracking down oral traditions, legends, private family papers and half forgotten events in distant Welsh national memory. His learned interpretations made him as the Sherlock Holmes of Welsh historians.

Though neither a historian nor Doctor Watson, my duty as the eldest son is clear. My father often said "The duty of a historian is to make his findings open to all". In 54 years of marriage my dearest Mamma supported my father's work. My wife Caroline does the same for me. So as you read my father's work spare a thought for the two remarkable women who made our family publications a reality.

Hugh Charles-Jones

EDITOR'S PREFACE

WHEN WE STARTED to look out suitable material for this book, it was like dipping into a tin of mixed sweets and choosing at random. We have seven archive boxes full of Carmarthenshire genealogical material, essays and talks by Francis Jones. The breadth of his research and knowledge of the county, where he lived and worked for so many years, is astounding.

We have endeavoured to pick out a far-reaching selection of material to cover the wide spectrum of Carmarthenshire life and character. It has not been easy. At the eleventh hour I typed up the article on the Gwyns of Gwempa. Today I found another article – new to me, handwritten, and I seriously considered inserting it. Only the knowledge of the ire this would raise in the hearts of the typesetter, the indexer and my husband stopped me.

To Francis, every day was filled with boundless possibilities for further knowledge. No time was wasted, no encounter unproductive. Every sheet of paper in the archives is covered back and front, often between the lines of a set of Minutes of some august organisation, with spidery writing, setting down the results of a meeting with a Carmarthenshire person with their personal memories of family or home, or with notes for an article or pedigree. Francis would enter any driveway, knock at any door, always sure of a welcome. We find, as we retrace his footsteps, that this welcome is now given to us as we labour to publish just a small fraction of what we hold. We are very grateful for your support. Brawdy Books is not a huge faceless corporation; it is two people with a loyal and hardworking band of outworkers to whom we owe a great deal.

Caroline-Charles Jones
Brawdy Books, 2002

N.B. As usual you will have to accept that the Welsh spellings are given as Francis spelt them in the articles we print. There will be several variations of spellings, e.g. Iscennen, IsKennen, Is Cennen, Llandeilo and Llandilo. Francis used the spellings he found in primary source material for the article, or as it was spelt in that century or because that was his preferred version. This shows the evolution of Welsh spelling through time. It is as he wished.

Caroline Charles-Jones
24 September 2002

ACKNOWLEDGEMENTS

OUR BOOK has many descriptions of houses and family histories. In house building and genealogies there are myriad details, any of which if incorrect can collapse the undertaking. This applies particularly to book publishing as it involves many people in different roles. In this our sixth book of Francis Jones's work, our grateful thanks to:

Andy Taylor for vital contributions and hundreds of solitary hours of demanding toil at the computer screen, equalled only by his tenacity under great pressure.

Grenville Barrett, generous with his time, enthusiasm and his photographic talent. Pam Davies, a stalwart in coping with proof reading tedium. Penny David for her excellent and kind contribution on Aberglasney. David Fielding of Carmarthenshire Life magazine for unfailing loyalty to our cause. The Historical Societies of Carmarthenshire, Pembrokeshire and Cardiganshire, The Welsh Historic Gardens Trust for generous help with publicity.

Thomas Lloyd – a stalwart friend of Francis Jones and a now a valued supporter of Brawdy Books.

Mrs. Madden who nobly coped with the ferocious discipline of indexing. Leon Olin and Sylvia Gainsford, for their usual superb draughtsmanship and illustrations worthy of the highest standards set by Francis Jones.

Richard Sheen, for his experience, humour and reliability. David Brunel White and Mrs. E. M. Lodwick for their excellent drawings originally created for the first edition of the *Historic Carmarthenshire Homes and their Families*.

Also to all the unnamed friends and colleagues who helped us along the way, and all our Patron Subscribers from the UK and over twenty countries world-wide. Without their support, not a word of Francis Jones's work would have appeared in book form.

Thank you all.

LIST OF PATRON SUBSCRIBERS

The Rt. Hon. Lord Aberdare, Elystan St. London.

Mrs. E. M. Austin, Penarth, Glam.

Mr. D. Ayers, Pill, Milford Haven.

Dr. D. L. Baker-Jones, Velindre, Llandysul.

Mr. H. J. G. Barr, Ashleigh Lane, Cleeve Hill. Glos.

Mr. Grenville Barrett, Cannon Hill, Bethlehem, Pembs.

Mrs. E. M. E. Barry, Shilton, Burford.

Miss S. G. Beckley,
     West Glamorgan Archive Service, Swansea.

Mr. S. R. Beesley, Price & Son, Haverfordwest.

Mr. D. F. Bevan, Ferryside, Carms.

Mr. A. ap I. Bowen-Jenkins, Ravens Park Lodge, Haverfordwest.

Mrs. G. M. Bowen, Blaenffos, Boncath, Pembs.

Mrs. P. M. Bowen, Mount Pleasant, Penffordd, Narberth.

Mr. M. & Mrs. R. Broad, Cumberland Park, S. Australia.

Mr. J. P. B. Brook-Little, Lower Heyford, Oxon.

Rev. R. L. Brown, Vicarage, Welshpool, Powys.

Miss E. M. C. Budd, Adpar, Newcastle Emlyn.

Phil & Sonia Budden, Penygroes, Llanelli.

Mr. O. Bushell, New Moat, Pembs.

Lord Carbery, Hayes Court, Wimbledon.

Cardiff University, Wales.

Miss Tileri Charles-Jones, Plas yr Wregin, Dinas, Pembs.

Mr. G. Charles-Jones, Plas yr Wregin, Dinas, Pembs.

Dr. R. E. Chilcott, Heathfield Rd., Keston, Kent.

Dr. W. E. Church, Bethersden, Kent.

Prof. D. Cohn-Sherbok, Bwlchllan, Aberystwyth.

Mrs. M. Colburn, Whitehorse St., Hereford.

Miss. J. Coleman, Abergwili, Carmarthen.

Mr. G. P. Coulter, Cocopan Drive, Altadena, U.S.A.

Mr. W. S. Croom-Johnson, Horderley, Shrops.

Mrs. J. Daniels, Conningsby Dr., Pershore.

Mrs. P. David, Falcondale, Lampeter.

Dr. D. R. Davies, Elmo Rd., Courtnay, B.C., Canada.

Dr. J. H. Davies, Stryd Fawr, Llandysul.

Mr. D. Davies & The Hon. Mrs. J. Davies, Cilgwyn Manor, Llangadog.

Mr. P. H. C. Davies, Stow Hill, Newport.

Mrs. E. K. Davies, Llanybydder, Carms.

Mrs. P. Davies, Argoed, Nevern, Pembs.

Dr. J. Davies-Humphreys, Flookersbrook, Chester.

Mrs. N. M. Delpech, Paskeston, Pembroke.

Gwyneth & Ieuan Evans, Dorlangoch, Brecon.

Mr. & Mrs. J. Wynford Evans, St. Fagans Dr., St. Fagans.

Mr. & Mrs. R. M. T. Evans, Box, Llanelli.

Mr. & Mrs. S. E. M. Evans, Llys-y-coed, Dinas, Pembs.

Mr. C. L. V. P. Evans, Lady Arbour Court, Eardisley.

Mr. D. L. Evans, Hillwood Road, Madeley Heath.

Mr. P. L. Evans, Mount Pleasant, Llangunnor. Carms.

Mrs. M. M. Evans, Myrddin Cres., Carmarthen.

Mrs. S. C. Fraser-Hungrecker, Harbord St., London.

Miss. H. A. Formby, Ysceifiog, Holywell.

Mrs. S. Francis, Penbanc, Fishguard.

Dr. D. P. Freeman, Dept. of History, University of Wales, Swansea.

Mrs. I. O'Connor Fullard, Cwmann, Lampeter.

Mrs. N. L. Gainsford, Rhos-y-Caerau, Pembs.

Mrs. S. J. Gambold-Jackson, Temeraire, Weymouth.

Mr. D. K. Gardiner, Sefton Park Rd., Bristol.

Dr. D. M. George, Darlow Dr. Biddenham, Bedford.

Mrs. C. George, Milton Meadows, Milton, Pembs.

Col. R. H. Gilbertson, Lampeter Velfrey, Narberth.

Mr. R. W. Giles, Marlborough House, Cardiff.

Mr. D. R. Gorman, Alder Drive, Hoghton, Lancs.

Mr. Alan V. Griffiths, Dol-llan, Llandysul.

Mrs. M. A. Griffiths, Blaencorse, St. Clears.

Mr. T. Gwyn-Jones, Hamstead Park, Berks.

Mr. E. D. Harries, McCarthey's Rd., Maleny, Queensland, Aust.

Dr. D. J. Harris, London, Ontario, Canada.

Mrs. S. Henry, Hayston Road, Johnston, Pembs.

Mrs. K. M. Hocking, Boxgrove Rd., Guildford.

Mrs. E. A. Horne, Millais, St. Quen, Jersey.

Dr. P. Howell-Williams, Llanfair Rd., Rhuthin.

Mr. C. I. Howells, Copse Edge Ave., Epsom.

Mr. E. E. Hughes, Juberri, Principat, d'Andorra.

Mr. J. V. Hughes, Rice St., Port Talbot.

Mr. & Mrs. J. Isaac, King Edward Rd., Swansea.

A. James, Gowerton, Swansea.

Mr, & Mrs D. J. James, Maesycrugiau, Pencader, Carms.

W. J. James, Plas Gwyn, Haverfordwest.

Mr. I. H. Jenkins, Dombey Rd., Poynton.

Mr. P. K. Jenkins, Latimer Rd., Llandeilo.

Mr. & Mrs. A. M. John, Myndd-y-Garreg, Kidwelly.

Mr. G. T. John, Rhydarwen, Llanarthney.

Miss A. L. Jones, Park Terrace, Carmarthen.

Mr. D. K. Jones, Eastgate, Cowbridge.

Mr. D. M. Jones, Tal-y-Werydd, Aberarth, Aberaeron.

Mr. R. Jones, Garsdon Mill, Malmsbury.

Mrs. M. Kellam, Can y Gwynt, Llanarth.

Mrs. B. J. Kirkwood, St. Ives, N.S.W., Aust.

Mr. A. Lewis, Llansaint, Kidwelly.

Mr. G. T. Lewis, Cholsey, Wallingford.

Ms. M. E. K. Lewis, Plas Ffrwdfal, Pumpsaint, Carms.

Mr. D. Lloyd, Staverton Leys, Rugby.

Mr. T. Lloyd, Freestone Hall, Cresselly.

Mrs. M. K. Longden, Hucclecote, Gloucester.

Ms. I. Lund, Clarksville, U.S.A.

Mrs. M. Madden, Aberystwyth.

Sir David Mansel-Lewis, Stradey Castle, Llanelli.

Mr. & Mrs. C. Mason-Watts, Noyadd Trefawr, Cardigan.

Miss. C. McCann, Llansaint, Kidwelly.

Mr. H. P. G. Morgan, Sienna Lodge, Ynystawe, Swansea.

Mr. T. L. Morgan, The Grove, Ickenham.

Mrs. J. Morgan, Carnachenwen, Pembs.

Mrs. P. Morgan, Cwrt, Penrhyncoch, Ceredigion.

Mr. D. T. Morgan-Jones, St. John's Lodge, Woodbridge.

Mr. & Mrs. H. Morse, Tonteg, Pontypridd.

Mr. I. N. Nagai, Sengawa-machi, Tokyo, Japan.

National Museum & Galleries of Wales, The Library, Cardiff.

National Library of Wales, Aberystwyth.

Rev. T. Oldham, Riverside Mews, Cardigan.

Mrs. M. Osborne, Shilton.

Mr. D. Owen, Ridgeway, Newport, Gwent.

Miss E. A. Y. Parry, Tirydail Lane, Ammanford.

Mr. D. N. Patchett & Mrs. L. A. Parry-Patchett, Tirydail Lane, Ammanford.

Mr. & Mrs. J. Pearce, Carrow Hill, St. Brides, Pembs.

Mr. R. & Mrs. P. Garnon Peters, Glentana Rd., Victoria, Canada.

Mr. & Mrs. G. Philipps, Cwmgwili, Carmarthen.

Mr. R. D. Pryce, Trevethin, Pwll, Llanelli.

J. D. Prytherch, Lower Plenty, Victoria, Aust.

R. J. Prytherch, Clifton, Bristol.

Mr. R. Pugh, Cwmoernant House, Carmarthen.

Dr. A. R. Rees, Tithe Barn, Rustington, W. Sussex.

Mr. A. & Mrs. M. Rees, Oaklands Swiss Valley, Llanelli.

Mr. L. Rees, Cerbid House, Solva, Pembs.

Mr. W. & Mrs. B. A. Rees, Craddock St., Llanelli.

Mr. J. Reynolds, Y Gelli Werdd, Erw Hir, Carms.

Dr. W. J. St. E-G. Rhys, Plas Bronmeurig, Ystrad Meurig.

Miss M. A. Richards, Marlborough House, Llandrindod Wells.

Dr. & Mrs. P. Robinson, Haverfordwest, Pembs.

Mrs. G. Rowland, Ennismore Ave., Guildford.

Mr. J. C. B. Rye, Brithdir Hall, Berriew, Powys.

Mrs. S. E. Savage, Hall Road, Hull, E. Yorks.

Dr. E. Scourfield, Mayfield, Sully, Penarth.

Mr. R. Sheen, Penrallt Mill, Llechryd.

Mr. M. A. Shepherd, Meadowgate Lane, Spalding.

Mrs. K. Silcox-Butt, Franks Hall, Horton Kirby, Kent.

Mrs. A. M. B. Skipper, Baldenhall, Malvern.

Mr. I. F. Skyrm, Broadheath, Tenbury Wells.

Dr. G. O. Stephenson, Parc Henri, Dryslwyn.

Mrs. M. J. Stephenson, Penrherber, Newcastle Emlyn.

Mr. A. Taylor, Meiros Hill, Nantgaredig.

Eifwen & Raymond Thomas, Pen-y-graig, Llanedi.

Capt. & Mrs. G. J. Thomas, Ty Od, Newport, Pembs.

Dr. W. K. Thomas, Lancaster Ave., London.

Eirwen & Raymond Thomas, Pen-y-Graig, Llanelli.

Miss. J. M. Thomas, Clydfan, Llangynwr.

Mr. E. H. Thomas, Finchampstead Road, Wokingham.

Mr. E. R. Thomas, Yardley, Leominster.

Mr. D. H. L. Thomas, Whitley, Finchampstead.

Mr. J. Thomas, Charleville Mansions, London.

Mr. J. E. Thomas, Bowham Ave., Bridgend.

Mr. N. M. Thomas, Bromham, Chippenham.

Mr. W. J. Thomas, Church House, Llangathen.

Mrs. H. M. Thomas, Pyllan Fawr, Sennybridge.

Mrs. P. Thomas, Polstead House, Oxford.

Ms. Marilyn Timms, 73 Thayers Farm Road, Beckenham, Kent BR3 4LY.

Rev. J. Towyn-Jones, President, Carms. Antiquarian Society, Carmarthen.

Mr. M. Tree, Hendre House, Llanrwst.

Ms. L. M. Voyle, Queen Victoria Rd., Llanelli.

Mr. J. Walford, Rhoslyn, Talley.

Mrs. E. F. E. Warlow, Castle Way, Dale.

Ms. E. White, Rosewood House, Bath.

Dr. D. M. J. Williams, Park Rd., Barry.

Mr. D. F. Williams, Harrington Dr., Cheltenham.

Mr. P. Williams, Cavendish Meads, Ascot.

Mrs. A. E. Willis, Heather Close, Sarn., Bridgend.

Mr. G. H. C. Wilmot, Woodbridge Court, Langland Bay.

Mrs. M. Winnett, Trapham Rd., Maidstone.

Mr. T. Woolner, The Butts, Long Compton, Warks.

COATS OF ARMS

Robert Banks Hodgkinson Esq.

Banks Hodgkinson of Edwinsford

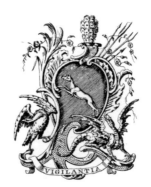

John Blome

Blome of Penybanc Ucha

Owen Brigstocke

Brigstocke of Llechdwnni

Campbell Davys

Campbell Davys of Neuadd Fawr

Morgan Davies

Davies of Cwm

William Dwnn

Dwnn of Penrallt

Terrance Vincent Fisher-Hoch

Fisher-Hoch of Plas Llansteffan

Charles A. H. Green

Green of Court Henry

Sir Geo. Griffies-Williams, Bart.

Griffies-Williams of Llwyn Wormwood

E. Gulston

Gulston of Derwydd

Hughes of Penymaes

Thomas Johnes Esq.

Johnes of Dolau Cothi

Jones of Pantglas

Lewes of Llysnewydd

Reginald Arthur Loyd

Loyd of Court Henry, Cilycwm

John William Lloyd

Lloyd of Danyrallt

Thomas Lloyd Esq.

Lloyd of Llanfihangel Abercywyn

Sir William Mansel, Bart.

Mansel of Iscoed

William Meares

Meares of Plas Llansteffan

Thomas Morris

Morris of Brynmyrddin

Mervyn Lloyd Peel

Peel of Danyrallt

Sir Jnᵒ Philipps, Bart.

Philipps of Clog y Fran

Philipps of Cwm

John Walters Philipps Esq.

Phillips of Aberglasney

Rees of Cilymaenllwyd

Walter Fitz Uryan, Baron Dynevor

Rice of Dynevor Castle

Stepney of Llanelly House

Morgan Thomas

Thomas of Lletty Mawr

John Vaughan Esq.

Vaughan of Golden Grove

Sir James H. W. Drummond, Bart.

Williams-Drummond of Edwinsford

Katherine Williams

Williams of Panthowell

*Brawdy Books are indebted to Thomas Lloyd, Esquire
of Freestone Hall, Pembrokeshire
for his kind permission to reproduce coats of arms
from his heraldic collection*

Chapter I

THE BROAD PICTURE

SOME ASPECTS OF CARMARTHENSHIRE IN THE 18TH CENTURY

THERE IS A GENERAL tendency when we think of history, to invest single great events with a far greater importance than they merit. I do not say that such events were not important – indeed they were of vital importance in themselves. Among these we find events such as the landing of the Romans 55BC, the Battle of Hastings, the Signing of Magna Carter, the fall of Llywelyn the Last, the Peasant's Revolt, the Battle of Bosworth, the Dissolution of the Monasteries, the Union of England and Wales, the Civil Wars, the Jacobite Rising, the American War of Independence, the French Revolution, the Battle of Waterloo, the Rebecca movement in west Wales, and so on.

These were important and significant events, but owing to methods of teaching history in the past, excessive emphasis was placed on them, with the result that they often appear as isolated incidents and so complete in themselves. They are apt to remain in our memories, not merely as signposts, but as incidents complete in themselves. It is a conception that requires revision, and indeed, correction.

What is really important in relation to these great events, are the conditions of life that led to them and the results that flared from them – in other words, cause and effect. Thus, to appreciate the significance of a single incident we must learn what went on *before* and what went on *after*. Thus incidents have to be placed in a context if they are to be intelligible to students of history. In other words, the study must involve a period of time, and it is clear that we must think of history as periods, and as far as Britain is concerned the century (with certain overlaps) provides a sound basis for the study and treatment of our history.

Now, certain centuries are more important than others, for the events that took place within them had greater and more abiding results. It is difficult to say which is the more important, for they are all important in themselves.

Wales in the 18th century has not received the attention and treatment that it deserves. One reason for this neglect is that, comparatively, it contains fewer of the spectacular single events that characterised other centuries, before and after. Its history is that of the groundswell rather than of great tempests, so that very few single events are impressed on the mind, which can immediately be identified with that century. Superficially, it seems a dull and prosaic period, punctuated by events that took place in distant parts and not immediately connected with country and home affairs. Yet there were stirring events on a national scale, and these had an effect on the whole kingdom, ultimately if not immediately.

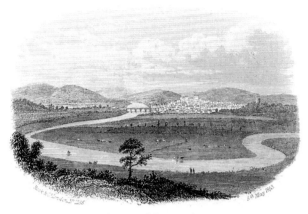

A view of Carmarthen

The 18th century is the gateway to modern Britain. It contains the genesis of institutions, customs and laws that regulate our lives today. Let us now, briefly, review the events of that century – a period full of interesting innovations.

First of all, there was a change of dynasty. With the death of Queen Anne the Stuart dynasty came to an end and was replaced by the German House of Hanover. This led to internal tensions for a large part of the population, particularly in Scotland and in the more conservative agricultural areas who remained attached to the Stuarts, which led to two abortive Jacobite uprisings, that of 1715 and 1745. But there was another and far more important result of the Hanoverian succession. George I was wholly German speaking and could not cope with the English language, and so relied almost entirely on his ministers in order to govern the country. Gradually this gave rise to one minister being considered as the chief or Prime Minister, in this case Walpole, who governed the country and advised the king, at the head of a group of ministers who became known as the Cabinet. Thus, here we have the origin of parliamentary government as we know it today. Although Parliament itself continued to be dominated by the House of Lords and the King could still make and unmake his Prime Minister, the power of rule was passing into the hands of Parliament, so that we had a constitutional Monarchy as we still have today.

During this century too, we find the basis of the two party system that was to become the characteristic of British politics. Although Members of Parliament continued to be drawn from an aristocratic class, they slowly formed themselves into two distinct factions – Tories and Whigs, i.e. government and opposition. The former were based mainly on the agricultural interest, and so to a greater extent were the latter, but the latter also contained industrial and mercantile interests, and a certain number of members with radical views, sometimes as extreme as those of what we call today, the "Left".

Religious movements during the 18th century – namely the rise of Nonconformity, and particularly the Methodist Revival, also influenced politics. Generally speaking, Nonconformity took a progressive view of politics, and supported the Whigs. In the 19th century these two parties became known as Conservative and Liberal.

Another incident that influenced 18th century political development was the French Revolution of 1789. On the one hand this strengthened the Tory viewpoint, particularly a little later, when the French attempted to dominate Europe; but it also strengthened the Whig or radical element. There were in those days, men who advocated the abolition of monarchy and the establishment of a republic, the disestablishment of the national church, and the introduction of a governmental system of a wholly democratic nature. Such extreme views were advocated in Carmarthenshire by Thomas Glyn Cothi in speech, poem and song, and many others. Thus the French Revolution influenced British political thought, and although it never developed into an extreme or violent movement, it nevertheless helped to emphasise the difference between Whig and Tory, Liberal and Conservative, and so perpetuated the idea of a two party political structure.

Another aspect, also with its results, associated with political outlook, was the advance of Education. Perhaps it is not quite right to speak of 'advance' – it would be more correct to describe it as 'establishment' and development. Prior to the 18th century, education had been confined to a few grammar schools, such as the Queen Elizabeth Grammar School in Carmarthen, grammar schools in Pembroke, Haverfordwest and Cardigan in west Wales, and the universities of Oxford and Cambridge, and Inns of Court, for those who wished for advanced education. However, a new movement, supported by people of all political opinion, had come into being – the Society for the Promotion of Christian Knowledge – SPCK – of which I shall have more to say anon. The object of this society was to bring to the poorer elements of society some basic knowledge of reading and writing, to be disseminated by local schoolmasters who taught in cottages and farmhouses, in the very homes of the people – both children and adults. The schools were not static, but circulating and were held at different places at different times. Though the main object was to extend Biblical learning and knowledge, it provided opportunities of wider study by those who were ambitious and able and in this way new ideas were absorbed and circulated among the poorer people whose education had been wholly neglected during the preceding centuries. This movement, led in Carmarthenshire by John Vaughan of Derllys, his daughter Madame Bevan of Laugharne, and Griffith Jones of Llanddawror, so influenced their countrymen, that we find in the last wills and testaments of the wealthier farmers, merchants, and landowners, provisions being made for the establishment of charity schools for the children of the poor. In Carmarthen town itself, a college had already been established for religious purposes, by the Nonconformists called the Academy, which later became known as the Presbyterian College, which only ceased to exist recently.

Added to this were the Sunday schools and also day-schools established by the Nonconformists, so that during this century basic education became available for all classes of people.

One of the results of this educational missionary work was a renaissance of literature, particularly poetry, both sacred and secular, composed in both the English and Welsh language. In this county we had famous hymn writers like Williams Pantycelyn, David Jones of Caeo, poets like John Dyer of Aberglasny, Erasmus Saunders of Clynfelin, and many more. Societies were elected, like that of the Ancient Britons, which later became the Cymmrodorion Society.

Certain overseas events should also be mentioned here for they were to have a profound, if not immediate influence on home affairs. Britain had always had to contend with the great rival powers of Spain and France on the world stage. The menace of the former had been removed during the previous century, but the latter remained a powerful enemy to our overseas aspirations. However, during the 18th century Britain had been able to destroy the French threat in large measure, and to establish her dominions in America, Canada, and India, and in other points of the globe, thereby laying the foundations of what was to become known as the British Empire. Neither must we forget one serious loss that Britain suffered during this century - namely the loss of the American colonies, which formed themselves into the United States of America. It must be remembered that Britain had established those colonies, and their inhabitants were wholly British in outlook, and that this withdrawal from the Empire was due to our own political ineptitude. It is hardly necessary for me to indicate the enormous importance of this event in our history, indeed in world history during the succeeding centuries.

The expansion of overseas trade is another facet of economic development of the 18th century. Trading posts were established throughout the world, new markets were found. This led to expansion of trade, and stimulated the home market, and led to two revolutions – the Industrial Revolution and the Agricultural Revolution – what we can call the truly acceptable face of revolution. These had already been set in train by internal causes, but were vastly stimulated by our overseas adventures. Both were developments that commenced to affect Carmarthenshire about 1750, and by 1800 had already become a major element in local life. The industrial revolution mainly affected south east Carmarthenshire. Industries such as coal mining, iron and tin works and lead mining, had been a feature of the local economy from early times, but had been carried on mainly on a minor scale by local landowners and tradesmen. However from 1750 onwards English entrepreneurs and industrialists, backed by London finances, started to take over, and through the investment of more finance and the introduction of more up to date machinery and management, works on a far more ambitious scale were established. This resulted in a rapid increase in population in the industrial areas, and ancillary industries followed in the wake of the basic ones. Thus Llanelly from a small village became a major town, and the village called Cross Inn became the flourishing town of Ammanford. This increase of population meant that there were more mouths to feed, more houses to be built, more homes to be furnished, so that agriculture was stimulated and market places became scenes of bustle and animation. An example of this is provided by the history of Buckley's Brewery. A small local farmer called Henry Child started a malt business, which slowly expanded with the increase of activity at Llanelly. He expanded the business, bought some public houses, and also built some small ships for the export of the products of Llanelly and its locality. His daughter and heiress married a Methodist minister called the Rev. James Buckley, a friend of John Wesley, and who helped to build the Methodist chapel in Carmarthen. His sons entered Buckley's Brewery, which continues to assuage the thirst of Carmarthenshire people. Apart from showing that alcohol can be next to godliness, this illustrates the effect of a prospering industry upon local endeavour.

As a result of such industrial activity, local banks came into being, and as early as 1786 the Lewis family opened a banking house in Carmarthen, which prospered with the continuing prosperity of the industrial development of south-east Carmarthenshire. Another, but less fortunate banker was Waters of Treventy, later of Sarnau, who established a bank at Carmarthen and Haverfordwest, but which later failed during a depression in the early 19th century.

Llanelli viewed from the north

Another feature of the 18th century that affected our county was the 'discovery' of Wales by English tourists. We are apt to think that tourism is something new, something which has come into being since the last war. Not a bit of it. In the 18th century tours in Wales became fashionable, and a number of tourists wrote an account of their visits, which often contain vivid and valuable pen-pictures of the state of the county at that time. Many were published, but many more remain in manuscript in the National Library of Wales and in the Carmarthen Record Office. With the increase of travellers, and also of trade, it became necessary to improve road communications, and during this century vast improvements were made, especially of the main turnpike roads along which the Royal Mail coaches ran. Thus, Carmarthenshire became less isolated, and more receptive to wider influences.

This brief review of the events and trends of the 18th century, will, I hope, indicate the importance of that century in Carmarthenshire life. Indeed, it was on the foundation established largely in this century that the consequent prosperity, not only of Carmarthenshire, but also of Britain was built. There have been many changes since that time, but the basis of most of our modern institution belongs to the 18th century.

This must form an introduction to a more detailed examination of some of the innovations and trends, which I have mentioned.

First of all, a few words must be devoted to Agriculture. Generally, agriculture had been fairly flourishing in Carmarthenshire. There were three main classes of farmers, namely,

1. *The gentry*. It is wrong to think of the gentry as being devoted only to fishing, shooting, and hunting, with occasional trips to the county town to sit in the Quarter Sessions or attend hunt balls. They were all practical farmers, farming the land around their mansions, usually directing operations themselves, occasionally employing a foreman or bailiff. They were largely responsible for the introduction of new methods and machinery from 1750 onwards, and encouraged their tenants to follow suit.

2. *Tenant farmers*. These were full time farmers whose whole life was bound to the concerns of the farms, and in many cases there was a tendency for the eldest son to continue the tenancy after his father's time.

3. *Freehold farmers*. They owned their own farms, and were also full time farmers, and the tendency here also was continuity of tenure within the family.

These farms on the whole were small in acreage, although there were a number of over 300 acres and more. During the 18th century there was a tendency (as in our time) to increase the size of the farm by absorbing the smaller units near, or adjacent to them.

On the whole farming had been fairly flourishing in Carmarthenshire, so much so, that farmers were able to enter the ranks of the gentry, or to send their sons on to the universities, enter them into professions like the law and medicine, and to live comfortably albeit simply. It was mainly subsistence farming.

Let us see what some of the tourists had to say on the subject of farming,

John Taylor c 1650 visited Carmarthen – "One of the plentifullest towns" he had ever visited. "Butter as good as the world affords is 2½ d per pound; a salmon 2½ feet long costs 12d; oysters are a penny for 100; eggs are 12 for a penny, and pears 6 for a penny."

In 1673 Blome wrote in *Britannia* – "Carmarthenshire, esteemed by some the strongest county in South Wales, and generally of a fertile soil, bearing good crops, hath rich meadows, which feed store cattle and is clothed with wood . . . the inhabitants are plentifully served with fowl and fish, especially salmon in great abundance".

A writer in 1741 refers to the county as abundant in corn, grass, cattle, salmon and woodlands; and later writers tell a similar tale.

The most fertile areas were the river valleys of the Taf, Cynin, Dewi fawr, Cywin, Gwili, Cothi, Gwendraeth, and especially the Tywi although there was always the risk of flooding.

Agricultural Societies

The earliest in Carmarthen was established in 1772 by Watkin Lewes of Penybenylog, Pembrokeshire, who owned estates in Pembrokeshire and Carmarthenshire; and was called "Society for the Encouragement of Agriculture, Planting and other laudable purposes". The society gave prizes for skill and enterprise, breeding of cattle, cultivation of the soil, crops, planting trees, and for cottage industries, like spinning yarn and knitting stockings, for fencing and making hurdles. The Society met four times a year, at the Cawdor Arms, Llandeilo (then called the Bear Inn), the Ivy Bush and Boars Head, Carmarthen.

Local landowners became pioneers of improvement – John Vaughan of Golden Grove introduced new machinery, ploughs, horse-rakes, etc., bought in London; George Rice of Newton (Dynevor), the Du Buissons of Glyn Hir, Mansel of Stradey and Johnes of Dolau Cothi were well known for the improvement they introduced to their farms. Most landowners carried out afforestation on a considerable scale.

Wages

Although the cost of living was relatively low, wages were also very low.

In 1794 –   head ploughman   £6 p.a.
2nd ploughman   £4 10 00 p.a.
A boy   £2 00 p.a.
Dairymaid   £3 00 p.a.
Junior maid from   £2 10 p.a. to £1 00 p.a.

They also received their food and keep, and also wool, and rows of potatoes in the fields. In 1787 at Golden Grove

Butler	£30 p.a.	Keeper	£12 12p.a.
House steward	£20 p.a.	Gardener	£25 5 p.a.
Footman	£16 16 p.a.	Woman cook	£26 5 p.a.
Coachman	£25 p.a.	Cow-boy	7d. per day.
Groom	£21 p.a.	Cow-man	10 d. per day.

By 1815 farm labourers received on average 1/- per day. Women as well as men worked out of doors. A tourist wrote in 1791, "Labour seems to be equally divided between men and women, and it is as common to meet a woman driving a plough as it is to see Taffy at the milk pail". Women's Lib. came early to Carmarthen.

One result of the industrial development in southeast Carmarthenshire and Glamorgan was to attract workers from the countryside. There was a constant drift of workers from the 18th century onwards, a fact often mentioned by contemporary writers, but this was partly counteracted by the introduction of labour saving machinery.

Afforestation

Carmarthenshire was famous for its great woodlands in the Middle Ages. Giraldus mentions among other local forests, the large forest near Kidwelly "well stocked with wild animals especially deer". In the 18th century a great many woodlands were felled. The development of coal mining led to a demand for pit-props, the iron and tinworks wanted wood to make charcoal, such as the ironworks in Carmarthen, Whitland Abbey, Kidwelly, Llandyfan, Cwmbran, Cwmdwyfran, Pembrey, and Llanelly. As the population grew the demand for new houses arose, for domestic fuel, furniture, fences, etc. During the war period, Carmarthenshire timber was used to build carriages for cannon, ships of war, and for merchant vessels, some being built on the Towy at Carmarthen Quay. In addition oak-bark was used in the tanneries around Carmarthen and other towns. So plentiful was the supply that much timber was shipped to Ireland and to English ports. From 1760 to 1800 Carmarthenshire lost great tracts of woodland including the forest around Kidwelly and extensive woods in Llanybydder.

CARMARTHENSHIRE.

Fine Timber.

To be Sold

BY AUCTION,

At the Bear-Inn,

IN THE TOWN OF LLANDILO-FAWR,

On Tuesday, the 6th of March next,

Between the Hours of One and Two o'Clock in the Afternoon, subject to Conditions of Sale to be there produced,

IN THIRTEEN LOTS, VIZ.

LOTS.	NO. OF OAK TREES.	WHERE GROWING.	PARISHES.	HOW MARKED.
1	257	Bwlchyffin	Llanfairarybryn	With a Scribe.
2	279	Do.	Do.	Do.
3	327	Do.	Do.	Do.
4	115	Dugoedydd	Do.	Do.
5	52	Ystradffin	Do.	Do.
6	249	Rhydygroes	Cilycwm	Do.
7	78	Do.	Do.	Do.
8	39	Do.	Do.	Do.
9	86	Glanrhossan	Do.	Do.
10	79	Glangwenlaes	Do.	Do.
11	73	Erwdiar & Wernddu	Do.	Do.
12	642	Abrogwr	Do.	Do.
13	4418	Wenallt	Saint Mary's, Kidwelly	Do.

ALSO,

To be Sold by Auction,

SUBJECT TO THE SAME CONDITIONS,

At the Black-Lion Inn, Newcastle-Emlyn,

On TUESDAY, the 13th day of MARCH next,

Between the Hours of Four and Five o'Clock in the Afternoon, in One Lot:

PARISH OF CENNARTH:

643 OAK TREES,

Growing on the Farm of Cillo-fawr, marked with Paint.

Lots 1 to 12, inclusive, are within a short distance of the River Towy; Lot 13 is within three miles of the town of Kidwelly; and the last-mentioned Lot is contiguous to the turnpike-road leading into the sea-port town of Cardigan, distant from that place eight miles.

The greatest part of this Timber is fit for Ship Building.

Philip Reynolds, of Nantgwynne, near Llandovery, will shew the first 12 Lots; the Tenant will describe Lot 13; and Richard Evans, of Newcastle-Emlyn, will point out the remaining Lot. Letters (post paid) addressed to either of those Persons will receive due attention.

14th February, 1821.

COUNTY-PRESS, LLANDILO: PRINTED BY JOHN DAVIES.

However, as selling timber was a paying business, the landowners continually carried out re-afforestation, so that within a few decades many of the woodlands were restored, and a more judicious policy of felling introduced.

In 1781, John Vaughan bought 5,000 saplings from a London nursery; John Colby a Pembrokeshire squire bought 60,000 2-year old trees from a nursery at Norwich in 1796; and Johnes of Dolau Cothi planted thousands of trees yearly. There was a famous timber nursery at Newcastle Emlyn run by a Mr. Hindes, which helped to supply local needs.

The Drovers – The importance of cattle and sheep to the Carmarthenshire economy.
During the 18th century, thousands of sheep were driven to Essex to fatten on the salt marshes before being sold, also cattle, pigs, even geese and turkeys. With the rapid growth of population in London and other areas, the Welsh cattle trade increased in importance. The roast beef of Old England is a misnomer – it should be of "old Carmarthen", for the Welsh cattle were the majority in the marts and fairs of the Midlands, the south-east and south-west of England. These animals were not valuable for their meat alone, for their hides provided material for tanners, leather-dressers, makers of saddles, pouches, shoes, belts, gloves, and other articles.

The Drovers were important people, for in addition to driving cattle they often acted as carriers of rents, paid bills for people who gave them cattle in lieu. They drove large herds so far as Leicester, Northampton, Gloucester, Bristol, Taunton, Weymouth, Oxford, Salisbury, Winchester, Guildford, Uxbridge, Ashford, Maidstone, Chelmsford, etc. They followed regular routes, and tried to avoid toll charges on turnpike roads. The cattle were often given shoes before starting out – Pumpsaint was a famous shoeing centre for North Carmarthenshire, also Llandovery and another was Tregaron. From Tudor times onwards the drovers had to be licensed annually by Quarter Sessions.

Mostly, they were of good character, and some were very prosperous, for they had cash resources in hand, and sometimes acted as moneylenders. To avoid risk of robbery, the drovers adopted a system of leaving at home the cash handed over to them and settling the accounts due to London creditors and others out of their cattle sales. By acting as agents and financiers in this way they anticipated some of the functions of modern banking. Indeed several of them established their own private banks. Amongst them was Banc yr Eidon Du (The Black Ox bank) because the notes were engraved with a black ox. This bank was opened in Llandovery in 1799 by David Jones, a local farmer's son and a drover. At his death in 1839 he left £149,000 in addition to a large estate. He was an ancestor of Jones of Blaen nos and Pantglas. His bank continued until 1909 when it was taken over by Lloyds Bank.

Dafydd Jones of Cwm Gogerddan Caeo (1711-77) was a successful drover who drove regularly to Smithfield. He became religious in later years and was a prominent member of the Independent Chapel at Crugybar, and wrote numerous hymns which are still sung today – Wele, cawsom y Meseia / Plant ydym eto dan ein hoed.

People living at a distance found the drovers particularly useful. Thus, John Vaughan who had inherited the Golden Grove estate, was an absentee landlord who lived in London, and received rents and other monies due to him from Carmarthenshire, with the help of the drovers. In October 1756 Lewis Lewis the agent wrote to tell Vaughan that "one David Jones of Cardiganshire [probably of Deri Ormond], a drover, will pay you £39.2.0. about ye 14th of the month . . . . I trusted him with cattle to that value at Abergwili fair". In due course Vaughan wrote to say – "Davy Jones's man paid £39.2.0 on your account here, and find they have great success in selling their cattle, and that he has paid about a thousand pounds to people here in Town [London]. Mr. Erasmus Saunders always takes care to have the money paid by the drovers or else gets bills gratis to send me as well as the other agents".

In December 1756 Vaughan wrote to Erasmus Saunders to say, "Timothy Jones the drover has paid me £200". In June 1761, Illtid Evans sent him £26 by William Jones, a drover, and later in the year Vaughan acknowledged the sum of £79.16.0 by the hands of Thomas Jones of Carmarthen, drover. In January 1762 Rees Price of Carmarthen wrote to Vaughan that "Our drovers are come home, but no money, and say cattle never sold cheaper than at the fairs in England, and beg leave to remit next year. Vickling with Irish beef has ruined our country" – which has a curiously contemporary ring.

It was a convenient arrangement on the whole. J. G. Philipps of Cwmgwili, Carmarthenshire's M.P. in the latter part of the 18th century, had to live much of his time in London so that he could attend the House of Commons. In those days the MP was responsible for his expenses – there was no salary and no free travelling, and no £10 a day for clocking in at the House of Commons, so that it was a heavy commitment for the member. Mr. Philipps often wrote to his wife in Cwmgwili for money. Mrs. Philipps would then contact a drover, and he would accept a number of cattle at an agreed valuation, and having sold them in English markets would pay the money to Mr. Philipps in London. Say the sum was £200, it was up to the drover to sell them at least for that amount, and if he got more for them which he invariably did, say for £250 – then he was in pocket to the amount of £50.

Isolation of west Wales - diminishing

During the second half of the 18th century the isolation of West Wales was being broken down. The expansion of industry and commerce made the provision of good roads imperative, and there was the added need for easier access to the markets in the industrial areas of SE Carmarthenshire and Glamorgan. Originally roads were looked after by the parishes but this was becoming inefficient, and so Turnpike Trusts were formed in Wales about 1750. Private Acts of Parliament authorised companies of landowners and people of means to take over stretches of roads and to repair and improve them. Capital was raised by issuing shares called Bonds or Tallies on which it was intended to pay 5% but it rarely paid that rate.

In 1763 the Carmarthenshire Main Trust was formed, and took over the road from Tavernspite – St. Clears – Carmarthen – Llandeilo – Llandovery – Breconshire border (the A40). It was along this road that the Irish mail-coach from London to Milford ran. Its first run took place in 1787. It was a crimson coach emblazoned with the Royal Arms, and the scarlet coated guard blew his long copper horn as the conveyance approached the inn yards for a quick change of horses. Toll-keepers had to be on the alert to open gates to allow the coach to dash through because the Royal Mail paid no dues. The Trusts paid their keepers who lived in the toll house alongside.

Other Trusts were the Carmarthen-Lampeter Trust, the Llandovery-Lampeter Trust, the Carmarthen-Newcastle Emlyn Trust, the Three Counties Trust, the Brechfa Trust and the Kidwelly Trust.

They improved communications, but in the following century ceased to be efficient, and finally their functions were handed over to the County Authorities.

Bridge Trusts were also formed to look after the numerous bridges. The Trusts often leased a gate or a group of gates to men who were known as toll-farmers. They paid a lump sum for a year, or whatever the term was, and recouped the amount themselves by the dues taken at the gates. Thus Twm o'r Nant, the well-known interlude writer, came to work with a timber merchant near Llandeilo who had secured the lease of the Abermarlais tollgate for £108 – Twm then took over the gate from 1783-1786.

Thomas Bullin, the entrepreneur, outbid the locals and acquired all the gates of the seven West Wales trusts; e.g. he paid £800 for the Whitland Trust, which was £300 more than previous lessees.

This system became less effective with increase of traffic and the heavier costs of maintenance, and in due course led to the Rebecca riots, aggravated by agricultural depression. Still in its earlier stages, the Turnpike Trusts had been reasonably effective in improving the roads. As a result some new and better bridges were raised over rivers – such as the Llandeilo bridge built by the famous bridge builder Edwards – and some of the improved bridges, maintained by the county rate in the 18th century, still serve the community.

A word must be devoted to the subject of enclosures, although strictly speaking, these belong to the early half of the 19th century. Enclosures in Wales were nearly all concerned with uncultivated lands and wastes of the hillsides and the marshlands of the coastal areas. In 1795 it was estimated that there were 17,660 acres of unenclosed lands in Carmarthenshire. Encroachment upon common and wasteland had been going on for many years, probably for centuries. Small upland farms had been enclosed and cultivated, and numerous cottages had been built on hillsides, on commons, and around the fringes of towns and villages. The squatters had claimed the rights enjoyed by freeholders, namely the right to pasture on the waste, to gather wood for fuel, the digging of turf and peat, and bracken for cattle bedding. Occasionally action was taken against the encroachers by Crown officials, sometimes the property was sold to them, and sometimes the local farmers and others took action against such squatters by demolishing their hastily raised habitations.

During the long war with France from 1793, and the increase in population owing to industrial expansion of which I have spoken earlier, food prices rose, and the value of cultivated land grew. Many of the smallholders on the commons accordingly sold out, and migrated to the towns, and the lands were incorporated in neighbouring farms. The tendency was towards larger farms, which, with the introduction of machinery were becoming a payable proposition. Accordingly, enclosures became necessary in order to increase lands for cultivation. It must be emphasised that enclosures were achieved perfectly legally either by common consent of parishioners or by Act of Parliament. The tales one often hears that enclosure was a form of brigandage by the well-to-do is utterly groundless. The first enclosure affecting Carmarthenshire was passed in 1807 involving 600 acres of marshland near Llanelly and by the mid-century most of the wastes and commons had been enclosed.

Carmarthen and the SPCK

The closing years of the 17th century, saw a religious revival within the Church of England, and led to the formation of numerous religious societies under guidance of local clergy. This led to the formation in 1698 of the Society for Promotion of Christian Knowledge (SPCK). Fortunately in West Wales it received strong support from the gentry, chief of whom was Sir John Philipps of Picton Castle (d1737), John Vaughan of Derllys (d. 1722), Bridget Bevan of Laugharne, Bishop Bull of St. Davids, Canon Edward Meyrick, vicar of Carmarthen, and especially Rev. Griffith Jones of Llanddawror.

Here again it is necessary to emphasise the association of the Established Church with this movement, for there is an idea that the clergy of the 18th century were a somnolent body little concerned with the aspirations and the welfare of their flocks. This was by no means the case, and the history of the SPCK indicates the breadth of their humanity and depth of their vision. Too little credit has been given to the Church for its educational and philanthropic work in Wales, and it is one of the pleasures enjoyed by historians who study original and largely unpublished documents, to discover contemporary evidence of the actions of men long since dead and forgotten. I shall never forget the pleasure I had many years ago, before the last war, in discovering a bundle of old papers that had belonged to the Rev. John Griffiths, a curate of the parish of Llandissilio on the Carmarthenshire – Pembrokeshire border, who enjoyed a lordly stipend of £40 a year which he augmented by profits from a small farm that he rented. Out of his meagre salary he bought a number of books, in English and Welsh, and established a small lending library to the benefit of this remote parish and the surrounding farms and villages. This was done entirely at his own expense, out of Christian charity and a desire to better the condition of his fellowmen. It was the first lending library establishment in west Wales by a private individual. The Rev. John Griffiths lived in 1760. He has been dead for over two hundred years, and today his name is known only to the laborious antiquary. Yet we can say, Da wâs, da a ffyddlon, buost ffyddlon ar ychydig. Dos i mewn i lawenydd dy Arglwydd.

But to return to the SPCK. Those associated with it were religious, social, and educational reformers. A diocesan library was set up in Carmarthen, furnished with books to the value of £60, and encouragement was given to the formation of parish libraries. The activities of the SPCK were widespread. It sponsored the translation into Welsh of religious books and the writing of new ones. These were circulated and distributed in thousands and were mostly written by Anglican clergymen. The Welsh Prayer Book was re-issued, and a large new edition of the Welsh Bible was provided in 1718, both were edited by the Rev. Moses Williams, scholar and cleric, born at Cellan, Cardiganshire, and who collected funds for the publication of the books. Another was Drych y Prif Oleredd published with the support of the SPCK in 1716, and written by the Rev. Theophilus Evans, born near Newcastle

Emlyn. In 1718 the first printing press in Wales was set up at Adpar, Newcastle Emlyn, by a Carmarthenshire man, Isaac Carter. He moved his business to Carmarthen some seven years later. In 1721 Nicholas Thomas opened another printing press in Carmarthen. Numerous Welsh books were issued from the two presses. From these beginnings Carmarthen developed into one of the major printing centres in Wales during the 18th century. John Ross also carried on a printing business in Lammas Street and Priory Street for over 40 years, and one of Ross's former associates began to print at Llandovery in 1764.

A major aim of the SPCK was to establish a charity school in every parish with the assistance of the clergy, gentry, and well-to-do residents, and to maintain the schools by their own local efforts. Although this ambitious programme was not yet fully realised, they succeeded in establishing quite a number of schools in Carmarthenshire – at Laugharne, Llanddawror, Llandybie, Llandeilo, Abercywyn, Llandovery, Llangadog, Carmarthen, Abergwili, St. Clears, Marros, Llanboidy, Penboyr, Pembrey and Kidwelly. Additional schools, conducted mainly by clergymen, were set up at Llanddarog, Llanelli, Llandyfaelog, Llandeilo, Llansadwrn, and Meidrim. The schools depended upon voluntary subscriptions, from which books and materials were purchased. The children were taught the 3 R's; the girls were also taught needlework, knitting, weaving and spinning, and the boys, about elementary farming and navigation. Much attention was given to scripture and religious instruction. The instruction was largely through the medium of English, but Welsh was used in the Welsh speaking areas.

Equally important was the work of Griffith Jones of Llanddawror, an early supporter of the SPCK. He was responsible for another aspect of education, and in 1731, with the support of Madam Bevan, he started the Circulating Welsh Charity Schools as they were called. They were an immediate success and by 1738 there were 37 circulating schools in West Wales. That year Griffith Jones wrote, "very few of these [pupils] could say so much as the Lord's Prayer when they first came to school: and many of them could in six or eight weeks' time, not only read tolerably, but repeat by heart all the Church Catechism in their native Welsh language, and make pretty good answers to plain and familiar questions concerning all the necessary points of faith . . . ."

The Circulating Schools were conducted for periods of about three months in various districts, usually during winter and early spring, when the scholars were not required for farm work. They were held in a variety of buildings – the parish church or vestry, an empty house, a private room, a barn, or an outhouse. All schools were free and often open to scholars of all ages, and the great majority were conducted in Welsh. Only reading and spelling, and the church catechism were taught, and special provision was made for evening classes for those unable to attend during daytime.

Griffith Jones also trained the masters for the schools. He set up a training academy at Llanddawror, and by the end of 1739 over 50 teachers had completed short courses there. The masters were required to be sober, God-fearing members of the Church of England, to be loyal to the King, to devote themselves to their work, "not strolling about needlessly and idling about the place". The masters were urged to be diligent and regular, and not to fall into guilt "and so be unable to answer before God, and moreover, be paid no wages". The

Bridget Vaughan

salaries of these itinerant teachers were much less than those paid in the former SPCK schools. They were paid two guineas a quarter, and sometimes received £3 or £4 per year. The SPCK gave generous support to the Circulating Schools. Among those who served as masters were Morgan Rhys of Cilycwm and John Thomas of Myddfai, both notable Welsh hymn-writers.

By 1740 there were 150 schools with over 8,700 scholars in south and west Wales. They spread to other parts of Wales. The peak years were 1757 (220 schools, 9,037 scholars) and in 1758 (218 schools, 9,834 scholars). Between 1737 and Griffith Jones' death in 1761, it was reckoned that there had been 3,495 schools with well over 158,000 scholars.

A word must be said here about Madam Bridget Bevan (1698-1779). Her father John Vaughan, a landowner, and deeply religious had been one of the strongest supporters of the SPCK, and a patron of Welsh literature. His home, Derllys, was a centre of religious, cultural, and political life, and it was in that atmosphere that Bridget was raised. She married Arthur Bevan, barrister at law and MP for Carmarthen Borough from 1727 to 1741. She too, was deeply religious and gave constant support to Griffith Jones and the Circulating Schools.

On his death in 1761, Griffith Jones left all the charity funds in his possession and the bulk of his own estate to Bridget, requesting her to continue the work of the Circulating Schools. She was then a widow of 63, and carried on the work energetically and successfully. Thus in 1763 there were 270 schools with 11,770 scholars, and in 1773 there were 243 schools with over 13,000 scholars. During the 18 years from 1761 to 1779 when Madam Bevan was in control the number of scholars in 3,280 schools was about 169,000 throughout Wales. When she died in her 81st year in 1779 she left £10,000 to form a trust for the continuation of the schools. But the will was disputed by two of her trustees, her niece, Lady Elizabeth Stepney of Llanelli, and her nephew Admiral William Lloyd of Danyrallt, Llangadog. The whole bequest was put in Chancery where it remained for 30 years, accumulating to over £30,000. But by then the schools had long ceased to exist because of lack of funds.

In 1809 a scheme was made to use the money to establish Welsh Circulating Schools on the lines of the National Society, teaching the 3 R's, to be known as "Madam Bevan's Charity Schools", and for children, only nine were functioning in Carmarthenshire in 1854 when the scheme ended, namely at Llanelli, Llanllawddog, Llanwch, Llandeilo, Llangain,

St. Clears, Eglwysfair Glyntaf, Llanfihangel Rhos y Corn, and Ystradffin. These schools had made a notable contribution to education, not in Carmarthenshire alone, but throughout Wales. We should be proud to remember that this was due to three Carmarthenshire pioneers – John Vaughan of Derllys, Griffith Jones of Llanddawror, and Madam Bevan.

During this century some interesting building took place. Manor houses followed a favourite plan – a straight facade; two or three storeys; rows of sash windows arranged symmetrically in the upper and lower storeys; in the centre, a small projecting porch supported on columns; the roof was covered with stone tiles, but in many instances with slate. There was little elaborate interior decoration, being generally restricted to simple painted panelling, overmantel, a moulded cornice and ceiling dome in plaster.

Another type was the cube, a square, sometimes with wings at either side, and/or, projecting to the rear – a good example being Upland mansion in Llandefaelog. Another example of the cube type was Furnace House built about 1750 by an owner who had benefited from successful participation in the tinplate industry. John Nash, who started his career in this town, built or improved several houses such as Dolau Cothi, Llysnewydd, Golden Grove, and also Carmarthen Gaol.

The 18th century farmhouse was exceedingly simple in design. Some were little more than cottages, but many were substantial stone built structures; they were strictly utilitarian and contained hardly any decoration.

Country cottages were very humble two-roomed structures, often thatched, but around the towns rows of more up-to-date houses were introduced by the masters of industry for their workers.

But generally speaking there was little architectural advance during this century apart from the houses of the well to do who either rebuilt entirely or made extensive improvements to existing structures. Yet by the end of the century there was a greater awareness, and as the agricultural and industrial revolution proceeded more money became available for improvements in domestic architecture, the main fruits of which were reaped in the 19th century.

Country Matters . . .

Leases And Rents

On 16 August 1718 Thomas Lloyd granted a lease of Gwaelod y Maes to David Harry of Kidwelly, yeoman, for the lives of lessee and his two sons, at a yearly rent of £22, and 3s. 6d. in lieu of duties, rendering a heriot or £3 when due; and on 29 January 1719-20 granted a lease for 21 years of messuages and lands (unnamed) to David William Bevan of Llangyndeyrn, yeoman, for a yearly rent of £3, and yearly duties of a pair of pullets or in lieu, 2 horses to carry hay and corn, 2 horses to carry coal to Alltycadno, a reaper in the corn harvest, to keep a hound, to grind corn at Alltycadno Mill, and to provide a man for one day to scour the mill pond; and on 21 February 1720-1, he granted a lease for lives of Tor y Coed bach to Thomas Evan at a yearly rent of £10, and among the duties was the keep of a hound and a cock.

Carmarthen Market in the 1860s

THE HUMAN ELEMENT IN CARMARTHENSHIRE HISTORY
ADDRESS DELIVERED ON 8 JULY 1964 AT ASHBURNHAM HOTEL

HISTORY IS THE RECORD of man's actions, observations, experience, and thought, and its range is bounded only by that of life itself. In one respect the earth is a vast graveyard; in another it is a teeming sphere of life. Every foot of our soil is a collection of historical documents written in the hand of God or the hand of man, and to discover and to interpret them is the function of the historian.

However wise, learned, or experienced a historian may be, he can never master the whole of this enormous field. All that he can hope to do is to become proficient in one or more aspects; he may become an expert on a particular period, a subject, a geographical area, certain trends.

In this respect our own county of Carmarthenshire offers splendid scope. It is not so large that the historian loses sight of the unity of his subject; it is not so small that he has to write "in blinkers" so to speak. Within the topographical unity of Carmarthenshire we have a diversity that contributes to the whole hill and lowland farming, rural crafts, coal, iron, steel, tinplate, and associated industries, we have a sea-board with ports and maritime interests, archaeological remains, cromlechs, earth forts of the prehistoric era, fragments of Roman civilisation, Norman castles, chapels and churches of the Age of Celtic saints, grey shells of monasteries, relics of courts of the Welsh princes, Tudor mansions, historic farmhouses, customs that trace their origin to the Laws of Howel Dda, and boroughs whose charters were granted over 800 years ago. Gliding on the waters of the Towy we can see coracles whose pedigree traces back to the ancient Britons who fished the same waters from similar wicker cockle-shells – the true "Pisces of Towy". These are but a few of the visible survivals of Carmarthenshire history. Our literary and intellectual remains are no less significant. The oldest manuscript in the Welsh language – *The Black Book of Carmarthen* – was compiled in our midst; the earliest Eisteddfod in Wales was held under the patronage of a Carmarthenshire prince; the first college in Wales was established in the county town (the old Presbyterian college), and eighteenth and nineteenth century printing presses of Carmarthen turned out more books than any other during those periods. The Rebecca movement bears witness to the high spirit of a peasantry which would brook no oppression, while the records of our volunteer and militia units provides evidence of the patriotism of the population in general.

It is only one aspect of this chronicle that I propose to discuss. History, considered in its basic form, is the story of the relations of men, or certain groups of men – with each other and with other groups – whether of a small parish, village, town, or whole county. That is to say, biographies of all manner of folk, humble and distinguished; social human history. It is this social human history that forms my theme.

When I came to Carmarthenshire in 1959, I found myself involved in two matters. One was the county – an area, as I have said, eminently suitable as a field of endeavour. The other was the written evidence scattered throughout its length and breadth – in the country-houses, in the offices of solicitors, auctioneers, professional and businessmen, industrialists, shopkeepers, innkeepers, in county and borough offices, in libraries, attics, and cellars – indeed it is true to say that practically every house in Carmarthen possesses at least one document of historical interest or importance. Numbers of people, with commendable public spirit, have deposited their documents in our Record Office. As a result, we are harvesting evidence of vital importance to present and future historians. These collections often supplement each other, and I shall show how part of a transaction described in the papers of one collection is supplemented by material found in other and totally different ones.

An example of this interaction is found in the history of the Towy. The river has been a significant factor in the life of Carmarthen. In early times it formed the eastern boundary of the kingdom of Dyfed which comprised what is now west Carmarthenshire and Pembrokeshire. The vale of Towy, was of strategic importance, for it formed the gateway to West and Mid-Wales. Through it ran a Roman road connecting the fort at Carmarthen to the valuable gold mines at Caio. Along this route the Normans penetrated and in the valley furious battles were fought between the Carmarthenshire princes and the mail-clad invaders. The construction of castles at Llandovery, Dynevor, Dryslwyn, Laugharne, Kidwelly and Carmarthen, indicate the military importance of the area. As the Towy is tidal, vessels of considerable burthen were able to reach Carmarthen on the flood tides, so that it became a flourishing port. Throughout the Middle Ages, and almost to our times, ships from as far away as the Mediterranean, north Africa, the Baltic, and America, landed

Roman and countrymen

cargoes at the quay and took any Welsh produce in their holds. The Mayor of Carmarthen still enjoys the title, "Admiral of the Port," The Romans and Normans departed, the castles crumbled into ivy-covered ruin, the river Towy flowed on, and in course of the centuries, as a result of good husbandry, the vale became known as "The Garden of Wales". From various sources we know that rainfall was heavier in those days than it is now, and that the river Towy was subject to frequent flooding.

The records of the Quarter Sessions contain references to such calamities. The entries were made by the Clerk of the Peace, in terse, matter-of-fact, unromantic legal terminology. On many occasions he records that bridges had been damaged as a result of floods, that Justices of the Peace were to superintend repairs which were not to exceed £20, or whatever the agreed figures were. We learn that a rate was levied to raise the money. But we are not told anything of the human side of the story.

However, from documents deposited in the Record Office by Lord Emlyn, we are able to recover part of the human element, and as you will see, some of it is of dramatic character. Several references to the results of the floods are contained in letters from agents of the Golden Grove estate to their master in London.

What scope these rustic dramas would provide for the pen of writers like Gwyn Thomas and Emyr Humphreys. Here we have the human aspect associated with the Towy which the cold factual record of the Quarter Sessions fails to afford. It is true that they involve peccadilloes. But human failings constitute essential ingredients of life, and the historian is oftentimes as indebted to the sins of the fathers as he is to their virtues.

The river was no respecter of persons. Rich and poor suffered alike, and after the great rain-storms of February 1795, John Vaughan of Golden Grove, the largest landowner in the county, wrote, "I lost 100 sheep in the meadow below this house, and seven acres of land carried away".

Even ordinary workaday activities on the Towy could impinge on national affairs. For instance between 1750 and 1770, and again during the Napoleonic Wars, the great oak forests that grew in the valley, were sold to timber merchants. In 1755 some 6,600 trees were sold for the considerable sum of £10,300. Gangs of men were employed by contractors to cut down the trees, which were then stacked along the banks between Kilsane and Dryslwyn. There they remained until there were indications of flood following on heavy rains. The tree trunks were then tipped into the river and floated away, guided by men in coracles, hired specially for the occasion. When the timbers floated as far as Carmarthen they were hoisted on board ships and carried to Milford Haven and Portsmouth where they were used to make men-o-war for the Royal Navy; and also to Chatham to be made into gun carriages for the Royal Artillery. It is an intriguing thought that some of the ships that ploughed the waves under Nelson, and the

gun carriages that galloped into action under Wellington, had their origin in the rural parishes of Carmarthen. Indeed one may be justified in saying that the battle of Waterloo was won, not on the playing fields of Eton, but on the banks of the river Towy.

As a result of facilities provided by the flood waters, ship-building yards came into existence below the Quay at Carmarthen, where vessels were built of sufficient burthen to cross the Atlantic, two of which are known to have indulged in the slave trade, at one time an occupation as fashionable as it was profitable. So it is that an acorn planted in the corner of a remote field finally found its way across thousands of watery miles to some distant haven which is "forever *Shir Gâir*".

As I have said, Carmarthen was one of the most flourishing ports in Wales. Foodstuffs, coal and culm, iron and tin, the product of farm, forge, and mine, were loaded at the quayside and despatched to England, Europe, and America. A sidelight on human frailty is revealed by the records of the borough of Carmarthen. The city fathers had to pass a by-law in 1805, to punish farmers, who were in the habit of placing large stones in casks of butter in order to increase their weight. The people cried out for food, and some Carmarthenshire farmers, it seems, gave them stones.

When we interpret the history of the river Towy in human terms, we see it, not merely a topographical feature, but an instrument of Fate which has brought to countless people, far beyond the confines of its banks, joy and tears, happiness and catastrophe.

Another aspect concerns the origins of movements, industries, political and cultural activities, religious and educational projects. There is a tendency to think in terms of the movement rather than of the individuals associated with it, inspired by the belief that the principle is greater than the person, that historical judgement should not degenerate into hero-worship. There is something to be said for this, but I feel it has been overdone in many cases. After all, we cannot understand the origins of any movement without knowing something about the feelings and impulses of the men and women who first thought about it, who initiated the process, who sowed the seeds which grew into the harvest that subsequent generations were to reap. In other words, we return to the basic factor – the human element.

The muniments of the Buckley family contain numerous details of the activities of their ancestors in the Llanelly area. Perhaps the most significant of these was Henry Child whose daughter married the first of the Lancashire Buckleys to settle in South Wales. Those acquainted with genealogy will know that from time to time a man of unusual ability and energy appears in the pedigree, who will establish the family fortunes or add materially to them. Such a man was Henry Child. He was born at Freystrop in Pembrokeshire in 1742, a member of one of those small and numerous gentry families at one time characteristic of West Wales. About that period, Sir Thomas Stepney of Prendergast near Haverfordwest, married one of the heiresses of the family who lived at the old mansion near the parish church of Llanelly, called Llanelly House. Stepney then settled there, and brought with him young Henry Child as his land agent. He proved active and competent, and some time afterwards, Vaughan of Golden Grove appointed him steward of manors in the Llanelly area. Child had an eye to business, and acquired a small malt-house in Llanelly. As a result of his work as agent he came into close contact with the tenants, mainly farmers, and so was able to find where the best grain grew, and to buy it for his own business. As a steward of the manors he had to arrange meetings of the court leets. He then took a public house, The Falcon, at which he held the courts. One of his duties was to see to perambulations of manorial boundaries – "beating the bounds" – after which he led the tenants back to The Falcon where cooling drafts of good ale awaited them. The Falcon too, became the venue for receiving rents, and Henry Child's bills to Squires Vaughan and Stepney, for meals and ale to the rent-paying tenants, have survived, and it is interesting to note that the bills for ale and spirits were over ten times as much as for the food consumed. Beating the bounds is thirsty work, but I have reason to suspect that Llanelly men were thirsty even *before* they set out on the journey. Now, John Vaughan and Sir Thomas Stepney, and afterwards his son Sir John, were prominent politicians, and Henry Child was not long in seeing how he could cash in on politics also. At election times the forty-shilling freeholders met at The Falcon, and then trooped away under Henry Child's guidance to give their votes at the hustings. His undertakings expanding, Child bought some farms, then launched out as a grain merchant. This venture prospered, and before long he obtained a lease of a wharf at Llanelly dock where he could export the corn he amassed, so became an export merchant.

As Llanelly was a growing town, more food was required locally, specially flour for making bread. Child, awake to the possibilities, in 1800 acquired a lease of Llanelly mill from Sir John Stepney, and the freehold of Felinfoel mill. The increase in population caused his businesses to flourish, particularly the brewing, and he built a bigger malthouse near to where the present Buckley Brewery stands. In 1795 he obtained a 60 years lease of the land for his brewery, at a rent of £5 per annum. He also opened out in new fields. He became an auctioneer, he leased the tithes of Llanelly parish, and also a barn where he received the goods in kind. He took part in public life and was nominated a commissioner for putting Acts of Parliament into operation. In 1810 Henry Child and his son William, were trustees named in the Act of Parliament for enclosing lands in Llanelly parish and for leasing the said lands and applying the rents to improving the town and port. He ruled his little empire from his home in what is now Thomas Street, near Thomas House.

Like the Stepneys he was a sympathiser of the Wesleyan movement. John Wesley stayed at his house while on visits to Llanelly, and for fifty years ministers were hospitably entertained beneath his roof. His religious nature is shown by the fact that the first Wesleyan chapel at Llanelly was built in Henry Child's garden in 1792.

He died in 1824 at the age of 82 years and the mural tablet to his memory in the chancel of Llanelly parish church, says: ". . . for more than half a century he patronized and promoted by his council and influence the interests of his town and its vicinity; he was the benevolent friend of the poor, uniform in his zealous attachment to, and liberal support of, religion, . . . an exemplary ornament of its virtues."

He had come a long way – agent, maltster, farmer, innkeeper, miller, auctioneer, steward of manors, wharf-owner, corn factor, exporter, and commissioner of acts of Parliament. His amazing energy, shrewd evaluation of possibilities, and intelligently-directed efforts, ensured him an established position in the life of Llanelly, and his philanthropy after he had acquired a well-earned competence, secured him a place in the affections of the community. Of his nine children, only one left issue. She was Maria Child, the ultimate heiress of her father, who married the Reverend James Buckley, a well-known Wesleyan divine.

The drive and energy of old Henry Child has been inherited in good measure by his descendants, who, over the years have expanded what was a local industry into a flourishing enterprise – so that in our times ambrosial draughts are still being brewed in the "land of the bards".

The Buckley muniments contain valuable material relating to the growth and development of the estates. For instance in 1824 Miss Elizabeth Buckley writes to her brother James, then in London. She says she was at two grand parties at Llanelly, and received invitations from Charles Nevill and Martin Roberts to go to concerts and so on. She ends her letter in this way – "Please to send me a small China crepe handkerchief to wear on my neck at tea parties: if China Crepe is out of fashion, any other kind that is light will do: it must not be large, *and put it down to Father's account*". Here indeed is a very human activity that youth of all periods have indulged in, a cross which fathers have so constantly borne.

Sometimes letters were sent from London to Llanelly, describing many strange and novel sights. In 1842, Anne Roe wrote to her cousin Mrs. Buckley, "Amidst the things we saw was the Thames Tunnel where we had a polite interview with Sir Something Brunell. We went to the further end of it, and were highly gratified. We saw Greenwich Hospital, and the poor maimed men going to dinner. It is a superb building and well worth notice. Madam Tussaud's magnificent collection of wax figures are well worth notice also . . .". I think the description "Sir *Something* Brunell" for one of the most distinguished engineers of the century, is a nice touch.

Another nice touch is contained in a letter of 1850 addressed to James Buckley, in which it is stated that Danygraig had been let to Mr. Nevill. The writer was pleased at this, and adds, "Mr. Nevill will made a good and safe Tenant". I feel that the shade of old Henry Child would have approved of the choice of a tenant whose rent-paying capacity was above reproach. A letter dated 1830 from a Mr. Fisher of London to Mr. James Buckley is of particular interest to Llanelly people, He says that he is a councilman of the Corporation of the City of London, and has persuaded the Lord Mayor, aldermen and council to use materials from Swansea and Llanelly for making the surface of Blackfriars Bridge. He says: "I don't mean cinders or iron dross, but the heavy hard copper dross, of which vast heaps I saw lying about when in South Wales, and I understood that the Proprietors would allow any one to take it away or even pay to get rid of it. I wish to know the lowest rate per ton for supplying 500 to 1000 tons during the next 6 to 8 months to be cast into barges alongside on the river below London Bridge, payment made on delivery. It might be brought altogether or as ballast or as part of the loading, say 20 to 80 tons at a time." It is an intriguing thought that the waste products from the Nevill copperworks at Llanelly helped to form the surface of a bridge that spanned the Thames over a century and a quarter ago.

I would like to revert to Carmarthenshire inns and their uses in olden times. Apart from providing food and drink the inn or tavern played an essential part in public life.

As I have mentioned they were used as places to collect rents, to entertain tenants, and to hold court leets. They were popular places for holding coroners' courts, and were often used by magistrates. There are instances of adjourned sessions of the County Quarter Sessions being held at the larger inns in Carmarthen and Llandeilo.

There is one aspect which has not received the attention it deserves, namely the tavern as a political weapon. The Whigs and Tories regarded the public house as a part of election machinery. In pro-Reform days polling took several days to complete, and the agents when it suited their book, would find ways and means for prolonging the polling so that it extended to a week or more. This they did by objecting to voters, whom they cross-examined at length, and so held up proceedings, while the sheriff, depending on the party to which he belonged, could declare the poll closed for the day in order to prolong the affair. This meant that the country voters, had to stay a night or two, even three or four, to await a chance to vote. Public houses owned by Tories would not serve Whigs with food and drink or give them lodgings, while Whig-owned houses treated Tories similarly. In the election of 1802, this proved disastrous to the Whigs. In Llandeilo, for instance, the Whig landlord, who was in financial difficulties, sold most of the inns he owned, and they were acquired by his political opponent, Lord Dynevor. Mr. Evans of Highmead collected over 60 voters in the Llangeler-Newcastle Emlyn area, all farmers, who trotted on sturdy ponies behind their squire, to vote for the man of his choice. On arriving at Llandeilo, the Tories seized their chance. They started delaying tactics, and the poll closed on that day without any of the Highmead contingent having voted. They found that no tavern in Llandeilo would give them food or put them up for the night, and Mr. Evans had to lead his angry and frustrated voters back over the hills to their distant homes. In days of subsistence farming, farmers could not afford to be away long from the farms, a circumstance often exploited by the local politicians.

Old diaries are full of interest and instruction. Like letters they were not written for public consumption, and often reveal innermost thoughts, fond hopes, ambitions, and disappointments of the writers; they are mirrors of the soul. Diaries are particularly valuable inasmuch as they contain information that can be found in no other source, and often add a liveliness to the factual and prosaic chronicle of human activity.

One such series of diaries belonged to John Johnes, one-time owner of Dolau Cothi in North Carmarthenshire, for the period 1788-1816, containing detailed accounts of day-to-day life. I can touch on a few aspects only. It is possible to obtain an intimate picture of the life of a Welsh landed proprietor during the period of the Napoleonic Wars.

John Johnes, was the only son of John Johnes of Dolau Cothi. Born in 1708 he entered the army at the age of seventeen and served in the 64th Foot (with a brief spell in the 60th) until 1791 when he resigned owing to visitations of the gout, a complaint from which his father had died. He then settled at his ancestral home and discharged the responsibilities of a country gentleman, as a magistrate, deputy lieutenant, and in 1803 as High Sheriff of the county. By his wife, Elizabeth Bowen of Maes Llanwrthyl, he had several children, of whom the eldest, also named John Johnes, became eminent as a barrister-at-law, Recorder of Carmarthen and Chairman of Quarter Sessions.

His letters and diaries reveal the deep affection he felt for his home and the locality to which he had now returned for good. Among his virtues was a constant solicitude for the welfare of his tenants. He met them at the "biddings" to which he always contributed, at the fairs, in the hunting field, at church, and on 17 July 1797 he sat amongst the congregation who had come to Cayo "to hear Rowlands preach". He shared objections to tollgates, and in a meeting held at Llansawel in January 1796 concerning the proposal for a toll on Llandilo bridge, John Johnes denounced it as "a handicap on ye upper part of the country". His home was "open house" to the gentry, clergy, and other neighbours, and no poor person was ever turned away from his gates. When he died in 1819, it was said of him that "he was the father rather than the landlord of his tenantry, he never oppressed or discouraged".

Like all his family he had a taste for antiquities, and in 1796 carried out excavations in the Cayo district which led to the recovery of early gold ornaments and relics belonging to the Roman period, and made an effort to acquire the fine collection of early Welsh manuscripts that belonged to Gwynne of Glanbrane.

But his main interests were estate management and farming, and he spent his life effecting improvements, encouraging his tenants to do likewise. He repaired the fabric of Dolau Cothi, employing John Nash who supplied the new chimney pieces and built a billiard room for him. His diary for 5 September 1794 reads, "Put up ye Billiard table and play'd the first game on it with my eldest sister". He improved the outbuildings, and rebuilt various houses on the estate. In July 1814 he agreed with a man called "Breeches Coch" for building a cow house (the thatching excepted) at Tanylan for £12. 12s. 0d. and gave him half a crown as "earnest," and in the September following erected a building at Abermangod mill to hold a carding machine at a cost of £46 4s. 7½d.

In 1794 he started to reorganise the gardens and built several glass-houses, where cucumbers, raddishs, onions, carrots, York and Drumhead cabbage, and "salading" were planted. Potato crops grew in both garden and fields and after picking were stored in specially prepared pits covered with straw and earth, protected by a fence. The fence was not always as effective as it should have been, and on 21 December 1812, he was angered with one Thomas through whose carelessness some enterprising pigs had enjoyed a glorious fortnight within the potato pit, the news having been conveyed to him "by the dairy girl", clearly no admirer of the negligent Thomas.

Large quantities of marl and peat ashes served as fertilisers in addition to farmyard manure.

Numerous entries contain valuable information about the prices of cattle. In 1794 he paid £6 5s. 0d. for a cow, and in the following year bought another for £6 15s. 0d. and a bull for £5 17s. 6d. Draught oxen were still used although horses were beginning to supplant them, particularly for ploughing. In 1794 he paid £11 for a pair of oxen, and the following year sold them for £4 14s. 6d.; in 1796 he received £26 9s. 6d. for a pair of oxen and a heifer. Several entries concern the shoeing of these animals.

By 1812 values had risen. In March of that year Johnes bought a pair of oxen for £24 from "William Davies the drover" to whom he gave 2 shillings "as luck". In 1814 he sold a pair for £30. Most of his milch cows consisted of the old Welsh blacks, but he had some other breeds as well, for in November 1795 he records the slaughter of "my Hereford shire cow".

The mountainous region in which he lived was favourable for sheep-rearing. In 1794 he bought 57 sheep and lambs at an average price of 8 shillings each. In June 1808 he sold seven small pigs for 8 shillings each. The only reference to horses is contained in an entry in July 1813, when he sold "my grey horse at Carmarthen fair" for £40 8s. 0d.

Like his more famous brother-in-law and cousin Thomas Johnes of Hafod in Cardiganshire, he took a keen interest in afforestation, and planted extensively in the vicinity of Dolau Cothi, along the hedges and roadsides, as well as forming new plantations at various other places on the estate. Between 1795 and 1813 he planted 4,917 trees, mainly larch, Scotch fir and oak. He was particularly active in 1808, and in March of that year Jack y Rhos drove the cart to Carmarthen Quay to collect 2,000 Scotch firs, 6 May Duke Cherry trees, 2 Orlean plum trees, two Morella trees for the garden wall, and a lonely Damson. On 13 March Jack delivered them to his master at Dolau Cothi, and within a fortnight fences were made and ground prepared for a new plantation at Penylanwen.

An entry on 13 March 1813 is of special interest, for it recorded that he planted 307 oak trees on the side of the road leading towards Llwynceiliog – "This plantation was made where I cut the oaks last year" an interesting example of re-afforestation.

Although these figures cannot be compared with the marathon performance of Johnes of Hafod who planted over one million trees it shows nevertheless that the landed proprietors of Carmarthenshire were conscious of the value and necessity of timber on their estates. In 1795, for instance, John Johnes had sold the groves at Maesyrhaidd and Llwynceiliog to Ben Davies for £800.

Wages paid to servants and casual workmen were carefully entered. In August 1794 he paid mowers 1 shilling a day; in October 1807 "Kitty of the Mill" received fourpence a day for 21 days toil. In October 1813 he paid 8 pence a day to casual labourers for work on the farm, which included making a ditch "around the Plantation". On Mrs. Johnes' behalf he paid "Jane of Llansawel, seamstress", 3 shillings for 6 days attention to the family wardrobe.

During harvest-time he received help from his tenants and neighbours, and after harvesting the wheat in August 1807, 39 people sat down to dinner at Dolau Cothi.

Interested in afforestation, John Johnes encouraged his tenants to plant trees, singly, in clumps, in avenues, sometimes in small groves. He himself gave a lead. For instance, in 1807-8 he planted 3,900 trees. In an entry in 1813 he says "I planted on the side of the road going to Llwynceiliog

307 oaks: this plantation was made where I cut the oaks last year", being an example of re-afforestation, in days when there were no government grants or aid. We learn about the wages he paid. In 1808 he had 6 outdoor servants, among whom the dairy girl received £3 10s. a year, the cow-girl £3 5s., and Little Tom the shepherd £2 2s. There were four indoor servants, the butler received £9 9s. a year, the cook £7 10s., the children's nurse and the housemaid £5 10s. each.

Sometimes a rift appeared in the lute. Under 3 November 1808 we read – "Catherine Allen the nursemaid hired herself last night for another year, but this morning she returned the earnest and left, although my wife expects a child"; and adds feelingly the words: "Catherine Allen is a sly bitch."

Another human touch is revealed in his dealings with the rat-catcher. He had suffered a great deal from rats which made serious inroads on his corn-loft. The entry read "I paid the rat-catcher 1 guinea. However, if he fails to destroy the rats, he is to come again to destroy them – gratis".

He possessed normal virtues and weaknesses as the following entries for 1797 reveal: I paid the smuggler 7 guineas: I drank too much brandy."

9 June. I took the oath of Justice of the Peace.

22 June. I paid the smuggler £3 10.

Diaries of Miss Hermione Jennings of Gellideg for the years 1865-71, provide a vivid picture of the life of a young lady of fashion, containing descriptions of assemblies and routs in Carmarthenshire, her presentation at Court, her first London season, visits to country houses and watering places, archery meetings at Llandeilo, dinners and house parties in west Wales. She was observant, pert, articulate, and her writing is like good conversation of some vivacious hostess out of Madam de Sevigny or Proust, who has known courts and men. Later she married Captain Barclay of the 63rd Regiment of Foot.

Attractive features of country house life in Victorian days are revealed in her pages. One is the scale of entertainment. It was by no means unusual to find as many as 20 or 30 guests, complete with maids and valets, arriving and staying three or four days. There was no wireless or TV or canned music in those days, and so impromptu concerts, charades, and plays were produced and the parts acted by the guests and their hosts, visits were made to places of interest, old castles, and churches, Twm Shon Catti's cave, and so on. These were the creative activities of people relying on their own abilities, the important art of self-help and self-reliance.

Among letters that have survived are a number written by a man who deserves to be better known in Carmarthenshire. He was the Reverend Thomas Beynon, born in 1744, died in 1833. The son of a respectable yeoman in Llansadwrn, he received his early education at Carmarthen Grammar School, and in 1768 was admitted to Holy Orders at Abergwili. He became incumbent of Llanfihangel Cilfargen, Llanfihangel Aberbythych, Llandyfeisant, Llanedy, and Penboyr, Rural Dean of Emlyn, Prebendary of Clyro in Christ College, Brecon, and Archdeacon of Cardigan. He took a prominent part in repairing churches, supporting circulating schools, was a patron of eisteddfods, and gave practical support to writers and antiquaries. In addition he was agent for the Golden Grove estate from 1780 to 1810. Many hundreds of his letters have survived and from them we learn about Turnpike Trusts, religious matters, food riots at Carmarthen, political battles of the day, education, sport, and especially farming and estate management. They abound in human touches, but I have time to refer to one only.

There had been a herd of deer at Golden Grove, since the days of Queen Elizabeth. During Archdeacon Beynon's

Deer stalking in reverse

time a fearful stag ran with the herd. Several roads passed through the park used by the people of the district and other travellers. The stag became the terror of the countryside. On seeing human beings it stamped, roared mightily and charged furiously towards them. Farmers and their wives had to run for their lives and leap like grasshoppers over protecting hedges; Mr. Beynon himself had more than once been the object of its aversion, and had complained to Lord Cawdor.

But no notice was taken of his complaints, However in 1805 the Archdeacon had a narrow escape. He wrote a stern letter to Cawdor describing how he had been forced to climb a tree to avoid the outrageous creature, and where he had been forced to remain for two whole hours. This proved too much for ecclesiastical dignity, and he now asked for the death penalty. Cawdor, who seems to have had an affection for the stag, replied that he was sorry about the affair, but felt that it would be a pity to destroy what was in fact a very fine animal. Beynon was not so easily put off, and in letter after letter reverted to the matter, while Cawdor found means to postpone a decision. Finally, in April 1806, Cawdor agreed to its destruction, and Beynon, and the whole countryside, breathed a joyous sigh of relief. Beynon's reply, full of gratitude, now that his old enemy was to be liquidated, ended with this classic sentence – "However, the Stag shall be preserved until your Lordship comes to the Country, for as he has been tolerated for so long it would be a pity to kill him till he is sufficiently *fat.*" Now, you see what I mean by the human element.

Business accounts, although they deal mainly with figures, percentages, profit and loss, need not be dry-as-dust affairs. We can often interpret them in human terms, and behind cold figures we can see hands hewing at the coal, attending the furnaces, or driving the plough. This is particularly true of old farming accounts. A friend who has a small farm in the Nantgaredig area has brought to me from time to time documents relating to the activities of his ancestors, going back to about 1750. He brings me, now a diary, now a bundle of old deeds, now a few letters, old wills, and so on, with the result that I have a pretty faithful record of the life of a Carmarthenshire farming family of the more modest kind.

These accounts were very detailed. A small herd of milch cow's was kept, about 16 in number on the average. No milk was sold as such, but was mainly used for making butter and cheese, and the skim milk fed to the animals. In the year 1889 he sold 1,200 lb. of butter for which he received £67 6s. 11d. The following year showed a much greater production, and he sold 2,154 lb. for £122 10s. 2d., the price varying between 8d. and 1s. 2d. per lb.

In 1895 Cheese sold at 1½d. to 1¾d. lb., and five years later varied from 1¾d. to 2d. per lb. In 1891 he sold a cow, "Cwrlen fach", for £8: a yearling bull for £9; and a black sheep and 2 lambs for £3 10s. 0d.

By the time I had read through the accounts I felt they had become my friends. In the cowshed were *Seren, Pinken, Cochen fach, Brithwen, Cwtwen, Penscwar, Llwydn, Gweno, Victoria, Beauty,* and *Susie Jane.* Among the horses – *Fly, Derby* and *Boss.* And three little pigs, *Betsy, Shanw,* and *Pet.*

He kept a servant man and maid. In the period 1840-99 the men received £16 p.a., and the maids from £8 to £11 per annum. They were not paid weekly, but the farmer was used as a bank upon which the servants drew as and when required. A very careful account was kept, and at Michaelmas the score was drawn up – *dydd o ddifyr bwyso* – and the balance still owing paid up. Here for instance is the way one of his men was paid over the year – new sleeves to waistcoats 1/4, to go home 2/-, repairing watch 10/-, medicine for warts 3d., Abergwili fair 10/-, Carmarthen races 1/-, Capel Mair Eisteddfod 1/-, for a bicycle £1, for Bible Society 3d., and 2/4 for a bottle of gin. Let us look at the payments to one of the maids – for clogs 3/9, for boots 10/-, for pinafore 2/-, kid gloves 2/6, for umbrella 9d., for calico to send home to mother 16/-, *ffair newydd Caerfyrddin* 1/-, for corsets 2/-, and for a small-tooth comb 6d.

Unless the human aspect is brought into the affairs of the bygone centuries – it need be only incidental touches, vignettes as it were – the 20th-century reader will find it difficult to feel at home in those distant times.

I have tried to give you glimpses of life in this part of Wales in days that are gone. I have tried to capture a scene where the passing moment lingers, a spot where Old Father Time, when he thinks nobody is watching him, sits down by the wayside to take breath. They are pictures of people concerned with domestic and homely matters. In the past, our history books have contained much emphasis on great and grand people, emperors and kings, generals and admirals, stirring events, battles on sea and on land. But this is only one part of the picture, for history is a rolling panorama of chanting landscapes and contrasts. We must seek for completeness. The retired Bishop at the coronation of a mighty monarch, but also the induction of a parish priest; the battle that changed the course of history, but also the religious revival that elevated the souls of the lowly; the wheeling of gorgeous squadrons that glitter in the sun, but also the merriment of little children in the playground of a county school.

History is not something remote, difficult, dead. It is alive, human, gay. All of us in our various ways are part of history. We are creating history, each one of us, at this very moment.

Perhaps in a hundred years' time someone will compile the history of the Society of Dairy Technology. He will describe its origins, state its objects, trace its development, and blazon its successes and achievements. He will relate how the Society held a meeting at Trinity College on the evening of 10 April 1972, and maybe he will add a footnote to say that it was addressed by a grey-haired antiquary who concluded by saying he was proud to have been privileged to address the members and wished their future activities all the success they deserved.

Training College, Carmarthen

"A LOCAL STUDY OF CARMARTHEN TOWN IN 1923"

CARMARTHEN is a town situated on the north side of the River Towy, about 16 miles from the entrance of the river into the Bristol Channel. The average height of land is about 60 ft. above sea level. Its latitude is 51' 8° n. and its longitude 4' 3° west.

The town or at least the castle, has been besieged several times. Its site forms the natural centre of a productive (agricultural) area, offers special facilities for defence, and commands the main route through which the traffic of the district passes. It is a centre from which authority, military, governmental and ecclesiastical is exercised. It is a market town also, and the farmers of the district bring their produce to be sold, and return with what they require from the many local shops and stores. Thus, being of model importance, Carmarthen has developed into a centre of instruction, and has also places of amusement.

Communication is adequate, there being a river, roads and railways. The last named is the most efficient means of communication, and just outside the environs of the town there is a railway junction. Here meet the main lines running up to London and down to Fishguard, and the branch line which leads to Cardiganshire and north Wales. The main line to Fishguard is a very important one and crosses the river by means of a draw-bridge.

The roads converge on Carmarthen and it is of great interest to note that the Carmarthen bridge, which is the main artery of traffic to the district outside the town, was originally built by the Romans. Its present condition is dangerous and it is proposed to erect a new one.

At one time the river was a very important route for communication. The town used to be a very good port and noted for its shipbuilding. However, since the making of larger ships, only the small boats are able to come up the river. Boats of about 100 tons bring flour, etc. to the town, and in order to pass the railway bridge the bridge has been made to open. Boats cannot proceed up the river unless the tide is a spring one; thus the tides control this means of communication. During the year 1923, twenty steamers and two sailing ships made 22 trips to the port; they came from different ports, mainly from Cardiff and Barry. The various cargoes consisted of corn, flour, granite chippings and general cargo.

According to the Census of 1911 the population of the district (including the Mental Hospital) was 10,221. The Census of 1921 showed a decrease of 210. Undoubtedly, this change is due to the number of local men who fell in the Great War. However, the estimated population to the middle of 1923 was 10,110, showing an increase of 99.

The River Towy presents an admirable example of a river meandering. A little way past Abergwili the river has left its original course, leaving an ox-bow lake, known as Bishop's Pond. The main valley is constantly liable to flooding, the floods spreading debris over the land. At the margins, however, the land is safer from flooding, and as it slopes up it escapes the cold mists which hang in winter over the river. These marginal lands are given over largely to grazing. Surrounding the valley is a dissected plateau, and on the slopes of the hills we see a few woodlands, some of which have been cut down.

History of the town

The name Carmarthen, or Caerfyrddin as it is called in Welsh, is popularly supposed to be derived from the celebrated Welsh sage, Myrddin Emrys, or Merlin Ambrosius, who dwelt here about the middle of the 5th century. However, it is older than the age of Merlin. It is pretty well agreed that the name is formed from the Welsh words "Caer", "mor", "din", signifying a fortified seaport. In English, caer is represented by caster, cester, or chester, and din by dun, don or town. Some say that the second syllable comes from the Latin "murus", meaning a wall, but the probability is that it is "mor" (Latin Mare), the sea, of which "myr" is an old plural form. The old Latin name of the town was Maridunum.

Little is known of the early history of Carmarthen, but it is said that a Roman station was founded here as early as A.D. 70. Welsh records ascribe the founding of the town to Macsen Bledig, born in Spain, and an officer of the Roman army in Britain, who revolted against the Emperor Gratian and was proclaimed emperor by the soldiers A.D. 383.

There also was a castle in the town, on the present site of the gaol. The north-west gateway and portcullis, flanked by two circular towers, are still entire.

When Speed drew a map of the town in 1610, the town wall seems to have been standing. He also marked the Priory, which was situated near the present Prior Chapel in Priory Street. There was a Friary in Carmarthen, standing where Dr. Bowen Jones's grounds are to be seen today.

The old town was the scene of many a bloody battle and the castle was besieged several times.

Entrenchments

A small entrenched position, near the Newcomb last in Llangunnor is supposed to have been formed by an outpost of Cromwell's army when it laid siege to the castle.

During the Civil War of the 17th century, Carmarthen was held for the Royalists. In the fields behind the Gas Works we see some fine earthworks that were thrown up as a defence. These walls of earth exist to the present day in perfect preservation, notwithstanding an act of vandalism, by which a length of the ditch was filled in. They are said to afford the finest example in the United Kingdom of earthen defences according to the strategic rules of the 17th century.

Carmarthen bridge

Local tradition says that the River Towy used to flow under Pen-y-Morfa and along by Pensarn. When the Romans came here they resolved to build a bridge in order to connect their settlements at Carmarthen and the west with the country on the east side of the river – in other words, their new road, Via Julia Maritama,

Nott's Square, Carmarthen

had to cross the river. Instead of building the bridge over the river, they built it on dry land (or rather near a marsh), and cut a new bed for the river, about 100 or 200 yards long, causing it to pass under the new bridge.

The bridge was built of small stones, and if one examines the arches it will be seen that it has been widened many times. It was widened 6 ft. in 1777, and the arch nearest the town was rebuilt in 1775. In 1828-1829 it was again widened and the recesses in the pillars, in which foot-passengers retired out of the way of traffic, were removed. A dwarf wall and railings were erected and later were replaced by those now on it. Only recently this bridge has been examined, and it has been decided to erect a new one, or put the present one in a suitable condition.

Rhyd-y-Gors

This name means "the ford of the marsh". It was situated near the present drawbridge of the Great Western Railway. Formerly, it was a small hill-fort built for the defence of the river passage. After the Roman period, its function as the guardian of the ford decayed. However, the name did not die out. Some time towards the close of the mediaeval period, a residence was erected on the opposite bank of the riser to the earthwork, and this building is still known as Rhyd-y-Gors.

Road Names

Priory Street, the road leading from St. Peter's Church to the most easterly point of the borough, takes its name from the Priory which used to be situated near by.

Dark Gate is so called because at one end of it there used to stand a gate of the town wall. From Dark Gate to St. David's Church is Lammas Street. Undoubtedly the name arises from the Feast of Lammas, which must have been observed by the friars of the neighbouring Friary.

Friars' Park is the name given to the little lanes that lead to the whereabouts of the old Friary.

Oysters for market

The names of Blue Street and Red Street are to be traced to the two political parties.

Spilman Street is in some way connected with the Spilman or Spelman family mentioned in some old local deeds.

Water Street had its name from the stream which now crosses under the road near the one-time turnpike gate, and Little Water Street from the water flowing from the hill side.

Dame Street, a mistaken refinement of Dam Street, is so called from a mill-dam at its upper end. Its present name, Mill Street, obscured the history of the neighbourhood.

Mansel Street is so named after Richard Mansel, who owned the ground.

Morley Street is named after a Mr. Morley, a cabinet-maker, whose premises extended from Lammas Street to St. Catherine's Street, which takes its name from St. Catherine's Chapel, which once stood near it.

Wood's Row is so called from an attorney whose offices were there.

Barn Row is named from the tithe barn that stood there.

Waterloo Terrace dates from the time of Wellington's victory.

Picton Terrace takes its name from Picton's monument which stands on the hill.

A barber named Jackson lived in Jackson's Lane; a cooper named Shaw lived in Shaw's Lane.

Richmond Terrace has been substituted by mistake for Richmead Terrace, a name suggested by Waendew, an adjacent meadow.

Morfa Lane (Morfa, a marsh), leads to the marshes formed by the river when in flood.

EXISTENCE OF RURAL INDUSTRIES

Today our country is an industrial country, the manufactures being carried on in factories. However, up and down the country we find in some places some old rural or peasant industries still existing. In Carmarthen and its neighbourhood about 50 years ago the occupation of a weaver was a very popular one, but this had declined since the factories have been introduced. Nevertheless, there are yet some rural industries existing in the locality.

In the town itself there are a few people who make baskets and other kinds of wicker-work and in the cottages of the rural districts we find many more folk engaged in the same practice. Many men do this work in their spare time.

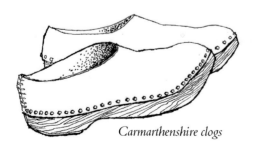

Carmarthenshire clogs

Again, clogs are made. The wood for the soles is obtained from the woodlands, and the leather is brought from other centres. Farmers and other country folk wear clogs when doing their work, and thus the clog makers do not find it difficult to have purchasers for their goods.

If one were to visit the market on a Saturday, one would see a stall of wooden spoons, etc. These articles are made in the neighbourhood of Whitemill.

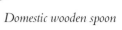

Domestic wooden spoon

Coopering is another occupation existing in Carmarthen. The coopers make the churns and wooden vessels needed by the farmers for the making of butter.

It is almost unnecessary to allude to the industry of fishing, because coracle fishing has for years been associated with the folk of Carmarthen.

There are two rope manufacturers in the town.

As the neighbouring countryside has many woods, the trees are usually cut down and sent to the colliery districts as pit-props, or are sent to the local saw mills to be sawn into planks etc.

SURVIVAL OF OLD OR CURIOUS CUSTOMS OR CRAFTS

"Mari Llwyd". There is an old, curious custom which still prevails in this area, especially in the village of Johnstown. It takes place during Christmastide and the first few days of the New Year. One person puts over his head the head of a horse made of wood or some other suitable substance, while another person goes behind him to form the back and the hinder legs of the animal. A white sheet is then placed to cover the two persons. This funny looking creature proceeds to the door of a house, and sings a very melancholy song, part of which is "Poor old horse, let him die". It can be imagined that this is a weird spectacle to find at one's door at night-time. Nevertheless, Mari Llwyd is not objected to, and those engaged in the performance go away the richer.

Blwyddyn Newydd Dda

Young folk still carry on the old custom of wishing people a Happy New Year (blwyddyn newydd dda). They go from door to door some time during the first twelve hours of the new year; they knock at the door and sing or say their greeting. As a reward they usually have money or sweetmeats.

Folklore – Old customs and ceremonies associated with deaths

"Sin Eating." Years ago, there was a very curious custom connected with the death of people, prevalent in this district. When dead, the person would be "laid out" in a coffin, and for a few days the coffin would be left open. In the meantime, a plate of food was laid on the breast of the deceased. An old man was called in to eat this food, for which action the eater received a small amount of money, perhaps a shilling. By eating this food it was commonly believed that the old man had eaten the sin of the dead person, thereby making the latter fit for the Kingdom of God.

This custom of sin-eating was not the only one associated with the death of people. Often, at the time of burial, the mourners were served with wine and cake. The wine was generally put into cups known as "funeral cups", two of which are to be seen in the Carmarthenshire Antiquarian Museum. To some extent this ceremony still exists. In some families, after the body of the dead one has been put to rest, those left to mourn the loss try to drown their sorrows by drinking as much liquor as possible.

ASSOCIATED WITH MARRIAGES

Weddings of years gone by were incidents of great interest. There were the large wedding processions, often consisting of five or six hundred persons, with the extinct Bidding; but those processions were headed by an inevitable wooden-legged flautist, and a club-footed fiddler, who by his ability to play seven tunes acquired a title "Ffidler saith twn".

Bidding

The Bidding is an old Welsh custom carried out in order to help the young marrying folk to set up a house. Of course, it was understood that when the contributors or any of their relations were married, the gifts were to be repaid. In order to make known the Bidding, the young people drew up a Bidding Letter, and sent it to their friends. Once the couple were united in matrimony, they were led to their new home by a huge crowd of people. These folk left the husband and wife when certain appointed men had seen the newly-married pair settled in their house. The following is a copy of a Bidding Letter.

> *Carmarthenshire, April 5th 1845*
>
> As we intend to enter the Matrimonial State on Thursday, the 9th day of May next, we purpose to make a *bidding* on the occasion, the same day, at the Young woman's Father's House, situated in the Village of Llanarthney, when and where the favour of your good and agreeable company is most humbly solicitated; and whatever donation you may be pleased to bestow on us then, will be thankfully received, and warmly acknowledged,
>
> *By your most obedient servants,*
> *John Jones*
> *Mary Thomas*
>
> The Young Woman, with her Father and Mother, Thomas and Sarah Thomas, together with her brothers, Thomas and William Thomas, desire that all gifts of the above nature due to them will be returned to the Young Woman on the said day, and will be thankful for all favours granted.
>
> The Young Woman's Parents will repay all gifts received on the above day.

Matrimonial spoons

In the Carmarthenshire Antiquarian Museum there are a pair of carved wooden "matrimonial" spoons over 200 years old – formerly used in this county. The two spoons are united in one; and the tradition is that on the occasion of a marriage, the bride and bridegroom were expected to drink from them together. If none of their contents were spilled, happy was their union; but if, on the other hand, some of the liquor was spilled, the result was not to be so pleasant.

Priodas Ceffylau (Horse Wedding)

Another old ceremony associated with wedding in this locality is that known as "Priodas Ceffylau". It was conducted after this manner: each person in the bridal party was provided with a horse, which he mounted. The party was then put in order of procession, the bride on her horse being placed far in front of the remainder of the procession. When all was ready, the procession set off, each member making his

"Get me to the Church on time" – the old way

or her steed gallop as fast as possible. The bridegroom did his utmost to overtake his beloved before she reached the church or place of marriage; and having arrived there, both were united in matrimony. This custom is still practised by Tartar nomad tribes and other primitive peoples in Central Asia today.

OTHER CEREMONIES, ETC.

Selecting the Mayor

For many years the Mayor elected was sworn in at his own residence, and not in the Town Hall. This is shown in the year 1651, when David Edwardes, Esq. was sworn in as Mayor of the Borough at his own mansion at Rhyd-y-gors.

On Charter Day, during a supposed cessation of the law, from sunrise to midday, burgesses were soundly beaten by the boys of the town, before they exercised their right of electing the Mayor.

Beating the Bounds

Every year it was customary for the Mayor and Burgesses to parade the boundaries of the Corporation lands in Carmarthen. This ceremony was known as "beating the bounds". When all this was over, the burgesses usually went to a certain inn, where there was a sumptuous dinner provided at the expense of the Mayor. At this meeting the Mayor and Sheriffs for the following year were elected, and the remainder of the evening was devoted to drinking and making merry.

The Admiral's Court

This was similar custom to the previous one. The Mayor acted as Admiral and Guardian of the river – from the Bridge to the Bar Pool. He boarded a ship in the company of the corporate officers, and together they proceeded in official pomp down the Towy, with the "silver oar". Should any obstruction be placed in the way so as to impede the navigation thereof, it was the Admiral's duty to see that the same was immediately removed.

Hiring and Pleasure Fairs

Pleasure Fairs are still held in Carmarthen. They are usually held on June 3, August 12 and November 14. The November Fair is known as "Ffair Cytuno" (Hiring Fair). It is at this fair that farm hands make a contract with certain farmers to serve them during the ensuing year. Hundreds of people, especially from the country, attend these pleasure fairs.

Punishments, etc

Of late, prisoners sentenced to death have been hanged in the gaol. Before the prison was built, those sentenced to the gallows were hanged at Pensarn, a little village situated on the other side of the town bridge.

Pillories and stocks were common sights in the town. One old inhabitant of the borough remembered a Welsh bard being put in the pillory four times for "doing something against the Government". At the old Market Cross there used to be the stocks – the terror of the disorderly. For a long while, the peace of the town was maintained by a single constable – Will y Lon.

Retribution. Pre Probation Officer era

Another old character, Old Shon Dwr, lived near the present market. It was his duty to take the sturdy vagrants that infested the country; he used to get them at the end of his cat's tail and whip them out of the town. This form of punishment ceased after Old Shon Dwr got more than he bargained for from an old sailor who had fought under Nelson. Man-traps were devices used to catch thieves or trespassers. They were concealed by the owner in a specified spot, and when the offender came along, he put his foot in the trap and was caught. Examples of these are seen in the local museum.

Another old custom was beating with rods of holly all persons found in the streets before noon on the 26th of December.

Omens and Charms

If the contracting parties in a marriage wore a borrowed article or garment at the wedding, their

Man (or person?!) trap

married life will be a happy one. A cat sitting with its back to the fire is a sign of snow.

A cat running about wildly is a sign of an approaching storm.

If soap falls on the floor when washing, it is a sign of a stranger coming to pay a visit.

If the fire will not light, the person's sweetheart is not in a good mood.

If, when a piece of bread and butter falls to the ground, the butter is nethermost, it is a sign of rain.

A person washes in a bowl of water, and another individual washes in the same water, if the latter does not make the sign of the cross in the water with his finger, and does not spit in the water, both persons will quarrel during the day.

When people move to another house, the first thing they take to the new house is a bar of salt. This ensures that the time spent in the house will be a happy one.

When the old oak tree in Carmarthen falls, it is said that the town will sink. This tree stands in Priory Street and is well propped up.

Public house signs and names, and their meanings

Carmarthen contains several old public houses and hotels. The largest of these are the Ivy Bush Hotel and the Boar's Head Hotel. The old saying "Good wine needs no bush" is said to refer to the old Roman custom of hanging a branch of ivy, the emblem of Bacchus, at the tavern door. The proverb implies that good wine would attract customers and advertise itself. Probably this is the reason for giving the hostelry in Spilman Street the name "Ivy Bush Hotel". Outside the Boar's Head Hotel there used to be a boar's head carved out of wood. This animal was hunted by many – it was a popular sport to do this – and hence the name given to the hotel. Similarly, the Stag and Pheasant received its name.

It is worth noticing the number of drinking houses named after certain occupations. We find in Carmarthen the Butcher's Arms, the Farmer's Arms, the Weaver's Arms, the Tanner's Arms, and the Cooper's Arms. Probably these ale-houses originated as meeting houses for the respective workmen, e.g. the weavers in the district gathered together in the Weaver's Arms to talk about business. The meeting was made more pleasant by having a good supply of ale at the disposal of the tradesmen.

A few examples of Carmarthen dialect

"To take a king abroad" – To take a king to pieces.
"I don't know what all" – I do not know what altogether.
"Dyn bach net" – A tidy, decent man; a good sort.
"Wy'n nabod e net" – I know him well.

Peculiar Welsh words and phrases

Besco, Cleber, Carco, Cawdel, Clwtyn, Clocsar, Crasfa, Cwn (chicks), Comjees, Dansherus, Loitran, Pwno, Pring, Shouc, Shape, Tyle, Tablen, Mor dwp a sledg, Gad dy brancs, Ffor co, Dan sac, Boddron, Browlan, Cwmws (perpendiculas or exact), Pinshin, Swmp, Swil (bath or a masher), Trwsho, Twmlo, Sprotian, Tywyll pitsh, Cerwch ona, Sang-di-fang, Tacle, Bechi'n galw.

Carmarthenshire Castles

The castles of Dryslwyn, Carreg Cennen, Newcastle Emlyn and Dynevor were built by the Welsh princes of Dynevor. The other Carmarthenshire castles were built by Norman overlords. That of Carmarthen, was a royal castle, built by the King before 1109, and was the first stone castle to be built in Wales. The County Record Office was once housed within its walls.

Chapter II

LAW ORDER AND DISORDER

Ave Atque Vale

A Brief Review of the History of the Quarter Sessions in Carmarthenshire

SO FAR AS WALES IS CONCERNED the year 1535 is the start point of the history of Justices of the Peace. They were introduced by the act of 27 Henry VIII, c.5 (1535) which provided for the appointment under the Great Seal of Justices of the Peace, Justices of the Quorum, and Justices of Gaol Delivery, who were to act within the Crown lands in Wales. The next stage was the Act of 27 Henry VIII, c.26, usually referred to as the "Act of Union" whereby Wales was united to England, and the separate jurisdictions – lordships Marcher and Crown lands – abolished, and the country formed into shires along the English pattern. The final stage was the act of 34-5 Henry VIII, c.26 (1542), which contained a section (54) stating that Justices of the Peace for the whole of Wales were to be appointed by the Lord Chancellor on the advice of the President and Council of Wales and the Justices of the Great Sessions, or by any three justices of whom the President had to be one. At the same time the Quarter Sessions and the Great Sessions were established for Wales. The latter functioned until July 1830 when they were abolished but the former continued to function until the end of 1971, a period of 429 years. The Quarter Sessions were abolished by The Courts Act 1971, which established with effect from 1 January 1972 a new court, The Crown Court, to try indictments and to exercise other jurisdiction previously exercised by courts of Quarter Sessions.

From 1542 the number of Justices of the Peace to each county was statutorily limited to eight, but this proved unrealistic, and the maximum limit was never observed, so that in 1581, for instance, Carmarthenshire had as many as twenty-five. The 17th century saw a further increase in their number, and in 1693 the King was empowered to appoint as many Justices of the Peace as he pleased. In the 18th century, the heyday of the squires, their numbers swelled considerably, so that in many counties, including Carmarthenshire, they eventually numbered over one hundred.

The Quarter Sessions met four times yearly, and in addition to their Judicial functions, the civil administration of the country was in their hands. It is true to say that the rulers of Wales, from this time onwards were the Justices of the Peace operating collectively through the Quarter Sessions. Edicts of central government could not be implemented without the co-operation of these unpaid administrators, and examples exist where they rendered totally ineffective certain acts of parliament which they felt were not in the interests of the inhabitants of counties in which they lived. It was a form of "Home Rule", when the Welsh were ruled by the class best qualified to do so, namely the old landed gentry, from whom the overwhelming bulk of the Justices came.

Maitland's dictum that the office of Justice of the Peace is the most distinctively English part of all our government institutions is one with which no informed person will disagree. The work of Justices as individuals is important, but more important still was their work as a combined body within each shire. It is through the co-operation of the Justices of the Peace that the Quarter Sessions became the effective instrument of the judicature throughout the land of Britain.

Two functions

I wish to emphasise again the Quarter Sessions had two distinct functions. Judicial and administrative matters were dealt with separately. Firstly, the Sessions dealt with criminal and civil cases. In other words, it had a purely judicial function, this aspect of its work continued until it was superseded by the introduction of Crown Courts. Secondly, the Sessions dealt with the civil administration of the county, and a glance at the records of Quarter Sessions will show that this was undoubtedly the greater part of their duties, a situation which continued until the Local Government Act of 1888 placed administration in the hands of the County Council elected exclusively to undertake that duty.

Few people today appreciate the important part that the justices played in the history of the county from 1542 onwards. Commenting on the introduction of Justices of the Peace in Wales, Trevelyan writes in his *History of England,* "supported by the strong arm of the central Government the Justices of the Peace were able to rule in the wild hill regions where feudalism and brutalism had run riot for centuries. These magistrates, under the system inaugurated by Henry VIII, were not Englishmen imported to hold down the natives, but Welsh gentlemen who were the natural leaders of the people".

Before the end of the Elizabethan age, the Justices of the Peace were an essential part of governmental machinery, and gradually became the rulers of Wales. The competence of their main court, the Quarter Sessions, was wide and vague. They could and did exercise "general authority". Their powers were not confined to criminal cases, but extended to adjudicating on certain civil cases. They were ministerial and executive officers as well as judicial, made their own regulations and enforced them. By the reign of James I the affairs of the shire were wholly in the hands of the Quarter Sessions, the supreme authority. Between 1688 and 1835 the Quarter Sessions assumed a legislative authority, enjoying complete autonomy. The Justices acted in three ways – as individual magistrates sitting alone (sometimes in their own parlours), jointly with a few colleagues in a division of the county, and collectively in general Quarter Sessions. It was a case of "Home Rule for Wales", where the land was governed and administered by Welshmen who lived on their own freeholds among their own folk, fully aware of local conditions, and, on the whole, a humane and responsible body of men. We must remember too, that there were very few "professionals" to help them, there was no organised bureaucracy, so that the Justice was no mere figurehead. He was hard worked and hard working.

Selection and number of Justices

For many centuries property ownership was a requirement for election to the Bench, originally land worth £20 annually (a large sum in Tudor times), and although in Wales this figure was lowered, land ownership remained the basic qualification. George Owen, the Pembrokeshire historian (died 1614) tells us that in his time "the justices and the chiefest gentlemen in every shyre that beare that office, with sum learned in the laws", adding, doubtless thinking of those with the lower landed qualifications, "dyvers men lyving are climbd upp to the bench by whom as the sayd statute sayeth the people will not be ruled". Thus it became the preserve of the landed gentry, but from the early 16th century industrialists, manu-facturers, and well-to-do tradesmen were added, but these always formed a minority. From the earliest part of the 18th century clergymen were added to the Bench. In the 19th century, and particularly in the twentieth, the field of selection was considerably widened, so that by today the Justices are representative of all sections of the community. So deeply entrenched was the notion of property-owning, that when the Justices of the Quarter Sessions were discussing the provisions of the proposed Local Government Bill, they resolved (26 April 1888) "That the County of Carmarthen recommends that the qualification for County Councillors whether elected or selected be the ownership of property or residence within the County". That "ownership of property" is placed first in these requirements is a significant indication of their way of thinking.

Those appointed to be Justices had to take statutory oaths in open court, and to present certificates that they had taken Holy Communion in the parish church according to the rites of the Established Church. In 1802 William Paxton, esquire, took the oaths as a magistrate; in 1803 there was a spate of new magistrates – David Heron Pugh, William McClary, Howell Price, Jenkin Davies, the Revd. Lewis Lewis, the Revd. Daniel Bowen, R. I. Starke, Herbert Evans, the Revd. Evan Holliday, Evan Jones of Dolwilym, William Skyrme, Llewellyn Parry of Gernos (Cards.), and Lord Kensington. In 1825, Sir William Champion de Crespigny Bt., of Rhosduon Fawr, Pencarreg, took the oath as a landowner of £100 per annum; in 1836 the Revd. Llewelyn Lewellin, D.C.L., Principal of St. Davids College, Lampeter, and in 1864, a *rara avis,* Henry Ridgard Bagshaw took the oath as required from him as a Roman Catholic to enable him to act as a magistrate for Carmarthenshire.

At the accession of a new monarch, the Justices again subscribed to the customary oaths. At the Quarter Sessions held on 14 July 1830, it was ordered that all magistrates were to take oaths of allegiance, supremacy, and abjuration, to His Majesty King William IV.

Their loyalty was further expressed in numerous congratulatory addresses to the sovereign and other members of the Royal Family. In 1837 they sent an address of congratulation to Queen Victoria on her accession to the Throne, and an address of condolence to the Queen Dowager on the death of his late Majesty. In 1842 they sent loyal messages to the Queen, Prince Albert, and the Duchess of Kent, on the occasion of an attempt on the Queen's life by one John Francis (a man with no Carmarthenshire connections). In 1862 they sent an address of condolence to the Queen on the death of

The Prince Consort. A more felicitous occasion was the marriage of The Prince of Wales, which drew from the justices in Quarter Sessions assembled the following address on 9 April 1863:

"Most Gracious Sovereign. We your Majesty's Justices of the Peace in Quarter Sessions assembled, approach your Majesty with sentiments of affectionate loyalty requesting that Your Majesty will be pleased to accept our sincere congratulations upon the occasion of the marriage of His Royal Highness The Prince of Wales with a Princess of the Royal Line of Denmark. We offer up our heartfelt prayers that the mutual affection which was the germ of that happy union may daily increase and that the guardianship of heaven may shield their Royal Highnesses from all events which may have ever a tendency to disturb their future happiness. We fully anticipate that the happiness which we fervently hope may ever attend their Royal Highnesses' path through life may shed a beneficial influence over the sorrow of which your Majesty has been so heavily afflicted and that the affectionate efforts of their Royal Highnesses will ever be directed to aid and support your Majesty in the conduct of the arduous affairs of State and to afford comfort and solace to the hours of leisure, relieved from the duties of the elevated position in which your Majesty's wishes have been so successfully realised by exertions to promote the welfare and happiness of your people throughout your Majesty's extensive dominions."

In January 1879 an address was forwarded to console with Her Majesty upon the death of the Princess Alice. In April 1864 they sent addresses of congratulations on the birth of Prince Albert Victor to the Prince and Princess of Wales, and a similar address to the Queen. The 50th anniversary of the Queen's reign in 1887 provided a further occasion for a congratulatory address.

Meeting places

From medieval times to our own, the Justice of the Peace would sit with his fellow-Justices in general Quarter Sessions for his native shire. In theory all Justices were entitled, indeed expected, to attend, so that when fully assembled, the Court of Quarter Sessions with its Bench of Justices, juries, officials, clerks, lawyers, and prisoners, may have numbered a hundred or more. During the last century the number of Justices who attended the Carmarthenshire Quarter Sessions numbered between 6 and 35. In 1863 for instance, the Chairman sat at Carmarthen flanked by 33 Justices. The accommodating of such number inevitably created a problem, and the Carmarthenshire records often mention extensions having to be made to the Shire Hall. During the 19th century the work of the Sessions increased rapidly, with the result that it became necessary to appoint numerous committees to deal with matters in detail and report their findings to the General Quarter Sessions, where they were either confirmed or referred back. Some Justices failed to attend as regularly as they might, whereupon the Clerk of the Peace placed an asterisk opposite the names of defaulting members when he prepared the minutes. This custom annoyed some of the Justices, none more so than Sir Richard Jennings of Gellideg. Accordingly at the Quarter Sessions held on 7 April 1881, Mr. Jennings got on his feet and gave notice that at the next Sessions he would move that the custom of placing stars opposite the names of gentlemen who failed to attend committees be discontinued. The Clerk of the Peace gravely entered the notice of motion in the records of the court. The next Sessions were held on 24 June 1881, and how the Clerk must have chuckled when he entered this minute – "Mr. Jennings's motion to discontinue placing stars opposite the names of gentlemen who failed to attend committees was not moved, *because Mr. Jennings was not present*".

In well organised Sessions, the first day was taken up in reading a proclamation of recent statutes, and charges read to the jurors and officials. The hearing of presentments and trial of cases would follow on the succeeding days. A case would normally be tried on the day following the indictment, sometimes not until the next Sessions. However, the administration of county matters, what would be called local government today, occupied most of the time of the Sessions.

The meetings were usually held at the shire halls in Carmarthen and Llandeilo, alternately. But they were by no means always held in these towns or in shire halls in the earlier days. For instance on 1 February 1740 the meeting was held at the Old Plough Inn in Llandovery, when James Price of Cilgwyn the newly elected Clerk of the Peace subscribed to the customary oaths. At the end of that Sessions it was decided that the next Quarter Sessions be held in the inn kept by the widow Chapman in St. Clears, and in the autumn of 1749 they were held at The Red Lion, Llandeilo, when the innkeeper received 40 shillings "for the use of his house to hold the Quarter Sessions" and in the summer of 1752 they were held at Llandeilo in the house of one Thomas Beynon who received two guineas "for the use of his room to hold this Sessions". The Winter Sessions of 1801 were held in a house in Spilman Street, Carmarthen, and the Spring Sessions of the following year at the Bear Inn, Llandeilo, and the Summer Sessions of 1802 at the house of Vaughan Horton, J.P., in King Street, Carmarthen. During the 19th century they were held in the shire halls of Carmarthen and Llandeilo.

Cases

All manner of cases came before the Quarter Sessions, the most important ones being sent on to the Court of Great Sessions (which operated from 1542 to 1830) or to the Assizes. They included homicide, assaults and violence (particularly numerous), burglary and theft (there seems to have been a high percentage of nimble-fingered folk in the county), riots, theft from wrecks, forgery, and so on. When an offence merited heavier punishment, the cases were sent to the superior court, that of the Great Sessions. Thus on July 1809 a writ of *certiorari* was produced for removing to the Great Sessions the indictment found against eighteen men for unlawful assembly, riot, and demolishing two limekilns in Pendine parish and in January 1812 a similar writ removed the indictment against Rees Goring Thomas for failing to repair the churchyard wall of the parish church of Llannon, to the superior court.

Some of the punishments may seem harsh to us today, but doubtless "fitted the crime" in a somewhat rough age – imprisonment with hard labour, transportation, "sent to the hulks", whipping, fines, and so on. Thus in 1749 Daniel James, gaoler, was paid £1 for whipping Enoch Charles, a convicted felon. The gaoler himself was no angel, for in the

Spring Sessions of 1750 he was fined £5 "for his Insolent Behaviour to the Court now sitting". In 1752 Morgan William a shoemaker of Llangadog was fined half-a-crown for "keeping a Disorderly House". In 1797, nine men were indicted for "a Riot and Disturbance at Llannon, against the authority of the Magistrates there assembled, and the hindrance of justice, and in 1801 the Quarter Sessions offered a reward of 20 guineas for discovering the author of a "Threatening Handbill" sent to magistrates in the Laugharne and St. Clears districts. A writ of *certiorari* was produced in the Summer Sessions of 1811 in respect of one Thomas Richards of Llandingat "for disquieting and disturbing the congregation assem-bled at a Meeting house" [place of worship] and for an assault. A more serious case was that of William Prosser who in 1821 was committed for contempt of court and tampering with the Grand Jury. In the Spring Sessions of 1797 it was ordered that the High Sheriff apprehend five men for plundering the wreck of the Swedish vessel, *Hedevig Charlorta,* on the coast of Laugharne. Some officials were not beyond reproach, particularly Richard Penry, a constable of Llanedy parish, who was prosecuted in 1797 for forgery, namely altering the figure 6d. to 18d., in a pass granted to a vagrant by Nathaniel Morgan, J.P. Men were also fined for failing to attend for jury service after having been summoned to do so, thus in 1834 Thomas Rees of Abercover and William Yalden of Vauxhall were each fined 40 shillings for not appearing to serve on the Grand Jury.

Local officials were punished for failing to attend the Sessions, such as Morgan David, chief constable of the upper division of Cayo, and Samuel Charles, constable of Kidwelly, who were fined 40 shillings apiece in 1751 for non-attendance. Where good reason was shown the names of certain men qualified to be jurors were struck off the list by order of the magistrates. In 1750 Peter Rutherch of Llandeilofawr, and in 1794 John Zacharias of Conwil Elfed, gentle-man, were excused further service as they were over 70 years of age and infirm. In 1801, David Jones of Bailybedw, Llanllwni, was excused, "being deaf", and in 1825 William Hancock of Moche, Llanstephan, was granted a writ of ease, "he being liable to fits".

In the Summer Sessions of 1801, Mary Price of Llangunnor was found guilty of stealing a blue, red and white striped petty coat, a check linen apron, and a spotted shawl handkerchief, of the total value of 4s. 2d., and sentenced to 6 months in a solitary cell in the House of Correction, and kept to hard labour. For stealing a silver tea spoon valued at 10 pence, in 1801, David John of Cilrhedyn, yeoman, was ordered to be delivered to Sergeant Lewis of the 46th Regiment of Foot to be conveyed immediately to the said regiment then in Ireland, and in the same sessions Priscilla John of Llanarthney was sentenced to 12 months solitary confinement with hard labour for stealing two ducks.

Another form of punishment awaited William Davies, convicted for theft, who was conveyed from Carmarthen Gaol to Portsmouth harbour to be delivered on board the *Lyon* hulk in 1800; and in the following year Hannah Williams, similarly convicted, was conveyed to the hulk *Nile* lying at Spithead. Harry Lloyd, a labourer of Llanfairarybryn having been found guilty of stealing articles valued at 14 shillings in 1821, was sentenced to transportation for 14 years to one of His Majesty's Dominions beyond seas.

On the other hand, a curiously modern ring is provided by an order in the Sessions of 1822 when the Court ordered that a stove be obtained for the lock-up at Llandovery, "necessary for the comfort of those that may be confined therein". In 1795 the County Treasurer was authorised to spend £5 to provide coals for "the poor prisoners now confined in the County Gaol". Neither were the spiritual needs of prisoners overlooked, and in 1810 it was ordered that "six or eight Godly books" be provided for them.

Numerous references are found to Rebecca rioters, and in 1840 the gaoler was authorised "to purchase a caravan for the conveyance of Prisoners" – forerunner of the Black Maria. On 31 March 1840 the Justices authorised the payment of £1 7s. 6d. to James James, constable for keeping prisoners in custody and attending them before magistrates "on suspicion of destroying the gate and toll house at Evelwen". This was the first tollgate to be destroyed by the apostles of violence who became known as Rebecca rioters. The situation deteriorated so much that on 4 January 1843, the Quarter Sessions decided to apply to the Secretary of State for the Home Department for a military force of 50 men to be sent from Brecon to St. Clears and neighbourhood, and to be under the direction of the local magistrate and 50 special constables to be selected at the Petty Sessions at St. Clears

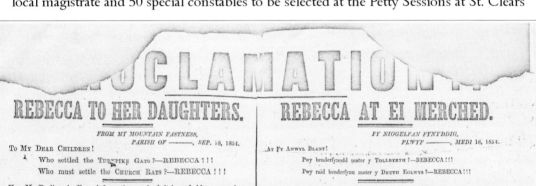

from the farmers of that neighbourhood, and placed under the Inspector of Police. That 30 of the most effective Pensioners in western Carmarthenshire be sworn as special constables and placed under such command as the magistrates at the St. Clears Petty Sessions should appoint, and finally, that the Secretary of State for the Home Department issue a free pardon to any accomplice or accomplices "in the late outrage, who will give evidence to conviction against the perpetrators of such outrage". The cost of combating the Rebecca rioters, partly borne by the county, proved heavy, and in October 1843 the Quarter Sessions agreed that on account of the distressed state of the ratepayers, the Vice-Lieutenant be requested to represent to the Government that the Government should bear the expense of the Metropolitan policemen sent to Carmarthenshire "during the outrages and disturbances and the destruction and demolition of turnpike gates and toll houses by incendiarism".

An echo of the landing of the French at Fishguard occurs in the January sessions of 1798, when the gaoler received 3 guineas for his "trouble and attendance for three weeks watching the French prisoners in the County Gaol".

Movements of paupers and "strollers" to their home parishes was vigorously enforced as they were a charge upon the rates if allowed to remain. Sometimes punishment accompanied the order, as in 1805 when Elizabeth Banner of the parish of Mathry, Pembrokeshire, and her infant male child turned up in Carmarthenshire without means of subsistence. She was brought before the Quarter Sessions who ordered that she be kept in the House of Correction to hard labour for seven days, and afterwards, together with her child, to be conveyed to her parish of settlement, Mathry. Bastardy matters also came before the Justices. In 1820 and 1822, two randy schoolmasters, David Jones of Brechfa and William Evans of Llangathen, were sworn as putative fathers and to be responsible for financial provision for the infants, and in 1826 two persons from Cilycwm parish with the splendid classical names of Sil Silvanus and Mary Augustus, who had loved not wisely, but too well, found themselves facing a grave Bench anxious to keep the rates down. Such illicit joyousness could be expensive, as John Theophilus of Llanfynydd, adjudged father of Dinah Davies's twins, found in 1796 when he was ordered to pay to the churchwardens of Llanfynydd £9 for Dinah's lying-in, and 3 shillings towards the maintenance of the infants. What tragedy lies behind the following entry in 1836 – "Pay Rebecca Lewis, sexton of Llangadock, 5 shillings for disinterring the body of John Thomas, an illegitimate child supposed to have been poisoned".

County Administration

We now turn to a more happy side of the Quarter Sessions, namely administration of the county. This touched practically every aspect of life – the levying of rates, care of public buildings, the constabulary, recruiting for the armed services, militia affairs, appointment of officials, licencing of inns, registering of Nonconformist Meeting Houses, weights and measures, prices and wages, care of records, enclosures, Judge's lodgings, bankruptcies, and so on. The following examples illustrate the variety of subjects that exercised the Justices in Quarter Sessions.

Officials

First of all, let us look at the officials. By far the most important was the Clerk of the Peace. He was appointed by the *Custos Rotulorum*, and most of the routine work of arranging the Quarter Sessions fell on him, such as drawing up indictments, arraigning prisoners, making out warrants and orders, keeping lists of jurors, and recording judgements of the Court. He kept the records but that duty he sometimes delegated to a Deputy-Clerk where such existed. The salary he received was derisory, but it must be remembered that the office carried fees, and normally the Clerk carried on a private legal practice as well.

On his appointment he had to appear before the Justices in Sessions to take the necessary oaths. On 1 February 1749 James Price of Cilgwyn, Myddfai parish, having been appointed Clerk of the Peace, before the Justices of the Quarter Sessions held at the Old Plough Inn, Llandovery, took the oaths of Allegiance and Supremacy, the Test and other oaths, and produced evidence that he had taken the sacrament on Sunday after divine service and sermon, according to the several Acts of Parliament. On 28 December 1834, the Court record reads "Edward Jones of Llandovery, gentleman, produced his Appointment of Clerk of this County under the hand and seal of the Rt. Hon. George Talbot Rice, Lord Dynevor, *Custos Rotulorum* of the said county, and it was ordered that he should take the oath of office and also the oaths of Allegiance, Supremacy, and Abjuration, and he took the same accordingly in open Court". As I have said, the Clerk of the Peace was allowed to carry on a private practice; and received the normal legal fees for work carried out on behalf of the Quarter Sessions which were often considerable. As time went on the tendency was to raise the Clerk's salary and to limit his legal fees. In 1829 the Sessions resolved that in future the Clerk be allowed £200 a year "in lieu of fees from this county, money orders excepted", instead of £100 a year as had been agreed in 1799. In 1835 they resolved that he be allowed £270 yearly in lieu of fees, but exclusive of expenses incurred by him in bringing actions pursuant to the order of the Justices, and he was to receive a further £80 yearly for expenses and trouble imposed on him by the Reform Act in respect of registration of electors, and they resolved further that he should be recompensed for any extraordinary work undertaken by him pursuant to any future act of parliament. In January 1853 the Sessions revised the scale, and resolved that £350 yearly "was a fair and proper sum to be paid to the Clerk of the Peace for his salary", exclusive of fees on prosecutions and other legal business transacted on behalf of the county, or stamp duties, fees to counsel, or costs in relation to the Rural Police.

The Justices kept a wary eye on salaries, over which they exercised rigid control. Their attitude is exemplified in a resolution made in 1830, which read, "Ordered that no salary now payable to any person out of County Rates and under the Control of the Magistrates, be from henceforth increased without notice given of such intended increase at the Quarter Sessions previous to the Session in which such increase shall be proposed, and no such notice or increase to be made at any adjourned Sessions, and that notice be inserted in the newspaper belonging to the County".

The County Treasurer, appointed by the Quarter Sessions, was less well off. In 1823 Thomas Jones was appointed (*vice* David William Stephenson, deceased) at £40 yearly, and providing sureties in £2,000 for due performance of the office. When Richard Rees took up the post in 1836, his yearly salary was the same; and in 1850 Charles Henry Hughes, attorney at law, was appointed County Treasurer at £50 yearly, and also Treasurer of the Police Rate at £30 yearly, he providing a bond with sureties in the sum of £3,000. In 1825 the County Solicitor received a yearly salary of £80, and in 1840 his successor was appointed at a salary of £105.

There were other officials who became more numerous as the work of the Sessions increased, ultimately leading to the establishment of a full-time bureaucracy. Among them were the County Gaoler who received £60 in 1794, the Governor of the House of Correction at £105 in 1806, the Court Crier at £15 in 1809, the Surgeon of the County Gaol at £30 in 1812, the schoolmaster at the Gaol at £20 in 1837, the Hall-keeper at £10 in 1823, Bridgemaster for the county at £30 in 1812, "upon giving up all other employment", and an Inspector of Weights and Measures in 1846 with a salary of £70, and to receive a moiety of all fines levied, and ten per centum of the fees. Pensions were granted to those who retired. A pension of £50 was granted in 1825 to Benjamin Waugh on his retirement as Gaoler and Master of the House of Correction, and in the following year John Moses was "discharged from the situation of Turnkey in consequence of old age and infirmities attendant thereon, and allowed a pension of £15 pa." Care of bridges had long been an amateur and part-time concern, but the increase in trade, and subsequently communications, demanded a more professional attention, and in 1848 Richard Kyrke Penson of Oswestry, Salop, Civil Engineer, was appointed full-time Bridge Surveyor for the whole of Carmarthenshire (he engaging to resign a similar appointment for Cardiganshire) at a salary of £150 p.a. including travelling expenses.

Other officials not directly under the Justices were obliged to qualify themselves for their posts by taking statutory oaths and delivering sacramental certificates to the Quarter Sessions. From 1807 onwards the Portreeves of Laugharne and of St. Clears regularly qualified themselves in this manner. In April 1808 William Lloyd of Laques, Esquire, took the oaths as High Sheriff of the county. In 1831 the Revd. Joshua Davies took the oaths to qualify himself. In 1808 Thomas Williams qualified himself as an officer of excise, and Hector Rees as 'Waiter and Searcher' at the port of Llanelli. In 1853 Hugh Williams, Esquire, duly qualified himself as "Recorder of the Borough of St. Clears".

A large number of clergymen similarly took oaths and made the declarations to qualify themselves for ecclesiastical appointments. In 1831 the Revd. Joshua Davies took the oaths to qualify himself as Prebendary of Llandygwydd. Cards.; in 1833 the Revd. Rice Rees, M.A., Professor of Welsh in St. Davids College, Lampeter, as rector of the sinecure rectory of Llanddewi Velfrey, Pembs.; in 1838 the Revd. David Lloyd Herbert Thackery Griffithes Williams of Llwynhelig, as rector of Penboyr and perpetual curate of Llanfihangel Aberbythych; the Revd. William Harries of Abersannan as vicar of Llanfynydd, and the Revd. John William Pugh of Greenhill as vicar of Llandeilofawr in 1841; the Revd. John Jones as perpetual curate of Llanreithan, Pembs. and the Revd. Richard Bowen Jones, B.A., as rector of Cilymnenllwyd *cwm capella* Castle Dwyrhan and in 1850 the Revd. Samuel Jones as perpetual curate of Eglwysfair-Glyntaf.

Deputations of gamekeepers, usually men of standing, were also recorded in the Sessions. In 1750 the Revd. William Harries of Laugharne, clerk was appointed by Sir John Philipps, Bart., lord of the manor of Llanddowror, and William Plowden of Plowden Hall, Salop, lord of the manor of Oysterlow Grange, to be gamekeeper within the said manors.

Records of Court

A matter that greatly exercised the mind of the Clerk of the Peace was the care and preservation of Court records. The person responsible for the records was the *Custos Rotulorum*, usually appointed from the most prominent Justices, but he normally delegated the work to the Clerk, who ensured that they were kept safely and would be produced when necessary. These were statutory papers, and apart from the legal necessity for their conservation, were required for precedents and references to help in current administration. From the historian's point of view, they are invaluable, and a satisfactory history of a county cannot be written without consulting them. In 1794 the Quarter Sessions papers include a payment of £13 2s. 6d. to David Rees, Deputy Prothonotary, "being his bill for a room to keep the records of the County for twelve years and a half at the rate of £1 1s. a year", and £2 12s. 6d. for a deal chest to keep the documents. In 1796 the Clerk of the Peace was ordered "to enquire for a fit and proper place to erect a Record Room and that he enter into a negotiation for the purchase of such place", and in the following year it was laid down that the cost of building such a room should not exceed £160. Accordingly the room was built within the Shire Hall, and in 1798 David Rees was paid £7 7s. for "his trouble in removing the records from the old record room to the new one", and £5 towards "keeping fire in the record room for the preservation of the County records", and "two old presses" in the Shire Hall were allocated for their reception. Apparently they were not enough and in 1801 the Clerk received ten guineas to procure new presses "for keeping and preserving the records of this Court".

It was decided to build a record room in the shire hall at Llandeilo as well, and in 1802 the Quarter Sessions accepted a plan by the famous architect, William Jernegan of Swansea, for such a building at the cost of £1,200. Jernegan completed the work in 1804; and Court ordered the payment of £30 to Thomas Harry, mason, "for facing the Record Room of the Shire Hall in Llandeilo with fine stone work".

In 1836 the Quarter Sessions gave directions "for placing an Iron Chest in the Shire Hall in Carmarthen to keep the records of the County". An entry in the Minute Book, for the Sessions held on 30 June 1887, read, "The Clerk of the Peace drew the attention of the Court to the dilapidated condition as to binding and otherwise of the Books containing the Minutes of the Court from the year 1748 (the most ancient among the Records of the Court) to 1878, and he was instructed to obtain an estimate for binding and indexing the same". On 20 October following an estimate for the work from Messrs. Hadden, Best & Co., was submitted to the Justices and accepted. These volumes, including that of 1748, are now preserved in the County Record Office. It is pleasant to be able to say that in 1959 a proper Record Office was established with two large strong rooms for the reception of documents, and which has been appointed by the Lord Chancellor as the official repository for statutory and other documents in Carmarthenshire.

County Buildings

The Shire Hall at Carmarthen, and its amenities (or rather, the lack of them), often exercised the minds of the Justices, and the Quarter Sessions records contain numerous references to the matter. In 1808 the Justices ordered that the seats of the Jury Box be raised, presumably for the benefit of minute jurors, and at the same time that "Brass hooks for hanging the Magistrates' Hats on, be procured and put up", and that a stove and ventilators be placed in the hall. Ventilation was still unsatisfactory in 1810, when it was ordered that the Deputy Prothonotary "do provide a Presbyterian for the Hall chimney at the Expense of this County". Lest some Nonconformists wilt at this order, I must add that a "presbyterian" in this context was a kind of iron hood designed to make the chimney "draw". Problems of accommodation afflicted our forebears no less than they do us today. As the business of the Sessions increased, a cry for more space arose. On one side of the Shire Hall was an inn that rejoiced in the sinister name of "Devil's Tavern", kept by one David Morris. In October 1820, the Justices decided to buy the premises for £570, and to incorporate it with the Shire Hall, which was done accordingly, and the Grand Jury room was built on its site. In 1828, another tavern, called "The Falcon" near the Shire Hall was acquired for similar incorporation. A third tavern, the "Plume of Feathers' escaped cannibalisation and continues to assuage the thirst of burgesses. To pay for these extensions and improvements, the Justices borrowed £2,500 in 1828, and made a contract with David Morgan of Carmarthen, architect, for carrying out the projected works. Gas lighting was beginning to come to west Wales, and in 1822 the Justices ordered that a gas light be placed "in front of the Hall" and another "at the foot of the steps". The Shire Hall was completely rebuilt and enlarged in 1829. Some of the basements, and the kitchen remained unoccupied for some time, until some enterprising burgesses "squatted" there, apparently without the knowledge of the Justices. When they discovered this in March 1838 they ordered "the persons living in the kitchen of the County Hall be immediately sent away".

The problem of space continued to vex the Justices, and in 1861 they undertook further improvements. Not everyone approved of this project, and on 4 November 1861, Rees Goring Thomas, J.P., gave notice that he would propose at the next Quarter Sessions that the improvements going on at the Shire Hall be abandoned, and a new Shire Hall and Judges' Lodgings erected on the Castle Green (i.e. just in front of the present County Hall), a site which had been offered by the Earl Cawdor. However, nothing came of this proposal.

The Shire Hall at Llandeilo is of much later date. In August 1800 the Court studied plans of premises in that town which they proposed to buy for the purpose of "erecting a County Hall and a market place therein for the use and at the expense of the County" but influenced by the incidence of taxes and rates, the Justices decided not to proceed in the matter until "a reduction in the Militia of the County" had taken place. However, in 1802 the Justices approved of a plan for building a shire hall on a site presented by Lord Dynevor, and an adjoining stable presented by Thomas Stepney, esquire. The building was to include provision for keeping the records, and also for securing prisoners for trial. The hall was eventually built. In 1848 it was put to a use not foreseen by the builders, and a minute of the Sessions held on 6 January of that year reads, "Ordered that the use of the Llandilo hall be granted for the performance of Divine Service therein during the time the church at Llandilo is being built". Several improvements were made to the building later in the century. The Justices were enemies to all forms of waste, as the unconsciously humorous entry in 1858 indicates – they ordered that "the useless stove" in the Llandeilo hall be removed for use in the county gaol.

Judge's lodgings

Mention of Judge's Lodgings directs our attention to another aspect of the administrative work of the Quarter Sessions, for the County officials were responsible for looking after visiting Judges of Assize. All aspects of the comfort of such legal luminaries were studied. In 1820 for example David Morgan, carpenter, received £10 for constructing water closets for the judges. In 1829 the Clerk of the Peace was instructed to agree with Thomas Jones and William Moss of Carmarthen, for furnished lodgings, for 21 years at the allowance of £20 for each Quarter Sessions. But this arrangement did not last long. Complaints about such accommodation are evidently nothing new. In April 1833 the Justices in Quarter Sessions considered that the Judge's Lodgings were "Inconveniently small, of which repeated complaints have been made", and ordered five magistrates, John Jones, John George Philipps, Grismond Philipps, John Lloyd Davies, and Thomas Morris, "to select the most commodious and best calculated appartments that can be found in Carmarthen for that purpose". In July 1834, as a result of the recommendation, the Justices agreed to use the house of Richard Spurrell in King Street for the Judge, at £40 per annum, and any further sum that the Government might allow. In 1839 the rent was increased to £50, and Spurrell's house remained the Judge's Lodgings for many years.

The Walls of Carmarthen Castle

The walls of the ruined castle of Carmarthen often engaged their attention, particularly as they were occasionally considered a threat to life and property. There had been some complaints in 1802, and in the Epiphany Quarter Sessions the Justices ordered Richard Owen, mason, to survey the castle walls and repair them "at the expense of this county". In 1804 an order was made to build "a depot" in a tower of the castle. In 1811, the condition of the walls again caused concern, and two Justices were ordered to inspect them and to repair

defects. As a result of their report, a committee of Justices was formed in the following year, empowered to make contracts for necessary repairs, while the damages "occasioned by the failing of the said wall" were to be settled by the committee and compensation paid by the County Treasurer. Among the sums paid out was £73 to one George Richards for damage caused to houses by the falling of the wall.

Old Carmarthen Castle

The Gaol

In 1789, the year the Bastille fell, the rulers of Carmarthenshire erected their own "Bastille" in the form of a Gaol within the area of Carmarthen castle, entered through a fine entrance designed by no less than John Nash. References occur in the Quarter Sessions records to subsequent repairs and extensions made to it. The development of industry and rapid growth of population, alas, increased the criminal work of the Courts, and the Goal became a "full house". In 1867 large extensions were made, and the adjoining ground, part of the site of the old castle enclosure known as Castle Green, on which stood a smithy and six cottages, bought from Lord Cawdor for £1,300.

There are numerous references to the administration of the gaol, extensions, improvements to the fabric, appointments of officials, payments, etc. A few examples must suffice to indicate what went on. In 1795 the County Treasurer was ordered to pay up to £1 10s. 0d. to buy necessaries for "old Gwen Owen" and David Evans, two prisoners in the gaol and also to provide oakum "or other proper article to set the prisoners in the House of Correction to work". New hinges and locks, the latter "of best construction", – for doors were continually being bought. In 1849 the Sessions ordered that the menu for Class I convicted prisoners should consist of a pint of gruel for breakfast, a pound of bread for dinner, and a pint of gruel for supper.

On an old plan of the gaol an area is marked as "Trebanda", the meaning of which escapes my comprehension. In 1831 the Clerk of the Peace contracted with George Howell, mason, for repairing "the Trebanda" in the county gaol, and keeping it in repair for seven years, at the cost of £40 8s. 0d., the work to be "certified workmanlike" by David Morgan, architect. Less mysterious was the treadmill, and contracts for the building of such a fabric "with one pair of stones and two boxes for prisoners" were invited in 1832. Numerous orders were issued in 1839, namely that boards should be placed in front of the treadmill to prevent prisoners seeing passers-by, but to be placed "so as to admit air"; that one or more tin or copper ventilators be placed at the sides of the mill, that convicts were not to receive letters or visits from friends during the first six months of imprisonment except "under peculiar and pressing circumstances", that a dark cell be fitted up for the punishment of "refractory prisoners" and that boards be placed on the outside of windows in the female debtors ward "as may prevent them seeing males walking in the yard". In 1844, £90 was paid for enlarging the treadmill. More ominous was the work undertaken in 1845 by James Griffiths, smith for "making new oak doors for the gaol, and flagging *under the drop*".

Other buildings for which the Quarter Sessions were responsible were the House of Correction, alongside the gaol, and the lunatic asylum kept for some time in a building against the inner walls of the old castle. New accommodation for these unfortunates was arranged in due course. In 1839 a committee of magistrates was formed to discuss with similar committees from Pembrokeshire and Cardiganshire the possibility of erecting a Lunatic Asylum for the three counties, which later was brought to fruition. The building became too small to accommodate the patients satisfactorily, and in April 1876 it was ordered that £278 17s. 0d. be granted towards furnishing the mansion of Job's Well for the reception of pauper lunatics. In October 1878 the Sessions ordered that the Committee in Lunacy be

Rhydygors

authorised to rent Rhydygors mansion for three years at a rent not exceeding £100 and rates and taxes of which Carmarthenshire should pay a due proportion with the other counties, and two years later Lord Emlyn gave notice that at the next Quarter Sessions he would ask the Court's sanction to be given to the Joint Counties Lunatic Asylum for taking Rhydygors for 21 years at £100 per annum.

The building of lockups, especially after the establishment of the constabulary, became an additional duty of the Sessions. Of course they were in existence before this, for in 1794 we read that the burgesses of Llandovery were presented in the Sessions "for not keeping a public gaol commonly called *a Lock up House* for confining, securing, and keeping in safe custody all offenders and prisoners taken up in the said borough". There were numerous lock-up houses in the county with an official in charge of each. In 1830 one Thomas William was appointed keeper of the lockup at Llangadock, at a salary of £3 p.a.

Militia

Militia matters, recruiting for the armed services, gazetting of volunteer officers, payment of allowances to wives of militiamen, stores, accommodation, etc., also came under the Sessions. In 1795 the Justices ordered the Treasurer to make payments to High Constables of the Hundreds, and the clerk of the Petty Sessions for "raising men for the service of His Majesty's Navy". In January 1799, the Treasurer was ordered to pay £2 8s. 0d. to the Clerk of the Peace for inserting in the *Gazette* the appointments of Lord Cawdor as Colonel of the Carmarthenshire Militia, Major Williams, and other officers of the unit. They paid for the conveyance of baggage of both regular and militia units in the county, and this formed a recurring item until about 1875. In 1795, the Justices ordered that 16s. 6d. be paid to a carter for carrying the baggage of a troop of the Somerset Fencible Cavalry from Carmarthen to the Breconshire border, and 8s. for carrying the baggage of a troop of the 38th Dragoons from Carmarthen to the Pembrokeshire border, and 12s. 9d. for carrying the baggage of the Carmarthenshire Militia from Carmarthen to Llanelli. They were responsible for building the barracks, and a magazine for the storage of gunpowder. These were heavy charges on the county, and finally the Government took over all military responsibilities, and on 5 January 1877 the Quarter Sessions transferred the Carmarthen Barracks and the acre of land on which it stood, to the Secretary of State of the War Department.

Rates

One of the most important aspects of Quarter Sessions work was the levying and collecting of rates. The Treasurer advised the Justices on the total sum required. The Clerk and Treasurer then drew up a list of the hundreds and parishes, and, based on population, calculated how much money each parish should contribute. The actual extraction was carried out by the Overseers of each parish, who handed the money over to the High Constables of the hundreds, and they, in turn, handed it to the County Treasurer.

In addition to a general rate, certain areas were ordered to pay a specific rate as and when necessary. In 1750 the Justices ordered that a rate of 4d. in the pound be assessed on the inhabitants of Llannon for repairing highways within that parish. In 1794 they ordered the Clerk of the Peace to issue a warrant to raise a rate of 9d. in the pound on the inhabitants of Glyn in Llangyndeyrn, towards repairing a road in the hamlet and also to reimburse the surveyor for purchasing land to widen the road, and they nominated Daniel Jones of Gwndwnbach to be assessor, collector, and treasurer for the rate.

The general rate contained a good deal of information concerning the rateable value of each parish. For instance in 1822 the Clerk of the Peace issued his warrant to every chief constable of each hundred and commote to raise £600 for a county stock. This sum was then subdivided down to parish level, according to the order of the court, by five Justices – John Jones, Lord Dynevor, the Hon. George Rice, John Edward Saunders, and Robert Waters – as follows:

Kidwelly commote (7 parishes)	£65 13s. 4½d.
Iscennen commote (6 parishes)	£39 1s. 6d.
Carnawllon commote (4 parishes)	£37 5s. 6d.
Cathinog hundred (9 parishes, and part of a parish)	£68 18s. 9d.
Caeo (Cayo) hundred (6 parishes and part of 3 parishes)	£80 0s. 9d.
Perfeth hundred (6 parishes and part of two parishes)	£79 11s. 6d.
Elfed hundred (13 parishes and part of one parish)	£82 12s. 9d.
Derllys hundred (24 parishes and part of one parish)	£148 15s. 10d.

Although retaining their identity as ecclesiastical parishes, by today, several of them have been absorbed administratively into the larger civil parishes.

Dissenters

The Justices in Quarter Sessions were responsible for licensing dissenting ministers and also registering houses wherein Dissenters could worship. The large number of entries in the second half of the 18th century onwards indicates the growth of Nonconformity in Carmarthenshire. A few must suffice. In 1749 six houses were registered as "meeting houses for dissenting Protestants", namely Argoed in Bettws parish, a house in the village of Llanfairarybryn, Llwynwhilog in Llanelli parish, Cilygell Ganol in Pencarreg, a house in Laugharne, Bwlchgwynr in Ciffig. The Chairman of the Justices who granted these applications was Griffith Philipps of Cwmgwili, a landowner well-known for his humane and liberal tendencies. Maurice Griffith attended the Michaelmas Quarter Sessions in 1750, when he made his Declaration and subscribed his Assent to the 39 Articles of Religion,

Chapel Y Babel, Llangunnor

except the 34th, 35th, 36th, and part of the 20th, in order to qualify as a Protestant Dissenting Teacher, and took the Oaths and subscribed the Declaration against Transubstantiation. This formula was applied in all such cases. In 1752 "the new house lately built near the Strand" in Laugharne, was registered as a place of worship for dissenting Protestants; in 1797, Ty'r Bont at Llangendeirn was registered; in 1801 a room and stable adjoining, in Llandovery, was registered in favour of Dissenters of the Baptist denomination. The formula was invariably the same in these cases for instance, in 1799 a meeting house erected on the tenement of Alltddu in Llandeilofawr parish "for preaching the Gospel and administering the sacrament by a certain set of people calling themselves Protestant Dissenters be registered by the name of Salem Chappel". Sometimes the name of the denomination is given, such as, in 1803, Trefach in the chapelry of Eglwysfair a Churig (Independents), in 1806 Conwyl Elfed Meeting House (Independents), Cwmsarnddu in Cilycwm (Baptists), and Llanpumpsant Meeting House (Methodists), in 1809 Philadelphia in Llangunnor (Presbyterian). Some of these meeting places were built as chapels, others were held in houses, such as "a certain house in the village of Mydrim called the Poorhouse" registered as "a place fit for religious worship" in 1811. Only one case of rejection has been found. The Session for October 1801, records "Forasmuch as it appears to this Court that the House called Bremenda in the parish of Llanarthney is a Farmhouse, it is therefore ordered that the motion for registering the same as a place for Divine Worship, be rejected". A case where cattle and corn came before prayers and hymns.

Roads and Bridges

The care and maintenance of roads, bridges, and footpaths – extremely important in a rural economy – proved to be one of the heaviest of the duties of the Justices of the Quarter Sessions. In addition to receiving reports and presentments, and issuing orders for repairs, the justices made contracts and carried out inspections. They often paid for repairs out of their own pockets, and were reimbursed by the County Treasurer after the sum had been approved in Quarter Sessions. In 1749 the justices ordered that 14s. be paid to Thomas Lloyd of Wenallt, J.P., expended by him in repairing Cowin Bridge. Several payments were made in 1794, *inter alia*, £4 6s. 0d. to Morgan John for "gravelling" the New Bridge by Llandovery, and £5 5s. 0d. to Thomas Vaughan for "repairing the battlements" of Pontantwn bridge. Presentments were made against parishioners of the county for failing to see that bridges and roads were maintained, and many of them refer to bridges on the boundaries with neighbouring counties. At the July Sessions of 1790 a presentment was made against the inhabitants of the county for failing to repair the one-half part of the Carmarthenshire side of Ponteglwysfair bridge over the river Taf which was on the boundary with Pembrokeshire, but this was discharged in the autumn sessions of 1794, the repairs having been effected. In 1833 the parishioners of Egremont were presented for not repairing the road from Maenclochog (Pembs.) to Narberth, from 'the road which crosses the river Cleddef called Feidir Dwr' ending at Egremont bridge, being 902 yards long and 10 feet wide. The illogical zig-zag boundary between the two counties at this spot was productive of much trouble to the administrators. This topographical lunacy still exists. In 1795, John Thomas, Bridgemaster for the county, submitted an estimate of £9 15s. 6d., for repairing Spydders Bridge, and "the long walls from the bridge to the Ladies Arch" and the magistrates ordered that John Rees of Cilymaenllwyd, J.P. be requested to employ persons to under-take the work; and later in that year the inhabitants of Llandurry were presented (and acquitted) for not repairing the high-road from 'Nantygro on the confines of Llangyndeyrn and Pembre' to the junction with the Kidwelly turnpike road "adjacent to the south end of Pont Rees Spwdwr." This would seem to explain the strange name "Spudder's Bridge" – Pont Rees Pwdwr (the bridge of idle Rees). Some landowners magnanimously gave lands so that bridges

John Ogilvy's Road Map, Carmarthen to Aberysiwyth, 1675 (1698) edition

could be made and roads improved; in 1801, Sir Watkin Lewes gave land so that a new bridge could be built over the river Cowin on the highroad from Carmarthen to St. Clears.

In 1825 the sum of £12 was given to Thomas Howell of Glaspant, J.P. to be paid out, under his inspection, for repairs to bridges at Cwmcych, Pontedwst, and Cwm Morgan. The Justices stood for no nonsense in the matter of upkeep of roads. In 1807, when the parishioners of Llanelli neglected to repair a road three miles long and twelve feet broad, from Llandaven to the river Loughor, they were fined £100, and Charles Nevill, gentleman, was ordered to see that repairs were properly carried out. Footpaths were as much of a headache to the Justices then as they are to the County Council today. Rights of way were jealously guarded. For instance in 1800, Ann Griffith spinster and John David yeoman, both of Llanddeusant parish, were presented for "stopping up and placing a certain dead hedge" across an ancient common and public footway from the market town of Llangadock towards Brecon and through a close of land called Ca Evan Saer being part of the tenement of Aberllechach in the hamlet of Maesffynnon. On this occasion the Justices were either somnolent or merciful, for they only fined them 6d. each. The outcome proved different for the parishioners of Cilycwm and Llanfairarybryn, guilty of not repairing "a common and ancient foot bridge", over the river Towy near Glanrhyd, in 1807. They were fined £60, which sum was to be applied to the repair of the neglected bridge. Fingerposts claimed attention in 1806 when Mr. Thomas Bishop was ordered to procure "Directing Posts" to be put up for the new road near Llandovery ford. The Justices were responsible, too, for the only drawbridge in the county, near the mouth of the river Loughor, a responsibility they shared with the Glamorgan Justices. In 1846 the Carmarthenshire Justices paid 3s. 6d. a week to one John Jones "for opening and shutting a Draw Bridge at Loughor", and scraping and repairing its surface.

Use of Welsh Language

In view of what is happening today, it is interesting to note that Carmarthenshire was a pioneer in bi-lingualism for official purposes, and the records provide numerous examples of the implementation of this policy. In 1796 the Justices ordered that the Revd. Thomas Price be paid £6 6s. 0d. for translating Form of Prayers into the Welsh language for the use of prisoners in the county gaol, and for printing several dozens of such forms. In August 1804 the Sessions ordered that 200 copies of the Salmon Fishery Act be printed in Welsh and English and distributed over the county. In April 1806 they ordered that regulations concerning the driving of carriages should be printed in both languages and posted in public places. In 1822 they ordered that the fifth clause of the new Turnpike Act be printed in both languages, and ten years later ordered the County Printer to print 400 copies of "Caution to the drivers of Carts" in Welsh and English. In 1834 they ordered that 1,000 handbills in Welsh and 1,000 in English be prepared by the Clerk, setting forth the material clauses from the Act of 4 and 5 William IV, cap 49, concerning weights and measures, to be handed to the Chief Constables of the Hundreds who, in turn, were to pass them to clergymen and petty constables. In January 1836 the Justices appointed Samuel Evans, a Carmarthen printer, to be "Interpreter of the Court and to be engaged in all matters unless the parties agree to the contrary". In 1840, the Court ordered that Lord Normanby's letter addressed to the Lord Lieutenant, concerning "Blasphemous Publications" should be translated into Welsh, printed as handbills, and circulated by the clerks of the different Petty Sessions. In 1841 the Justices ordered that 12s. be sent to the District Society for Promoting Christian Knowledge, to buy Welsh testaments for use in the county gaol, and the following year paid 19s. 4d. to provide Welsh and English Common Prayer Books. In 1866 they ordered copies of an Order in Council to be printed in both languages. Of this attitude towards the language by our former administrators, the squires of Carmarthenshire, may be truly proud.

Cultural attitudes

The Justices were not indifferent to cultural matters. In July 1867, they resolved "That the promoters of the next Carmarthen Eisteddfod be authorised to use the Shire Hall at Carmarthen for the purposes of Social Science and meetings", and in the following October decreed "That the Shire Hall in Carmarthen be at the service of the Penny Reading Society, until countermanded, provided no damage is done thereby to the hall". There is no indication that permission was ever withdrawn. In 1875 they authorised the Cambrian Archaeological Society to open "a bricked-up doorway in the old castle at Carmarthen", and having carried out an examination, they were to close the doorway up again. The Justices had acquired several pictures, mainly portraits, to hang in the Shire Hall, and took good care of them, so that they have survived to our day in excellent condition. In the minutes for 11 October 1829 we read "That the Thanks of the County are peculiarly due to the Reverend Edward Picton, Clerk, for his very handsome present to the Subscribers to the Column in Memory of his Brother, the late Sir Thomas Picton, and particularly to the Lord Lieutenant and Magistracy of the County for a full length Portrait of that lamented Hero . . . That every care be adopted to preserve to future Ages this splendid likeness of the form and features of a Man the Memory of whose heroic deeds will live for Ever in the recollection of his grateful Countrymen and whose praise so Justly merited will always excite the pride and Emulation of Britons in general and Welshmen in particular". In 1881 the Justices accepted the County Surveyor's recommendation that pictures in the Carmarthen Shire Hall should be cleaned and varnished, and ordered accordingly.

Other activities, somewhat less cultural, took place in the hall on occasions. Dinners were held there, but these were discontinued by order of the Justices. In 1867 they granted permission to the Revd. D. Archard Williams, Archdeacon of Carmarthen, who had applied to hold a bazaar for three days in the basement of the Shire Hall, but added that no bazaars should be held there after that. The fact that the Archdeacon was a Justice of the Peace himself may have had some bearing on the success of his application.

Friendly societies

A large number of these useful organisations sprang up in Carmarthenshire from 1750 onwards. They were required by law to be registered with the Clerk of the Peace and entered among the records of Quarter Sessions. They were mainly run by men for men, and did a lot of good, especially in alleviating difficulties when people were suffering from ill-health. However, Carmarthenshire seems to have led the way in "Women's Lib", as shown by the

THE NAGS HEAD

MEETING OF THE FEMALE SOCIETY 19TH. OCTOBER 1799

Women's Lib?

Quarter Sessions order of 16 January 1798 – "That articles of a Friendly Society held at the Sign of the Nags Head in the town of Llandovery, called The Female Society, be filed"; and on 9 October 1799 "the Articles of a Friendly Society held in Llangadock called The Reputable Female Society be filed". Among the men's friendly societies were "The Gomerian Society" meeting at the Red Lion in Llan-dybie, "The Llanelli Brotherly Society" meeting at the Barley Mow, Llanelli, and "The British Faithful and Friendly Society" meeting at the sign of The Cross Hands at Llannon – all of which were in existence in 1846. There were Ancient Britons, Loyal Britons, Royal Britons, True Britons, Cambrian Union, Cambrian Benefit Society, Llanelli Brotherly Society, Loyal and Liberal Society, the United Brethren, the Welfare Society, and many more.

Constabulary

The administering of the constabulary became an important aspect of the work of the Sessions. The first reference to the establishing of a force in Carmarthenshire occurs in a resolution of the Quarter Sessions held on 10 April 1839, and is worth quoting in full since it illustrates the attitude of the Justices, landowners to a man, to its control.

It reads as follows:

> "The Court having taken into consideration a communication from Her Majesty's Secretary of State for the Home Department as to the establishment of an efficient constabulary force appointed and controlled by the Magistrates of each county, would afford much better means than now exists to allay every disturbance that might possibly occur, *but they view with alarm* any intention of vesting in any other body the right of appointing such force, as taking from them the only effective means of acting as conservators of the Public Peace and imposing upon them and their Tenantry the costs of maintaining an establishment without giving them a voice in its formation."

In the event, the Constabulary, its recruits, direction, and administration, remained in the hands of the squires, and, it may be said, a very good job they made of it.

On 25 July 1843, the Justices resolved: "That a Rural Police be appointed for this county under the Provisions of the Act 2 & 3 Victoria, cap. 93, and that, subject to the approval of the Secretary of State, to appoint one Chief Constable, 6 Superintendents, and 50 Constables at the following rates of pay:

> *Chief Constable* – £300 p.a., plus £150 allowance for 2 horses, house rent, and travelling expenses.
>
> *Superintendent* – £120 p.a., plus £34 for a horse and travelling expenses.
>
> *Sergeant* – £1 2s. 0d. a week.
>
> *Constable* – 1st Class £1 a week, and 2nd Class 18s. a week.

The money for the first three months of the Force's existence was to be raised by a rate of one penny in the £ upon the sum of £324,100, which was the annual rateable value of the county at that time.

On 28 June 1843, Captain Richard Andrew Scott was appointed Chief Constable, and on 4 March 1845 Major Kenneth Alexander de Koven was appointed Deputy Chief Constable.

The administration of the constabulary took up a great deal of the time of the Sessions, and the new organisation developed into an effective force. Its numbers increased, new lock-ups were built, and the incidence of crime was kept down. The Chief Constable suffered a shock in 1850 when his salary was reduced to £250. After that the wages increased, but somewhat tardily. In 1866 the Chief Constable's salary was increased to £350, in 1873 to £400. On 8 April 1875 Superintendent William Philipps was appointed Chief Constable, *vice* R. A. Scott, deceased, and his salary fixed at £400 inclusive of travelling expenses.

Chairman of Quarter Sessions

Originally, the *Custos Rotulorum* (appointed by the Lord Chancellor) was presumed to preside over his fellow justices, although the law made no provision for a chairman. It became customary for the Chairman to be appointed by the Justices from among themselves, and generally speaking he was no more than the spokesman for the Bench, but where the Chairman enjoyed a great local prestige, and was particularly active in the discharge of his duties, and possessed a strong personality, it was possible for him to impose his views on his fellows. Carmarthenshire was fortunate in the quality of its chairmen, who regularly attended at Sessions and took a prominent part in county life. Among these was John Johnes of Dolau Cothi who resigned in 1873, having been Chairman for nearly 20 years. He was a much loved figure, owner of an extensive estate, Welsh-speaking, and thoroughly conversant with all aspects of country life. He was followed by an Anglo-Saxon, Hardinge Stanley Gifford, Q.C., M.P. for Launceston, an Inner Templer, one of the most distinguished lawyers the country has produced. He resigned the chairmanship of the Carmarthenshire Quarter Sessions in 1885 when he was created Baron Halsbury, and went on to higher appointments – Solicitor General 1875-80, Lord Chancellor in 1885-92 and 1895-1905. He became a Privy Councillor, and in 1898 was advanced to the dignity of an earldom.

Much more could be told of the Quarter Sessions and its work. How it conducted itself during the Rebecca Riots, how it combated the great cattle plagues in 1751 and 1865-67, how it opposed the Government's plan to impose a toll on lime (much used by Carmarthenshire farmers), how it governed prices and wages, and administered the county generally.

In this essay I have emphasised the administrative aspect because the Municipal Corporation Act of 1835, the Poor Law Amendment Act of 1854, and particularly the Local Government Acts of 1885 and 1894 which created County, Parish, and District Councils, resulted in the elimination of most of the powers and duties of Quarter Sessions in the administrative field. Since 1888 their functions have been almost wholly concerned with the dispensation of justice, and their judicial powers expanded steadily with the increase of the number of offences summarily punishable. Accordingly, we are apt to forget that it was once an all-purpose instrument without which the country could not have been governed adequately from the reign of Henry VIII to that of Queen Victoria. I am not exaggerating when I say that the most important single influence on the lives of the people of Carmarthenshire in post-medieval times was the Justice of the Peace.

REFERENCE
[1] In 1880 it was ordered that the "old mad house" be converted into a police station.

Gaol News . . .

Tuesday 15 September . . . Euge Buckley a untried prisoner – in Irons at 5 o'clock a.m. for making a noise in his cell and disturbing the old [sic] Gaol from 3 o'clock a.m. by Knocking his Bed stead against the walls of his cell

Wednesday 16 September . . . the *Carmarthen Journal* and *Welshman* reporters and the *Cambrian* do called and I gave the particulars respecting Mary Ryves ["an Idle and disorderly person taken into custody on 7 September] which I consider she is a imposture according to the papers which she has in her possession and she has been Travelling the country so long to obtain sufficient money to carry her to New South Wales to her husband as she call him, but as fast as she git it she spend it in drink for she acknowledge in this Gaol that she received about seven pounds between this and Merthyr and she came here without a shilling in her pocket, H. Lawrence Esqr. called and examined Mary Ryves and his worship was the same opinion as myself respecting her which I informed his worship that I reported it to the *Welshman* and the *Journal* and the *Cambrian* Reporters to endeavour to put a stop to her.

Saturday 19 September . . . Euge Buckley a untried prisoner refused to make use of his Gruel at supper this evening.

Sunday 20 September . . . Charles Davies and David Thomas put in to the refractory cell on Bread and water for fighting on the Sabbath day.

One for the road

MR. GULSTON, MR. PEEL, AND THE JAVELIN MEN

CARMARTHENSHIRE READERS seeking information about High Sheriffs of former days, are fortunate to possess two substantial volumes written by James Buckley of Castell Gorfod, published in 1910 and 1913. We are aware that a particular man has served the office of High Sheriff, attended on judges of Assizes, obligingly entertained them and other law functionaries, public figures and personal friends to sparkling luncheons and dinners. We are aware that the sheriffs were attired in a special uniform, displayed heraldic cognisances on trumpet banners, and were attended by javelin men. In short, we know about the externals, but as for what went on "behind the scenes" leading to these colourful occasions, little is known to the general reader. Hence, it was a matter of good fortune to come across correspondence concerning the shrievalty in 1860, and although extending to only sixteen letters, they provide vivid glimpses of how a sheriff arranged affairs as he prepared himself for the year ahead. The letters form part of the Derwydd muniments now preserved in the Record Office at Carmarthen.

Although the sheriff's main function continued largely in the traditional mould, nevertheless several changes had taken place in methods employed by different holders of the office. One such change broached in 1860 concerned the use of javelin men, which had an effect on the sheriff's responsibilities and, incidentally, his privy purse. Among other matters discussed in the letters were sureties, the shrieval oath, deputy and under-sheriffs, dress, carriages, lodgings. References to the javelin men are especially interesting since efforts were afoot around 1860 to render them obsolete by transferring their functions to the County Police Force. Later, this was accomplished, so that the javelin men's presence became optional and purely ceremonial.

All the letters, save one, were addressed to Alan James Gulston, then living at Teignmouth, Devon, so that correspondence between him and others concerned became an essential feature of the proceedings. Having been "pricked" High Sheriff for 1860, he was now preparing himself for the task ahead. Of English origin the Gulstons were engaged in commercial concerns, their connection with Carmarthen-shire having been formed by the marriage in 1767 of Joseph Gulston of Ealing (later of Knuston Hall, Northants.) to Elizabeth Bridgetta daughter of Sir Thomas Stepney, Bart. She became heir to her brother, Sir Thomas the 9th and last baronet, Groom of the Bedchamber to Frederick, Duke of York, for 30 years, and who died without issue in 1825. Her son, Joseph Gulston (named after his father) inherited in due course, and died in 1779 when he was succeeded by his son, also named Joseph Gulston, who resided at Derwydd and Knuston Hall, and became the first of that name to become High Sheriff of Carmarthenshire, in 1827. A note written by his grandson tells us a little about him and his shrievalty – "Joseph Gulston only stayed at his ancestral home of Derwydd for a single period of about three weeks, and upon his departure his orders were carried out for the demolition of some forty or more rooms, part of the old place, which were in very bad repair, and, much to be regretted, a sale of the old furniture in these rooms was ruthlessly effected. As High Sheriff in 1827 Mr. Gulston drove four grey horses in his coach and met the Judge at Carmarthen Bridge with 24 Javelin

Taliaris

Men in full liveries and their Javelins, Trumpeters, and Banner Men" (Carms. R.O. Derwydd MS CA/14).

By his wife, Anna Maria Knowles of Egham, Surrey, he had a son and heir Alan James Gulston (born 1813) chosen to be High Sheriff for the year 1860. Gulston, who had served as a captain in the 47th Regiment of Foot, lived for some years at Derwydd before moving to Devon, and was recipient of the letters printed below. Finally he moved to Guernsey where he died on 8 August 1866, and his body brought back to Carmarthenshire for burial at Caledfwlch, Manordeilo, where his widow, who died at Llandeilo on 23 January 1887, was also buried. The only child, named Alan James Gulston after his father, became a Justice of the Peace, a Deputy Lieutenant, developed into a keen antiquary, and in time succeeded to Derwydd. When James Buckley, High Sheriff in 1895, died in office, the remainder of his shrieval term was served by the last named Gulston.

Among friends most ready and willing to help Mr. Gulston was William Peel of Taliaris (also called Taliaris Park) a few miles from Llandeilo. His forebears, Lancashire folk, had engaged in the manufacture of cloth, and lived at Pale Fold and Church Hank near Blackburn. William's father, Robert Peel, a successful calico manufacturer, decided to invest his profits in realty, and a few years before 1820 bought the Cwm Elan estate in Radnorshire, serving as High Sheriff of that county in 1821. He then decided to move farther afield. Carmarthenshire was the choice, and in 1834 he bought the Taliaris estate of 3,048 acres, for £65,000. The purchaser died in 1838, and was succeeded by his only son, William, the helpful correspondent of Gulston. Born in 1802, William Peel was educated at Brasenose College, Oxford, and two years after his father had purchased Taliaris, married Anna Maria eldest daughter of a neighbouring landowner, John William Lloyd of Danyrallt, Llangadog, by whom he had ten children. He was appointed a Justice of the Peace, Deputy Lieutenant, and in 1843 served as High Sheriff. He died in 1883.

William Peel's letters to Mr. Gulston, based on his own experiences, reveal ways and means that enabled him to conduct shrieval duties without dipping too deeply into his pocket although his resources were such that no anxiety need have attended his earthly career. One of the ever recurring items of the correspondence was the bodyguard, the javelin men, who in earlier days kept order in courts of law. In modern times their numbers were limited to twelve, sometimes ten, but by today they are virtually unknown. Present-day sheriffs should be thankful they did not live in the reign of Charles I, as indicated by John Evelyn in his diary for 1633 – "The year my father was appointed Sheriff [of Sussex], he had 116 servants in liveries, every one livened in green action doublets". *Autres temps, autres moeurs.* The letters reveal William Peel as a very practical man, possessing a lively wit garnished with a gentle cynicism.

Another correspondent meriting mention is Dr. John Propert, M.D., a leading medical man of that period. His father, Thomas Propert of Blaenpistyll, Cardiganshire, descended from the ancient family of Propert of St. Davids, Pembrokeshire. The doctor became closely associated with the Metropolis, and is chiefly remembered as founder of the Royal Medical Benevolent College, Epsom. When he wrote to Gulston he was living at New Cavendish Street, London, and in his letter quotes some experiences of "my friend and neighbour Mr. Jennings your immediate predecessor in Carmarthenshire" (Richard Jennings of Gellideg, High Sheriff 1859). It is noteworthy that three generations of the worthy doctor's kinsfolk, all lawyers, have been closely involved with the shrievalty in west Wales – Richard Thomas Propert Williams, Deputy Sheriff of Pembrokeshire, an office later held by his son Edgar Propert Williams, while his grandson, Mr. Howell Propert Williams, has himself been the Deputy Sheriff of Dyfed.

As the letters speak for themselves, I have refrained from comments or discussion on their content, and I offer them here in their entirety. Where necessary I have added in the text a few words in square brackets, hoping they will be of assistance to the reader. All the letters concern the period January to February 1860.

January 21 1860. George Brace, 25 Cavendish Square, London, to A. J. Gulston.

> *My dear Sir,*
> On Monday I hope to be able to write to you about Dr. P, and the extent of his *substantiality*. In the mean time I draw your attention to the necessity of casting forward quickly as to the arrangement necessary to be made as I presume you will not follow in the wake of a late far famed Major who would not receive Bain William, told a fib, committed himself, and was fined. Query – Carriage, Court Suit, Javelin Men-Tenants, Banners, Arrangements for Lodgings, Reception of Judge &c &c &c. I hope Dr. P will prove to be the owner of many dirty [acres], as the risk of a Welch Sheriff is great – he is responsible for the *honesty* and *propriety* of conduct of *every* Officer who executes a Writ (don't be *vastly* alarmed) and *you* can only have the counter indemnity of the Under-sheriff and his friends who will be bound. You as Sheriff have also the risk and expense of trying all *interpleaders* applications, up to the final attendance at the Judges Chambers, as the Judges at Chambers rarely, if ever, give costs from the belligerents. The Under Sheriff does of course all the drudgery, but through Whiteman, to whom I have written, some expenses may be kept down.
>
> *Very truly yours,*
> *G. W. Brace.*

P.S. Time may [?press] – It would save a few posts if you permitted me to write appointing P. Lewis, on the required and satisfactory security being given, this supposing the Doctor be *apparently* substantial. I have a letter today from Glascodine stating the roadway over Griffith level leading to the station, is giving way. I have written to Glascodine, Capt. Griffith and Whiteman, I can do nothing about Miss Gulston's Estate, before I have the will.

January 22 1860. John Whiteman, Llandilo, to George Brace, Esq., London. [copy].

Dear Sir,

In reply to your enquiries of yesterday respecting the realized property of Dr. Protheroe. I am informed he has three large farms in Llangathen parish, viz, Pentre Davies, Cwmmagyl, and Cylddery, the exact amount of rent I cannot ascertain but is supposed to be about £350; also a farm called Ynyslass in Llanarthney parish and one in Llandebie parish called Brynny with some collieries, sup-posed rental of these farms £230. These form the principle features of Dr. Protheroe's property, and it is generally believed the property is not mortgaged; there was a mortgage of £800 held by old Mr. Jones the owner of the Castle Inn, Llandilo, but that is said to be paid off.

I am dear Sir, Your Obedient Servant,

John Whiteman

January 24 1860. William Peel, Taliaris Park, to A. J. Gulston.

My dear Gulston,

I hate notepaper, so this half sheet of blue with plenty of room on it. I am sorry you are Sheriff but it can't be helped.

Well, I will give you what information I can, and have searched out my accounts during my Shrievalty in 1843 of which I give you every item, but things are much altered since that Becca year 17 years ago! and the last Under-sheriff could give you better information than I can. However there are few things on my list except the clothes and bills for keep of the 12 Javelin men which can I think be cut down as I succeeded a man who very properly clipped pretty close, and as you will see did not bleed very freely to these brigands' lances which they endeavoured to stick in at all parts. Now for advice. As to Chaplain – some people bring their own fancy man to confess them; you and I would require that privilege if we could afford it, but we must put a constraint over our feelings and forego the luxury which is expensive, as you must board and lodge him all the time and you cannot present him with less than 5 or 10 guineas each assize, if you take him from his home and appropriate him solely. [On] the first assize I took our respected minister, Mr. Williams of the parsonage whose ghostly counsel and advice was highly comforting and wholesome, and he gave me a very long sermon, cheap I should say at the money to a Dives but dear to a Lazarus like me smarting from the wounds caused by the stings of that nest of hornets into which a sheriff of necessity thrusts his head. Well the second time I was more economical in my soul's luxuries, and hired that excellent Divine, the Vicar or Rector of Carmarthen, to preach to me and the judge, and derived great benefit therefore as did I have no doubt his Lordship the Judge did also, and this at the more moderate sum of £2-2-0 with which he was well satisfied and I dare say none the worse for the loss of the virtue that had gone out of him into the Sheriff and Judge. Perhaps one guinea might be a proper remuneration, but as that is the common parsonial fee given by the trade to each other on the wholesale principle I fancy a sheriff must pay the retail price, and then you have done with him too – not so with your special retainer, who says your grace whilst you stop. You are aware perhaps that if, under a recent act of parliament, the Sheriff wishes it and the Justices in Quarter Sessions assembled allow it, he may have the use of the Police Officers and be altogether relieved from the necessity of providing and clothing 12 Javelin men, saving himself the expense of about £100, and with javelins, swords, and belts, £40 more. (I borrowed the swords and belts from Mr. Phillips of Aberglasney, and saved myself that sum through his kindness.) Well, I dare say you knew that Lord Emlyn proposed last Quarter Sessions that the Sheriff should have the use of the police and that the Chief Constable should be ordered by the courts to supply policemen to the sheriff for that purpose. Lord Emlyn was told he was out of order and must give Notice of a motion to that effect at the next Quarter Sessions, which I think he did, and I have no doubt if he does it will be carried. Now I suppose the Quarter Sessions come off before the assizes in which case you will probably, the motion being carried, ask for the police and save the hundred pounds or £140 as the case may be. As to a carriage I have nothing but a little [   ], and I know of no one to apply to for the loan of one, indeed I do not think there is either a chariot or a Coach in the county. But if you cannot hire one at less expense, I have a plan in my head for getting a chariot cheap that would answer the purpose, at least, if I were Sheriff I should be content with it.

The scheme is this – about two months ago I bought a chariot from Thomas of Llwyn Madoc [Brec] for five pounds! but I had to fetch it home, and we found it too heavy for our horses, it cost £400 when new, and had only done very little work for about 3 years; in fact had not worn out its first tires of the wheels and then laid by for about 15 years; it has no driving seat, but a rumble behind; the lining of the richest green silk having never been exposed but dressed in brown holland all the time just as it came out of the coachmakers' hands; it is as good as new. Cleaver could paint the under carriage and varnish the body very well and make it look very handsome. Now, you might do it up for the use of it and thus both of us be served, eh? But unfortunately Mr. Maskelyne took a fancy to it and as I only bought it to break up and found its wheels and axles (which last are crooked) not exactly suitable for carts as I intended, I let him have it for what I gave and the toll bars fetching it, and a man's maintenance. Now, from what he said in his letter the other day it seems to me that he did not like his bargain because there was no driving seat and it only holds three in-side (what chariot ever did?). You have a coach house at Llandilo to put it in I think, and if you like the scheme I would write and offer him what he gave me for it and the carriage up to Swindon and expenses he paid from Llwyn Madoc: altogether about £8 – my price cost £5, expenses from Llwyn Madoc to Taliaris and tolls, say 6s. 6d., carriage to Swindon £2 13 6. It would cost you £2 13 6 from Swindon to Llan-dilo, and painting by Cleaver. You would also be liable for the year's tax I suppose, if they find you out (£3). I have sent to Cleaver to know what he wants for painting under carriage, varnishing body, and painting crest if required. Perhaps after all you can have one cheaper. £5 5 0 the job each time. I know nothing about it under £10. After you have done with it I will give you £3 for it, to break up, and not a penny more, or you can sell it to anybody else or burn it. You must make up your mind quickly, and as you determine I will ask Mr. Maskelyne for it or not – quickly because I think he will be breaking it up if you do not. I suppose you would try to hire in Gloster or Bristol – carriage down here and back twice over, say £8, or keep it and pay 4 to 5 months' hire. Horses, Ivy Bush generally supplies decent enough 4, and wear jackets I think you find of your colour and buttons. Frock coat costume quite the thing to meet judge in. As to Lodgings, sheriff takes them there being as you know no decent room or attendance at any Inn in Carmarthen, look out in time. You only want them for yourself and servants, Under Sheriff will not trouble you. I shall have the honour of attending on your highness during your gestation and delivery if alive and well, and if you will come to me during the week before the campaign opens, will help you about, down to Carmarthen and all that. I do not know who your under sheriff will be, but if you choose a Llandilo bird he will be handy to consult, being near; if at Llandovery, you will have the train to carry you. Carmarthen will be too far off I should say. I suppose you must have a responsible man whatever else he maybe; he shall have access to you at all reasonable hours, but I won't promise to lodge him, but shall be highly delighted and so will Mrs Peel to have you with us. And now I will conclude having spent the whole day in collecting the information I have given. So, Good Night and kindest regards to all. Yours very truly, William Peel. [PS] I sent to Cleaver to know what he would charge for painting carriage. Mr. Cleaver says he cannot

Taliaris Park

give an estimate but must see it first. He would only charge bare wages, for arms and crest he would charge 10s. for the two if not such a great deal of work. I fancy he would want £6 for the whole, crests included. Please correct my letter, I am too tired to read it over again.

[Appended to the letter is William Peel's "Expenses for one of the two Assizes held in 1843", as follows]:

Trumpeters fee for blowing their cracked instruments	£5	5	0
Their board and lodgings	£2	5	0
Wine at lodgings for self and friends,			
Port, Sherry, and ale, ½ doz. of each	£2	18	0
Ringers. I would offer them £1 1 0 beforehand.			
If refused say let it alone	£2	2	0
Sawdust for the hall	£0	10	0
Judges clerk supposed a usual fee, and Judges servants			
as under, and opposite, opening Commission £2 2 0,			
Part acted by the butler, train bearer 10s 6d.			
Butler 10s 6d an imaginary being, coachman 10s 6d.			
I fancy this can't be helped	£3	13	6
Mr. Davies draper, week's lodgings, £5 5 0			
Provisions, candles etc, £2 4s 6d.			
Ditto paid my servants, £1 15 8			
Confectioner, cofee, biscuits, fancy bread, £1 4 2	£10	9	4
Rent of Stable £1 10. Horses hay, Corn £2 7 8	£3	17	8
Innkeeper Ivy Bush, wine and biscuits for Sheriff			
and his company going to escort judge	£5	0	0
Lodging Javelin Men 6 days at 3s 9d per day, £11 17 0.			
For their horses, hay and grass and their servants			
taking back their horses (they walked home) £4 13 0,			
dinner at Cross Inn on road home again	£17	6	6
Wands 5s 6d, Clerk Sexton 10s, Chief Constable 3s			
on going to Church to hear sermonat assizes	£0	18	6
Chaplain's fee, the rector or vicar of Carmarthen	£2	2	0
Clothing for 12 javelin men and 2 trumpeters at £5 a man	£70	0	0
Calendar printed on vellum £2 10 0. I refused to pay	£0	0	0
Tailor claimed £5 for a suit of clothes.			
I paid him as I only served one			
assignment at my own expence	£2	10	0
Turnpikes, meeting judge	£0	8	0
Say for other incidental expences	£5	0	0
Total Expense of one Assize	£134	5	6

N.B. If you have not your banners ready painted, by you (though I think you have your father's) they will cost about £10 10 0, though perhaps much cheaper now, my father paid that sum for his 35 years ago!!

January 26 1860. J. Prothero Lewis, Llandilo, to George Brace, Cavendish Square, London [Copy].

> *Dear Sir,*
>
> I was called suddenly from home yesterday which prevented my writing to you. I beg to propose as sureties my cousin David Prothero Esq of Llandilo, M.D., and my brother-in-law David Davies Esqr of Bryneithin near Llandilo who may perhaps be known to you as Mr. Davies of Froodvale. They are both men of substance and I trust you will be satisfied with them. I do not know whether you would like to act as the Sheriff's agent in London. If so I should be glad and feel obliged by your letting me know by return of Post. I had desired my friend Mr. Clarke of Clements Inn to call upon you to make all necessary arrangements (he is I believe known to you) and if you should not feel disposed to act in the matter he will do so. The Sheriff will have to take the oath of office which may be done before any justice of the Peace of the county in which he resides after he has received his Warrant. The oath is to be written on Parchment and when taken, to be sent to the Clerk of the Peace to be filed. The Under-sheriff's appointment must be in writing and a duplicate forwarded to the Clerk of the Peace. I will ask Mr. Clarke to get all this done as you are unwell, unless you prefer preparing the necessary documents yourself. It will save time if I get the whole matter arranged between Mr. Clarke and yourself. As soon as the appointment is made out I will see the Under-sheriff of the last year as to the transfer of the Writs etc.
>
>

I am dear Sir,

Yours truly J. Prothero Lewis.

January 30 1860. C. Henry Raimond, 25 Cavendish Square, London, to A. J. Gulston, Teignmouth, S. Devon.

> *Dear Sir,*
>
> I forward you a letter (copy) from Mr. J. P. Lewis of Llandilo to Mr. Brace. The Mr. Clarke he makes mention of is of the firm of Gregory Sons and Clarke of Clements Inn, Solicitor. Mr. Brace is much worse, dangerously so.
>
>

I remain dear Sir,

Yours very obediently

C. Henry Raimond.

January 30 1860. William Peel, Taliaris Park, to A. J. Gulston.

Mr Dear Gulston,

I could not get the en-closed from Nathaniel Davies (Justices' Clerk) till too late for Post though I sent for it. It does not give us much information but I fear that the Qr Sessions which would have suited your purpose will be held after the assizes, as if there is an adjournment held it would only be for trying prisoners and thus clearing the Gaol of the minor cases and not for County business. I sent you the Carmarthen Journal giving the account of the Cardiganshire Qr Sessions, what was said and done there. By that account it might appear that it rested with the Courts to direct whether the Sheriffs should have the use of the police instead of his javelin men, but I have not seen the Act and it may be that the Sheriff has the right to the use of the police without the permission of the Court though from what was said I fear not, however get the Act from your Stationer and see. If the Court of Quarter Sessions be held, as I fear it, well after the assizes, and the authority to use Police be necessary, I am afraid there is no chance of getting the assistance as the Magistrate could only grant that when there assembled. And if you have to provide men for the first assize all you would save at the next would be their keep, £17 to £20. The next thing to be done is if obliged or inclined to provide your own javelin men is for you, if so inclined, to ask our Friend at Aberglasney to send his swords and javelins which I was told would save from £20 to £40.

Yours in much haste,

William Peel

January 30 1860. John Whiteman, Llandilo, to Allan J. Gulston, Esqr., Teignmouth, S. Devon.

Honoured Sir,

Herewith I send copy of a letter sent to Mr Brace on the subject of Dr Prothero's property, since which I am in-formed the rental of the whole of his landed and house property amount to £1900 per annum. I am very sorry to hear Mr Brace is again ill. Little David Davies shall be at Bristol, at the time appointed to receive the horses with strict orders to bring them to Llandilo, and I will prepare a place for them to be at grass and in at night with good hay, as you wish. I am Honoured Sir, Your Obedient Servant, John Whiteman. PS. The Javelins, Cutlasses, Banners, etc, etc, are all at Llwynyberllan but will require a little doing up. I have this day received a letter from Mr Brace's clerk informing me that Mr Prothero Lewis of this town is appointed Under-sheriff and I have also seen it in The Welshman newspaper. At your convenience you will please say if I am to have the Javelins etc repaired and done up.

January 30 1860. Lord Emlyn, Golden Grove, Llandilo to "Dear Mr. Sheriff".

As the first man in the County and representing H, *and* as an old warrior, *and* as principal landowner and House owner in Llandilo. I have no doubt you have some difficulty in making up your mind how much you will give to the Llandilo Voluntary Rifle Corps, and as we are to have a meeting next Saturday I should be proud to be able to announce that you wish to join us and become an Honorary Member. We cannot let you off for less than £1. £5 would be very handsome but there is no limit upwards. We really shall be obliged for a small contribution as there are a good many expenses to be met. I wish you would come and live somewhere about here. We want neighbours very badly. Lady Emlyn joins me in these wishes and begs to be remembered to Mrs Gulston.

Yours very truly,

Emlyn

January 31 1860. William Peel, Taliaris Park, to A. J. Gulston.

My Dear Gulston,

Being in Llandilo today I got our Clerk Val [?Natl.] Davies to look me out the act of Parliament containing the enactments relating to the substitution of Police for Javelin men. After a hunt we ran it to earth under an act to amend law relating to Police. There is only one clause which treats on the subject, a copy of which I send to you. From this you will see that as I supposed it is only by the direction of the magistrates in Qr or General [Session], which means the same thing, that the Police can be substituted, and this through the worst luck in the world, it quite vexes me, you cannot avail yourself of the police services as the Assizes will as far as we can make out take place before the Qr Sessions. I saw Cleaver today as to painting carriage if it is to be had, he says about £6 for painting, and Crests about £1 the two. I only said a friend of mine thought he might possibly bring a carriage that wanted painting and I wanted to know what he would charge if he had the job. It is just a toss up whether carriage is to be had or not, but if it is it will answer the purpose unless you are prouder than I am. Nevertheless you may probably hire one or be able to send your own down at less money. No harm in my mentioning this choice of evils to you – "It is only a choice of evils from the cradle to the grave", said my medical man when he said I had better not ride, I can't stand that said I. Well sir be ill and ride or be well and give up your horse "its only a choice etc etc. . . . ["] I have no time to write just now, hence my loquacity, List of game killed at Taliaris this year – 137 partridges, 70 pheasants, 32 hares, only 14 woodcocks, 3 wild ducks, 1 teal, a dozen snipes, and 401 rabbits.

Yours William Peel.

[Enclosures].

Extract from the 13th and 14th Charles 2nd. Chap. 21, Sec. 1. Parts 1, 2, and 3 of section, of no importance. 4, And also that no Sheriff shall after the 1st day of February (1663) have more than 40 men servants with Liveries attending upon him in the time of the Assizes, nor under the number of 20 men servants, in any County whatsoever within the Kingdom of England, not under the number of 12 men servants in any County within the Dominion of Wales. 5, upon pain that every Sheriff offending in any of the premises contrary to the true meaning hereof shall forfeit for every default the sum of £200. *Extract from the 22nd and 23rd Victoria, cap. 32. Sec 18.* It shall be lawful for the Justices of the Peace of any County in General or Quarter Sessions assembled if they shall think fit to direct that a sufficient number of Police Constables of the said County shall be employed to keep order in and within the precincts of the Court of Assize and the Chief Constable of the County shall thereupon employ a sufficient number of such Constables for such purpose and in that case it shall not be necessary for the High Sheriff to provide and maintain any Javelin men or other Men Servants with Liveries at the Assizes, anything contained in the Act of the 13th and 14th years of His Majesty King Charles the 2nd Chap 21 notwithstanding.

February 1 1860. J. Prothero Lewis, Llandilo to A. J. Gulston.

Dear Sir,

Mr. Brace wrote to me some days ago stating that you had kindly promised to name me as the Deputy Sheriff for this County for the ensuing year. Permit me to thank you for your kindness. I trust you will never have occasion to regret having done so. I had desired my Agents, Messers Gregory, Son and Clark of Clements Inn, to put themselves in communication with Mr. Brace and to get the necessary documents prepared. I was much grieved to hear that Mr. Brace has been so ill that my Agents have been unable to see him, and in a letter received from them today they tell me that he is now in a most dangerous state. They state that they expected a letter from Mr. Thos Brace or Mr. Colt desiring them to carry out this matter. Under these circumstances I have taken the liberty of requesting Messers Gregory and Co to communicate with you, and to forward you the necessary papers. I named my cousin Doctor Prothero and Mr Davies of Bryneithin as Sureties in the Bond to be given by me. They are both men of property and character and I trust you will be satisfied with them.

I remain Dear Sir,
Yours very faithfully,
J. Prothero Lewis.

February 8 1860. Gregory Son and Clark, Clements Inn, to A. J. Gulston, 5 Dean Crescent, Teignmouth, Devon.

> Sir,

We had been in communication with our late respected friend George Brace prior to his melancholy death touching your appointment of Sheriff and the appointment of your Under-sheriff. We had also been in correspondence with our friend Mr J. P. Lewis of Llandilo and at his desire forward to you the form of Oath which is required to be taken by Sheriffs of Welsh counties. This Oath must be subscribed by you and sworn before a Justice of the Peace for the County of Carmarthen or before one of the Barons of the Exchequer in London. Please therefore to consider which will be most convenient to yourself and should you decide on coming to London we will willingly afford you every assistance. After this Oath has been taken it must be sent to Mr Lewis in order to be filed by the Clerk of the Peace. We also send you the Appointment of Mr J. P. Lewis as your Under-sheriff, in duplicate – these in like manner have to be lodged with the Clerk of the Peace. We also enclose the Appointment of ourselves as Deputy Sheriffs in London, this has not to be lodged but may be returned to us. We also forward you the Deed of Covenant between the Under-sheriff and yourself which has been already executed by Mr J. P. Lewis and his sureties and will require execution by yourself at the 1st seal. You can retain it.

> *We are Sir, Yours obediently,*
>
> *Gregory Son and Clark.*

Detail of Javelin

February 10 1860. John Propert, New Cavendish Street, London to A. J. Gulston

[This notepaper is headed 'Royal Medical Benevolent College, Epsom. Office: 37 Soho Square, London, W. With an engraving of the College.]

Most happy shall I be my dear Sir if I can afford you any assistance or information. I have just seen my friend and neighbour Mr. Jennings, your immediate predecessor in Carmarthenshire, and he informed that there is a clause in a recent Act which authorizes the employment of the Police to keep order at the Assizes, consequently superceding the Javelin Men, but as yet it has not been acted upon nor does he think that it will in our Country especially.

What I did was, I dressed up twelve of my tenants, or their smart young sons, I gave them an useful suit consisting of a blue frock coat, a blue waistcoat and trowsers, with a scarlet strip on the outside, I gave also a pair of boots and of course a hat and black stock with my crest button on, which, as well as the scarlet strip they took off as soon as I had done with them, which left them with a handsome suit of useful clothes which they still [use] and are very proud of them and only wear them on high days and holidays; the halberts and swords were lent me by an old schoolfellow at Cardigan; and altho' I entertained the Judge and the Grand Jury, Bar, etc. at two splendid dinners, one at each Assize, my whole expense did not exceed £300! I met the Judge about two miles out of town with, of course, my Javelin Men who had much the oat of a squadron of Dragoons! Your under Sheriff will afford you every information you may require. I sincerely hope that your amiable Lady is by this [time] strong and well again and I trust the Almighty will support your beloved Parent through her very very severe trial.

With kind regards, I remain, my dear Sir, most truly yours,
John Propert.

February 13 1860. J. Prothero Lewis, Llandilo, to A. J. Gulston.

Dear Sir,

I will make out a list of the different fees usually paid by High Sheriffs. These are some fees, which I hear, some of the late *High Sheriffs have declined paying.* I will ascertain what these are on Wednesday, and you may rely on my taking every care that you shall be put to no unnecessary expense. I hope you will be able to take the Oath very soon, as in strictness the Oath must be taken before the Sheriff can enter on the duties of his Office. I hope to see Mr Whiteman in the course of the day.

I am, Dear Sir, Yours faithfully,
J. Prothero Lewis.

February 14 1860. John Whiteman, Llandilo, to A. J. Gulston, Teignmouth.

Honoured Sir,

I herewith send you patterns of Mr James, London House, Cloths and But-tons for Javelin Men's clothing, with the price of each, including every requisite to complete the suits. Mr Thomas tailor's price for making up is £1 3s. 5d. each, total £2 4s. 6d. or £2 1s. 6d. each suit. I was at Carmarthen yesterday and the estimates I obtained there were much higher, the lowest I herewith send £3 3s. 0d. Mr James, London House, will furnish very *good hats* at 8s. each, inferior from 5s. to 7s. The Javelins and swords are all found excepting the Belts for the swords, merely a black leather strap (required). The swords require a good deal of cleaning. The Banners were very dirty, some of the colours turned black. I have had them cleaned as well as possible, the silk is very tender (from age). I thought they might do with care. I send them by this day's post for Mrs Gulston's inspections. I find the regular charge of the Trumpeters is 2 guineas a day each, and their clothes (provide for themselves, I think they can afford to do so). I looked at the Sheriff's Lodgings at James Puddicomb, Draper, Guildhall Square. (Davies does not let lodgings.) The charge is £5 5s. 0d. per week for the *room alone,* the use of Linen, Plate, etc are all extra – the late Sheriff paid £7 10 0 including those things. The charge at the Ivy Bush Hotel is 2s. 6d. per day for Sitting Room, 2s. 6d. bedroom, all other things the same as any gentleman coming to the Inn. You can have rooms in the private Lodging House attached to the Inn which ever you would prefer at the same price. I hear many Sheriffs have lodged at the Inn. Their charge at the Ivy Bush for 4 horses to meet the Judge, etc is £3 3s. 0 d. per day, this includes all charges, Post Boys etc. Mr. Corner, landlord of the 6 Bells [St Peter Street] will do it for £2 5s. 0d. including Post Boys; he has done it for several Sheriffs. I find it is customary for the Post Boys to have Jackets found them of the same cloth as the Javelin men. The two last Sheriff's Javelin men had horses. Some of the Judges have gone to Carmarthen by *Rail,* when that is the case, horses are not wanted. I have consulted P. Lewis and he will endeavour to find out which way the Judge will come. If we are obliged to have horses, I must contrive to send them back the same day. The charge at the Old Ivy Bush for board and lodging the Javelin Men is 4s per day each man (and no beer). At the Six Bells 3s. 9d. and a pint of beer to each meal, 3 meals per day. You do not name the style or cut of Frock coat, the Tailors wished to know as a guide for their price. I suggested Single Breasted to be buttoned up close with an upright collar with hook and eye inside, so as not to show the neckhandkerchief. I thought it would correspond with the military effect of the red stripe on the trowsers and cockade. (Scarlet cloth would be very expensive cut in stripes.) I have suggested scarlet braid an inch wide, Mr James and the tailors think it will look as well as scarlet cloth. The Frock Coat made in this way comes much cheaper. But all these matters are submitted for your consideration. Any thing that I can do to lessen the expenses and to further your wishes will have my utmost attention.

I have the honour to be, Your Obedient Humble Servant,
John Whiteman.

February 15 1860. Gregory Son and Clark, Clements Inn, to A. J. Gulston, 5 Dean St, Teignmouth, S. Devon.

Sir,

We some days ago received the appointment of Under Sheriff and Deputy Sheriff signed by you, but with their dates in blank. The first act to be done by you as Sheriff was that first mentioned in our letter, viz the taking of your Oath of office, and which as we in that letter said must be taken either before a Justice of the Peace of Carmarthenshire or one of the Barons of the Exchequer in London. As the duties of the office of Sheriff are disarranged for want of this step, may we solicit you that the most convenient course is to run up to London and get this Oath taken. Mr Lewis the Under-sheriff is getting very anxious about it as he cannot accept the charge of the prisoners or of any of the un-executed Writs.

We are Sir, Yours obediently,
A Gregory Son and Clerk.

Undated

After 5 February, 1860. William Peel, Taliaris Park to A. J. Gulston.

My dear Gulston,

I have been in London the last week and on my return found your letter of the 5th which my wife did not forward to me, thinking I should return sooner than I did. Hence the delay in answering it. I shall be very glad to see you whenever it suits you to make your appearance here, as I am not going from home that I know of. I returned from London last night, a horrid cold journey, found a slight sprinkling of snow when I got here. I fancy the Judge will be delivered or rather the train will be delivered of the Judge at the Station of the Carmarthen and Cardigan Railway which branches off from the South Wales Railway station, and comes in right into the town behind the Ivy Bush where your carriage will meet him. As to four or a pair of horses I fancy you would meet him with four if it were out of town and take him away again with the

same, but it is not everybody who uses four in any way. The last man was a Commerical party who had just bought a place; his habitat London, and not having before had a standing in this market, thought it well to bring himself and his goods in with four horses to his waggon. I had a pair only but not posters being horses then worth about 80 apiece (or a 100 now), in fact my two hunters – showy bits, and other

Javelins on parade

people using their own have had a pair only. If I could get a respectable pair of Post horses I would myself have only a pair at the Station, being in the town one would have a good excuse for the alteration, but it is a matter of taste. The Judge could not complain of a double Brougham and pair and you would have for your reason if you did not care for expense yourself, that you were cutting things as low and near as could be for the sake of the poor devil who would have to follow you in the same profession. As to the dress of the Javelin Men – I gave them a tailed coat (not frock), a striped groom's waistcoat, drab cloth breeches and gaiters and a hat – livery buttons on all except the gaiters, and 10s Hats with Gold Bands. I should say 7s. would do now in these days of silk hats. As to the livery buttons, I made agreement with the tenants that they should all return me their buttons and gold bands (which are none the worse for wear) and found my coachman in buttons and bands for 12 years. And I gave them common buttons in their place which cost very little. I also gave them better gold bands to cost 4s. 6d. instead of 2s. 6d. at which last named price they would have been worth nothing afterwards. You remember my advice to borrow swords and javelins of Mr Phillips. All this remember too is only according to my shabby ideas and what I did for myself: You may wish to do more grandly. The Javelin Men through the tailor hinted that shoes at my expense would be very "nice things to have", but I told him if they waited till I found them, as I supposed they had shoes of their own, they would have to make this pilgrimage barefoot. The sheriff need not as in some counties make his own entrance in procession into the town from his own house, so you can send your carriage to Carmarthen direct, which will save you posting etc.

Give please our united kindest regards to Mrs Gulston and your young people, and believe me,

Very truly yours, William Peel.

P.S. As I mean to have the honour of escorting you to meet the judge, I will take you down in my dog cart. Keep your under-sheriff well in hand, they are often anxious their principal should do the thing well "while he is about it as it only comes once in your life". If you have Phillips's swords and javelins you will have to trim the latter with fringe of your own livery colour, and if you can't put this neatly back again, put new on as I did for him.

[ ] February 1860. William Peel, Taliaris to A. J. Gulston.

My dear Gulston,

Since I wrote to you yesterday I have come to the conclusion that I shall be able to lend you my new carriage which I think will be sure to be ready about the 25th of this month, or at any rate before the end. It is in London. It is a roomy sociable landau holds 4 inside, 2 on the box, and has a rumble behind. When I write to you first saying I could not lend you one, it was because I had not the vehicle to lend but last week I was in London on some business and I saw one I liked and bought it thinking I should not be in town again for some time and I might never again have the opportunity of getting one so cheap. It is second hand but had not been used more than three months and then very little indeed, if the Coachmaker had not told me I should have taken it for a new one. I am having a little alteration made in the painting and a rumble added, but it is promised me certainly by the time I mention. *And* I am sure it will be ready as all I am doing is to had *[sic]* a white line picked out on the green ones, and the crests and fresh hand polished. As it has been standing in the shop this winter, was built last year, it is a very smart affair. I did not mention it yesterday as I had not consulted Mrs Peel whose carriage it is, and I thought she might not like the thing to be knocked about in an Inn Yard. But that amiable lady says she will lend it to you with pleasure, provided which is a *sine que non* that you provide a private lock up Coach House in Carmarthen for it, and have a servant with you, which of course you will, who will *superintend* the cleaning as she would not trust it to the Post boys to clean. Well now, Mrs Peel having done *fairly* as far as her part goes. I will do my share and fit you out, Cinderella wise, with a Coachman and pair of horses if you like to have them. But Coachman and horses must go together because one of my horses though gentle as a Lamb with Joseph is furious in a crowd with a stranger. Joseph too would look after the cleaning of the carriage and you would thus have no responsibility to Mrs Peel on that score. My horses are not as you know large ones but are handsome and good, took me to Neath without baiting last Saturday, 28 miles in 3½ hours under rather than over. My harness is brass and in very good condition, if you would go to the expense of frontlets for the bridles of your own colours and saddle cloths under the pads. It would help the appearance and not cost much. I can then drive you down to Carmarthen, and you will only have to pay for those standing at the Inn and the man. The pair horses 11 shillings a day, and the man 4s. 6d. or thereabouts. You will then escape Rees's charge for the horses and dressing his postilions. Which you will have to do. On Joseph you will have to hang your own livery but he is a commonsized man and you can have it made loose and it will come in sooner or later for a servant of your own. Now if you like to avail yourself of these things, either the carriage by itself or carriage, coach-man and horses, on the terms stated, they are at your service for this assize and if I am alive for the next too. It is not because I am jealous of your making a splash. I can assure you but I think a fellow like a High Sheriff fallen among thieves has special need of some Good Samaritan to pour oil on his wounds and set him on his own beast. By the bye as I will be with you at the assizes if there is a bedroom to spare in your lodgings will you bespeak it for me as the Inns you know are execrable.

Thine most true, William Peel.

[P.S.] I mentioned the matter to Joseph in strict confidence which I know he will observe because I could not offer to lend him without [certainty].

A further missive, in another part of the Derwydd MSS, addressed to Mr. Gulston at Teignmouth in February 1860, contains a splendid drawing of four horses in dress harness "manufactured for His Highness the Pacha of Egypt" by Urch and Co., 84 Long Acre, London, doubtless hoping to find a purchaser in the Carmarthenshire Sheriff.

How the letters and advertisements influenced the High Sheriff is not known, but a note written by his son Alan Stepney Gulston, provides some information of what resulted. Having recorded that his father 'took the oath of fealty on Ash Wednesday 22 February 1860', he proceeds – 'The Spring Assizes was opened on 6th of March and lasted for five days, the Judge being Sir John Barnard Byles, knight. Mr. Gulston was attended by 24 Javelin men and like his father he drove grey horses. In May 1860 Mr Gulston took "Woodland" [now known as Clyne Castle, Glam.] the seat of Mr Graham Vivian, near Swansea, from which he started on the 10 July 1860 for Carmarthen when on the 11th of July Sir M. W. Bramwell, Knight, arrived by rail from Haverfordwest and was received by the High Sheriff and his Javelin Men (all wearing swords), the High Sheriff in the uniform of a Deputy Lieutenant, and his Chaplain in full canonicals. The "Commission" was opened on the 12th July, when, there being no Criminal cases and no Civil cases, the High Sheriff presented the Judge with a pair of white gloves in honour of the "Maiden Assize". There being only two Assizes held at that time in each year, the duties of the High Sheriff came to an end'.

The scribe, Alan Stepney Gulston, born in 1844, was the eldest son and heir of the fore-going. Educated at Harrow and Merton College, Oxford, he settled at Derwydd which he restored very considerably, preserving as many of its surviving features as possible. He became a well known local antiquary, member and sup-porter of the Carmarthenshire Antiquarian Society, and contributed useful material to its *Transactions*. He filled several public posts, was a Justice of the Peace, a Deputy Lieutenant, Captain in the Royal Carmarthen Artillery Militia (1867-81) and in 1895 High Sheriff. The previous Sheriff, James Buckley, of Bryncaerau Castle, died in his year of office, on 2 September 1895, and Alan Stepney Gulston was appointed on 3 October following, the third successive member of his family to fill the post. He appointed David Long Price of Talley as Under-sheriff and the Rev. David Davies, M.A., vicar of Llandybie, as chaplain.

As a good antiquary he believed in describing his shrieval activities, and recorded: *Winter Assize.* On Thursday 7 November 1895 I drove from Derwydd to Carmarthen (15 miles) and on Friday afternoon the Judge notified that he would "arrive privately".

On Saturday the 9th the High Sheriff (in full uniform of a Captain Royal Carmarthen Artillery Militia), the Under-sheriff, and Chaplain (in full canonicals) drove to the Judge's Lodgings accompanied by 24 police, etc, bells ringing, trumpeters and banners – thence with the Judge, the Honourable Sir John Compton Lawrence, knight, to St. Peter's Church for service and a 15 minute sermon by the Chaplain; thence to the Guild Hall to a full fanfare of trumpets when the Commission was duly opened; only a few short cases standing for trial, All was over at 1 p.m. and at 2 o'clock the High Sheriff partook of Luncheon with the Judge when, after courteous adieux he drove home to Derwydd.'

'*Spring Assize.* On Saturday 19th January 1896 I started 3 p.m. from Derwydd and drove to the Ivy Bush Hotel, Carmarthen, and dined with the Honourable Stephen Coleridge. On Monday the 20th at 5.30 p.m. I drove in full uniform with the Under-deputy Sheriff James John Esq., and Chaplain, to Carmarthen station, carriage and pair, coachman, groom, two trumpeters, and 14 Police with Inspector to meet the Judge, the Honourable Sir John Charles Day, Knight, arriving from Lampeter, and on Tuesday 21 January 1896 drove in state to the Guild Hall at 11 a.m. when the Commission was duly opened, and after the Judge had delivered a most complementary charge to the Grand Jury, I presented the Judge and six officials with a pair of white gloves to commemorate a 'Maiden Assize' in a similar manner as did my Father some 35 years before. After which I gave a state Luncheon to about 40 persons, Champagne ad lib, cigars and coffee, being supported by my brother George, Sir James Drummond, Bart., and the whole of the Grand Jury, the Bar, and officers of the Court, the Borough Mayor, etc, The Lord Bishop of Swansea, Honourable C. Fielding, Judge's Marshals, etc, etc. I drove home on that day to Derwydd leaving Carmarthen at 3.30, and so my duties as High Sheriff came to an end'.

As we can see, the Javelin men had departed, their place taken by the Police. The two Assizes had become the basic pattern of shrieval participation.

Alan Stepney Gulston of Derwydd, recorder of the shrievalty in late Victorian days, died without issue on 9 September 1919. His wife, Agnes Margaret (née Anderson) had pre-deceased him in 1913. Derwydd passed to his niece, Miss Agneta Annie Justinia Stepney Gulston, M.B.E., J.P., daughter of his younger brother George. She died unmarried, and Derwydd was inherited by her kinsman, Mr. Ralph Stepney Gulston. (The house has since been sold. Ed.)

I am grateful to Miss Susan Beckley, B.A., Carmarthen Archivist for all her help, and especially to her Assistant Miss Elizabeth Twist, B.A., for placing her palaeographical expertise at my service and helping to unravel difficulties that attended the arrangement of some of the letters.

SHERIFFS OF WEST WALES 1540 - 1603

No student of Welsh genealogy can have failed to notice one remarkable phenomenon regarding the ruling families. Despite political subjection and heavy defeat on the battlefield, the native royal and noble families survived to an almost miraculous degree. The measure of this survival is clearly indicated in the shrievalty lists from 1540 to 1603. In Carmarthenshire, during those years, 58 High Sheriffs came from Welsh families, and only 7 from families of non Welsh origin; of the former, 25 claimed descent from the ancient princes, and 27 from medieval chieftains. In Pembrokeshire, the southern half of which was completely anglicized, 37 High Sheriffs were of Welsh origin, 27 of non Welsh origin; of the former 31 claimed descent from Welsh chieftains. This survival persisted throughout the succeeding centuries, and the fact that today the Lords Lieutenant of both Carmarthenshire and Pembrokeshire are descendants in the male line from the 11th century Cadifor Fawr of Blaencych must remain one of the most intriguing footnotes to the history of the ruling families of Dyfed.

Country Matters . . .

About 1700 Pembrey drew the notice of a distinguished antiquary, Edward Lluyd, whose observations containing some interesting facts about the locality were quoted in Richard Fenton's *Tours in Wales* as follows –

"Penbre Court, ye Seat formerly of the Butlers and afterwards of the Vaughans, and now belonging (in right of his Lady) to [William] Ball, Esqr, whence it descends to my Ld Ashburnham's Lady . . . Diwlais Brook divides this parish from Llan Elhi, springing at Croslaw Mountain and falls into the sea . . . Here are 2 lakes close together called Swan Pool where there are plenty of Eels, and in the Winter store of Fowls such as Ducks and Teal, sometimes wild Swans or Elks and wild Geese. The adjoining one, stored with Turbot, Bret, and Sole. They take here a large sort of Fish called Friers or Monk Fish (in Hereford, Gloucester, and Worcester, whither they carry them, Soucing Fish) about May, June, and July. This Pool (or Pools for both may be called one) is called Swan Pool because the Lord of the Manor (Mr. Ball) has thereon about 40 swanns. Before the hard frost there were about 8o, which all died to 6".

An irrigation ditch extending from the area of the farms of Towyn Mawr and Penybedd to the burrows near the present golf-course, is nowadays marked on maps as "Swan Pool Drain", a far cry from the days when the pool harboured elegant swans of the masters of Pembrey Court. Reference to "the Swann pools at Pembrey" occurs in manorial records of 1642.

THE SCALES OF JUSTICE

Report on the Order Book 1569-1627

Description of the Manuscript

HE MANUSCRIPT volume under consideration contains ordnance and decrees made by the Common Council of the borough of Carmarthenshire between the years 1569 and 1627. It contains 44 parchment folios (88 counting both sides) plus one end page, and apart from a little fraying at the top of the last two folios, is in good condition. It is bound in black calf skin, ornamented with tooling of one panel within another, clearly the work of a local leather-worker. The overall size of the book is 10½ inches by 8½ inches. The entries (which are not in chronological order) are made in the style of calligraphy known as the "Secretary hand", the headings and titles of the sections being done in large ornamental script, that on folio 13 being an excellent example. Fine examples of ornamental capital letters, adorned with the figure of a man, a little dog, a bird, and mythical figures occur on folios 5, 11, and 15. The headings are mostly in Latin which was normally used in official and legal documents of the period, but the text is in English. Then are also glossaries and marginalia contributed by contemporary hands.

Provenances

This is an archive produced by the Corporation in the normal course of its business, and the essential definitive record of its proceedings. How it strayed from official custody I not know, but on folio 1, a small square of paper has been stuck, bearing the words "Em Alcwyn Evans MSS. Orig(inal) Doc(ument) No. 8". This shows that it had come to his hands, and was afterwards considered to be his possession. Alcwyn Evans was an erudite antiquary, living in Carmarthen, who published various papers on the history of the town based on the manuscripts of the Corporation. He had studied this particular manuscript very carefully, and entries made in his own neat handwriting occurs on thirty-eight of the folios. He died in 1902, and the subsequent history of the manuscript is unknown, until its reappearance in Sotheby's sale room where it was bought back for the Corporation on 20 November 1973.

Content

The book contains the orders issued by the Common Council at its various meetings, and are signed by the Mayor, the Recorder, and members of the Council. The great majority of the members signed, which speaks well of the literacy of the burgesses in those days. The earliest entry was made on 4 May 1569 when Lewis Davies was Mayor, and John Entail, Recorder. The orders were preceded by the formula that the Mayor and Common Council "did order, condiscend and agree as fellows," etc., and often adds "with the grave advyse" of the Recorder. Among the officials mentioned in addition to the Mayor and Records, and Deputy Mayor, Aldermen, Justices of the Peace, bailiffs, chamberlains, sword-bearer, sergeant, and common attorneys, all of whom were appointed in open Council, usually in

Town Hall, Carmarthen, 1861

August. All meetings were held in "the guyldhalle' and the Mayor was to ensure that all orders were put in execution "as God shall gyve him grace and love".

The entries concern numerous aspects of the administration of the borough and throw light on the way of life of the burgesses from 1569- 1627. No one was to be admitted a burgess unless he had dwelt in the town for twelve months, or to have the freedom, unless he had completed a seven years' apprenticeship, or any burgess or freeman's son who the Mayor "thinks will be a goodly person" could be given the freedom and admitted on payment of 3s. 4d. while a "foreigner' could secure his freedom of the borough on payment of £5 (Order, 1582).

Three names were annually submitted for the office of Mayor, and the election made in open Council. The procedure, detailed in an order in 1569, stated that the three nominees be presented for election "upon Jesus daie next being the 7th daie of August next according to the auncient custom used". In 1594 it was ordered that on every Monday after the Feast of St. Michael the Archangel the "auncient or eldest alderman was to be elected one of the Justices of the Peace for the town for the ensuing year; and that the Mayor was to be the other Justice.

Special powers were granted to Aldermen, and in 1582 all Aldermen were empowered to commit to prison, summarily, any person or persons "fighting, quarellinge, scoldinge" or otherwise disturbing the peace or behaving contrary to the Queen's laws, and sergeants, constables, or any other burgess were enjoined to assist the alderman making such arrest and committal. Any person making an assault or affray "with bludshed" was to be fined 7 shillings, and "for any dry blowe" given he was to pay two shillings and sixpence. In 1583 it was ordered that aldermen be exempt from jury service.

Particular instructions were laid down as to the dress of councilmen, and in 1582 it was ordered that every Common Councilman was to attend meetings "apparaled in their gownes" on pain of a fine of half a crown, and the bailiffs were to attend in their gowns on every Court day, on pain of a similar fine.

On 11 March 1585 it was ordered that the Common Councilmen should go in their scarlet gowns to the Mayor's house, and "in decent and comlie order" accompany the Mayor to morning and evening prayers at church; and on days when Courts Leet or Quarter Sessions were held in the town, they were to attend him to the Guildhall, and attend him to service in the Mayor's chapel; and it was further ordered that burgesses worth £20 in land or goods, should before next Easter provide "a comlie fur" and similarly attend the Mayor, or to be fined 2/6 for non-attendance and 20/- for not providing themselves with "comelie gownes". The sword bearer was also to attend, and his wages to be raised from £2 to £4 per annum so that he could be "comelie appareled".

An order made in 1594 shows that the Statute against Liveries passed in the reign of Henry VII, was being contravened, and the Council decided to enforce it. Accordingly on 10 July 1594 the following order was made - "That whereas divers of the enhabitants and burgesses of the towne are retayned and weare Liveries to certain gentlemen, by colour whereof divers mysdemeanours and offences are by them committed" for avoiding of which inconveniences it is ordered that none of the burgesses and inhabitants shall henceforth retain or wear any liveries of any person or persons whatsoever, except some of the gentlemen of H.M. Privy Council, the Lord President of the Council in the Marches of Wales, the Bishop of the Diocese for the time being, the Justices of H.M. Great Sessions of the County of Carmarthen, or some of the Council of the said town, "upon pain of being disenfranchised of their freedom and libertie within the foresaid tone". However, a later Mayor, Morris Lloyd, caused the order to be disallowed, but it was re-imposed in November 1597.

Apparently election days could be a source of anxiety to the authorities, and in 1581 it was ordered that persons causing disturbances and tumults on election days were to be fined, and further ordered that no person or persons were to lift any candidate "on their shoulders or backs" in order to ensure his election as an officer, and instead were to behave in seemly manner, and to "freely yeild their voices in quiet, honest, and decent sort" in favour of the nominated candidates.

On 15 November 1597 the Council ordered that henceforth the town was to be divided into wards, namely, (1) The Gell Street, Dam Street, and Water Street, in the Lower Franchise, and to be called Gell Street. (2) St. Mary Street, Key Street, and Bridge Street, to be called St. Mary Street Ward, (4) King Street, Lower Water Street, and Spilman Street, to be called King Street Ward (5) Priory Street and the Upper franchise to be called Priory Street Ward. Each ward was to be governed by an alderman with full powers to govern same.

Seemingly, the "law's delays" is an old problem, and on 17 April 1581, the Council laid down rules as to the procedures in the town's law courts. Time governing the bringing of actions was laid down, officers of the corporation were not to be sureties, jury returns were to be properly made, and should any attorney cause delay or misbehave, he was to be fined four pence to the poor men's box, or else not to be admitted to practice in the court.

Several complaints had been made about the use of unauthorised weights and measures where "stolen wool" was weighed, and on 7 May 1576 the Council ordered that all wool was to be weighed only "at the common beam, and by the common balance and weights" appointed by the Mayor, who appointed Richard Jenings, Sergeant, to be overseer of the weights. The Mayor was to receive one penny for every stone so weighed.

All transgressors were to be fined half a crown for every stone of wool weighed elsewhere in the town. In 1585

stricter control was made over the sale of fish, and ordered that fish-boards be erected "nighe the conduit in the market place", and that all fish should be sold there, under pain of forfeiting the fish; and as it had been reported that certain fishermen sold fish from the river Towy at an excessive price, they were to sell them only at the said fishboard under pain of a fine of £5. Mention of the Conduit directs us to the order issued on 3 March 1586 by Mayor Thomas Nuthead, who stated that "divers disordered persons very undecently and without good order" washed foul and unclean things at the Conduit, and watered horses, mares, and cattle, washed foul buckets, pails, looms, barrels, clothes, roots, fish, flesh, and "other filth" there, and henceforth they are to desist upon pain of imprisonment or a fine of twelve pence.

Apparently, the presence of pigs could constitute a nuisance to the burgesses, and on 5 October 1576 it was ordered that "no manner of swine great or small, unless lawfully

ringed and yoked shall be suffered to go to lie in any open street or streets within the said town of Carmarthen", and the owners were to pay a fine of fourpence for each offending swine.

The book also mentions charities that the Mayor was to administer. In 1601 one Hugh Atwell, parson of St. Tewe in Cornwall (formerly parson of Coverley, Devonshire) left the sum of 30 shillings to the town of Carmarthen "to keep the poor at work" for ever; and Alderman John Fisher of Carmarthen gave 20 shillings "to remain for ever to keep the poor of the said town at work".

It seems that wedding gifts were not always in the public interest according to an order issued on 10 November 1583. It states that people used to bring gifts to young couples being married at the parish church, which encouraged many to marry in the hope that such gifts and offerings might enable them to support themselves, but as some did not receive sufficient gifts they were driven to extreme poverty and, together with their children had to be relieved by the Council. Accordingly it was ordered that after next Christmas Day, no townsfolk were to offer gifts or benevolence to any persons to be married, on pain of a fine.

Sunday observance exercised the town fathers, as was shown by an order made on 9 June 1583, which reads, "Whereas divers persons repairing to the church to hear Divine service, forgetting their duties to God and their obedience to Her Majesty's laws, do many times when the minister is reading Divine service, walk in the churchyard and there very unseemly behave themselves in walking and talking to the offence of the well-disposed and to the evil example of others; and whereas also divers persons keeping taverns within the town do in time of Divine Service, permit and suffer divers persons frequenting their said houses to sit tippling during the Divine Service", in future all such transgressions were to be fined fourpence for each offence.

A particularly interesting order was made on 15 November 1567, which reminds us of the custom of burials within pariah churches. So numerous were such burials

in St. Peter's church that they incon-
venienced the worshippers, and the
Council took action. To avoid annoyance
by the multitudes of burials within the
church, it decreed that henceforth the
churchwardens were to place the burgesses and their wives in pews according
to their degrees, callings, and abilities and
that no burgess, wife, or child be buried
within the church, except those born in
the town and who had executed some
capital office such as Mayor, Recorder,

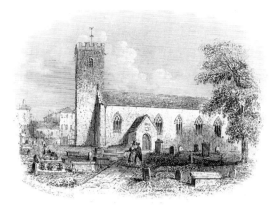

St. Peter's

Town Clerk, Bailiff, or one of the Common Council, such persons to pay to the
churchwardens, over and above the accustomed fees for burials, the sum of 6s. 8d. towards
paving and other repairs of the church, and if the churchwardens neglect this duty they
are to be amerced 6s. 8d.

I trust that these few examples will provide a flavour of the character of this book,
which has now returned to its parent archives, to remind us of the labour, of bygone
councillors of Carmarthen, and to enable modern historians to render more complete the
exciting history of this ancient borough.

Bureaucratic Costs . . .

Rice Williams took a prominent part in public life, and between July and September of
1676 received the honour of knighthood. His account "touching the passing of his
patent" has survived, and reads as follows:

Paid the Attorney General for his fiat for the
ad quod damnuni 17s.

To the Cursitor for the *ad quod damnuni* £1 12 0.

Mr. Pingey of the Petty Bag Office for filing
the *ad quod damnuni* and two copies
thereof, £1 2 6.

Writing the petition fair 2s 6d.

For the King's Warrant to Dr. Wynne £6 5 0.

The Solicitor General for the Grant £5 7 6.

The Clerk of the Patents £2.

The Solicitor's clerk 3s.

The Waiter at the Secretary's office 5s.

At the Secretary's Office for the King's hand
to the grant £6 5 0.

The Signet Office £7 8 8.

For the Privy Seal £7 8 8.

The Waiter there 5s.

Mr. English for my Lord Chancellor's receipt
£1 6 6. At the Patent Office for ingrossing the
Patent £4 13 0.

At the Hamper Office £14 13 4.

For my passing [putting?] the Patent £20.

For waterage several times at Whitehall 6s.

CHAPTER III

CARMARTHENSHIRE LITERATURE AND PROPAGANDA

SOME CARMARTHENSHIRE WRITERS

THE *Dictionary of Welsh Biography* records the names of 365 men and women born in the county of Carmarthen. Of these, 201 that is, over a half, were writers or connected with literature in one form or another. A review of literary activities within the county, and of the factors that influenced, and in some ways determined, the style and content of the output of Carmarthenshire writers, may be of interest.

First, let us look at the Middle Ages. An important factor in medieval cultural life was the existence of the royal house of Dynevor. It must be remembered that Carmarthenshire was the home, the capital, the headquarters, of the ruling dynasty, located from time immemorial in the Tywy valley. The princely courts of Dynevor, Dryslwyn, and Carreg Cennen had sheltered and maintained household bards and had welcomed the travelling poet and story-tellers, keepers and creators of the oral and written learning of those days. The Laws of Hywel Dda – a monarch who ruled this very region – provide evidence of the high status enjoyed by literary men, while the poems of the later *Gogynfeirdd* illustrate the value and extent of royal patronage in the 12th and 13th centuries. The first Eisteddfod of which we have record in Cardigan in 1176, was held under the auspices of a Carmarthenshire prince, the great Lord Rhys of Dynevor.

When the Welsh princes rode into the twilight in 1282, the bards were bereft of the benefactors that had sustained them so liberally for so long. But bardism did not wither, the bards did not hang their harps on the willows. The Welsh noble families – the *uchelwyr* – remained, and their patronage enabled the native learning to survive. Bledri ap Cadifor of Cilsant known as Bledri Latimer, who acted as interpreter between the Welsh and the Normans, is believed to be the Blederious, writer of romances mentioned in the works of Gerald the Welshman.

Despite the penal laws of Henry IV which proscribed as "rhymesters and wastrels" those who sang of the glories of their race in the Welsh tongue, they continued to find sanctuary in the halls of an aristocracy whose lineage formed the theme of so many of their songs. Bards, storytellers, and genealogists like William Egwad of Llanegwad, Ieuan Deulwyn of Pendeulwyn (fl. c. 1460), Syr Harry Mastr, Ieuan Tew Ieuanc, Dafydd Gorlech, and Lewis Glyn Cothi enlivened the 15th century with the melodious cadencies of the old minstrels and the creative vigour of the Renaissance. About the year 1450 a great Eisteddfod was held at Carmarthen when an enlightened nobleman, Griffith ap Nicholas of Dynevor, descendant of that Urien Rheged of whom the Cynfeirdd had sung, adjudicated the bardic contests. On this occasion the metres were revised and new regulations made to guide the bardic fraternity.

That other prop of learning in medieval Carmarthenshire – the Church – must not be overlooked. The monasteries of Talley, Whitland, Kidwelly, and the Grey Friars and the Priory of St. John in the town of Carmarthen, were the centres of the only truly literate people of their day, that is, men who had received disciplined education and whose calling demanded the constant use of the learning they had absorbed. We know from the poems of the bards and from reports made during the Dissolution, that these monastic houses owned many beautiful manuscripts compiled with loving artistry in the scriptoriam and assiduously studied in the repose of the cloister. Among these is the 12th century *Black Book of Carmarthen,* the earliest surviving Welsh manuscript, one of our most precious literary treasures and compiled within the Priory above the banks of Tywy.

In 1948 a friend of mine bought a 14th century parchment roll in a London sale-room, and on examining it I made out the faded words: *"Rowch honn y gwrtt Brodyr Kaer Verdiun"* – Place this in the court of the Friars of Carmarthen.

The turbulence of the period, the Norman-Welsh struggles, the rising of Glyndwr, and the Wars of the Roses were responsible for the destruction of many learned works. Generally, religious bases were respected during the fratricidal strife, but a number suffered at the hands of the spoiler, and what the hounds of war had started was soon to be completed by the iconoclastic enthusiasm of the zealots of the Reformation who professed to see in an illuminated manuscript the expression of ancient superstition, and in a coloured rubric, the mark of the Beast.

Although the dissolution of the monastic houses dealt a blow to scholarly pursuits, the new spirit of enquiry and adventure that marked the 16th century compensated in some way for the loss of the former religious patronage. During the Tudor period the Welsh gentry organised itself and established a pattern of behaviour that proved advantageous to cultural interests. Substantial land-owning families emerged – by the year 1600 there were 120 gentle families in Carmarthenshire – who sent their sons in increasing numbers to the Universities of Oxford and Cambridge and to the Inns of Court. Jesus College, Oxford was an early favourite, and between 1602 and 1673 four Carmarthenshire men became its Principals. Among properties in the county acquired by that college was the old Priory, and when leased to Grismond Williams in 1781, a considerable portion of it was still standing, being used as a chapel by the dissenters of Carmarthen – a situation not wholly devoid of irony.

Great houses like Dynevor, Edwinsford, Bryn y Beirdd, and Court Henry welcomed the savants of the new age. At Ystrad Ferthyr, Gruffudd Dwnn (died 1570) amassed a fine library, and his home became a literary club where scholars from all parts of Wales came to

Edwinsford

enjoy the hospitality of the cultured squire and to engage in poetic disputation with their intellectual equals like Gwilym Hiraethog, William Lleyn, Owen Gwynedd, Harry ap Rhys, Thomas Fychan, Sir Owen ap Gwilym, and William Salesbury who discussed with his host his plan to translate the Bible into Welsh. At Abergwili lived Bishop Richard Davies, one of the greatest of the successors of St. David, whose scholarly works were no less felicitous than his spiritual ministrations, and whose name is still revered as one who helped to bring to his largely monoglot flock the solace of Holy Writ in the only language that they understood.

There can be little doubt that the translation of the Bible was the greatest single factor in perpetuating the Welsh language for it encouraged writers to employ the vernacular as the vehicle of their thoughts and industry. This, together with two other developments in the 17th century, namely the emergence at Nonconformity and the establishment of the Circulating Schools of the S.P.C.K., exerted a notable influence on the literary output of Carmarthenshire, and gave it a distinctive religious flavour which has characterised it to this day.

The publication of *Canwyll y Cymry* by Vicar Prichard of Llandovery in 1681, had a profound effect on the religious feeling of the community, and stimulated local writers to compose works on similar themes.

Nonconformity was becoming an integral part of Carmarthenshire life and books and pamphlets streamed from the printing presses to swell the religious literature that became a feature of the 18th and 19th centuries. The contribution of hymn-writers must be specially mentioned. Over seventy came from this county, some who wrote or published whole volumes of hymns, others who are remembered on the score of a single composition. The rollcall is an impressive one and includes such men as David Charles of Pant Dwfn near St. Clears and his son of the same name, Dafydd Jones o Gaeo, David George Jones author of *Bydd myrdd o ryfeddodau,* and the immortal Williams *Pant y Celyn, Y Per Ganiedydd.*

The Established Church did not lag behind. Bishops of St. Davids like Burgess and Thirlwall nobly forwarded the love of learning that had been the concern of earlier shepherds like Bishop Richard Davies and Bishop Laud. Among the parish clergy, we might name the Revd. John Evans (d. 1780) one of the founders of the Honourable Society of Cymmrodorion, and the Revd. John Dyer of Aberglasney (d. 1757) whose poem "Grongar Hill" has a haunting beauty that is ever new.

No survey of local literature is complete if it neglects the printers and publishers. Carmarthenshire was extremely fortunate in this respect, and in the eighteenth and nineteenth centuries flourishing printing houses arose in Carmarthen, Llandovery and Newcastle Emlyn, associated with the names of Isaac Carter, John Ross, the Evanses, Rees of Tonn, the Spurrells, and Owen Rees who became a partner in the national publishing house of Longmans in 1794.

The contributions of editors of journals and newspapers, both religious and secular, deserve far greater respect and recognition than has hitherto been accorded them. Among these were David Owen of Llanpumpsaint ("Brutus"), editor of *Yr Efengylydd* and the *Haul* a fiery controversialist and a prolific writer, the accomplished David Rees of Capel Als,

Grongar Hill

Llanelli, editor for 30 years of the *Diwygiwr*, and John Edward Jones first editor of *Yr Ymofynydd*. Their success was not confined to sacred literature, and several became editors of national publications of secular character. Such was Sir William Davies who came from Talyllychan, the distinguished editor of the *Western Mail* who died in 1935. For over 150 years two weekly newspapers, the *Carmarthen Journal* and the *Welshman* provided a valuable forum for literary expression in addition to recording current events.

The names of Carmarthenshire poets were household words, bardic names like Dewi Emlyn, Iago ap Dewi, Rhuddwawr, Nathan Dyfed, Watkin Wyn, Job, Gwili, and Dyfnallt. They wrote in Welsh, but there were several who wrote in English, like Sir Lewis Morris of Penbryn, for example. There were eminent *eisteddfodwyr* like Archdeacon Thomas Beynon of Llandeilo, and Evan Jones, Gernos; *novelists* like Ann Beal; *political writers* like Thomas Glyn Cothi, and David Jones, "Freeholder"; *Bible commentators* like Peter Williams; *historians and antiquaries* like Joshua Thomas, David Jones, Canon John Fisher and talented Gwenogvryn Evans; and *ballad men* like Levi Gibbon, Dewi Dywyll, and Ben Simon, rustic troubadours whose natural gaiety delighted the less sophisticated audience. In our own day the works of authors like Dr. D. J. Williams, Nantlais Williams, Gwenallt, Gomer Roberts, and John Harries of Bettws, testify to the virility of Carmarthenshire literature.

Not all were *great* writers by any means, but all were endowed with those most precious of gifts that Nature can bestow upon man, namely the creative mind and the responsive spirit. Many were men of little or no formal education, yet they produced original thoughts and speculations that continue to delight and instruct us to this day. These gems were sometimes small and unpolished, but like all gems they held sparkle and an inner light. Few were professional writers in the sense that they derived their livelihood from the product of their pens. There were clergymen and ministers who devoted their leisure hours to writing; there were farmers and tradesmen who did likewise – George Lewis (d. 1858) shoemaker and poet; John Jones (d. 1837) barrister, historian, translator, author; John Howell (d. 1830) weaver, schoolmaster, musician, editor, poet; David Evan, known as "Dewi Dywyll" tailor, publican, and poet; and J. W. Nicholas, solicitor, Clerk of the Peace, novelist, essayist. Here was an infinite variety. In the realms of letters, each was a prince in his own right.

The present state of the long, unbroken literary tradition of Carmarthenshire augurs well for the future. The National Eisteddfod has been held five times in the county during the last century, and now it has come for the sixth time, to Llanelli. It is agreeable to reflect that the Patron of the Eisteddfod, Her Majesty the Queen, is a descendant of that Lord Rhys, the Carmarthenshire prince who first patronised the first Eisteddfod of which we have record, over seven hundred and eighty years ago.

AN ELECTION SONG

UNTIL THE SECOND REFORM BILL Parliamentary representation was very largely in the hands of the great families of the country. The appeal at elections was personal rather than political, and it is quite usual to find candidates in their addresses expressing their intention to live up to "the highest traditions of my family". This is the note struck in most of the addresses that I have seen.

For many centuries the counties and boroughs of Carmarthen, Pembroke, and Cardigan have been well represented by the widespread house of Philipps, but their success was not achieved without the support of other great landowners. A candidate could only be sure of victory if he could enlist the support of landowners who controlled many votes on their estates, and if a successful candidate afterwards had the misfortune to alienate the sympathies of his friends, the chances were that at the next contest he would lose his seat, In west Wales the political labels of Tory and Whig had little significance. What mattered was the "grouping" of the great family interests.

In the 18th century the Philipps family of Cwmgwili and its relations the Philipps families of Picton Castle, Penty Park, and Coedgain, dominated the politics of the ancient borough of Carmarthen. In 1784 John George Philipps of Cwmgwili, eldest son of Griffith Philipps, was elected member and represented Carmarthen until 1803 when he accepted the Chiltern Hundreds. He held it as a "safe" seat for most of the time, but in 1796 he was seriously challenged by an outsider whose only connection with Carmarthenshire was by marriage. This was Magens Dorrien Magens of Hammerwood Lodge, Surrey, a member of a well-known London banking house of the day. He had married, in 1788, Henrietta Cecilia Rice, eldest daughter of the Rt. Hon. George Rice by Cecil, Baroness Dynevor, and so was allied to a family of considerable influence in

the county. Supported by the Dynevor interest he opposed J. G. Philipps and was returned member for the borough on 27 May 1796. Philipps, however, presented a petition which was successful, and on 7 November 1796, he was declared elected by a majority of twenty votes over Magens.

Once more the house of Cwmgwili was supreme, having defeated the very considerable interest of Dynevor.

As may well be imagined this was the occasion of much rejoicing on the Philipps side, and a week or so afterwards a poem was circulated extolling the virtues of the victor.

An election song, a broadsheet copy of which I have in my possession chronicling a later election, equally acrimonious, between Philipps of Glangwili and Jones of Ystrad thought to be in the 1831 contest, is given below.

A Man of Olden Time!
Composed in Dame Street

Behold, the glorious day is come!
   Squire Jones is our Member!
The lovely rose in season's come,
   It is July and not December!
And all that did against him stand
   Their names I'll not relate, Sir;
He won the day by real fair play,
They raised him to the chair, Sir.

The fifth day of July, Sir,
   The like was never known, Sir;
The nobility of counties three
   Came flocking to the town, Sir.
The Red and Blue they triumphant wore
   To celebrate our Member;
All windows lined with ladies gay
   To magnify his honour.

When he ascended to his chair
   The town did roar like thunder;
St. Peter's, with one assent,
   Cried "Jones is our Member."
His own footman before him rode
   In sailor's dress, indeed, Sir,
A gay-dressed May-pole in his hand
   Mounted on a war-like steed, Sir.

Sir John Owen, I do declare,
   A man of high renown, Sir,
He down from London came with speed
   To grace Carmarthen Town, Sir.
Squire Morgan, of Quay Street,
   Did in his chariot ride, Sir,
He stood between us and our foes,
   And lowered down their pride, Sir.

Iscoed (old house)

There's Mr. Lewes, of Llysnewydd,
    And Lewis, of Llanayron,
Mr. Picton, of Iscoed,
    And also Mr. Beynon;
Mr. Timmins, of King Street,
    He friendly played his part, Sir,
– was true unto his friend
– to the ark, Sir.

Captain Mansel, of Iscoed,
    A man of courage bold, Sir,
He was so true unto his trust,
    He would not be controll'd, Sir.
Henry Lewis, of Quay Street,
    With heart and hand was willing
Our true-bred Welshman to promote,
Likewise, Lloyd Llewellyn.

Health and wealth to Squire Jones
    Likewise to our Sheriff Powell,
William Jones, of Spilman Street,
    And likewise Walter Howell.
There's Grismond Philipps, I do declare,
    He did behave so loyal;
And Mrs. Philipps, of The Parade,
    Gave them a plain denial.

Robert Waters, of the Bank,
    And likewise Edward Davids,
Saunders, of Glanrhyn-fawr,
    And Captain Stephen Phillips;
All friends were loyal to the Town,
    God bless them all together;
It was his right for all their spite,
    I hope he will reign till death, Sir.

Squire Jones, of Ystrad Lodge,
    The truth I will declare, Sir,
He was brought up within our walls,
Which makes us hold him dear, Sir.
    He is the third generation in this town,
That I can well remember;
Makes me cry out in all my heart,
"Brave Ystrad Lodge for ever!"

The time is come I wish to see,
    And now I will retire;
I have seen the flower of all the land
    Enjoy our hearts' desire.
He will lower down their pride,
    He will right the poor,
Nor slight the meanest member;
I'm quite at ease, I will sit and sing
From hence until September.

Llysnewydd

CHAPTER IV

EMINENT PERSONALITIES

CARMARTHENSHIRE CHARACTERS

SIR RHYS AP THOMAS was the third son of Thomas ap Gruffydd, eldest son of Gruffydd ap Nicolas of Dynevor (called the "Eagle of Carmarthen"), a descendant of a knight of King Arthur's Round Table. He was born in Abermarlais, Carmarthenshire, in the year 1451. When young, Rhys was placed in the tutorial care of Edward Lewis, a clever scholar from north Wales. After Rhys' father and two brothers had died, he succeeded to their fortunes, and soon assumed an influential position in south Wales. He opposed Richard III, and gave much aid to Henry Tudor, Earl of Richmond, who afterwards became Henry VII. The valorous conduct of the noble Welshman on the field of battle is well known. It was his battle axe that settled the fortune of Bosworth's eventful day by felling the "bristled Boar". Sir Rhys held many offices, and he was "little less than a prince in his native country". His estate was a large one, including twenty castles. He married twice. He spent his latter years at his favourite residence, Carew Castle, Pembrokeshire, and died there in 1527, at the age of 76 years. He was buried in the monastery of the Grey Friars, Carmarthen. Later, his remains and those of one of his wives were removed to St. Peter's Church. The place of his rest in this church is marked by a tomb, a large sculptured mass.

Tomb of Sir Rhys ap Thomas

Lewis Glyn Cothi, lived between 1447 and 1489. Poet
Born in Llanybydder parish within the confines of the Royal Forest of Glyn Cothi. One of Wales's greatest 13th century poets, and wrote numerous poems in praise of Carmarthenshire men. He was a Lancastrian, and a friend of Jasper Tudor, Earl of Pembroke.

Sir Richard Steele, the famous essayist, was born at Dublin on March 12th 1671
He lived for some time in the farmhouse of Tygwyn, Llangunnor, near Carmarthen. He removed to a house in King Street in the town, where he died on 1 September 1729. He was buried in St. Peters Church in the vault of the Scurlocks.

General Sir William Nott

Another famous personage of bygone days. He was born at Neath, but the home of his boyhood and youth was at Carmarthen. His services in India will never be forgotten, and after retiring from that country he came to Carmarthen. His health was fast failing, and he died on 1 January 1845, and was buried in a vault at St. Peter's churchyard. A monument stands in Nott's Square in memory of this noble soldier.

Dr. Robert Ferrar, Bishop of St. Davids, was martyred in Carmarthen on March 30th, 1555, for not denouncing the Protestant faith during the Marian Persecution. There seems to be sufficient reason to believe that the bishop suffered near the Market Cross (in the present Nott's Square). A tablet has been attached to Nott's Memorial in memory of this martyr. When the Market Cross was taken down, the stone which supported the stake to which the martyr bishop was bound, was removed to Lammas Street, and in 1843 was transferred to Abergwili Church, where it now forms the apex or finial of the spire.

Sir William Vaughan, 1575-1641, Farmer, Coloniser, Author

Of Torycoed in Llangyndeyrn parish. He was a great farmer, introduced new systems of husbandry, and wrote a book on agriculture and estate management – the first book published in Britain on that subject. He established a colony in Newfoundland (at his own expense) in 1617, which he colonised with Carmarthenshire emigrants. He was knighted in 1628. Buried at Llangyndeyrn in August 1641.

Madam Bridget Bevan, 1698-1779, Philanthropist and Educationist

Born at Cwrt Derllys, daughter of John Vaughan. She was a patron of the Welsh Circulating Schools and the S.P.C.K., and applied her great wealth towards the education of Carmarthenshire people. She was one of the strongest supporters of Griffith Jones, rector of Llanddowror, another great educationist. She married Arthur Bevan, barrister-at-law afterwards the Recorder of Carmarthen and Member of Parliament.

John Vaughan of Golden Grove, 1757-1804, Landlord and Farmer

Born at Plas Llandybie. Lord Lieutenant 1781-1804, the youngest Welshman ever appointed to that office. A great farmer, he introduced new methods of farming on his vast estate, breeding, new corn rotations, afforestation, etc, so that the vale of Tywi, when many of his estates lay, became known as "The Garden of Wales".

Sir Thomas Picton
Born Poyston, Pembrokeshire, August 1758
Though a Pembrokeshire man, he was better
known as a Carmarthenshire man. He was
a great soldier, being a Lieutenant-General
in the British Army. He fell at the Battle of
Waterloo and was buried in London.
A monument stands at the top of Johnstown
Hill in memory of this brave soldier.

Oliver Cromwell in Carmarthenshire
During the Civil War in May 1648 Cromwell was in the Carmarthen area on his way
to besiege Pembroke Castle. He is said to
have stayed at Cwmcastell in Newchurch
parish, a few miles from Carmarthen, where
a watch-pit was made. General Laugharne,
the Parliamentary commander captured
Carmarthen castle, and placed a garrison in
it. Guns were hauled to the top of the keep
to dominate the town. When Cromwell

The first Picton monument

reached Newchurch he was met by a body of farmers under the owner of Trawsmawr.
A scheme to capture Cromwell had been made by the squires of Pantycendy and Plas
Howell. This failed, and in their flight, pursued by Cromwell, the owner of Trawsmawr
was killed. This took place near Knightsford.

Cromwell's affinity with Cwmcastell was a family one. His ancestor Sir Richard
Williams, who took the name of Cromwell, was the son of William ap Morgan of
Cwmcastell in Newchurch, Carmarthenshire.

During the 1648 campaign Cromwell visited Golden Grove, home of the Earl of
Carbery, where he was entertained by the Countess. Tradition says that whilst at Golden
Grove he shot a stag in the park and until the last century there remained there a tree
called Cromwell's tree, on a branch of which he is said to have rested his gun when he
shot the stag. On his return to England he presented her with some stags for her hospitality.

James Howell, son of the vicarage
Three-hundred-and-thirty-six years have gone by since the death of James Howell,
Historiographer Royal to Charles II, and author of the ever popular *Familiar Letters*. Generally
speaking, little of his other activities seems known to those who quote his name. Nevertheless,
he was a remarkable man, equally at home in the Courts of Europe as in the lodgings of
scholars, secretary to embassies, secret agent, a royalist who boldly told Cromwell that the
monarchy must be restored, author, pioneer of spelling reform of the English language,
and one of the earliest writers to make a livelihood from literature and journalism.

James Howell, fourth child of the Revd. Thomas Howell, vicar of Abernant and Cynwil in Carmarthenshire, was born about the year 1594. He received his early education at Hereford Free School under "a learned though lashing master" as he feelingly describes him, and he proceeded to Jesus College, Oxford, in 1610 where he graduated three years later. He spoke of his college days with affection, and to him Oxford was always "my dearly honoured Mother".

His description of himself as "a pure cadet, not born to land, lease, home, or office", and having no "other patrimony or support but my breeding", illustrates the difficulties of a younger son. However, his "breeding", attractive personality, and capacity for mastering languages, more than compensated for the lack of inherited possessions.

After leaving Oxford, Howell was appointed steward of a glassware manufactory, and in 1616 went to the Continent on behalf of his firm. He travelled through Holland, France, Spain, and Italy, studying methods of glass making and securing the services of expert workmen. He learnt to speak and write the languages of the countries he visited, an accomplishment that was to stand him in good stead in future years.

On his return to London, about 1621, he decided to seek a post where his linguistic talents could be employed to greater advantage. For a short time he was a tutor in the family of Lord Savage, and during 1622 accompanied Lord Altham's son on a tour in France.

Towards the end of 1622, Howell was commissioned to go to Spain to obtain satisfaction for the illegal seizure of a richly laden vessel belonging to the Turkey Company. His audiences with the King and Ministers of State proceeded satisfactorily, until the cancellation of the "Spanish match" between the Prince of Wales and the Infanta prejudiced all chances of a final arrangement. He was at Madrid when the Prince was presenting his suit and became friendly with members of his Household.

In 1624 he secured the post of Secretary to Lord Scrope (afterwards Earl of Sunderland), Lord President of the North, and took up residence at York. Through his master's influence, he was elected Member of Parliament for Richmond in Yorkshire, but his excursion into politics was of brief duration.

On Sunderland's death in 1630 he found himself without regular employment, but succeeded in securing temporary posts. In 1632 he was Secretary of an embassy to Denmark, and during his sojourn at the Danish Court secured privileges for an English trading company. In 1635 he spent some time at Orleans on state business, and after 1639 acted as a secret agent for Strafford, then Lord Deputy of Ireland.

In 1640 Howell turned his energies to creative writing. Despite his bustling life he had maintained an interest in literature and knew many leading writers of the time. He was especially friendly with Ben Jonson, to whom he presented Dr. Davies's Welsh Grammar, together with a poem of his own composition in praise of the book. One letter he sent to Jonson contained "a choice story" he had heard in France, "for you to put upon your loom and make a curious web of". When the poet died Howell composed an elegy on him.

Between 1640 and 1666, he published over 60 books, pamphlets, and numerous poems and letters. Many were composed in the Fleet where he was imprisoned for his loyalty from 1643 to 1651. A stout Royalist, he wrote tracts advocating the restoration of the monarchy, even in Cromwell's heyday. His *"Instructions for Forreine Travel"*, dedicated to Prince

Charles, seems to have been prophetic in its dedication. Subjects like *Royal Marriages of Great Britain, History of Louis XIII, Account of the Low Countries, Venice, Naples, and Spain*, reveal his knowledge of continental states. He compiled dictionaries and grammars of foreign languages, and made numerous translations from Latin, Italian, French and Spanish authors. He wished to reform English spelling along phonetic lines, and advocated the elimination of redundant letters, like the final vowel in "done" and the removal of "u" from words like "honour".

None of his works is more popular than *Epistolae Hoelianae*, the "*Familiar Letters*", an intimate stream of contemporary gossip which continue to delight the reader even after the passing of three hundred years. They show his literary style at its best, light and aphoristic, and containing a wealth of descriptive and anecdotal material. Among people to whom he addressed letters were his brother Dr. Thomas Howell, Bishop of Bristol, Dr. Field, Bishop of Llandaff and afterwards of St. Davids, Sir Kenelm Digby, Lord Herbert of Chirbury, the Duke of Buckingham, Lord Conway, the mercurial Sir Sackville Crow (of Westmead, Laugharne), and the Earl of Pembroke with whom he claimed distant kinship based on a tenuous link in the higher reaches of his family tree, visible only to a Welshman of strong genealogical passions.

He touches on all manner of topics – ancient prophesies, the Inquisition, Algerian pirates, continental morals, foibles of kings, battles, miracles, scandals, the Grand Turk, plagues, churches, heralds, and Welsh mountain ponies. He advises us against litigation – "Law is a shrewd pick-purse". English ale is an elixir, apparently – "While Englishmen drank only ale they were strong, brawny, able men, and could draw an arrow an ell long". He describes a letter on the beverages of various nations as "a dry discourse upon a fluid subject". He appreciated the power of the pen, and told Jonson, "The fangs of the bear and the tusks of the wild boar do not bite worse and make deeper gashes than a goose quill sometimes". Experience had taught him patience – "Though princes's guerdons come slow, yet they come sure". He found no reason to revise this view. Following the Restoration, Howell received, for his loyalty, a gift of £200 from the King who also appointed him Historiographer Royal with a salary of £100 a year. These favours, and the money he derived from writing, enabled him to spend the remainder of his days in ease and comfort.

James Howell died in London, and was buried on 3 November 1666 in the Temple church where a fine monument was raised to perpetuate his memory. The tomb was badly damaged by Hitler's bombs in May 1941.

A GENTLEMAN OF WALES

Lines attributed to Cadoc the Wise

His manservant diligent.
His maidservant civil.
His son honourable.
His daughter cleanly.
His kindred faithful.
His friend true.
His steed trained.
His greyhound fleet.
His falcon courageous.
His oxen strong.
His kine well marked.
His sheep heavy limbed.
His hogs large.
His family intelligent.
His home well kept.
His bard learned.
His harpist respectable.
His mill close at hand.
His church a long way off.

His house weatherproof.
His homestead compact.
His land productive.
His bed soft.
His wife chaste.
His food wholesome.
His drink sparkling.
His fire alight.
His clothes warm.
His neighbours peaceable.

His lord mighty.
His king just.
His spiritual father wise.
His God merciful.

The Seven Necessary Qualifications of a Gentleman

1. To be a Bard at his Table.
2. To be a Lamb in his Apartment.
3. To be a Hermit in Church.
4. To be a Peacock on the Street.
5. To be eloquent in Disputation.
6. To be a Tutor in his family.
7. To be a Lion in the Field.

REFERENCE
Llanstephen MS 159, 1697/8.

THE UNWELCOME BRIDE

IN JANUARY 1715, a Chancery suite brought by Sir Edward Mansel against his widowed daughter-in-law Catherine, suggests that her entry into the family had been less than welcome. He stated that his late son James Mansel "being very young, a minor wished to marry Catherine the widow of Alltycadno," "a very shrewd person", but the baronet was opposed to the union. However, for a time James and Catherine kept their engagement secret, but eventually had to negotiate with the reluctant Sir Edward, and the agreed settlement (allegedly a verbal understanding not executed by deed), provided the bride with ample provision should she be predeceased by her husband. The wedding took place in 1711. In the event James Mansel died in 1714, intestate because Catherine had ensured that he should not have facilities to execute a will, or so it was said. When creditors of the deceased asked for their dues, Catherine refused to pay saying that he had left neither realty nor personalty. She asserted that Sir Edward and Lady Mansel had pressed her to marry their son, because she had been left very well off by her previous husband, Thomas Lloyd, and assured her that Sir Edward's estate would probably come to James; whereupon she was "induced to harken to the said courtship", and at length married the young man. But Sir Edward declined to honour the verbal agreement, stating that Catherine had taken good care to retain "a firm hold" upon her own estate when she married. Unfortunately the verdict is not recorded. Catherine lived until 1733 when her administration was granted.

Dirleton

ALAN STEPNEY GULSTON – SOLDIER, SQUIRE AND ROMANCER

ALTHOUGH DERIVING descent and possessions from a Welsh heiress, the Gulstons remained very much an English family and had not settled or lived for any length of time in Carmarthenshire. The first to settle there was Joseph's son, Alan James Gulston. Educated at Winchester he served as an officer in the 47th Regiment of Foot, and in 1841 married Augusta Catherine Giveen, an Irish lady. He succeeded to the Carmarthenshire estate in 1842, and decided to settle there.

Mr. and Mrs. A. J. Gulston came to stay at the Cawdor Arms Hotel in Llandeilo. They took a short lease of Abermarlais where they took up residence. After 1852 Gulston bought Lwynyberllan a modest house near Llangadog bridge, from George Peel, and decided to make alterations and extensions to his new purchase before settling there. Whereupon the family left Abermarlais, and rented Coomb Royale in Devonshire for a time, and afterwards moved to Woodlands, in those days a pretty little place near Swansea. During this period they often came to Llwynyberllan (which had been let to a Captain and Mrs. Hall) for fishing and shooting.

In 1859 Mr. Gulston made considerable changes at Llwynyberllan which he renamed Dirleton. Many were surprised that he did not restore Derwydd. According to a contemporary, Derwydd at that time was "a fine old mansion, very much out of repair, but capable of being made very nice and comfortable: however they entirely dismantled the house and brought all the pictures, etc. to Dirleton". Gulston accepted the responsibilities of a landed proprietor, becoming a Justice of the Peace, Deputy Lieutenant, High Sheriff (1860), and captain of the Llandeilo Volunteers.

But he did not ignore Derwydd by any means. In 1868 he employed B. Bucknell of London to produce plans for repairs and improvements which included provision for the main entrance to be in the centre of the enlarged residence, at a cost of £600. This does not seem to have been carried out, for in September 1870, the architect George Gordon Page of Bedford Row, London, produced an ambitious plan for alterations and additions, making provision, in accordance with Gulston's instructions, for incorporating the old house and repairing it wherever possible. Of course, the additions were entirely new, but some materials from the existing mansion were to be used, for instance the tiles from the old kitchen were to cover the floor of the new.

Nevertheless. Gulston continued to make Dirleton the main family home, and in 1872, bought the adjoining estate of Dan-yr-allt for the considerable sum of £173,000. For various reasons, Gulston decided to let Dirleton house, and went to live in London, and afterwards in Guernsey. In 1881 Dirleton was sold to John Peel. In that year Alan James Gulston died at Guernsey, and his body was brought home for burial at Caledflwlch church near Llandeilo.

He was succeeded by his eldest son, Alan Stepney Gulston who had been born at Abermarlais, Llansadwrn, in 1844. He was educated at Harrow School, and afterwards at Merton College. Oxford, where he graduated B.A., and like his father became a Justice of the

Alan James Gulston of Dirleton

Peace, Deputy Lieutenant, and High Sheriff (1895-6), and served as a captain in the Royal Carmarthenshire Artillery Militia until 1881. He was lord of the manor of Llandeilo Patria and Villa, held on a lease under the Bishop of St Davids. He married in 1886, Agnes Margaret Anderson of Marston Lodge, Cheltenham, by whom he had no issue. He died on 9 September 1919, and was buried at Caledflwlch.

Alan Stepney Gulston was deeply interested in his Welsh ancestry, the Stepneys and particularly the Vaughans, and adopted the additional surname Stepney by Deed Poll dated 19 May 1886, being afterwards known as Alan Stepney Stepney-Gulston. He determined to restore Derwydd to its former glory and to use it as a residence. A man of cultivated tastes, an excellent artist, he wrote poetry of no mean merit, was versed in antiquities and all branches of historical studies, becoming President of the Carmarthenshire Antiquarian Society and Field Club. We must also remember that he was a romantic.

Part of Derwydd house was ruinous when Mr. Stepney Gulston decided to restore the whole structure, to preserve the earlier portion, and to extend it to include amenities of a modern kind. He commenced operations about 1888, and the result is the house as we

Alan Stepney Gulston of Derwydd

know it today. His undoubted devotion to the place has ensured the preservation of some interesting features of the old fabric.

Alan Stepney Gulston settled at Derwydd, and soon some startling items of knowledge began to circulate, many of them appearing in newspapers and other journals. We learn that it was "probably in very early days the site of a druid's retreat" as indicated by the name Derwydd. The house had been "eight hundred years in the same family", and "traces of a dry moat" had been discovered. It had been a much larger house until about 1820 when a portion of it containing "upwards of 40 rooms" had been demolished. It had been one of the "seats" of Sir Rhys ap Thomas who had lived there "in his young and

Bookplate – Joseph Gulston II

romantic days" with a lover, the nubile Gwenllian, sister of the abbot of Talley, no less; a room was shown to visitors, "the King's room", so called after Sir Rhys had entertained Henry Tudor there with "a carousal for several days" while on his leisurely march to Bosworth. But royal associations went back much further, for we hear that King John had been a guest there in 1210. During the 17th century "it was a sheltering place of Cromwell's troops"; in front of the building was a "tournament court" where gallant knights in armour performed before admiring audiences. A "barracks" was once attached to the house, and about 1800 the "militia" carried out drills there. The hall, in fact was the "banqueting hall, having been so used since the days of Sir Rhys ap Thomas"; a space or alcove on the ground floor was actually "a pre-reformation chapel". In true Victorian style the ghost of a Miss Gwen Vaughan haunted "Sir Rhys ap Thomas's room", and glided through the house revealing herself only to unmarried men, being evidently the possessor of some Freudian complex.

There had been "a feud" between two Vaughan brothers, one of whom lived at Derwydd, the other at Golden Grove. A daughter of the former fell in love with a son of the latter, but the stern parents would have none of that nonsense. After clandestine meetings the lovers formed a plan to elope on horseback; however, a woodman of Derwydd learnt of their design, and being a particularly nasty fellow, informed the maiden's brother. When they tried to elope they were followed at a wild gallop by the brother who hurled his "truncheon" at them, striking and killing the lovely maiden. Her shade now appears just before the death of the "head of the family", sometimes at the "ghost-window" at Derwydd, or standing with outstretched arms near a great stone at Rhyd y ffynnon where calamity had overtaken her in the days of flesh. Apparently this tale was well-known amongst "the peasantry around Derwydd", and could be vouched for by a bachelor blacksmith named Vaughan, "one of his ancestors having been a natural son of a member of the Derwydd family".

It is an impressive recital, and although Queen Elizabeth I never slept at Derwydd, we need not think the worse of it for that omission.

But one searches in vain, not for confirmation, but for any reference to these exciting associations prior to the late 1880s when Alan Stepney Gulston renovated the house and, evidently, refurbished its traditions. His own notes and "hand-outs" to Welsh newspapers are the earliest references known to the laborious antiquary. The only excuse I have for referring at all to these lively fictions, is because most of them have been enshrined in the pages of a learned journal. This was after members of the Cambrian Archaeological Association had been entertained at Derwydd by the hospitable Mr. Stepney -Gulston, and when Mr. Stephen W. Williams, F.S.A., gravely informed the assemblage that the old part of the house had been lately rescued from falling to ruins by his host and that "most of it is 12th century".

Derwydd

THE LIVELY MRS. JOHN BROWNE OF FFRWD (FROOD)

FROM HIS OWN family's standpoint, the elder son John Browne made an extremely good marriage when on 26 July 1683 he led to the altar of Llangyndeyrn church, Mary Vaughan the eccentric daughter and one of the ultimate coheiresses of Philip Vaughan of Plas Trimsaran by his second wife Sage, daughter of John Mansel of Stradey. Mary was described in family papers as having "considerable portion in her own power".

The acquisition of a well-dowered bride proved no bed of roses for John Browne. Mary's family were opposed to the union, considering the Brownes to be parvenus, alleging, with some justification, that the bridegroom's father was mean and miserly. Indeed, later Mary herself was to describe the marriage as "a great condescencion" on her part. The young couple lived at Stradey (which belonged to Sage, mother of the bride) until the death of old Francis Browne in 1701, when they returned to Ffrwd.

Mrs. Mary Browne was fond of London which she often visited accompanied by her husband. Their last visit took place in 1703, a melancholy occasion, for on 24 June of that year John Browne died at Kensington "rather suddenly, of the distemper", having survived his father by less than two years. His body was brought home and buried at Llangyndeyrn on 4 July. Administration of the goods of old Francis Browne left unadministered by his late son John, was granted on 25 August 1704 to John's widow. There were three children – Francis, Sage, and Dorothy.

Several unexplained circumstances attended his sudden demise, rumours flickered, with the result that Mrs. Browne was suspected with having poisoned her hapless husband. However, the suspicions could not be proven, and she walked away from the court with traces of a faint smile on her comely countenance.

That was not all. John had died owning, in addition to the Ffrwd estate, personalty valued at over £2,000. There was no sign of any will and it was widely believed he had died intestate. Shortly after the funeral Thomas Lloyd of Alltycadno (who had married the deceased's aunt, Jane Browne) called to condole with the widow, and no mention was made of a will. Eight months later, to 'his astonishment, he heard that Mrs. Browne 'had just proved her husband's will, and that the son had been disinherited. "Suspecting ill practice", Lloyd came to Carmarthen on 9 September 1704, and meeting Mrs. Browne in the street (she lived in that town from time to time), asked her about the will and whether it was true that the son had been disinherited. She seemed concerned that he was so interested, and explained that her name was used in the will only as trustee for the son, then a minor. Lloyd suggested she should execute a deed to declare the uses of the trust to avoid possible lawsuits. She agreed, and they went together to Nathaniel Morgan, attorney, who prepared the document, which Mrs. Browne then flatly refused to sign. When shown the probate will, Lloyd noticed it was in Mrs. Browne's handwriting, and did not believe the signature to be that of John Browne with which he was familiar.

This led to a Chancery suit, in course of which some very remarkable evidence was given by witnesses in March 1708. One John Edwards who "did then teach school" in Plas Trimsaran where Mrs. Browne's elder sister (Lady Dorothy Mansell) lived, had a strange tale to unfold. Late in 1703, and without warning, Mrs. Browne arrived in the schoolroom and chatted amicably with the pedagogue who had never met her before, and said she would call again as she had some business for him to perform for which he would be "well rewarded". Soon, she came again, said she understood he could copy all manner of handwritings, that she had some which might be beyond his capabilities, and then produced papers containing the signatures of Richard Stepney, Charles Dalton, John Browne, also her own, and invited him to see what he could do. Thus challenged, he set about the copying which he accomplished "so precisely" that Mrs. Browne nodded approvingly. When he turned away for a moment to speak to one of the scholars, she took from her pocket "a piece of paper folded in an unusual way or cornerfold", and prevailed on him to write the signature "John Browne" on one of the folds. She then picked up the papers and departed. Later she was back again, saying it seemed a pity for a man of his learning "to stay in so poor a place", but if he would accompany her to London she would recommend him to Lord Blessington who would find a good place for him. The pedagogue was surprised, "knowing of no kindness he had done her"; however, business prevented him from going. About New Year's Day 1704, one John Thomas Hugh showed an alarmed Edwards a letter he had received from Mrs. Browne, in which she wrote that if Edwards "offered to speak or discover anything of counterfeiting of hands" she would use the rigour of the law against 'him, and that by the law of England he would be hanged. He left Trimsaran hurriedly, and heard nothing more until 23 March 1707 when Margaret wife of John Thomas Hugh, "a near relative" of Mrs. Browne (who by then had married Henry Sellery) tried to persuade Edwards to return to Plas Trimsaran "where he would be well taken care of". It was clear that Mrs. Browne wanted the pedagogue completely under her control. He was not to talk. But talk he did, to some tune, when called to depose in the suit.

The will of "John Browne, gentleman, of Istradey", dated 25 May 1690, was indeed in the handwriting of Mrs. Browne, and bore the alleged signature of testator. He bequeathed all the realty "to his "dear beloved wife" Mary Browne, her heirs and assigns, *for ever;* to his son Francis, all the books "in my study at Frood"; to his daughter Sage, £500 when she became 25 years of age; his wife to be sole executrix, and guardian of the children until they became 28 years of age. The will was proved at Carmarthen in 1703.

The formidable dame claimed that the bequest of the realty was the result of an arrangement deriving from hostile experiences with her own family, the Vaughans. Her kinsfolk, she said, had been deeply opposed to the marriage, and in a position to prejudice her portion and prospects in respect of the Trimsaran estate. To counteract this and to indemnify her, Francis Browne and his son John (the bridegroom) promised 'to settle on the bride all they possibly could "suitable to her great condescencion in the said marriage, and so far as they were able, to make amends from what she might suffer from any of her relations". As a result of the marriage she actually "suffered very much by the displeasure of her nearest relatives". And not only that, for Francis Browne afterwards proved less liberal than she had been led to expect, took a dislike to his son whom he tried to deprive of the inheritance, and threatened to settle all on his grandson (John Browne's son, Francis). Evidently Mary was not regarded an ideal mother by old Francis Browne, who took her children Francis and

Sage into his care and brought them up. After the grandfather's death in 1701, efforts were made by Thomas Lloyd of Alltycadno and John Philipps of Carmarthen, both hostile to Mrs. Browne, to take the young Francis into their guardianship. It was these unhappy situations, Mrs. Browne asserted, that had prompted her late husband to make his will in her favour.

After dragging on for several years the suit came to a head in 1714 before a judge and jury at the Hereford Assizes. Following the verdict, the alleged will which had remained in the Probate Registry at Carmarthen had to be handed over to the judiciary, and on 7 June 1714, Nathaniel Morgan the Deputy Register applied to his superior, the Registrar of St. David's diocese, for power to do so. He wrote – "The will of John Browne of Froode in this county, gentleman, deceased, has been contested in several courts of Law and Equity, at last by a directed issue out of Chancery on a tryal at Hereford, the Jury found it a forged will, which was since decreed confirm'd by my Lord Chancellor I was served on Saturday last in the Evening to deliver the said will to Mr. Rd Philipps the Plaintiff's *(sic)* sollicitor in order to be brought to London . . . The real and personal Estate of the deceased might be worth about £6,000."

The words of the Decree read "But as to the said real Estate, the pretended Will of the said John Browne appearing a gross forgery, his Lordship doth order the proper officer in whose hands the said original will now remains do deliver the same to Mr. Rd Philipps the Defendant *(sic)* Browne's sollicitor to be by him brought before the Register of this Court there to remain subject to the further order of the Court. I desire you will send me your answer per first post, that I may pursue your Directions in this affair . . . ", and asks him to ensure that the office was indemnified for handing over the will. *(NLW, Ottley Papers.)*

We do not know whether the lady, having been adjudged guilty of "gross forgery", was punished, but it is clear that the Ffrwd estate passed to John Browne's only son. Documents relating to the affair contain hints that Mary was not devoid of eccentricity, and her cavortings prior to her second marriage appear to support this.

If elements of tragedy attend the circumstances of her first marriage, elements of comedy certainly attend those leading to her second. The scene opens in the year 1703 with the arrival in London of one Henry Sellery, a young Irishman of the slenderest means, and his aunt Mrs. Mary Cole, a widow allegedly owning an estate in Lisburne. They took lodgings in Pall Mall, and shortly became acquainted with a Robert MacNeale and Elizabeth his wife, also hailing from the Emerald Isle, who lived in nearby Bury Street.

One day in June 1704, soon after dinner at which Henry Sellery was a guest, a visitor called on the MacNeales. She turned out to be a lively widow, Mrs. Browne of Ffrwd no less! As he was to depose later, Sellery "liking her person and being pleased and enamoured with her company", enquired of the MacNeales of the bewitching lady's "circumstances in the world". They declared she was a rich widow worth £20,000, adding they had great influence with her so that she was altogether in their power and would marry whomsoever they pleased. Whereupon he declared his interest, and the MacNeales said they would arrange the match provided he paid them 200 guineas immediately after the wedding. They added they had similar influence with Sellery's aunt, Mrs. Cole, and would persuade her to settle her Irish estate on him if he paid another 200 guineas, and they even produced a document to that effect to be signed by Mrs. Cole, which they showed the bemused Mr. Sellery. At this stage Mrs. Browne had not revealed her London address to the suitor, who, a few days later asked the MacNeales for it, but they declined until he had signed a bond in their favour in £400. About mid June Mrs. Cole returned to Ireland.

Mr. Sellery was not the only aspirant to the fair widow's hand. A sea-dog, one Captain Berry, proved particularly importunate, paying ardent attentions to her, and on bended knee implored her to marry him. She refused, because as she later said, in many ways he had "behaved badly" to her. The rebuffed captain departed, taking her gold watch with him, set out to sea and was not seen again. Another, and more exalted suitor was Mr. Mitton, Gentleman-Usher to H.R.H. Prince George of Denmark, who courted her with some intensity, but after a while he too had to depart with a flea in his ear.

A few more fences lay ahead of Mr. Sellery, but in the end Irish charm proved irresistable. He had bought a quantity of jewels, but had been obliged to deposit them with the MacNeales as security for money he had borrowed. One day he asked Mrs.

MacNeale if she would entrust the jewels to him so that he could show them to Mrs. Browne whose person they would adorn after his debt had been discharged. This, he felt could not fail to impress the widow. Mrs. MacNeale complied, having made him "swear an oath on the Holy Evangelists" that he would return them. Accordingly he called on his inamorata who was delighted and asked to be allowed to retain the jewels until the morrow. The infatuated greenhorn agreed. But when he called on the following day he found that the bird had flown. Mrs Browne had taken a coach post-haste to Wales – taking the jewels with her!

This led to a flare up in the MacNeale household, and Sellery was sternly bidden to retrieve the jewels or else the law would be invoked. The harassed man wrote to Mrs. Browne imploring her to return them. This brought no reply. Further letters couched in similar vein met with no better response. After several months of despair, constantly assailed by Mrs. MacNeale's threats, and fearful that his marital prospects would come to nought, Sellery took a coach to the west and eventually found his way to Ffrwd. There he was entertained most hospitably by the charming widow who explained that her sudden departure was prompted by Mrs. Cole's failure to sign the document conferring her estate, worth £10,000 on Mr. Sellery. But now Mrs. Browne received him into favour again, and agreed to return with him to London and bring the disputed trinkets with her.

On their arrival in May 1705, Sellery deposited the casket with a now mollified Mrs MacNeale, but soon after he entreated her to hand over the jewels again for a short time otherwise he would lose Mrs Browne and the annuity of £500 she had agreed to bestow on him. This was done. However, Sellery made no effort to repay a sum of £215 or to return the jewels by way of security.

At last the suitor's tightrope walk came to an end. His blandishments brought the required assent, and on 17 August 1705 Henry Sellery and Mary Browne widow were married by Licence at St. Benet's church, Paul's Wharf. This Wren church stands close to the College of Arms, and memorials to bygone heralds continue to adorn its walls. The prenuptial settlement was executed on the eve of the wedding.

Despite wedding bells, the bridegroom's debts to the MacNeales remained undischarged and the jewels continued to bedeck the person of the heroine of Ffrwd. Writs were issued. To escape them, the Sellerys took up abode "in a privileged place within the liberty of Whitehall". Eventually Mrs. Sellery offered terms, that provided the MacNeales allowed her and Henry to return to their house as lodgers, she would restore the jewels or otherwise pay the debt. This was agreed, the Sellerys came to Bury Street, but no sooner had they settled in, than they suddenly left, taking the jewels and leaving the debt unpaid! Mrs. Sellery returned hot-foot to Ffrwd, while Mr. Sellery remained in London where "he sculked and kept himself private in privileged places in this City" beyond writs and bailiffs.

Accordingly the MacNeales took steps to procure a warrant of arrest from the Green Cloth, but before it could be effected Sellery escaped and rejoined his wife in the comparative safety of rural Carmarthenshire. The persistent creditors then obtained an escheat in order to outlaw him.

How the affair ended is not clear. Probably the debt was cleared eventually, allowing a relieved Henry Sellery to settle with his wife, for some time at Ffrwd, then at Pibwr, and in Carmarthen, with occasional visits to Ireland, while Mrs. Sellery's jewellery continued to bedeck her person and to dazzle her friends. The marriage lasted for some thirty-five years, but I have not found a single reference to either man or wife during the last thirty-one years. This is remarkable for it is inconceivable that the mercurial Mrs. Sellery should have lapsed into respectable obscurity in so complete a way.

Through the kind offices of Mr. Roland Thorne, Mrs. Sellery's will, proved in London, has been made available to me. The last will and testament of "Mary Sellery, alias Browne, wife of Henry Sellery, gentleman, now living in the county of the borough of Carmarthen", was made on 20 April 1743. Testatrix states that she made the will under a power contained in the settlement executed before her marriage to Henry, and also "by other powers given and reserved", and continues "I desire to be buried in the parish church of St. Peter, Carmarthen, near the grave of Lady Vaughan of Terracoed, and I give £50 for my interment, escutcheons, and scarfs"; to her daughter Elizabeth, wife of John Lloyd, gentleman, "my gold watch and rings, and £500 to be met partly from mortgages from John Jones and

Griffith Harry of Llangunnor, and partly from debts due from her late son and godson Francis and John Browne; to her grandchildren Edward, Elizabeth, and Margaret Browne, £500 apiece; to Sir Thomas Stepney, Bart., John Stepney, esquire, and 'his son Thomas Stepney, Justina Stepney and Mary Stepney, and her nephew Sir Edward Mansel, £5 each to buy a ring; mentions "my son Francis Browne, esquire, deceased, and my godson John Browne, gentleman, of Frood"; to her grandson John Browne she gave "all my realty and personalty", he having been executor of his late father; and appointed "my friends and relations" Sir Thomas Stepney and his son John to be executors. Her husband was totally excluded from the will. Had they parted?

Even at this final phase, difficulties continued to attend her affairs. The surviving executor renounced and the grandson John Browne, the residuary legatee, refused to accept administration, which was then granted in London on 1 August 1745 to John Wilson, esquire, a creditor of testatrix. Neither was Mrs. Browne buried as she desired in St. Peter's Church, and the registers contain no mention of her. She seems to have always attracted the lightning.

THE HARRIES OF FFRWD

AMONG later tenants of Ffrwd was the highly respected family of Harries, progressive farmers, faithful supporters of Ebenezer chapel at Crwbin. Household service (*dyletswydd teulu*) was regularly held before breakfast, attended by the family and servants; a portion of Holy Writ was read, followed by a hymn and an *adnod* recited by one of the congregation. Among the numerous servants was "Henry'r osler" whose secular concern was the welfare of his master's horses. For some reason Henry had taken a dislike to Mrs. Harries, a very handsome woman by all accounts, and he constantly sought ways and means to annoy her without making it evident that he was the mainspring of her discomfiture. During one such assembly Mr. Harries called upon the nipper (*gwas bach*) who had just entered into service, to recite a Biblical verse from memory. The lad responded with commendable alacrity, and with suitable emphasis declaimed as follows *"Fel modrwy aur yn nhrwyn hwch yw menyw lan ddisynwyr"* (Like a golden ring in a sow's nose, is a beautiful but brainless woman). A little pucker appeared on Mr. Harries's brow, and when the meal was over he quietly asked the *gwas bach,* who had taught him. "Henry'r osler sir" came the innocent reply. Shortly afterwards a chagrined ostler was seen tramping away, pack on shoulders, to seek a farm where the housewife was of more homely mien and less liable to excite his spleen. Some years later the Harrieses removed to Dryslwyn Fawr, Llangathen.

CHAPTER V

THE DUCHESS AND A CAVALIER

THE ETHOS OF GOLDEN GROVE

THERE ARE FEW areas in Wales where Place and People have combined to produce a more coherent and vivid representation of continuous Welsh history than the settling of which Golden Grove is centre. Here in the parish of Llanfihangel Aberbythych we stand in the very heart of the ancient kingdom of Deheubarth, the decisions of whose princes affected the lives of people as widely separated as the farmers of remote Genau'r Glyn, the herdsmen on the Precelly slopes, and the fishermen on the banks of Llwchwr.

I would like to draw your attention to the physical setting, to the Places, after which I shall have something to say about the People who lived here.

Below us lies the Vale of Tyvi through which Roman legions marched from Carmarthen to the gold-mines of Cynwyl Gaeo, flanked by the rolling plateau of Cantref Mawr to the west and rugged Cantref Bychan to the east: within our sight are two castled residences of the princes of Deheubarth: from this very spot a 13th century peasant might have heard the war-horns at Coed Lathen where a Norman force was routed in 1257, or the strike of hatchets as masked raiders demolished the tollgates in the days of the young Queen Victoria. Within a few hundred yards of this spot, some of the finest devotional works in the English tongue were written, while a nearby eminence inspired the poem whose descriptive periods still enthral those who contemplate the brow of Grongar Hill. Should a Roman centurion, a prince of Dynevor, a freeman of Llettygariad, or a miller of Cilsaen through Merlin's potent magic, suddenly appear amongst us today, they would have no difficulty in recognising the old familiar landmarks, for this valley and its hill-slopes have endured substantially unchanged, there are no towns and villages where none stood before, and the landscape remains mercifully free of those scars that industrial development has inflicted on less fortunate areas in South Wales.

The rich soil and sheltered pastures of this valley have resulted in a flourishing husbandry which justifies our calling it the Garden of Carmarthenshire. From here we catch glimpses of the Towy winding through the green meadows like

Dynevor House

Dryslwyn Castle

some unfinished poem, a river that rises in the Cardiganshire hills, and flows through the entire length of this county. The valley was the gateway to west and mid Wales, and the modern highway known as the A40 follows a route along which men have tramped since pre-historic days.

Within sight of Golden Grove, stands the grey ruin of Dynevor Castle, capital of Deheubarth, cradle of a spirited race of princes who ruled over the region comprised of the modern counties of Carmarthen, Cardigan, and Pembroke. The first known eisteddfod in Wales was held in the town of Cardigan under the auspices of the Lord Rhys of Dynevor, and that after the overthrow of the dynasty in 1282, it was in Cardiganshire among Cardiganshire people, that a branch of the family was able to maintain itself – in Iscoed and Gwynionydd – and to retain in large measure those franchises that had long been the prerogative of Welsh royalty.

Further south we can see Dryslwyn Castle, another fortress of the princes, and further east, over the hill behind us is Carreg Cennen perched on a mighty crag reminiscent of some Rhineland stronghold. These castles protected the heart of the kingdom.

Nor must the churches be excluded from this brief survey, churches whose names take us back to the Age of Saints – Llandeilo, Llandyfeisant, Llangathen, Cilfargen, Llanarthney, Llandybie, Llanegwad, and in addition numerous holy wells that continue to bear the names of men who first brought the solace of Christianity to these hills and glens. Potted around them on the, slopes amid the heather and the gorse, are many cairns and monoliths marking the graves of an earlier folk the character of whose strange, twilight

Saved from the flood

gods is suggested by the name of a rocky eminence in this parish called Craig Derwyddon.

A visitor to Llandeilo about the year 1800, stated that more country residences were concentrated in this small area than in any other part of Britain. This is very true. It is a gallery of architectural history, a land of old houses, homes of the ancient gentry, casting an aristocratic air over the whole countryside, forming a pattern of social life that lasted for over 500 years before economic and political forces conspired to destroy them in the present century.

Of the 20 mansions that existed here in 1800, only one is tenanted today by a descendant of those who lived there in that year.

Some have disappeared from the face of the earth like Tygwyn near Llandeilo; this was the home of the Philipps family before moving to Cwmgwili, and belonged to the Vaughans of Derwydd, and today nothing is left except a mere mound of rubble among the thorn and bramble bushes. Middleton Hall, home of the Myddletons and later of the Abadam family, was burnt down.

Golden Grove

Just below Llangathen church, which you can see from here, is Aberglasney, former seat of Sir Willis ap Thomas one of the first sheriffs of Carmarthenshire, then of the Rudds, one of whom was Bishop Rudd whose splendid monument is in the parish church, and more latterly of the Dyers.

Below Llangathen, almost racing us, across the river is Berllandywyll, which has close associations with Cardiganshire. For over a hundred years it was the home of the Lloyds who moved there from Castle Hywel. They liked the place so much that they eventually sold Castle Hywel and made 'Berllan Dywyll' – 'the secluded orchard', beautiful name – their permanent home. The Lloyds were a numerous family, and some of their descendants are still with us. Berllandywyll is now a farm.

Just below it, Cilsaen bridge spans the Towy. In olden days the Vaughans of Golden Glove maintained a ferryboat here at their own cost. The boat has gone long ago, but the cottage by the bridge is still called Glan y bâd. Another mansion which became a farm is Rhydarwen. It is one of the oldest houses in the district. There is little in its appearance to indicate its earlier character, but inside are some original spandrils dating from the early Tudor period, which show six coats of arms, a carving of the head and shoulders of a man and woman, and a hunting scene executed with great spirit. Another mansion, now a farm, is that of Cwrt Brynybeirdd, 'Hill of the Bards', home of a branch of Sir Rhys ap Thomas' family, a remarkable house, in the form of a hollow square, with a courtyard in the centre.

About 10 of the mansions are farmhouses today. Two have become institutions – Tregib near Llandeilo, former home of the Gwynn-Hughes family, is a religious seminary, and Golden Grove a Farm Institute. Three continue to discharge their traditional function – Newton, now called Dynevor Park, home of Sir Rhys ap Thomas K.G., and now of his direct descendant Lord Dynevor: Derwydd, an old seat of the Vaughans and lately the home of their descendant, Miss Stepney Gulston, and lastly Court Henry in Llangathen, home of the Lloyds, descendants of the Lloyds of Bronwydd, another link with Cardiganshire.

Such then is the setting – the Places. I have left Golden Grove to the last, because the history of the house is inseparable from the family that inhabited it.

I shall now turn to the People. What is important is not the length of the pedigree, but the contribution of the whole family. The family tree is not merely a perpendicular affair stretching back to the romantic mist, but a lateral affair embracing all relations, both male and female descents. This is well borne out in the Golden Grove Manuscripts to which I shall refer later. Some time ago I received two excellent examples of this in pedigrees from Capt. Hext Lewis and from Mr. Lloyd of Cynghordy. These pedigrees included details about the cadet branches and recorded the descendants of the womenfolk as well as the sons, together with biographical details of their achievements and contributions. In other words they were *family histories,* which did not confine themselves to the main line, but included all relatives.

This attitude is enormously important. If there is anything at all in heredity, then this is the way to investigate it, and the only way in which we are likely to assemble the necessary evidence. The social historian must ever be grateful to the Welsh preoccupation with people.

Having said this, I will now discuss the fortunes and misfortunes of the families of Golden Grove, first the Vaughans, and afterwards the Campbells, Lords Cawdor.

The Vaughans

Descended from the Princes of Powys, the Vaughans settled in Carmarthenshire in 1485 and from the days of the Tudors to those of the Regent, they were its leading family. There is a royal air about these Vaughans. They served in the King's wars at home and abroad, by land and sea: one accompanied the Prince of Wales in Spain on the occasion of the wooing of the Infanta: instinctive royalists, six drew the blade for Charles I in whose service two became generals; the senior line was advanced to the dignities of a barony and an earldom, and five members received the accolade of knighthood; they represented the shire, with the exception of three parliaments, from 1593 to 1689, and with the exception of two parliaments, the borough from 1621 to 1725; eleven became High Sheriffs of their native county; on sixteen occasions Vaughans filled the mayoral chair, and on ten, the shrievalty of the borough of Carmarthen: pioneers of agricultural reform, a Vaughan of Golden Grove advocated improved methods of tillage as early as 1571, another was the first Welshman to write a treatise on farming and estate management in the reign of the first Elizabeth, and under her successor founded a colony to further his dreams. From this house came a Lord President of Wales and the Marches, a Governor of Jamaica, and a President of the Royal Society, while the last of the line at Golden Grove held the high office of Lord Lieutenant of this county.

Sharp deterrent

Nor were they indifferent to the republic of letters. The Vaughans extended a timely patronage to the learned Jeremy Taylor who survived a turbulent decade in the seclusion of Golden Grove where he wrote about eighteen of his finest books: a Vaughan gave his friendship to James Howell, author of the *Epistolae Hoelianae,* and fostered the genius of Dryden, of Aubrey, Evelyn, Butler, and Beaumont. Conscious of their heritage they nurtured the traditions of their forebears, and it was the direct intervention of a Vaughan of Golden Grove that persuaded an English king to extend his patronage to the

Welsh language, several of them were authors of poetry and prose. The establishment of schools in south Wales during the 17th and 18th centuries owed much to the interest and practical support afforded by a father and daughter of this talented stock namely John Vaughan of Derllys and Madam Bridget Bevan. They extended their liberality to religious life, were patrons of churches in more than the ordinary sense, and several Carmarthenshire churches still use plates engraved with the name and arms of Vaughan.

The family occupied numerous country houses. At the height of its affluence the parent estate, that of Golden Grove, comprised over 50,000 acres, 27 extensive manors and lordships, and five castles, and when these are added to the lands of the many branches it can be truly said that nearly half of Carmarthenshire owned a Vaughan for landlord.

This family, the greatest in South Wales, produced legislators, courtiers, consuls, pioneers, possessed great wealth and high social standing, "pounds sterling and the strawberry leaves", yet today not a single descendant bearing the surname Vaughan remains in the land wherein they had dwelt for over 400 years. The last member of the family died at The Parade in Carmarthen in 1928. She was Miss Ada Jessie Vaughan.

But the virtue of a family does not reside solely in its possessions, or in the length of its pedigree, but in its contributions to its times. Although the Vaughans were by no means constantly successful in the measures they advocated nor always wise in the causes they promoted, yet they never failed to give leadership or to place their undoubted talents at the service of their countrymen. By whatever yardstick they are measured, the Vaughans of Golden Grove emerge as a justification of that category of people which so long guided the local concerns and national destinies of the British state.

The first of the family to settle in Carmarthenshire, was Hugh Vaughan, a descendant of the former Princes of Powys. He married Jane daughter of Morris ab Owen of Cwrt Bryn y Beirdd, a second cousin of Sir Rhys ap Thomas of Dynevor. This marriage proved of the greatest importance to Hugh Vaughan. After the Battle of Bosworth in 1485 Rhys ap Thomas, his relations and friends received rewards from Henry Tudor. On 22 September 1485 Morris ab Owen of Bryn y Beirdd was appointed Steward of the Lordship of Kidwelly, and his son-in-law Hugh Vaughan became Forester of that lordship. Hugh subsequently received grants of land and became established as a minor landowner. Through the influence of Sir Rhys ap Thomas he was appointed Groom of the Chamber to King Henry VIII.

Loyalty to the Crown, the acceptance of relatively minor official posts which gave local prestige and provided a starting point to higher things, finally sealed with a Court appointment. Here was the familiar pattern governing the re-emergence of the long pedigree native élite from centuries of uncertainty to burgeon into energetic, enterprising

Kidwelly Castle

The treasure train

Tudor gentry in whose hands local administration and parliamentary representation remained until the end of the 19th century.

Then came another episode that had a profound affect upon the Vaughan fortunes. In 1531, Sir Rhys ap Griffith, grandson of Sir Rhys ap Thomas, was executed for treason, and on 1 April 1532 the King appointed Hugh Vaughan, Groom of the Chamber and Forester of Kidwelly, to be the Keeper and Receiver of the rents and forfeited lands in the comotes of Kidwelly, Carnwallon and Iskennen. The importance of this appointment will be appreciated when I tell you that it was upon the wreckage of the vast possessions of the unhappy Sir Rhys ap Griffiths, that the Vaughans largely built an estate, the extent of which no subsequent land-owner in south west Wales, with one exception, has ever equalled, much less exceeded.

Hugh Vaughan lived at Kidwelly, and had one son and eight daughters. The son, John Vaughan, obtained Crown leases of lands that had belonged to Sir Rhys ap Griffith, and between 1541 and 1574 he acquired leases of the lordship of Dryslwyn, the fishery of the Towy, and extensive properties in Kidwelly, Iskennen, Llanstephan, the town of Carmarthen, Llangain, Llanelly, Pembrey and St. Clears – lands which were afterwards bought by his grandson. He was also appointed Receiver of the lordship of Kidwelly.

He took a prominent part in public life – Bailiff of Carmarthen in 1553, Mayor in 1554 and 1563, and also High Sheriff of Carmarthenshire in 1563. When he occupied the mayoral chair, the bard William Lleyn addressed a poem to him. He was M.P. for Carmarthen Borough in 1558, and sat for the County from 1571 till his death in 1574.

John Vaughan was the builder of Golden Grove in the period 1565-1570. It was built on a virgin site, for no references to Golden Grove or Gelli Aur have been found in earlier documents. The house stood on the low ground near the present old gardens in the valley below.

When John Vaughan died in 1574 his family had become one of the most important in the county. His son Walter Vaughan added to the family fortunes; he followed his father as M.P., was High Sheriff of both Carmarthenshire and Pembrokeshire and Mayor of Carmarthen. In 1576 he was one of the founders of Carmarthen Grammar School. He added to his estate both by purchase and by taking further Crown leases. He was interested in coal mining and worked extensive mines in Kidwelly, Llwynhendy and Llangennech. He was twice married, firstly to Mary Rhys of Dynevor, and secondly to Lettice Perrot. He died in 1596, and left 15 children. This quiverfull was remarkable for its talents and achievements. Five of the sons swooped like hawks on the heiresses of Carmarthenshire estates, married them, and founded vigorous families of their own at Torycoed, Llanelly, Derwydd, Cwrt Derllys, and Lletherllesty. Five of the brothers served as High Sheriffs and two as Members of Parliament, three of them were knighted, and one became an Earl.

One of the brothers, Sir William Vaughan of Torycoed, became an M.A. of Oxford and a Doctor of Philosophy of Vienna University. He wrote a large number of books, and founded a colony at his own expense in Newfoundland in 1616 and named the new farms after his Carmarthenshire properties.

It was the eldest son, John Vaughan who reaped the richest harvest. Educated at Oxford and the Inner Temple, he married Margaret daughter of Sir Gelly Meyrick, right hand man of the ambitious Earl of Essex. This was a good marriage for Vaughan, for his wife's dowry amounted to £1,500, and his father-in-law promised to use his influence to secure him "great preferment". In 1599-1600 Vaughan served in Ireland with his father-in-law and was knighted by Essex for his services. The stage seemed set for a brilliant future, when the newly dubbed knight found himself in the midst of a tempest that overwhelmed his sponsors. The Earl of Essex overplayed his hand and ended his life on Tower Hill beneath the headman's axe, a fate shared by Sir Gelly Meyrick in 1601.

As a son-in-law of Sir Gelly and as a follower of Essex, Sir John Vaughan came under suspicion. All his papers were searched, he was arrested and questioned, but as no evidence of complicity in the revolt was discovered, he was released and ordered to return to his Carmarthenshire house. After Sir Gelly Meyrick had been arrested, Vaughan acted with great shrewdness. Secretly and by night he sent waggons to Sir Gelly's Pembrokeshire and Radnorshire homes, and carted all his silver plate, his jewels, tapestries, and other treasure and concealed them in the deep cellars of Golden Grove. This treasure was said to have filled 20 great trunks. Lawsuits were conducted for years against Sir John Vaughan, but he managed to retain the lot, and when pressed by the lawyers admitted only to having taken articles to the value of his wife's dowry which he said that Sir Gelly still owed him.

He weathered this ugly storm, and the advent of the new dynasty proved a help. From 1601 to 1616 he lived in Carmarthenshire and added to his estates. He took a leading part in public life, and when a plague struck Carmarthen town in 1603, the Great Sessions were held at Golden Grove. He made friends with the supporters of the new King and through their help obtained some appointments, and was made a member of the Irish Privy Council. He was an ambitious and able man, and soon an opportunity presented itself that converted him from a local landowner into a magnate who deliberated in the highest councils of the realm. He was told that the King was going to create his son, Charles, to be Prince of Wales. This meant that a Household would be created for him. Vaughan set to work immediately. He wrote a letter to Sir Henry Nevill asking him to help him to obtain a post in the Prince's services. He also wrote in December 1614 to Lord Somerset asking for his influence and enclosed a present of £100 which he asked him to accept as a Christmas box. He canvassed old friends and cultivated new ones, and venison and game from the parklands of Golden Grove graced many a table in Whitehall.

His manoeuvres succeeded. In February 1616 he was knighted by the King, and in the following month secured the important post of Comptroller of Prince Charles' household, which he held till the prince ascended the Throne in 1625. He thus became the ruler of the princely household, the friend and guide of the future King. He accompanied Charles to Spain in 1623 when he went courting the Infanta, guided his studies, and stood with him on all ceremonial occasions.

In 1621 he was created Baron Vaughan of Mullingar in the Irish peerage. Vaughan was Member of Parliament for Carmarthenshire, and his elevation to the peerage raised constitutional issues – did this promotion debar him from sitting in the Commons? The intervention of Sir Edward Coke resulted in the findings being declared in his favour, and Lord Vaughan was able to sit in both the House of Commons and in the House of Lords, apparently without any reluctance. It was the first time this question had arisen and that it should have concerned a Welshman from Golden Grove, is of interest to us today.

During his office as the Prince's Comptroller, Lord Vaughan had spent nearly £20,000 out of his own pocket. After Charles became King these services were rewarded, and in 1628 he was created Earl of Carbery. He had come a long way and had weathered many storms. In 1630 he bought vast crown properties in Carmarthenshire which the King was selling in order to raise money, and so added considerably to his estates. He died in 1634 at Golden Grove and was buried in Llandeilo Church. Here I should mention that in 1617 he rebuilt the church of the parish of Llanfihangel Aberbythych at his own expense.

Before I discuss the life of his son, the 2nd Earl, I would like to digress and say something about his remarkable brother-in-law, John Protheroe of Hawksbrook, near Carmarthen. John Protheroe was a scholarly squire with scientific inclinations and married Elinor Vaughan, the Earl of Carbery's sister. Protheroe was the first man to experiment with the use of coal instead of charcoal for reducing iron ore, and he and the Vaughans obtained a Patent from King James to do this. He was also a great astronomer and helped Harriot and Lower to produce the first telescope in Britain. He was connected with the discovery of the Circulation of the Blood in a somewhat sinister manner. Two doctors had been working independently of each other on the circulation of the blood. John Protheroe who was interested in the subject was friendly with both doctors. Warner suddenly came on the truth, and in great excitement told Protheroe about it, but before he could publish his findings Harvey forestalled him. Warner afterwards complained bitterly – saying that one day he saw Dr. Harvey and Mr. Protheroe deep in conversation, and when he approached them the conversation stopped abruptly. Shortly after this Harvey brought out his books and Warner was convinced that Protheroe had passed on the information to him. It is also interesting to note that John Protheroe's granddaughter was the famous Lucy Walter the lady friend of Charles II. Thus the present Duchess of Gloucester who is her descendant is also a descendant of the Vaughans of Golden Grove.

Richard Vaughan, the 2nd Earl of Carbery added to the honours of Golden Grove. He was knighted in 1625, and succeeded his father as Earl of Carbery in 1634. His first wife was Bridget Lloyd the heiress of Llanllyr in Cardiganshire. Through her he acquired the Llanllyr estate, and after his wife's death in 1636 he sold the Llanllyr estate to David Parry of Noyadd. At Llanllyr was the famous Hirlas Horn which had been presented by Henry VII on his march in 1485 to Bosworth. This came into the Earl's possession, and was brought to Golden Grove, and it remains to this day in the possession of Lord Cawdor, the ultimate heir of Golden Grove.

When the Civil War broke out in 1642, Carbery was appointed Lieutenant General for the three west Wales counties, and in the following year the King created him Baron of

Emlyn in the British peerage. However in 1645 Carbery was defeated and retired to Golden Grove. In 1648 Oliver Cromwell himself called there on his way to Pembroke, and for the hospitality he received sent two stags as a present to Lord Carbery who kept a herd of deer.

In 1645 when Cardigan Castle surrendered to the Roundheads one of the prisoners was Dr. Jeremy Taylor. Through Lord Carbery's influence he was released, and afterwards he lived for ten years at Golden Grove where he kept a school for the sons of the Royalist gentry. Lord and Lady Carbery encouraged him to write and it was here that the most famous of his books were composed, such *as The Golden Grove Moralised, Holy Living* and *Holy Dying*. After the Restoration he became Bishop of Down in Ireland.

The Hirlas Horn

With the Restoration Carbery re-entered public life, and became President of the Council of Wales and the Marches, and Lord Lieutenant of all the Welsh Counties, thus he was virtual ruler, Viceroy, of Wales. He held the post until 1672. In 1676 a number of West Wales gentry wrote to him complaining that not enough books were published in Welsh, and asking for his help in the matter. Lord Carbery immediately saw the King, who, a week later, appointed "The King's Printer for the Welsh Language". This is the first time that an English King extended his patronage to the language of Wales, and it is of particular interest to know that it was done at the request of Richard Vaughan, Earl of Carbery. The 2nd Earl died in 1686 aged 86 and was buried at Llanfihangel Aberbythych church.

The 3rd Earl of Carbery, John Vaughan was born in 1639, and educated at the University of Oxford and the Inner Temple. He was knighted in 1661, became a courtier and a friend of Charles II. He was a man of liberal outlook, and in his younger days gave support to the Quakers, and in July 1664 he was arrested at a Quaker meeting and thrown into gaol, but was released when he pleaded privilege as a Member of Parliament.

He had an only child, a daughter, Anne, who married the Duke of Bolton. They lived mostly in London. During this time three quarters of Golden Grove was burnt down. The Duke of Bolton had agreed to let one of his poor relations live there in 1729, and sent a letter to the butler to air the rooms for his reception. A careless servant maid lit the fires and sparks from one of them fell into the room and the house was badly damaged. It had been an enormous house consisting of over 50 rooms. The remaining one quarter was then used, and in 1754 it was partly restored, but to nothing like its former glory. On that occasion the rooms were made much larger.

The Duchess and her husband parted in 1732, and she spent the remainder of her life at Golden Grove, Windsor Castle where she was a Lady in Waiting, and in London. One interesting entry in her household accounts shows that on every St. David's day she paid 1/- for a leek to be worn in honour of the patron saint.

She died without children in 1752 and left the Golden Grove estates to her cousin John Vaughan who settled there and largely rebuilt the house.

Three further generations of the family lived at Golden Grove the last of them was John Vaughan, born in 1757, educated at Harrow, and from 1771 to 1775 he studied in the German university of Gottingen. His only brother Charles Richard Vaughan entered the army as a Cornet in the Innskilling Dragoon Guards.

In 1776 John Vaughan came to live at Golden Grove and spent much of his time in sporting activities, being an enthusiastic fisherman, an excellent shot, and a fearless horseman, hunting with both Carmarthenshire and Cardiganshire foxhounds. He entered public life when very young. In 1779, when 22 years of age he became Whig Member of Parliament for Carmarthenshire which he represented until 1784. On 25 March 1780 he became Lord Lieutenant, at 23 years of age being the youngest Welshman ever appointed to that important post. It is interesting to note that his father was still alive when the appointment was made. The father died seven months later, and John Vaughan inherited the Golden Grove estate. His brother, the Cornet of Dragoons, died six years later, unmarried, and John Vaughan, as the sole representative of his family found himself the owner of seven estates in Carmarthenshire – Golden Grove, Llandybie, Piode, Lletty Gariad, Bremenda, Gellydywyll, Penllwyngwyn, and the reversion of Berllandywyll, making eight in all; and in right of his wife, a share of the Abermarlais estate, and the mansion of Westmead: an estate at Shenfield in Essex, and a leased country mansion, called Harnish, in Wiltshire. He also owned lands in Llandyfriog, Cardiganshire, and in Cilgerran. He was lord of 27 manors, and owned five castles. He had been born not merely with one silver spoon in his mouth but with a whole service.

In 1781 he married Elizabeth Letitia Jane Maude, only child of Sir Cornwallis Maude, Baronet, who was

An ACT for Explaining a Power contained in the Settlement of the Dutchefs of Bolton's Eftate, on her Marriage with the prefent Duke, and making the fame more Effectual, for the Purpofes thereby intended.

created Lord de Montalt in 1783 and Viscount Hawarden in 1791. He was utterly devoted to Letty as he called her. A delicate creature, very frail, short-sighted, she was an invalid for most of her life. She died in 1796, aged 39.

John Vaughan took a prominent part in public life and was an active politician, of liberal, advanced ideas, and a constant supporter of the Whig party.

He improved the house of Golden Grove. It was decorated by the brothers Poletti, and he paid John Nash £10 10s. 0d. for making a plan for a bath, this being the first sum of money ever received by Nash as an architect. The house then consisted of 22 rooms, with 104 windows.

Antiquarians have reason to be profoundly grateful to him. Vaughan was deeply interested in history, and he spent a great deal of money in arresting the decay of the masonry of the castles of Newcastle Emlyn, Carreg Cennen, Dryslwyn and Kidwelly. He built a wall around the foot of Dryslwyn castle; in 1796 he mended the walls of Kidwelly castle, and had a padlock placed on the castle gate, as he said "to prevent idle people getting in and doing mischief". He was mainly responsible for building Newcastle Emlyn market house. He also added to his library and many of his bills contain the titles of the books he bought, a large number being historical works. Pictures, especially engravings attracted him, and he bought very large numbers such as Hogarth's prints, Continental views; and employed an artist from London to paint Carmarthenshire scenes for him. Among the pictures he bought, was one in a gilt frame for which he paid £2 5s. 0d. in 1786, entitled "The Credulous Lady", I would give much to see this portrait, for that type of womanhood I feel is now almost, if not quite, extinct. A man of cultivated taste, he bought a good deal of Wedgewood and of Swansea china all specially decorated with the Vaughan coat-of-arms.

He kept a large household staff. When he died in 1804, he had 24 servants, not counting woodwards and agents on various parts of his estates. Among his servants was Williams the Harper to whom he paid a salary of £36 a year, a very large sum in those days. He was among the last of the Welsh harpers. At election times Vaughan used to send him to Carmarthen to play in the Whig public houses to encourage the voters. His music possessed potent qualities, for at one election when a Carmarthen barber, a Tory, entered the pub where Williams was playing, his Whig audience hurled themselves on the intruder and half strangled him. His music evidently did not soothe political breasts.

Vaughan was a progressive farmer, and subscribed 20 guineas annually to the Carmarthenshire Agricultural Society of which he was President. This society was the second of its kind in Wales, founded in 1772, and its founder was a Cardiganshire man, namely Watkin Lewes of Abernantbychan. Vaughan was particularly keen on afforestation, and hardly a year passed without many

Golden Grove today

hundreds of trees being planted. In 1731 for instance he planted 5,000 trees. He encouraged local carpenters and blacksmiths to invent and improve agricultural machinery, and spent vast sums on improving his breed of cattle. In addition to his herds, he also kept wild cattle and a herd of deer in this park.

He built several canals around Golden Grove, and even planned to build one from Llandovery to Carmarthen, and from Llandeilo to the river Loughor.

His two closest friends were Lord Cawdor of Stackpole Court and Col. Brigstocke of Blaenpant, who were very kind to him especially after his wife's death. Among English visitors to Golden Grove was the author Dr .John Moore, who frequently brought his family with him, to stay for several weeks during the summer. One of his little boys became a soldier, known to history as Sir John Moore, killed at Corunna in 1809.

Not a drum was heard, not a funeral note,
As the corpse to the ramparts we carried.

It is interesting to recall that part of his youth was spent in this very district. John Vaughan died on 19 January 1804, at the age of 47 and was buried in the family vault at Llanfihangel Aberbythych church.

Robert Frost once said "There are three great things in this world, there is religion, there is science, and there is gossip". Carmarthenshire is still one of those places where the science of gossip is pursued religiously, and John Vaughan of Golden Grove provided the county with dramatic material for the exercise of a native talent that was to add one legend more to a land already rich in legends.

John Vaughan had made his will in 1786. He left his estate to whatever sons he might have by his wife, in tail, and in the event of having no sons, then to his daughters, and in the event of having no children at all, then to his wife Mrs. Letty Vaughan, and after her death to his friend John Campbell, Lord Cawdor.

Such was the will, clear, positive, and perfectly in order. Now let us look at the succession. John Vaughan had no children by his wife, so there were no heirs of the body. Mrs. Vaughan had died in 1796, before her husband, so she could not inherit: of the legatees, Lord Cawdor was the only one living, and so inherited the Golden Grove estates.

Now John Vaughan had other relations. He had a half-sister (his father had married twice) a Mrs. Watkins who had married a Breconshire parson and had a large family. He had second-cousins living in London, "poor relations", called Mrs. Comyn, Mrs. Basewall and Mrs. Lewis. In Carmarthenshire he had kinsmen, distant cousins, like the Vaughans of the Parade, Carmarthen, to whom I referred earlier, the Davies' of Coomb, the Stepneys of Llanelly, and also the Brigstockes – all of whom had hoped to get a slice of the cake, but all had been excluded. The will was a bombshell. I have noticed that a desire to acquire more money is a feeling that resides in every human breast, it may slumber but it is never entirely asleep, and will leap into feverish activity at the slightest tinkle of a coin or the rustle of a banknote. John Vaughan's will was like the clanging of the bells of a thousand fire-engines, bringing to life emotions, imaginations and gossip, which, it would be wrong to say is totally forgotten, even after the passage of over 150 years. The relations started lawsuits, and the buzz of conversational hornets enlivened the tea-tables of Carmarthenshire.

One fiction stated that John Vaughan and John Campbell, when very young men, had made a Grand Tour of Europe together. Before they set out each had made a will in favour of the other should any accident befall them. After the Tour the wills were to be destroyed. Vaughan destroyed his friend's will, but the canny Campbell carefully preserved Vaughan's. Another version makes it a trinity, for Thomas Johnes of Hafod is said to have been one of the party and made a similar will.

This of course is complete nonsense. John Vaughan did not make his will until 1786, about six years after he had been married.

Another tale says that John Vaughan and Campbell went to the wars in India, and made wills, in each other's favour, another complete fabrication.

Another tale says that John Vaughan lost £100,000 at cards, and that Campbell helped him out: also that Campbell lent large sums of money to Vaughan on other occasions. This I can prove is totally inaccurate. Vaughan never owed Campbell a penny – and what is more Campbell was never in a position to help anyone financially owing to his own very heavy commitments. Now, who was John Campbell, Lord Cawdor, and what was his connection with John Vaughan?

The Campbells descended from the ducal Scots house of Argyll, and by the female line from those Thanes of Cawdor made known to a wider audience through the genius of Shakespeare. The first to settle in Wales was Sir Alexander Campbell who in 1689 married Elizabeth Lort, heiress of Stackpole Court in Pembrokeshire. The marriage of heiresses was in the blood, for John Campbell the son followed in the matrimonial footsteps of the father. He sought his bride in Cardiganshire, and found her in Mary Pryse daughter and heiress of Lewis Pryse of Glanfread, a member of the ancient family of Gogerddan. The next in line was Pryse Campbell who married Sarah daughter of Mr. Edmund Bacon, premier baronet of England, and their son John Campbell became Lord Cawdor and inherited the Golden Grove estate. Pryse Campbell was Member of Parliament for Cardigan Borough, and his son John with whom we are now concerned was also Member of Parliament for Cardigan Borough from 1780 till 1796.

John Campbell was born in 1755, and was thus two years older than Vaughan. Campbell was educated at Eton, Vaughan at Harrow – hardly an auspicious beginning to a beautiful friendship. Both men had similar tastes – they were Whigs and supported each other whenever there was an election: they were famous as progressive farmers and as improving landlords, and co-operated to introduce new methods into local agriculture, public affairs and political life attracted them: they were enthusiastic sportsmen – there was a pack of hounds at Golden Grove and another at Stackpole – they were keen antiquaries, being extremely learned in subjects like sculpture, painting, literature: they were firm friends and it was to Campbell that Vaughan always went for advice. And it was to this friend that he left his estate. Cawdor is best known for his conduct during the Landing of the French at Fishguard in 1797 when he became a local hero.

Thus in 1804 Lord Cawdor owned four estates – Glanfread in Cardiganshire, Stackpole Court in Pembrokeshire, Golden Grove in Carmarthenshire, and Cawdor Castle

An unexpected archaeological dig

in Scotland, at one time totalling over 101,000 acres. He acquired Golden Grove by a perfectly straightforward bequest. He was a lucky man.

Apart from inheriting the estate, Lord Cawdor cleared up John Vaughan's debts, which amounted to £141,000. His son was created Earl Cawdor and Baron Emlyn in 1827. It was in 1827 that the foundations of this present house was built. The old Golden Grove was pulled down, and today there is nothing above ground to indicate its former site. We know exactly where it was. A few years ago a tractor going merrily through a glade on its lawful occasions, suddenly and alarmingly sank into the ground, and in this way the huge arched cellars of the former plan were re-discovered. These were the cellars in which great treasure had been hidden in Elizabethan days. When, with a hopeful mind, I examined the vaults some time ago, I failed to find a single coin or jewel – the Vaughans, the Cawdors, and Principal James had been here too long. The present building was built by the celebrated architect Wyattville, a solidly built product of the 19th century.

It is unnecessary for me to dwell on the achievements of the subsequent Lords Cawdor. From 1813, they have produced four members of Parliament, three Lords Lieutenant and Keepers of the Rolls, two Privy Councillors, and a First Lord of the Admiralty. One of the family earned the highest award for courage, namely John Vaughan Campbell who won the Victoria Cross in 1916.

I have shown that Lord Cawdor is descended from the Cardiganshire family of Pryse, and that he once owned the Glanfread estate. The Cawdors are thus intimately connected with the three counties of old Deheubarth. Recently I made a detailed investigation of the pedigree of Lord Cawdor. I found that he is a descendant, in blood, of Henry Tudor afterwards Henry VII, and also from The Lord Rhys of Dynevor, Prince of Deheubarth. It seems a form of historical judgement that the Hirlas Horn, once owned by Henry Tudor, should at long last have come to the hands of his descendant, the Lord Cawdor.

JOHN VAUGHAN, THE THIRD EARL OF CARBERY

"Nothing in his Life became him like the Leaving of it"

JOHN VAUGHAN, second but eldest surviving son of the 2nd earl, received his early education at Jeremy Taylor's School, before matriculating on 23 July 1656 at Christ Church, Oxford, whence he proceeded to the Inner Temple in 1658. He was created a Knight of the Bath on Charles II's coronation in April 1661, and with his elder brother Francis made a member of the Council of Wales and the Marches.

Sir John Vaughan entered public life on 8 May 1661, when he was returned as Member of Parliament for Carmarthen Borough which he represented until 1679, when he took the seat for the County and held it until 1681 and again from 1685 to 1687. He started political life as a courtier. He supported the King's party on 14 February 1667-8, which stated its intention "to undertake to get the King money" – consequently known as one of the "Undertakers" – in a parliament antagonistic to royal demands. In 1672 he again took the King's side in a debate on the security of the Protestant religion, and in 1677 was described as one who had betrayed his country by advocating a standing army "under the command of The Biggotted Popish Duke", that is the Duke of York, afterwards James II. He had been forward in pressing Clarendon's impeachment in 1667, being one of the first to make an attack on him. Vaughan did not merely assail Clarendon in order to please the King. Clarendon had been responsible for limiting the powers of the Council for Wales when Carbery was President, and so could expect little sympathy from the Vaughans. He was colonel of a regiment of foot in 1673-4.

A man of liberal outlook, he was a prominent member of the Kit-Cat Club where the "Whig" view predominated. In. his younger days he gave support to the Quakers whose principles appealed to him so that in July 1644 he was arrested at a Quaker's meeting held in Mile End Green and thrown into Newgate gaol, but his plea of privilege as a member of parliament secured his speedy release. His experience did not deter him and he continued to be sympathetic towards Quaker matters until he succeeded to his father's title in 1686. In later life he became strongly Protestant and an exclusionist.

His Quaker sympathies may have had something to do with the attentions he paid to Gulielma Maria Springett, a woman of great beauty and of saintly character, whose mother, widow of Sir William Springett, had remarried to Isaac Pennington the Quaker. According to John Aubrey, Lord Vaughan courted Gulielma for "her fortune, quality, and good humour"; however, she preferred the suit of William Penn, the Quaker founder of Pennsylvania, whom she married in 1672.

In 1674 Lord Vaughan (so-called when he became heir apparent on his elder brother's death in 1667) was appointed Governor of Jamaica, since the Earl of Carlisle to whom the post had been offered had been unable to accept it. The appointment carried a salary of £1,000 per annum. Among those he invited to accompany him was his friend and countryman John Aubrey, who wrote on 9 April 1674, to Anthony Wood – "I am like to be spirited away to Jamaica by my Lord Vaughan, who is newly made Governor there, and mighty earnest to have me goe with him and will looke out some employment worthy of a gentleman for me".

His governorship took an unhappy turn right at the beginning. His countryman, the colourful Sir Henry Morgan, had been appointed as lieutenant. Vaughan, who suspected the mercurial temperament of his subordinate, decided from the outset to keep him under control. The partnership proved tempestuous, and in the end disastrous to Vaughan. They embarked in separate ships on 8 January 1674-5, Vaughan giving strict injunctions that Morgan's vessel should keep close touch with him throughout the voyage. Whether by design or through the vagaries of the weather, Morgan's ship took another course and reached Port Royal on 5 March, some nine days before the Governor.

Vaughan landed on 14 March at the same port where the ladies and gentlemen of the island welcomed and entertained him to a banquet of eleven courses and "73 dishes of succulent spiced fishes, birds sweetly stuffed, fowles roasted and so tender their flesh parted in the fingers, meate in great quantity, pastries with sufficiency of herbes". He then drove to the Governor's palace in Spanish Town, the banquet having done little to subdue the smouldering anger he felt towards Morgan whose early landing had made his own somewhat of an anti-climax.

Strife broke out between the principals immediately. Morgan was popular, a hail-fellow-well-met, a *bon viveur,* inclined to make the best of things as they were, while Vaughan was reserved, cautious, idealistic, bent on reforms, particularly the suppression of piracy and privateering. The Governor's temperament, his sensitivity about matters of precedence, proved unsuited to the task that lay before him. He failed to secure the co-operation of the rumbustious deputy, while his attitude and language revealed a lack of tact, and his actions, that he possessed little executive capacity. He addressed a complaint to the government at London, recommending Morgan's release from his duties, but no attention was paid to it. Matters went from bad to worse and in 1676 he wrote direct to the Lord Privy Seal (the Earl of Anglesey) making serious accusations, complaining that his difficulties were exacerbated by the constant conflict with Morgan whose intrigues even endangered the peace with France and Spain that Vaughan had been instructed to preserve. This again was ignored. Finally, on 13 January 1677-8, the Earl of Carlisle superseded him, and in March 1678, he returned to England.

Vaughan's pro-consulship had been a failure. Among the complaints of his conduct was that he had "made haste to grow as rich as his government would let him" and that he had trafficked in slaves. A letter written shortly after his death, over 30 years later, by Ralph Palmer to the Viscount Fermanagh, states that Vaughan "had redeemed his estate and amassed wealth by the government of Jamaica, where he carried many gentlemen of Wales and sold them for slaves as he did his chaplain to a blacksmith . . ." Does the following entry in *The Golden Grove Books* refer to one of these unfortunates – Morgan Gwynn of Glandywely "accompanied John, Lord Vaughan to Jamaica and never returned"? However, no evidence to support these allegations has been found.

Vaughan never again became prominent in Welsh affairs "but passed the latter part of his life in retirement, enjoying a fine fortune together with the estimation of the country", and renewed his cultural interests as "a man of fashionable ability and taste". However, it would be wrong to conclude that he withdrew himself entirely from public life. He continued to sit as Member of Parliament, representing Carmarthen Borough until 1679 when he exchanged for the county which he represented until 1687. He was a Lord of the Admiralty in 1683-84 and again in 1689-90. Although a courtier, he did not identify himself with the later policies of James II, neither did he attend his parliament in May 1689. After the accession of William and Mary his political life was one of total eclipse, due probably to his lack of ambition and ability rather than to any continued sympathy with the fallen Stuart King. His political views were "progressive" if his membership of the Kit-Cat Club is any indication. He was one of the thirty-nine members of that famous club, where an engraving of his portrait (painted by Kneller) hung.

His further public appointments were secondary in importance and honorific in character. In 1685 he was appointed a Deputy Lieutenant of the counties of Carmarthen, Cardigan, Brecon, Radnor, and Glamorgan; in 1702, Vice-Admiral of South Wales; in 1707, *Custos Rotulorum* of the counties of Cardigan and Carmarthen, being also a Justice of the Peace of the latter.

The amateur approach to public affairs is in harmony with the dilettantism that marked his private life. Like all the Vaughans he was a patron of the arts, a lover of learned conversation, of scientific disputation, and of academic controversy; and he encouraged enquiring minds and creative instincts. He had known philosophers like Boyle and Glanville. One of Dryden's earliest patrons, from as early as 1664, Vaughan composed some commendatory verses which prefaced that poet's *Conquest of Granada* (1670-2), and in 1678 the grateful Dryden dedicated his somewhat Rabelaisian poem, *Limberham,* to his noble patron. He encouraged John Aubrey whose works contain several references to him. Aubrey wrote to Anthony A. Wood in 1680, "I have engaged the Earle of Dorset, my Lord Vaughan, to write verses, and they will engage my Lord Mowgrave and the Earl of Rochester". He gave his friendship to John Evelyn who was present at the annual feast of the Royal Society on 30 November 1687 when "we continued my Ld Carbery president another yeare", and on 7 May, 1693, he "dined with my Ld Mowgrave where was Ld Shomberg, Carbery, Maclesfield & divers other persons of quality". Beaumont dedicated his *Treatise on Spirits and Apparitions* (1705) to him, saying that "his Lordship's great genius to a contemplative life which raises human nature to an excellency above itself and highly influences the economy of this word, had naturally induced him to dedicate his book to his Lordship".

His interests were not confined to literature, for navigation, discoveries, experiments of a scientific character, and mathematics, attracted him, and he acquired unique manuscripts composed on some of those subjects. Among his collections were some papers of the famous Thomas Harriott who had received valuable assistance from a Carmarthenshire man. This was John Protheroe of Hawksbrook near Bancyfelin, who had married a sister of the first

Earl of Carbery, and became the grandfather of the lively Lucy Walter, a subsidized lady-friend of Charles II.

With such interests, it is small wonder that he received the fellowship of the Royal Society, and his abilities were further recognized when he became President of that distinguished institution for the years 1686-89.

The third Earl's somewhat complex character is not easy to assess. To Pepys (*Diary* entry 16 November 1667) he was "one of the lewdest fellows of the age, worse than Sir Charles Sedley", the latter being notorious for a careless attitude to moral niceties, and the same diarist recorded that in 1681, Lord Vaughan and some companions visited Henry Saville, the ambassador, and engaged themselves in "talking blasphemy and atheism, drinking, and perhaps what is worse". Here, it would appear, we have a true son of the Restoration, no better and no worse than his contemporaries. If we can accept Pepys's strictures, then Carbery's character resembled that of his brother, the rakish Francis. Pepys, of course would have known him personally, and it is interesting to observe that he succeeded Pepys as President of the Royal Society.

Carbery's failure to make a success of a high appointment provides a parallel to the life of his father, the second Earl who failed as Lieutenant-General in 1644 and as Lord President in 1672. Perhaps the very catholicity of the third Earl's interests and tastes may have constituted an impediment to his career. These were so varied and diffused that they may have hindered a single-minded concentration on the work in hand, necessary to bring any enterprise to a fruitful conclusion. All along, his attitude is that of a cultured amateur, a gentlemanly scholar, qualities clearly reflected in his portrait by Kneller still hanging on the old dining room wall in Golden Grove.

Few references have been found to the latter part of his life. In May 1690, it was reported that the Earl of Carbery and the Marquess of Carmarthen were among the peers who attended the consecration of the Archbishop of Canterbury. He lived mainly at his home in Chelsea, later known as Gough House, with occasional visits to Golden Grove to inspect the woodlands in which he took a special interest.

Carbery married twice. The first wife, Mary, was the daughter of Humphrey Browne of Green Castle, near Carmarthen, High Sheriff in 1655, who died in 1660. When her brother, Christopher Browne died at the age of 8 years, Mary became sole heiress of the estate. She died childless, at the age of 18, sometime before November 1672, and administration of her goods was granted on 14 October 1674. About the latter date, Vaughan sold Green Castle and the remainder of his wife's estate (which she had conveyed to him absolutely) to one Richard Brett of St. James's, Middlesex. He was married, secondly, at St. Martin-in-the-Fields, on 10 August 1682, to Anne Savile, then aged about 20 years, eldest daughter of George Savile, 1st Marquess of Halifax by Dorothy daughter of Henry Spencer, Earl of Sunderland. By the marriage settlement dated 3 August 1682, Anne brought a dowry of £10,000 to her husband who settled a jointure of £2,300 per annum to her. By "Nan", as she was known in the family, he had three children: George born 6 October, and baptized 30 October 1683, at St. Martin-in-the-Fields, who was buried on 7 May 1685; Charles, died in infancy; and Anne, born in January 1689-90. The Countess did not survive the birth of her daughter, and was buried at St. Andrew's, Holborn, on 23 January 1689-90.

The Earl survived his second wife by some twenty-two years, and never married again. He died in his coach while travelling from London to Chelsea on 16 January 1712-13, aged 73. An escort of Grenadiers of the Guards and Her Majesty's mounted trumpeters accompanied the cavalcade when his body was borne to rest in St. John the Baptist Chapel in Westminster Abbey on 28 January. He left no sons and his honours died with him. By his will, dated 25 May 1710, and proved 2 February 1712-13, he bequeathed all his real and personal property to his only child, the Lady Anne Vaughan, and annuities of £150 to each of his unmarried sisters, the Ladies Frances and Althamia Vaughan.

BILL FOR THE FUNERAL EXPENSES OF LORD CARBERY 28 JANUARY 1712-13

Cawdor Collection in Carmarthen Record Office

"For the Funerall of The Right Honble John Earl of Carbery perform'd by The Society of Upholsters at Exeter Chainge".

Jan 28 1712	£	s	d
A double lid Elme Coffin & a leaden Coffin lined… with a Sarsnett Quilt & Ruffle		6	0
A large Outside Elm Coffin covered wth velvet & Sett of wth large Bullion nayles 4 pr of handles 9 Coronets & a fflower of gilt wth gold	18	0	0
A payre white kid gloves and a payre white Cotton stockins for My lord		5	6
A Depositum of My Lords Tables of Honr. Engrav'd on a Brass plate and gilt wth gold	4	0	0
For lineing the Coffin wth Searcloth to preserve the Body & putting up the Body wth sweete powders	2	3	0
A Herse wth 2 Horses & 8 men in mourning to carry the leaden coffin	1	2	6
A Herse wth 2 Horses & 4 Men in mourning to Cary in the velvet Coffin	1	2	6
A Roome for the Body hung in deep mourning with Velvet. A velvet Canopy & the ffloore covered	20	0	0
The next Roome in deep mourning wth Cloth and the Seates covered A velvet Canopy, a velvet Chayre of State & ffootstoole	8	0	0
The next Roome to that in deep mourning wth cloth and the Seates covered	5	0	0
The Hall in deep mourning wth Bayes	3	0	0

A Rayle Round the Body covered wth Velvet	1	10	0
24 plumes best black ffeathers for the velvet Canopys and Rayle	4	0	0
A velvet Palle the whole time	1	1	0
A Crimson velvet Capp & Coronett & black velvet Cushion		15	0
10 large silver Candlesticks & stands by the Bodyand Chayre of State	1	10	0
66 large Silver Sconces for the Roomes, att 2/-	6	12	0
16 black ditto for the Hall	0	8	0
91½ lb waxe lights & Tapers at 2/8 per lb	12	4	0
6 White wax fflambeaux for the Porters att the Gate & Dore		12	0
A Majesty Escucheon at the Head	5	0	0
A Standard of Great Brittain, A Guidon, A Greate Banner, 6 Banner Rowles, A Surcoat of Arms, Helmett & Crest, & Mantle, Sword & Targett, Gantletts & Spurrs caryd before The Body, & putt up in Westminster Abby neare the place of Intermt	42	0	0
5 Doz Silk Escucheons wth Coronetts for the Roome where the Body lay, The Poll, Cushion & Canopy halfe Empald, 6/-, and halfe wth the quartered Coates 7 /-	9	10	0
10 Doz (and) ½ Ditto vergd wth Silver for the next Roomes and the Hall, halfe impaled 3, and half with the Quarterd Coates 3/6	16	19	6
2 Achievments yd 1 Square wth Supporters & Coronetts for Chelsea House & Golden Grove ...	10	0	0
6 Men in mourning and long Cloakes to attend My Lords Body & a Page att the ffeete 4 dayes	7	0	0
2 Ditto to attend by the Chayre of State 4 dayes	2	0	0
4 Porters in mourning wth Gownes Staves & Scarves to attend att the Gate & Dore 4 dayes	4	16	0
A Herse drawne by 6 ffine fflanders Horses	2	0	0
46 of the Nobillitys mourning Coaches wth 6 horses each (besides the Lady Hallifaxes) to accompany the Herse att 22/6	51	15	0
A lead Horse covered in deep mourning wth a velvet Caparicon & black plumes of ffeathers	5	0	0
4 of Her Majestys Trumpetts on Horseback in theire lac't Coates and Accoutrements	4	6	0
38 Horsemen in mourning to ride before the Herse & to cary the Trophys att. 7/- each	13	6	0

24 ffootmen in mourning to attend the Herse & Coaches & to cary The Body att 3/6	4	4	0
6 Ditto to attend the Coronett & Cushions and lead Horse	1	1	0

2 of Her Majestys Serjeants, 2 Corporalls
    & 8 Granadiers of the Guards to attend the Herse
    and lead Horse from the Pall Mall
    to Westmr. Abbey ....
	2	0	0

23 plumes best black ffeathers for the Herse and Horses	4	0	0
Coverings for the Herse & Housings for the Horses of velvet	3	0	0

24 Buckram Escucheons
    vergd wth Silver 12 Shields, 6 Shafferroons,
    6 Banners 12 long Pendts. & 36 small Ditto
    for the Herse & Horses ....
	13	4	0

6 Silk Escutcheons 10 shields, 8 long Silk Pennons
    and 1 large Shafferroon
    for the led Horse ....
	8	2	0

4 Trumpett Banners upon Silk	6	0	0

100 White wax fflambeaux & 100 Men in black Coates
    & Capps to attend the Procession from Chelsea
    to Devonshire House att 5/- ....
	25	0	0

400 Branch Lights of white wax & 400 Men
    in black coates & Capps to attend the Procession
    from Devonshire House to Westmr. Abbey att 7/- .
	140	0	0

A ffine Cloake for the Chiefe mourner	0	10	0
6 Silk Scarves cover'd with ffrizanere ffor The Lords Supporters of The Palle att 25/- each	7	10	0
4 long Crape Scarfe for The Sub Deane of Westmr. yt Officiated	0	16	0
17 best Hatbands for mourners Supporters of The Palle & Ministers att 3/6	2	19	6
18 pair Mens Shamy Gloves. att 3/6	3	1	0
6 Hatbands for my Lords Underservts 18/- 6 pair Dyed Topt Gloves for the same 12/-	1	10	0
5 pair Dyes Topt Gloves for The Lady Hallifaxes Servts	0	10	0
22 Silk Scarfes for Gentlemen yt Caryd The Trophys The Queens Trumpetts & Managers at 14/-	15	8	0
73 Cloaks for the Rest of The Horsemen & Coachmen at 2/-	7	6	0
164 Hatbands for Horsemen Coachmen Postillions Porters ffootmen & attendants att 2/-	16	8	0
164 black Dyed Topt Gloves for the same att 18d.	12	6	0

	£	s	d
12 pair Ditto for 12 ffootmen yt attended the Herse ..	0	18	0
12 pair Dyed Drawne Topt Gloves for vergers & officers of The Abby att 2/-	1	4	0
24 pair Ditto for the Choyre & 8 pair for the Singing Boyes............	2	16	0
Crape for the Beadles Staffe & Chelsea love Ribbd Hatband & Gloves	0	7	6
49 pair Cullerd Topt Gloves poynted & welted wth black for the Lords & Gentlemens Servants	3	13	6
For hanging a Roome to receive the Lords Supporters of The Palle att Westmr Abbey in deep mourning with Cloth and the Seates coverd	4	0	0
12 large silver sconces for the Roome	0	12	0
Paid for the use of the Roome 20/- for Carpenters worke & use of Timber 12/-		12	0
Paid the Grave Digger by Order	0	5	0
Paid Mr Crump Herauld att Armes 5 Ginns	5	7	6
Paid 2 Hackney Coaches wth Company back to Chelsea	0	8	0
4 Men in mourning to attend the State 3 dayes	1	16	0
8 Men in mourning besides my Selfe to attend the ffunerall	2	0	0
ffor Irons to putt up the Trophys in the Abby and workmanship	2	5	0
ffor covering 2 Outside fframes in mourning for the 2 Achievmts Cramps & Nayles	1	5	0
	£585	14	0

ffor my owne attendance & Coach hire what yor Honr pleaseth

Received March ye 26th 1713 of The Rt. Honle The Lady Ann Vaughan the sume of five hunderd & Eighty Pounds in full of the bill & all demands ffor the Society of Upholsters.	£580	0	0

Witness Rand. Baron, an upholster.

Golden Grove (old)

ANNE, DUCHESS OF BOLTON
1690-1751

Mistress of Golden Grove

THE LADY ANNE VAUGHAN occupies a significant position in the history of the ancient Carmarthenshire family of Vaughan of Golden Grove, inasmuch as she formed the bridge, so to speak, between the original owners who had been established there for many generations and the cadet line which succeeded to the property in the 18th century. By her marriage she entered the highest rank of the peerage and increased the already high prestige of her family, but by so doing she almost contributed to the destruction of those material possessions that her ancestors, by their ability and shrewdness, had patiently amassed over the years. On two former occasions, because of the turbulence of national affairs, the fortunes of the Vaughans had narrowly escaped shipwreck. A third calamity was again to threaten to overwhelm them, this time by the unpredictable course of a matrimonial venture of which the Lady Anne was the storm centre.

Anne was the daughter and heiress of John (Vaughan) third and last Earl of Carbery by his second wife, Anne Savile, daughter of George, first Marquess of Halifax by Dorothy Spencer, daughter of Henry, Earl of Sunderland. Her mother died shortly after her birth, and the register of St. Andrew's Holborn records her burial on 23 January, 1689-90.

Nothing is known of the little girl's upbringing apart from the fact that she was privately educated by a pious governess to whose influence her lifelong interest in books, pictures, and *objets d'art* may be attributed. As she grew older she brought great comfort to her bereaved father who showered the most affectionate attentions on her. She became also an object of especial interest to a wider circle, even to many who had never seen her, and impecunious noblemen and ambitious matrons noted with satisfaction the progress of this sole heiress to vast possessions.

Anne had barely left kindergarten when her father's friend, thirty years her senior, claimed her hand. This was Charles Talbot, Earl of Shrewsbury, who had been advanced to the dignity of a dukedom in 1694; he was an experienced, if not successful, hunter of heiresses. It had been rumoured in 1676 that he was to marry Mrs. Downes "sister to him killed last year at Epsom". In February 1692-3 he had journeyed "into Glamorganshire to marry Mrs. Thomas an heiress who hath £4,000 per annum and £2,000 in money". But the nobleman

John Vaughan Esq.

discovered that rich widows can be hard bargainers, and his suits came to nought. About 1695 he told Carbery that he had noticed a common quartering in the Vaughan and Talbot escutcheons, and hinted that their distant kinship might perhaps be transformed into a far closer one. Though by no means adverse to the proposition of one who was an intimate friend, Carbery felt disinclined to commit the future of his daughter at this stage. But Shrewsbury was nothing if not persistent, and in October 1698 the renewal of the suit was noticed by a contemporary who wrote "it's discoursed again that the Duke of Shrewsbury is to be married to the only daughter of the Earl of Carbery". The siege of the Lady Anne continued for some years. In August 1699 Luttrell reported that "the Duke of Shrewsbury, now well in health, and lately come to town, 'tis said to be married to the only daughter and heiress of the Earl of Carbery", and on 5 March, 1699-1700 Lord Bellmont wrote to congratulate Shrewsbury on the prospective union. The outcome seemed inevitable and in September 1700 Lord Lexington was informed that "the articles are at last adjusted with old Carbery". However the congratulations proved premature, the certainties but empty shadows, for the negotiations broke down.

The reasons for the failure of the suit are not known, but a letter written on 9 September 1700 by John Methuen to James Vernon seems to suggest that indifferent health may have had something to do with it – "I am pleased to hear the match of the Duke of Shrewsbury proceeds, hoping his health is then in some good condition and that his thoughts will be turned towards this world." Whatever the reason, Shrewsbury abandoned the pursuit of Carbery's daughter, and whether the state of his health improved or not, matrimony finally overtook him in 1705 when he married at his lodgings at Augsburg in Bavaria, a determined widow of foreign extraction. Anne returned to her dolls and primers, and we hear of no further matrimonial angling until after her father's death.

The Earl of Carbery died on 16 January 1712-13, aged 73. By his will, dated 25 May 1710, he left all his property, both real and personal, to his only child and heiress, with annuities of £150 to each of his two maiden sisters the Ladies Frances and Althamia Vaughan. The will was proved in London on 2 February 1712-13 by the executors, Richard Vaughan of Derwydd and John Vaughan of Derllys, to whose special care the late earl had entrusted his young daughter. A contemporary observer noted that, "though he has left his daughter £4,000 per annum besides a great personal estate, was contented rather to keep all he had gotten for himself, than to dispose of her well in marriage with any part of it, or the settlement on or after his death though 84 (*sic*) years old". Whatever Carbery's reason may have been for not disposing of his daughter in marriage, it appears not unlikely that he had discouraged or postponed such an event.

The Lady Anne's directions conveyed through her trustee, Richard Vaughan, to Morgan Davies of Dryslwyn, her Carmarthenshire agent at this time, provide an insight to her character. On 20 January she ordered Davies "to put himself and all the Domestick and household servants now at Golden Grove into Mourning and that he should Inform himself what Bountys and Charities were used to be distributed or bestowed upon poor Indigent people upon the death of other her Ladyshipps Ancestors at Golden Grove, and that her Ladyshipp will have this looked upon as her Father's own Act because she believes if he had made the Codicill he intended these things would have been directed and provided for therein".

On 27 January, the eve of the Earl's funeral, Lady Anne assured Morgan Davies that she "would alwayes shew a particular Regard to all her Father's Faithfull Friends and Servants and for the present Encouraged him to proceed cheerfully in the Execution of all those powers and commissions granted him by my Lord her Father", and instructed him to examine the estate accounts with the assistance of an experienced accountant and Mr. Arthur Price the attorney, telling him "that he might depend upon fair usage, for her Ladyshipp designed to give it [the account] in Charge to the Accomptants that they should take Equall care not to doe wrong to any person as to doe her Right, and if any matter were dubious they should rather determine against her Interest *It being her Ladyship's principle rather to Suffer than to do Wrong*".

On 12 February, she asks Davies to forward a rental of the estate, to be filled in on a special form she encloses: she wishes it so "for she finds it troublesome to apprize her selfe to my Lord her Father's Bookes being according to the scheme of Merchants Accounts which is dark and Abstruse to such as have not been long versed in them", she wants "Clearness and Plaines" in the accounts, and as she intends to come to Golden Grove in the summer, he should consider steps for her reception – "She has noe Saddle horses nor Furniture here for her servants and therefore you must send word in Time how far you can

---

THE
CASE

Of the Right Honourable the Lady *Anne Vaughan*, touching the *Pre* and *Post*-Fines in *South Wales*.

T H A T the Crown by an undoubted Right and antient Prerogative, is legally intituled to certain Fines upon the Alienation of Estates by Fine or Recovery.

T H A T those Profits arising to the Crown, are commonly called the *Pre* and *Post* Fines; but upon Alienations by Recovery, a *Pre*-Fine only is to be paid.

T H A T the *Pre*-Fine is paid for the Crowns granting the Original Writ, on which such Fine or Recovery is grounded ; and the only Rule prescribed by Law for the rating or ascertaining the *Pre*-Fine, is to admit the Party to compound the same at abont 2 *s.* in the Pound according to the yearly Value of such Estates, which *Pre*-Fine being thus ascertained, the *Post*-Fine (which is sometimes called by the Name of the King or Queen's Silver, of the Fine which is paid *Pro Licentia Concordandi*) is always as much, and half as much more as is the *Pre*-Fine.

T H A T those *Pre*-Fines and *Post*-Fines in the Six Counties of *South Wales*, have together with the Profits arising from the Original Seal been antiently and usually Leased, and let to Farm by the Kings and Queens of this Realm, at the certain Yearly reserved Rent of 134 *l.* 4 *s.*

The Grandfather, or Great Grandfather of the Lady *Anne Vaughan* purchased the said Lease ; which by frequent Renewals hath continued in her Family ever since, except that the same, amongst other the Estates of her Family, was Seized and Sequestred in the late times of Usurpation, for their Loyalty and firm Adherence to the Royal Family, through the whole Course of the Civil Wars.

T H A T the yearly Profits and Advantage of the said Farm are not greater than what are usually made

"Clearness and plainess" in the accounts

accomodate her from Golden Grove. Her Ladyship hath six black horses for her Coach, but for fear any Accident or Mischance if you have any strong Colts of their Colour at Golden Grove it may be adviseable to break one or two of them and in case no mischance happens in soe long a Journey they may be sent to Market without loss or prejudice."

Anne was 23 years of age when her father died, eligible, wealthy, owner of the largest estate in south-west Wales, so that we are not surprised to read in a letter written on 27 February 1712-13: "There is such running after my Lord Carbery's rich daughter as you never saw. My Lord Lumley makes the greatest bustle . . . My Lord Winchester and My Lord Hertford are also in pursuit." The chase was soon over, for on 31 March 1713 we hear that "My Lord Winchester is to be the happy man that marries my Lady Ann Vaughan." The rapid progress towards the altar, barely two months after the restraining hand of Carbery had been removed, strengthens the view that the father had been disinclined to part with her.

The "happy man," Charles Pawlett. Marquess of Winchester, the 28 year old son and heir of the Duke of Bolton, was a well-known gallant of that sophisticated age. There is ample evidence that the prospective bride and her kinsfolk were highly satisfied with the arrangement. The attitude of the bridegroom is less clear, but what does emerge with distressing clarity is that he was actuated and animated by the most mercenary of motives, regarding his wife merely as a financial convenience and her estate as a means of liquidating those liabilities that his follies had incurred. Fortunately for Anne, she found champions to whose vigilance the Golden Grove estate owed its continued existence. Indeed, had it not been for them, the tale of Golden Grove would have ended here. They were her cousins. Richard Vaughan of Derwydd, his brother John Vaughan of Derllys, both barristers-at-law, knowledgeable in legal intricacies, the latter a Member of Parliament, both of them men of affairs, alert, proud of their ancestry and devoted to the Lady Anne. When John and Richard Vaughan died, in 1722 and 1724 respectively, another cousin, Richard Vaughan of Shenfield, became her champion, and after his death in 1729, his son John proved as vigorous a protector as ever his father had been, although, as we shall see, his motives may have been less disinterested.

At the time of his marriage Lord Winchester was in debt to the extent of £4,000, heir to a ducal title and an encumbered estate. By the marriage settlement executed on 20 and 21 July 1713, Anne agreed to pay a lump sum of £15,000 to the Duke of Bolton, and to settle the Golden Grove estate on her prospective husband and their issue, and in default of issue to the wife and husband in survivorship, with remainder to such person or persons as Anne should name; the Duke was to be responsible for paying his son's pre-marital debts; Anne was to receive £1,500 per annum and the rents from certain parts of the Golden Grove property reserved to her sole use; power was given to husband and wife to make leases during their joint lives of any parts of the estate at such rents and on such terms as they should think fit. Anne's trustees were all kinsfolk of the house of Golden Grove – Sir Thomas Stepney of Llanelly, Sir Edward Mansel of Trimsaran, Sir Nicholas Williams of Edwinsford, baronets, Griffith Rice of Newton, the Richard and John Vaughan of whom we have spoken earlier – to whom the following lands were conveyed: Golden Grove and demesne, the castles of Kidwelly, Emlyn, Dryslwyn, Carreg Cennen and Llandovery, the lordships and manors of Kidwelly, Carnwallon, Iscennen, Emlyn, Elfet, Widigada, Traian March, Traian Morgan, Traian Clinton, St. Clears, Dryslwyn, Cilsaen, Alltygaer, Llanfihangel Cilfargen. Llandovery, Perfedd, Hirfryn alias Llanfairarybryn, Faerdref, and Felindre Sawdde, with their appurtenances. In order to make up the sum of £15,000 agreed upon, Anne mortgaged part of her realty for £6,000 on 18 July 1713.

The settlement signed sealed and delivered, and the £15,000 duly handed over, the marriage took place on 1 August 1713, and the newly-weds settled down in Winchester's London house in Marlborough Street. The father-in-law having got his hands on the dowry showed no desire to carry out the contract by paying his son's debts, a circumstance that caused Anne to say later that she would not have remained content with a mere £1,500 per annum had she known how the Duke was going to behave. Lord Winchester lost no time in attempting to squeeze out further sums of money from his wife's resources, by arranging leases and trying to sell the considerable timber that grew on the Carmarthenshire estates. He laid hands on every penny he could find with the result that the small annuities due to Lady Winchester's two aunts, the Ladies Frances and Althamia Vaughan, could not be paid. Accordingly the annuitants borrowed the money from Rachel, Lady Russell, to whom they assigned the annuities on 13 April 1715. Lady Russell, a businesslike woman, obliged Winchester to give securities in the matter, which he did by granting her some of his wife's estates to be held by her until such time as he discharged the accumulated annuities.[2]

Lady Winchester's father, grandfather and great-grandfather had been enthusiastic advocates of afforestation, and as a result the best woodlands in the whole of south Wales were to be found on the Golden Grove estate at the beginning of the 18th century. Richard Vaughan, the trustee, declared early in 1714 that "there are woods on the estate fit to be cut and should have been cut many years ago had not an unaccountable regard in my Lady's ancestors for them made them averse to it". Anne had inherited this attitude, and during the negotiations on her marriage settlement had refused absolutely to grant power to cut down the woodlands in the vicinity of Golden Grove "which make the Beauty and Ornament of the Seat" as she put it, and had "ye preservation of a seat that had continued soe long in her Family soe much at Heart that she cannot think of doing any act which in consequence may tend to its Ruin and Defacement". Most leases show her desire in this connection, such as the clause in a lease for 99 years she granted on 2 October 1714 to David Evan Howell of Llangunnor, whereby he was to plant an ash and an oak every year during the term of the lease. Nevertheless, certain woodlands had been surveyed in her father's lifetime and timber earmarked for felling, and these she was quite willing to surrender. Winchester did not share his wife's concern for the timber or for the future of the inheritance, and as a result of his indifference the upstart family of Dyer of Aberglasney was able to encroach upon certain manorial rights vested in the Vaughans from time beyond which the memory of man did not run. The Golden Grove timber represented money. And Winchester wanted that money.

But there was much more to the misunderstanding than this. Well disposed friends watched the deterioration of relations with uneasiness and alarm. The Lady Halifax, and the Lady Russell whose first husband had been Francis, Lord Vaughan, tried to reconcile husband and wife, but without success. Although the union was no love match, this by itself need not have constituted a serious disadvantage, and many sensible partners united under similar circumstances, a normal feature of the matrimonial arrangements of those days, more often than not made a go of things and went together through life very prettily. However there was a marked difference of temperament between Anne and her husband; this together with the money difficulties of the latter, proved too severe a strain. Winchester became more importunate; Anne declined to produce the extra money at the expense of the estate. The Duke appointed an agent to view the woodlands, and Anne immediately ordered that no trees were to be cut, saying "I cannot in that particular depend upon the person my Lord has trusted". Matters went from bad to worse, "My Lord made her an early confession of his aversion" wrote Lady Mary Wortley Montagu, and within six months of the nuptials he left her.

In May 1714 Winchester instructed Richard Robinson of St. Andrew's Holborn, solicitor, to tell Lady Winchester "he would not live under the same roofe with a woman [should] use him so, and that he would let the house immediately", told him to prepare a deed of separation as speedily as possible, and to insist on her agreement to a sale of the timber "to go towards paying his debts". Robinson communicated with Richard Vaughan and asked him to convey these sentiments to Lady Winchester since he regarded them so "shocking and brutal" that he could find no heart to undertake the commission himself.

Richard Vaughan who had done his best to avoid a breach, now addressed a dignified and eminently sensible letter to Lord Winchester. He reminded Winchester that the late Lord Carbery "did very often in the most pathetick terms recommend his daughter and her interests to my care and friendship"; it appeared that the trouble had been occasioned because of "a mutual jealousie, of the want of that love, affection, and esteem which ought to be inseparable from man and wife"; indeed Anne had the highest regard for Winchester and his family, and had rejected offers of marriage from two noblemen, one of whom was prepared to let her possess and enjoy her own real estate "as well as £9,000 down," while the other was anxious to grant her a jointure of £2,000 yearly "as well as £10,000 down"; these offers she turned away because of her affection for Lord Winchester; by her marriage settlement she had behaved very handsomely, and her willingness to accept only £1,500 per annum for herself was further evidence of her generosity; she was not devoid of faults but none of them justified her husband's demand for separation.

Winchester would not listen. His debtors had somehow to be appeased. The giant oaks of Golden Grove, tantalising in their majesty, offered the solution. The woodman's axe alone could save him.

No compromise could be made. The deed of separation, dated 28 July 1714, assigned Golden Grove and its demesne, the Old and New Parks, and certain lands in the parishes of Llanfihangel Aberbythych and Llangathen, to Lady Winchester, while the profits and rents of the remainder of the estate were to be enjoyed by Lord Winchester so long as his father, the Duke of Bolton lived and after whose death the whole property was to revert to Lady Winchester, absolutely; she was also to enjoy her personal estate at the London house and at Golden Grove, to have coal from the colliery on the Great Mountain worked by William Price under a lease from the late Earl of Carbery, with full power to sell timber to raise money for repairing properties on the estate and for no other purpose; should Lord Winchester survive his wife, his interest under the marriage settlement of the previous year was not to be impeached by the provisions of the deed of separation; finally, she was to have no responsibility whatsoever for her husband's debts. The arrangement was weighted heavily in Anne's favour.

Realisation of the position soon brought Winchester to his senses, and three months after signing the deed he came to Anne, a reconciliation took place, and the terms of the marriage settlement became operative again.

Winchester was a man of some ability. Using his wife's interest he defeated, in 1714, Sir Thomas Powell in a contest for Carmarthenshire which he represented in Parliament until 1717 when he was called to the House of Lords as Baron Pawlet of Basing. In 1715 he was appointed Steward of the Royal manors of Carmarthenshire and Cardiganshire, Governor of Milford Haven, Vice-Admiral of South Wales, and Lord Lieutenant of Carmarthenshire and Glamorganshire, being re-gazetted to those lieutenancies after the accession of King George II, to whom, as Prince of Wales, he had been a Lord of the Bedchamber from 1714 to 1722. In 1716 he was appointed Chamberlain of Brecknock and of the counties of Brecon, Radnor and Glamorgan. He succeeded his father as Duke of Bolton on 21 January 1721-22, and received the Garter later in that year, and in 1725 became a Privy Councillor. Colonel of the Horse Guards (Blue) from 1717 to 1722, he was promoted Major General in 1739, and Lieutenant General in 1745 when he raised and commanded a regiment of foot for service against the Jacobites.

There can be little doubt that Anne was genuinely fond of her husband, and after the reconciliation they got on reasonably well, although the latter's enthusiasm seems occasionally to have been somewhat restrained. When Richard Vaughan sent seventeen leases for Anne's signature on 10 August 1715, his accompanying letter says, "the Town talks as much as ever of my Lord's Disposition towards your Ladyship, which they found on his never going down to you all this time, when he seldom or ever attends the House, but this (is) not true for he is there upon all the Grand Occasions which indeed happen not very often". He added that Winchester still owed a considerable sum on account of his last election as Member of Parliament, which he must pay if he expects to be chosen again.

Most of their lives were spent in London. Nevertheless Anne did not lose touch with Carmarthenshire. For many years she continued to pay yearly pensions to those servants who had outlived their working days, like Morgan Rees the former gardener of Golden Grove who received £5 yearly from her. She paid a yearly charity of £20 to the parson, churchwardens and overseers of the parish of Llanfihangel Aberbythych, for distribution among the poor. She insisted that the park wall be kept in repair, and that the herd of deer that roamed within should never be allowed to fall below 250 in number. In 1715 she was negotiating about letting the Great Park for £40 per annum, on a yearly tenancy, among the conditions being that the tenant should preserve the number of deer already noted and to buy "the wild cattle that are now therein". Her father's agent, Morgan Davies of Dryslwyn, was followed by Arthur Price of Dyffryn, an able attorney who managed the estate practically throughout the Duchess's life. Among officials appointed by the Duke, was Grismond Philipps of Cwmgwili as steward of the extensive lordships of Iscennen, Elfed and Widigada, Arthur Price as co-steward of Widigada from 1727 onwards, Phillip Jones of Llether Neuadd as a steward for the manors of Mabelfryw, Mabedrud, and Forest Glyn Cothi, and Rees Price who looked after the lordship of Kidwelly.

The bogey of debt continued to haunt the Duke who turned to Anne when occasions became pressing. Time and again she came to the rescue, going well beyond the terms of the marriage settlement to do so. Under their joint signature large numbers of leases were granted and the consideration monies and rents there-from handed to the anxious Duke; manorial rights such as escheats, were sold, the Pre- and Post-Fines in South Wales, which she held, were mortgaged for £3,700; she produced £700 out of her own purse on one occasion, and on another sold £1,100 worth of timber and £200 worth of stock at Golden Grove. She even paid annuities to legatees who had benefited under the will of the Duke's late father.

However, all these sums went with the wind, and despite his wife's assistance, he successfully kept solvency at arm's length. By 1724 his position had become really serious, and Anne came to his rescue once more to the extent of the large sum of £20,000. In order to raise this sum, the Duchess consented to an Act of Parliament to explain the power in her settlement, and to make it more effectual for the purpose of raising the money, as a result of which, Sir Peter King, Lord Chief Justice, and James Colebrooke of London, advanced the £20,000 on 25 March 1725, being secured by a mortgage on the Golden Grove estate at 4½ per cent, a charge that weighed heavily on the estate for over three-quarters of a century. These sums she raised to meet the Duke's occasions, and, as she expressed it, "to make him easy". By 1728 she had given her husband £28,500, exclusive of the £15,000 of the marriage settlement and the yearly rents and profits derived from his interest in her estate, and to do so had encumbered her inheritance to the extent of £37,000. She had even raised mortgages on her own account, to the extent of £1,000 and £745 from her kinsfolk John Vaughan of Shenfield Place and Miss Sophia Vaughan of Ormond Street, London, besides several other smaller sums secured by bonds and specialities. Despite the generous co-operation of his wife, the Duke neglected to attend to such matters as the repair of Golden Grove house and other properties on the estate he never visited, and even to pay certain fixed charges, conduct which ultimately brought further embarrassment to him and his Duchess. To him, Golden Grove was the golden goose, and the course of events, if allowed to continue, must inevitably have ended in a way similar to that in the fairy tale.

Had it not been for Richard and John Vaughan of Shenfield, the Duchess would have been bereft of her patrimony. However, they insisted that the Duke produced ample securities for the greater sums, and in 1725 had obliged him to give securities for the £20,000 out of his own properties. This proved a very sore point, and for many years afterwards the Duke tried all manner of means to cajole Anne to surrender these securities. On more than one occasion she inclined to weaken, but the watchful Vaughans and the trustees stepped in and averted the fatal step. The Duke complained often of her commerce with the Vaughans, alleging that by consulting them she merely added to her own legal expenses. When he got her alone he was able to make headway, as in 1726 for instance when "he made promises to her in private" and persuaded her to prevail upon her trustees to surrender the old lease of the Pre- and Post-Fines so that she could obtain a renewal on more favourable terms. She succeeded in gaining the co-operation of the trustees in the matter, and on 16 July 1726, the Prince of Wales granted a new lease, which the delighted Duke promptly mortgaged to one John Patlock on 28 September of the same year. Not content with this he initiated steps actually to sell the mortgaged lease, but to this the shorn Duchess returned a firm no.

A further complication now attended the Hogarthian career of this light-hearted nobleman. He fell in love with a bewitching actress of the London stage, one Lavinia Beswick, known more commonly as Lavinia Fenton. who had become the "rage" of London as Polly Peachum of *The Beggar's Opera*. In 1728 the infatuated Duke took her off the stage, set her up in a London house, and settled £400 a year on her. This situation added to his financial disorders, and he renewed his onslaught on the resources of Golden Grove. Towards the end of 1729 he left the Duchess declaring he would never live with her more. They never met again and communicated only through third parties.

The deserted Duchess remained in the house in Marlborough Street. On 7 February 1730-1, the Duke sent her a message by the hands of Lady Pawlet, stating that he wanted a legal separation and inviting proposals to the end.

The ensuing bargaining, protracted for over a year, was marked by proposals and counterproposals, claims and counterclaims, sometimes degenerating into recriminations and petty wrangles over quite minor matters. Constantly advised by her counsel Gilbert Horsman and John Wainwright of Lincoln's Inn, the attorney John Howell, Madam Bridget Bevan and of course the Vaughans, the Duchess emerges from the sorry strife with far greater dignity than the Duke. His main object was to induce her to give up his security for the £20,000 mortgage and to allow him greater power over the estate: in return, he undertook to advance her annual income to £2,000, and to provide her with certain personalty, including all her books at Hackwood Park (the Duke's Hampshire seat) and articles of furniture, plate, coach, liveries, family pictures and so on. She agreed to give up the security on condition that he resigned

Legal wrangles

all interest in her estate absolutely, provided her with ample securities against his debts, and paid her the interest of three quarters of £20,000 during his lifetime, a money payment of £500 down, and particular personalty which she specified in detail. Around these proposals, wordy warfare raged for many months. Prompted by her advisers the Duchess asked for details of the Duke's financial position, a view of vouchers and receipts, and the precise manner in which he would indemnify her estate against his debts. The Duke avoided committing himself in detail, often changed his ground, and tried to embarrass her by petty annoyances. When Arthur Price of Llandybie, the attorney who received the rents of the Welsh estates, called on the Duke, he was brusquely sent on his way with a flea in his ear, and when the Duchess took up the cudgels on behalf of the aggrieved attorney, the Duke denied any harshness, blandly saying that all he had in mind was to hurry the attorney back to Carmarthen so that he could apply himself to the affairs of the estate and to avoid further expense by detaining him "in Town". He stopped her supply of venison from his park. He interfered with her servants. He charged her with maligning his character, to which she spiritedly replied that "she had no need, and therefore did not require to asperse the Duke's character to justify her own, nor would it ever be in his power to lessen hers". She stood firm in her determination not to give up the securities, the crux of the whole affair.

In December 1731 he decided to remove the Duchess from London, away from the troublesome Vaughan relations and the lawyers so near at hand. Saying he wished to give up his house in Marlborough Street as a measure of economy, he asked her to move to Abberstone House in Hampshire which would be prepared for her reception and staffed with the necessary servants. She replied that her affairs would not allow her to leave London at the moment. To his renewed attempts to make her name a date for departure, she found a series of excuses to defer an answer.

This state of affairs might have continued indefinitely, had not word been brought to the Duchess that her husband was trying privately to sell a lease of a part of the Golden Grove estate. Acting on advice she promptly filed a Bill in Equity against him. When served with a copy of the Bill, the Duke flew into a towering rage, and accompanied by a footman drove to the house in Marlborough Street at about 2 o'clock in the morning. Although all

A Ducal "domestic"

were asleep he tried to burst into the Duchess's apartment by a back door. But this was locked, and the angry man hammered at it "with both hands and feet, very hard". He then sent his servant to the front door which was found to be locked also. When he repeated his visit in the following night he experienced a similar reception. Following this rebuff, he sent a private message to the groom of the chambers to see that the doors were unlocked when he came on the third night. Accordingly, that functionary instructed the Duchess's woman who told the chambermaid who told her mistress. The keys were again turned in the locks.

On 14 December the baffled husband ordered her to go to Abberstone. In her reply she reminded him that when a surveyor had examined the house some three years previously, it had been reported that the building was in such condition as to be unsafe for habitation, and added that the surveyor would give that testimony on oath if required.

But he was not finished yet. On 1 January 1731-2 he sacked the housekeeper, butler, cook, kitchen maid, housemaid and two footmen, who were sympathisers of his wife. This left only the secretary and groom of chambers, both of the Duke's "party". Thoroughly alarmed and feeling no longer safe, the Duchess slipped away on 3 January and took refuge at the home of her husband's sisters who had always been kind to her. Having received assurance from a lawyer of Doctors' Commons that her act would not entitle the Duke to proceed against her in the ecclesiastical courts nor prejudice her claim to alimony, she rented a house in London and set up on her own account.

Negotiations were re-opened early in February, the Lady Mary Moore, the Duke's sister, acting as go-between. He reiterated the demand for the surrender of his security for the £20,000, and made some attractive offers if she would agree to his main proposition.

Her advisers showed that the Duke had no power to make such offers. It was no good. He threw in the towel, having failed to obtain any further concessions beyond the terms of the marriage settlement of 1714. Indeed his chagrin induced some remorse, for his final words on 13 February to Lady Moore, which he desired should be transmitted to his wife were, "I hope they (i.e. the terms) are contributing as much as I can to her Happyness, as long as I live, and will in some measure make amends for so many years of misfortune". They did not meet again. The Duke remained with his inamorato who bore him illegitimate sons on whom the surname Pawlett was bestowed.

The Duke had been a poor manager and an unsatisfactory husband. When his debts became pressing he wrung money out of his wife, when that source failed he resorted to mortgages. When a mortgage was called in he cheerfully mortgaged another slice of territory to meet the occasion. And so it had gone on. Had he been more frugal perhaps, he might have avoided the octopus of debt that now enwrapped him.

The Duchess of Bolton passed the remainder of her life in London, with occasional stays at Windsor Castle where she had apartments. Why did she not return to Golden Grove embosomed among the trees which it had been her concern to preserve? There had been good reason. Both the Duke and Duchess were very much "London-folk," and it is doubtful whether they ever wished to spend any considerable time at the Carmarthenshire seat. In 1729 the Duke had given permission to one of his poor relations to reside at Golden Grove as it lay "in a Cheap Country," and sent orders for an apartment to be aired and prepared for his reception. But "the person Employ'd to Air the House left ye ffire carlessly, whereby the House was burnt down", as the Duke's answer to one of his wife's suits, testified. In fact, about three-quarters of the residence suffered, and by the frantic efforts of the servants some of its valuable contents were saved. Historians have reason to lament the loss of family muniments consumed in the blaze, and a later inheritor of the estate had to expend

A blazing hearth

much time and money in searching in the Tower of London for records of the numerous Crown grants that had been made to the Vaughans during earlier reigns.

A clause in the marriage settlement bound the Duke to "sufficiently repair and keep in good repair the said capital messuage called Golden Grove and so leave the same at the time of his decease, he being allowed to cut sufficient timber for the repairing the same that is not in any walks or any ways ornamental to the same messuage". Evidently he had not shown any active interest in the place before the conflagration, and certainly not afterwards. In 1736 the Duchess took counsel's opinion as to the best method of obliging the Duke to rebuild and repair the house, as well as the out-houses and offices, then described as being in a sad state. However, it was considered that even if he were adjudged guilty of a breach of covenant it remained doubtful whether the considerable sum required would be forthcoming from his hollow coffers, and his wife's trustees had not sufficient money to apply for the purpose so long as the Duke lived. During Trinity Term of 10 George II, an action was brought against him by the Earl of Chesterfield, one of the trustees of the marriage settlement, who stated that although the Duke was allowed to cut timber for the maintenance of the mansion, he had carried out no repairs, with the result that all the tiling, thatching, covering, walling, plastering, painting, wainscotting, flooring, doors, windows, etc., were decayed. The Duke answered that he had shown no neglect prior to the fire, and had found no time to attend to the matter since that unfortunate event. Without lord or lady the house mouldered and crumbled for another twenty years before an energetic heir restored it to a semblance of its former glory.

The peccadillos and defections of the Duke resulted in several protracted lawsuits which provide us with glimpses of what had taken place in earlier days, thereby rescuing from total oblivion some of the evidence that had perished in the flames. The case relating to a charity school at Bristol will serve as an illustration. As long ago as the days of Charles I there had been a fee-farm rent amounting annually to £129 6s. 9¾d. issuing from the lordship of Kidwelly and the commotes of Carnwallon and Iscennen, of which the Golden Grove family had been manorial lords since the time of the first Earl of Carbery. By a series of transactions which need not be followed in detail, the rent had become vested in Edward Colston, who, Bristol-born, had become a prosperous London merchant. Colston founded a charity School at his birthplace for the education of fifty poor boys, and on 25 November 1708 conveyed certain properties and the said fee-farm rent, to the Master, Warden, Assistants and Commonalty of Merchant Adventurers within the City of Bristol as trustees of the charity. The last Earl of Carbery and, in due course, the Duke and Duchess of Bolton paid the annual charge to the Bristol school. However, after Michaelmas 1736 payments ceased and when the Merchant Adventurers enquired into the reasons thereof, the Duke and Duchess denied that they were seized of the said lordships and commotes, and submitted that even if such payments had been made it had been wrong for them to have done so. Lack of deeds and writings prevented the Merchant Adventurers from distraining, and so they instituted a suit in the High Court of Chancery. The "law's delays" and the equivocations of the ducal pair, for once acting in unison, caused the suit to drag on for many years. Finally, the answers to the Duke taken at his house in Hanover Square on 9 June 1746, and of the Duchess taken at Windsor Castle on 11 August following, admitted that such a rent had once been charged on some lands within the lordship and commotes, but that they could not identify these particular lands. The defendants were able to impose further delays on the proceedings, but in 1749 the action ended, and on 24 June of that year the Court ordered them to pay arrears and costs which came to £1,406 10s. 6½d., and to continue the annual payments. The charge was still being paid by the owners of Golden Grove in the 19th century.

No part of the estate, however far-flung, was safe from the Duke. About 1745 he received £700 for some of the property in Jamaica, which had been acquired by the Duchess's father when Governor of that island in the time of Charles II. So vague and uncertain was the family about this particular matter that enquiries were still being made as late as 1808 as to the extent of the properties the Vaughans owned in Jamaica, one of which bore the name of Golden Grove after the Welsh home of the original owners. Despite the encumbrances and the weight of the Duke, perched on top like some Old Man of the Sea, the main estate held together.

An account book once belonging to the Duchess provides us with information about her social and domestic life from 1725 to 1752, and some entries contain clues to her character. She made annual payments towards the support of the Charity schools at Basing, Basingstoke, and Winslade, and from 1725 onwards paid considerable sums towards the salaries of the teachers and for providing clothing for the pupils. Her religious connections are indicated by the following payments – on 17 July 1725 she paid £8 being 1¼ years' rent for "the Pewes in Mareybone Chapell," on 27 September 1727 £8, a year's rent, for "a pew in Trinity Chapell," and on 14 May 1729, £18 10s. 0d. for "Her Grace's Seat and Servant" in the same chapel.

Many entries refer to her wardrobe, the very numerous references to the buying of stays and corsets, "strapping and girdles," suggest that fine ladies of those days were not unacquainted with besetting physical problems that our contemporary ladies are at such pains to combat. On 5 October 1727 she paid Francis France the sum of £25 "for Ermin for Coronation Robes". Other purchases include white kid gloves (bought by the dozen pairs), riding coats, silk hose, materials such as brocades, lawn, satins, flowered cambric, muslin, Indian sprigged muslin, velvets, hooped petticoats, "gold trimming" for aprons and for shoes, hoods, mantles, gowns, shifts, night-gowns at 3s. 6d. apiece, silk garters at 3s. a pair, 19 yards of flowered silk "for a sack" for £4 15s. 0d., and so on. From 1736 onwards evidence of retrenchment is shown by such entries as 1s. 6d. for cleaning silver lace, "dying a quilted petticoat" (2s. 6d.), altering a velvet hood and a hooped petticoat, dying gloves and stockings.

Nevertheless she continued to add to her wardrobe, and paid £140 10s. 5d. for clothes during the period November 1737 to June 1738, and numerous payments to mantua-makers.

Her love of finery led to an increase in the contents of her jewel box – £73 10s. 0d. "for jewels" on 17 October 1729; £11 4s. 6d. "for jewels" on 17 November 1731; £39 18s. 0d. for pearls which included four small pearl drops of 23 carat, two large ones of 19 Carat, and two of 10 carat in her ear-rings, on 11 April 1733; in March 1735 she bought two necklaces and a fan, in 1736 she paid 10s. 6d. for a pair of French pearl pendants, and 7s. for a French pearl necklace. To the period of comparative economy belongs the entry "6s. for 2 rows of false garnets to put on a necklace" (25 February 1737-8) and 2s. "for new mounting a black fan".

She was addicted to snuff, although it is difficult to believe that the vast quantities she bought, were all for her personal use, such as 8 shillings for a pound of snuff on 24 November 1736 and a similar quantity on 11 December following. The gold snuff box she bought for £40 on 18 June 1731, was later bequeathed to her friend Lady Hotham, and in 1737 she bought six "iron snuff boxes" for about 3 shillings apiece.

She bought a great deal of furniture for the house in Marlborough Street during the years 1726-1729. Francis Sheldon was responsible for many pieces, such as a fine India chest on a gold frame for £21, and making ducal coronets for gilt wall mirrors amounting to £44 14s. 0d. She furnished her bedroom with green valances, curtain and stuffs, had a new four-poster bed made with feather mattress and bolsters, and green hangings, and had crimson damask hangings made for win-dows in other rooms. Most of the furniture was

made of walnut and mahogany. In 1728 she paid £14 for a chimney-piece glass in a gold frame, two pier glass frames with extra gilding to them. Her mahogany dressing table cost £5 5s. 0d., two other mahogany tables £2 5s. 0d., and two tea-tables £7, a needlework screen in walnut frame £2 2s. 0d.; she bought two pairs of "brass arms" for £1 10s. 0d. in 1727, and two years later paid £6 for a pair of glass sconces "in gold frames and brass arms"; a fine Japan cabinet was acquired for the "blue damask drawing room," three large Japan chests and a coloured Japan cabinet for her bedroom, a walnut chest of drawers with a case of shelves with glass doors, a little tortoiseshell cabinet and an Indian corner cupboard. Some of these she took away to her new London house after the second and final separation from her husband.

A library in her London home and at her husband's Hampshire seat, Hackwood Park, contributed to her literary tastes. Among the books she herself bought were Clark's *Sermons* in ten volumes costing £7 7s. 6d. (June 1731), *History of China* in four volumes for one guinea (December 1736), and the accounts contain several entries such as "for books and binding" £8 15s. 0d. (April 1732). Among possessions later handed down to her heirs were many books and a quantity of silver, the latter being particularly well selected, showing an admirable taste and discrimination.

The considerable sums she paid for chairmen indicate that she walked very little when in Town. For example from 2 June to 2 July 1726 she paid £9 19s. 6d. to her favourite chairman, Abraham Meyrick, for carrying her and supplying flambeaux, and on 11 June 1735 she paid £30 2s. 0d. for chairmen for 28 weeks' service. In June 1730 she paid £36 14s. 0d. for a new Sedan chair. For longer distances she travelled by chaise, complete with driver, footmen, and postillions, provided for her by the Duke.

An entry on 1 March 1737, one shilling "for a leek," shows that she was not unmindful of her ancestry. On 30 March following she was delighted to pay fifteen shillings to a man "for bringing Phebe again when lost" – namely her little pet dog. On November 15 1736, seven shillings and sixpence were paid for a cage to hold her singing canaries.

The Duchess was well served by her house-steward, John Roberts, who with his wife, had been attached to her household since 1725, and perhaps before that year. Roberts spent all his life in her service and acted as one of the executors to her will. His accounts for the last year of her life contain a record of domestic payments which show that she spent her time between London and Windsor Castle. Among the entries for 1750 occur the following – £61 10s. 0d. paid in July, being half a year's wages to her servants; on 7 July money was disbursed "on charity to the poor at her Grace's going to Windsor"; £10 18s. 0d. was paid to Mr. Chappell the bookseller; her expenses for travelling from London to Windsor on one occasion included £2 10s. 1d. for diet, 7s. 6d. to servants at Houndslow, 12 shillings for horses and turnpikes, a total of £3 9s. 7d.; on 30 July, she paid 7s. 6d. for the cartage of twelve frails of raisins to Windsor Castle; her return from Windsor on 7 September amounted to £1 18s. 0d. In September 1750 she was unwell and took a trip to Bath to take the waters, but returned to Windsor early in October. The state of her health is indicated further by the entry made on 20 October that Roberts paid seven shillings to an attorney for engrossing codicils to her will.

She rarely received much more than £1,350 per annum derived from her own direct property in nine Carmarthenshire parishes, which consisted of rents paid by 170 tenants. The remainder of her estate was enjoyed by the Duke who rarely found himself in a position to pay her the annual £1,500 secured for her under the marriage settlement. Nevertheless she lived very comfortably, attended by twelve servants whose combined wages amounted to £123 per annum, in addition to which they received board and lodging, livery, extra allowances when travelling, and of course the coveted vails. Among the senior servants were John Roberts the steward (£30 p.a.), William Keen the butler (£12), Richard Minshull and William Dimond, the footmen (£8 each), a stewardess and housekeeper (£8 each), a cook (£10), and four other maids.

The following episode throws some light on the Duchess's character. Having no children of her own, she decided to leave the estate to her distant cousin, John Vaughan of Shenfield, who like his father, Richard, had proved such a good friend when the Duke was battering at the portals of her property. Extremely proud of her ancestry, she spent hours studying the beautiful illuminated pedigree that had been made for the Vaughans by heralds in the seventeenth century. This document, a *tour de force* of heraldic achievement, was kept in a locked box especially made, and when, nearly a century later, a gentleman who should have known better, tried to remove it from Golden Grove, he found the container too large to be placed in his carriage, and had to abandon his impudent enterprise.

So she chose John Vaughan to be her heir. The Golden Grove estates were to pass to him, and after his death to his eldest son Richard who had been born in 1726. Like so many women (apparently in all ages) the Duchess was quite certain in her own mind who would make the best wife for Master Richard, and set about engineering the event. Her choice fell upon another relative, namely the heiress of part of Derllys and of Derwydd, Elizabeth Lloyd, grand-daughter of John Vaughan of Derllys and niece of that Madam Bevan who had been a constant friend of the Duchess. Richard and Elizabeth were fifth cousins, but there was another and rather curious affinity that had resulted from the fact that the father of the boy had married the mother of the girl, both children being by previous marriages, as shown by the pedigree.

John Vaughan of Shenfield became a widower in 1730, and four years later Elizabeth Lloyd lost her husband. Six years after the latter event, the widower and widow married. The Duchess was delighted, and now saw all the more reason why the son and daughter of the parties should also be united in holy matrimony. Such a marriage would have been of the greatest advantage to the House of Vaughan, for it meant that the estates of Golden Grove, Derwydd, Derllys, Hawksbrook, all in Carmarthenshire, and Shenfield in Essex, would be combined, to produce not only economic and social power, but political as well.

The Duchess did not allow her own failure in matters matrimonial to inhibit her. She knew best. Here was an ideal situation. She set to work, first of all on John Vaughan, who, knowing where he stood in the Duchess's plans, readily agreed to her suggestion.

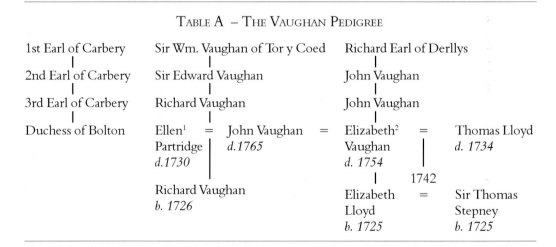

Table A – The Vaughan Pedigree

1st Earl of Carbery	Sir Wm. Vaughan of Tor y Coed	Richard Earl of Derllys		
2nd Earl of Carbery	Sir Edward Vaughan	John Vaughan		
3rd Earl of Carbery	Richard Vaughan	John Vaughan		
Duchess of Bolton	Ellen[1] Partridge *d.1730* = John Vaughan *d.1765*	= Elizabeth[2] Vaughan *d. 1754*	=	Thomas Lloyd *d. 1734*
	Richard Vaughan *b. 1726*	Elizabeth Lloyd *b. 1725*	1742 =	Sir Thomas Stepney *b. 1725*

On the other hand, Mrs. Vaughan, a vivacious, subtle, and individualistic woman, was less forthcoming, and avoided giving a direct answer, by indulging in vague politenesses without committing herself either way, which lulled the Duchess even if it did not wholly satisfy her. Having listened to these verbal cavortings, the Duchess said that perhaps they could discuss the matter in greater detail on a future occasion. Mrs. Vaughan replied airily that she would always be honoured to wait on Her Grace.

The fact was that Mrs. Vaughan had her own plans about her daughter's disposal. The Stepneys had been old friends of the Vaughans of Derllys, and Mrs. Vaughan had selected as her future son-in-law, Thomas Stepney, heir to a baronetcy and a very respectable property. Fully apprised of the Duchess's intentions, she determined to forestall her, and under conditions of the greatest secrecy, without even informing her husband, she effected the betrothal in 1741. The delighted Mrs. Vaughan, courteous as ever, then told her seventeen-year-old daughter to apprise the Duchess of the turn of events. Miss Elizabeth, in a delirium of happiness, wrote the letter from Derwydd. The emotions of Her Grace on reading the letter are clearly reflected in her answer:

"Madam – I reced your letter in wch you are pleased to inform me yt there is a match concluded on between you and ye son of Mr Stepney. I have a great esteem for Sr Thomas Stepney, who I look upon as a worthy honest gentleman, and wish him and his family very well, but must be excused if I give ye preference to my own family, wch is very natural, and I did believe your mama would have done so too, as it is her family, by birth as much as mine, and as she has since married into it again: whenever I have talked to her of your marrying Master Vaughan, she never made ye lest objection to it of any kind whatever, but, as I thought seemed in appearance to approve of it – if she did not, she had many opportunities (both before and since she married my cousin Vaughan) to have undeceived me, wch, as she never did, I and I believe all other people (except ye few who, I find, were admitted into her secret) did think she intended to dispose of you to no other than Master Vaughan when you both came to a proper and convenient age; however, tho perhaps I might once think myself intitled to such a share in her friendship as to have been made acquainted with her designs before they were concluded and upon ye point of being finished, yet I think I have reason to complain or wonder, since she did not think fit to acquaint her husband, who certainly of all others in the world had ye greatest right to her confidence. I don't at all wonder at your preferring Master Stepney before Master Vaughan, he having, as I am informed, ye advantage of being one year older than Master Vaughan, and consequently ye choice of a young lady turned of sixteen. I wish you much joy and happiness, and am, Madam, your most humble servant, A. Bolton."

The conventional politeness of the final words did little to temper the chiding sentences that preceded them.

After all, perhaps things happen for the best, and the balance that had been so artfully disturbed by the step-mother was fully restored by Master Richard Vaughan, who, a little before the Duchess's death, became betrothed to a Carmarthenshire heiress in whose veins ran the divine ichor derived from Golden Grove and whose hands carried a plump fortune of £30,000.

Accordingly, it was a smiling Duchess who penned her precise and careful last will and testament on 1 February 1749-50. She bequeathed all her realty and personalty to John Vaughan of Shenfield for life, with remainder to his only son Richard and his heirs in tail male, with remainders to John Stepney son of Sir Thomas Stepney of Llanelly and his issue in tail male, and in default to Eugene Vaughan of Plas Gwyn, with remainder to his son John Vernon Vaughan and his heirs in tail male, and in default to the Duchess's right heirs for ever. Charles Phillips and Arthur Price of Llandybie, Morgan and Gwynne Davies both of Coombe, and Thomas Phillips of Llanelly, were appointed trustees, and the said legatees John and Richard Vaughan, and John Roberts "Steward of my House," executors. That she had got over her disappointment about the marriage of Elizabeth Lloyd (now Lady Stepney) is shown by the fact that her son, John Stepney, was named as a remainder-man.

On 20 October 1750 she made two codicils whereby she left annuities varying from £4 to £50 to thirteen of her servants, and certain gifts to her friends. Among these were the following – to the Lady Gertrude Hotham she left "my gold snuff box set with a cornelian at the Top and another at the Bottom, the pictures of Gertrude second wife of the first Marquess of Halifax, and the picture of Lady Stanhope mother of the said Lady Hotham"; to Richard Vaughan "all my books"; to Mrs. Lucy Woodcock of Marlborough Street, £100, "my Gold Repeating Watch," and King William's last speech to Parliament worked in needlework: to Mrs. Dorothy Clarke, daughter of the late Revd. Dr. Samuel Clarke, five gold medals of the late King William, William and Mary, George II, of the late Queen Caroline, and the Duke of Cumberland, portraits of Lady Sundon and Mrs. Woodcock and a "reflecting Telliscope"; to Mary, Countess of Thanet, the portraits of George first Marquess of Halifax and his first wife, of William Marquess of Halifax, the Duchess of Roxburgh, Lady Essex Savile (the legatee's sister) and of Lord Bland; to Lady Mary Tufton, the portrait of her mother, the Countess of Thanet: to Mrs. Rice widow of Edward Rice, "my Gold Chased Etui," the picture of the Hon. Mrs. Townsend, and a little square enamelled picture set in gold of the Countess of Leicester (grandmother of both testatrix and the legatee); to Mrs. Angell Butler, 20 guineas; to Mrs. Sophia Vaughan "my gold chas'd Snuff Box"; and to my servants John Roberts and Mary his wife £100, a piece of silver, "my chagrin Pocket Book garnished with Gold," linen and furniture etc. at "my house in London and in my lodgings in Windsor".

By her second codicil she had expressed a desire to be "decently but very privately buried without any Pomp or Show in the Vault belonging to my Family in the parish church of Llandilovaur near Golden Grove". The parish register of Llanfihangel Aberbythych contains the entry, "Anne her Grace the Dutches of Bolton died Friday the 20 of September and inter'd Sunday the 13 of October in the year 1751," from which it would appear that her wish so far as the place of sepulture was concerned, was not carried out. She was 61 years of age at the time of her death.

No series of papers and letters have survived covering a lengthy period of her life to enable us to form a balanced estimate and evaluation of the Duchess's character and personality. To guide us we have certain scattered items, and these succeed in only giving us a part of the truth, and a part of the truth can often be misleading. They may provide indications, and, all other things considered, with glimpses of the essentials of a person's character; but a human being is an amalgam of contradictions. When materials are scanty and fragmentary all the biographer can do is to seek for a constant, a recurring factor, and register the rhythm of a song whose words may be denied him.

And what can we say of the Lady Anne Vaughan, Duchess of Bolton? Let a contemporary speak – "Educated in solitude with some choice books by a saint-like governess; crammed with virtue and good qualities, she thought it impossible not to find gratitude, though she failed to give passion; and upon this threw away her estate, was despised by her husband, and laughed at by the public" – such was the verdict of Lady Mary Wortly Montagu written in retrospect on 8 December 1754.

From the evidence preserved in the Cawdor muniments it would seem that this summing-up is really not far off the mark. How much her resistance to the would-be brigandage of her husband was due to her own spirit and how much to the hawk-like Vaughans, those cousins who neither slept nor slumbered, is not wholly clear. She was certainly no woman of the world as shown by her inability to retain her husband's affections or to modify his demands, and by her peevishness when Mrs. Vaughan of Shenfield had pulled the wool over her eyes in the business of Elizabeth Lloyd's marriage. The Duke had been able to persuade her to make considerable concessions – such as mortgaging the Golden Grove estate for £20,000, an act which may be interpreted either as culpable weakness or incomparable generosity on her part. That she desired to help him within reasonable limits is patently clear, and even at the final rupture when he was living in open adultery and the father of two illegitimate sons, she continued to act with a restraint unusual in such circumstances. Her gratitude to those who helped her, and kindness to her dependants in Wales, to her personal servants as testified by her will, and the loyalty shown to her by the Duke's servants during the sorry affair of 1731, suggest a personality capable of attracting affection. No breath of scandal touched her, and that in an age when scandal had lost its sting, when eccentric or amoral behaviour invited little more than amused smiles; not altogether free from family pride, her attachment to certain ancestral attitudes may have limited her capacity for dealing rationally with contemporary affairs and changed situations. Her portrait, painted by Kneller, still on the wall in Golden Grove, suggests an amiable but unexciting nature, composed but negative, presentable without vivacity. She was a good woman living in an age when goodness was not enough.

Some gossip that persisted in Carmarthenshire, recorded by Lady Hills-Johnes of Dolau Cothi on 10 February 1905 illustrates how truth can be distorted in course of oral transmission. She wrote that the Duke of Bolton owed a gambling debt to Lord Carbery who offered to cancel it on condition that Lord Winchester married the Lady Anne. The son, ordered to make the proposal on pain of forfeiting the unentailed part of the Duke's estates, did so, at the same time imploring Anne to reject him as he loved another. But she accepted him, whereupon he is said to have retorted, "Your wedding day will be the unhappiest day of your life". They parted after the wedding, but he obtained possession of her money, which obliged her to borrow from her legal adviser on condition that she bequeathed a certain sum to him. Finally, Lady Hills-Johnes tells us, the Duke had tried to burn down Golden Grove.

Now gossip is not history; and some of Lady Hills-Johnes's statements are incompatible with known facts. We do not know the preliminaries leading to Anne's marriage, but what we do know of her father's attitude towards previous suitors, and his wish expressed several times "in the most pathetic terms" for the trustee to protect her, by no means harmonises with the bargain over "the gambling debt," or with Lady Montagu's description of the gallants "in hot pursuit" – one of whom was Lord Winchester – *after* Carbery's death. Distortion is obvious. It is true that they parted for a short period soon after the marriage, but afterwards lived together for some fifteen years before the final breach; the reason for the fire at Golden Grove has been given earlier in this essay, nevertheless it seems to have been easy for ill-informed opinion adverse to the Duke to saddle him with the responsibility for it.

On the Duchess's death, her personalty and certain parts of the estate passed to John Vaughan, and the remainder of the realty continued to be enjoyed by the Duke who was entitled to do so during his lifetime. Just over a week after his wife's death, "the fair old-fashioned Duke of Bolton" as Horace Walpole called him, using words that may mean much or nothing, married his Lavinia who had comforted him for over twenty-three years without benefit of the wedding-ring. He died at Tunbridge Wells on 26 August 1754, aged 68, and was buried at Basing. Lavinia, Duchess of Bolton, died at West Combe Park, Kent, on 24 January 1760, aged 52 and was buried at Greenwich.

APPENDIX A

Some Notes from the Agent's Accounts

The meticulous and resourceful Arthur Price took over the management of the Carmarthenshire estate, and acted as agent for both the Duke and Duchess of Bolton from 1714 onwards. His beautifully kept rentals and disbursements of the Duchess's part, covering the years 1714-1751, are very nearly complete, and provide us with a valuable record of the property during a critical period in its history. Included among them are a few accounts relating to the Duke's affairs. The rents, on an average, came to some £3,000 per annum, of which the Duke received about £1,450, the Duchess about £1,350. The annual variation in the receipts, never very considerable, was due to leases falling in and new ones being granted at improved rents. Thus, in 1712, the total rental stood at £3,409. In 1726 the Duchess's part amounted to £1,311, in 1736 to £1,413, in 1746 £1,554. Additional revenue came from other sources such as *cymortha*, heriots, duties, manorial dues and incidences, tithes, mineral rights, sale of timber, etc. In 1737 for instance, the Duchess received £1,403 3s. 6½d. from rents, and additional monies from the sources mentioned above, bringing the total to £1,427 13s. 5½d. while the Duke received £1,552 0s. 9d.

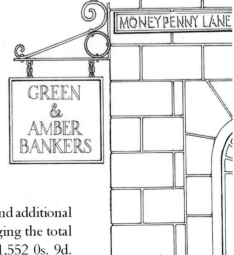

from rents, and additional perquisites bringing his total to £1,778 7s. 8d. Thus, the total rents for the year ending Michaelmas 1737 stood at £2,955 4s. 3½d. and, with the additional items produced a grand total of £3,206 1s. 1½d. Over and above this were sums received from the Fines of the Great Sessions in South Wales, which varied from about £300 to £500 per annum according to the amount of business transacted. The monies were sometimes carried to London by Carmarthenshire drovers, sometimes by the agent himself who made an annual journey, and sometimes by drafts drawn on London banks, especially on one banking firm with the delicious name of Green and Amber. In addition much game and produce was despatched by public coach from Llandeilo and also shipped from the quayside at Carmarthen. In December 1733 for example, "182 pounds of butter (were) sent to London for her grace's use, put at Carmarthen in 3 casks on board of a ship whereof Francis Morgan was Captain".

The Duchess sold a fair amount of cordwood from various woodlands to be made into charcoal for local industries, and also bark to the Carmarthenshire tanners. Robert Morgan who had an iron-works at Kidwelly and later at Carmarthen bought much of this timber. In 1736 she sold 122 long cords from Wenallt wood, near Kidwelly, to Robert Morgan at five shillings and sixpence per cord. In 1737 Morgan bought 81½ long cords at the same price, and in 1745 bought 98 long cords out of Wenallt wood and 65 long cords out of Forest farm, Llanedy, at seven shillings and sixpence per cord. Re-afforestation was immediately carried out, and the Duchess insisted that "young and tender saplings" be planted to replace the old. Her concern for the woodlands is shown by her action in 1738 when she persuaded Mrs. Phillipps of Bremenda, to whom the Duchess had rented property, to re-rent it back to her "for the better preservation of the wood growing there commonly called Bayly Glase Park Wood".

Among her disbursements was the yearly sum of £13 to a clergyman for serving the churches of Llanfihangel Aberbythych and Llandeveyson, while in 1742 the Duke paid £5 14s. 5¼d., being two-thirds of the cost of placing a new roof on Llangathen church, "the old roof in many places being quite fallen down," the remaining one-third being paid by the incumbent.

Entries also contain details of the annual charity to the poor paid by the Duchess. The sums she paid varied from £17 to £22, the average figure being £20. The charity was entirely in her pleasure, and was paid to the poor who were her tenants in Llanfihangel Aberbythych and other parishes. The agent's entry for 1737 stated that "only decayed tenants of Golden Grove or such who either themselves or their Ancestors were formerly Dependents on Golden Grove," were to receive the charity. She also made donations to those who had suffered misfortunes. In 1739 she relieved Evan Richard, a tenant in Llanegwad, who had suffered loss by fire, and in 1744 gave £8 to Thomas Thomas her tenant at Penddeulwyn in Llangunnor parish whose farmhouse "had been consumed by fire as to be made level with the Ground".

Although an "absentee," she took a personal and lively interest in details of her ancestral estate. Indeed the Duchess never once visited Carmarthenshire during the whole of her life, and the Duke came there only "on one or two occasions," when, as Lord Winchester, he was elected Member of Parliament for the county. On 7 February 1725-6, the Duke granted a lease to Thomas John Rees, gentleman (who then lived in the dairy house) of part of The Mansion house, namely "all that Room or Hall commonly called the Servants' Hall alias the Red Room being part of the Capital House of Golden Grove," the great barn and cowhouse formerly called the Coach horses' stable, the little stable, pigsty, the upper orchard adjoining the Great Park, and all gardens belonging to Golden Grove house except the Parlour Garden, the great lawn, and nine meadows in the demesne, for 21 years at £112 per annum, lessee to pay all rates and taxes except window tax. In 1729 the house was largely burnt down. In 1734, the Duchess paid one Richard William 15 guineas "for takeing Dimensions of Golden Grove house as it formerly stood," and "£1 4s. 5d. to the mason and carpenter who helped him". The window-tax on what remained of the house amounted to only 2 shillings per annum (1737 entry).

The careful accounts kept by Arthur Price provide evidence of the difficulties with which tenants, agent, and landlord had to contend in 18th century Carmarthenshire. Among the properties owned by the Golden Grove family was the farm of Messa Patria otherwise Bertwn, on the low coast between Kidwelly and Ferryside. A great deal of valuable land in the area had been lost during a catastrophic inundation in 1610, and the threat of encroaching waves remained a constant factor in the lives of those who lived on this low lying strip. Large sums were expended by the landlords during the 18th and 19th centuries to combat the menace. In 1735 the Duchess paid £39 14s. 9d. to erect "as a fence to preserve the House on Messa Patria ffarm and some of the lands thereto belonging from being laid waste by the Sea". In 1738, £9 5s. 6d. was paid "for a new wall at Messa Patria ffarm commonly called Berton lands in order to defend those lands and house from being ruined by the Sea," and a further sum of £61 19s. 7d. for building "the sea wall" to protect the lands "so sorely damaged by the Sea". In the following year, £34 0s. 8d. was paid to strengthen the wall, in 1740 the sum of £21 12s. 2d. had to be expended to protect the lands, dwelling house and outhouses "from the cruel mercy of the Sea," and in 1746 further work was "occasion'd by tempestuous weather and strong gushes of Wind driveing some Spring Tides to swell a deal higher than usual and violently to beat upon the ffence . . .".

Not only on the coast did the Duchess and her agent have to wrestle with the vagaries of the elements. Many miles inland, in the very heart of the county, the river Towy oftimes sprang into rage and inflicted grievous wounds on the most fertile acres of the estate. Many a melancholy tale did the agent have to unfold to distant masters. He writes, like Royalty, in the third person, referring to himself as the "Accountant". In 1737 he reported on a Llangathen tenant – "A greater probability of this tenant's breaking than of holding out; the frequent overflowing of the river Towy renders this rent so hazardous"; of another tenant, "the river Towy has already so far contributed towards his ruin that the Accountant fears his Grace will be a loser by him"; of another tenant on Towyside he says "because of that inconvenience, he left"; and of a meadow, Helyg Duon, just below Golden Grove House – it "lyes close to the Banks of the River Towy, some acres of its hay so damaged as scarce worth

Carmarthenshire floods

to be carried off," the tenant in poor circumstances "partly, if not chiefly because of the Inundation". Of the land around Helyg Duon, he writes in picturesque vein in 1738, "almost the whole ffarm is frequently seen as a Sea by means of the river Towy and the Mows of Corn swimming thereon as so many vessels". He complains of difficulty in obtaining tenants for the riparian farms, owing to "the incredible mischief" of the Towy, which causes "everybody to be cautious of medling therewith". Another tenant is far in arrears of rent although "the land is rich, as it is every where along that River's side, but because the River is so ill a Neighbour every one shuns it".

The trouble did not end there. When the capricious river burst its banks some tenants sought to make profit of the circumstances by secretly removing the livestock, claiming that they had been swept away by the swirling waters. They then said they could not pay that year's rent, and as there were no cattle, remedy by distress was not possible. Arthur Price, however, was alert to these machinations. In 1738 David Harry of Dryslwyn Fach, whose rent of £40 was several years in arrears, had recourse to invoking the aid of the river god to solve his difficulties. Price wrote "The Tenant here in a certain night when his whole Farm was, as it were, delug'd and covered with the water of the River Towy, conveyed all his liveing stock of every kind thence, and with the favour of the night drove them a dosen miles off the premises, which were afterwards found at divers places by the people the Accountant dispatch'd in quest of them, and by those people brought back again. Thus he secured the rent and was put upon the necessity of seeking another tenant, a seeking not easie to be successful in any where on the side of the said River, so apprehensive is every one of the damage by the fflouds thereof." In fact, these cattle were found on the very borders of Cardiganshire by the pursuers, who had raised a hue and cry throughout north Carmarthenshire. The hunt occupied four days, and "this extraordinary service, for which the Accountant craves an allowance," cost him £1 12s. 0d. What scope these rustic dramas would provide for the pen of D. J. Williams or Emyr Humphreys.

The tenants were a mixed bag. The majority were enterprising and industrious, but others were "idle," one "at intervals disordered in her Intellects," and some flitted by moonlight, one to far-off America. A particularly difficult handful was Mrs. Elizabeth Williams, who rented a house in Carmarthen town at £4 a year. Mr. Price writes feelingly in

The last asset

1738 – "Mrs Williams is dead. Tho' she came to an Estate of £300 a year above 20 years before her death, yet she died wretchedly poor, haveing in litigous Suits and other expensive methods reduced herself to such poverty as not to dare, for fear of Creditors, to stir out of her house for many years to her dieing day. At her decease she owed two year's rent, and to secure it, the Accountant seiz'd all the Lumber in the house, and had it not been for a distress of a Parrot and its Cage she left in the house, the rent had fallen short." One would have liked to have learnt more about this exotic bird that helped to redress the deceased lady's debts.

REFERENCES

[1] Transactions 1963, Part 1, pp. 96-145.

[2] The last of the aunts, Lady Althamia Vaughan, was still living in 1718, when Anne laid out £20 to buy "several things" for her.

MARITAL PROBLEMS AND A MEDIEVAL WILL

REFERENCE TO Llandeilo Abercywyn occurs in the latter part of the 15th century when its ownership was finally determined by heiresses. The then owner, John Wogan, last in the main line at Picton Castle, spent most of his life in Ireland, and died some years before 1420 leaving four daughters, one of whom, Katherine Wogan, received Picton Castle as part of her inheritance. She married, firstly, a kinsman, Sir Henry Wogan, who died without issue about 1437; secondly, in 1438, Owain Dwnn of Mudlescwm, Carms. The latter venture gave rise to some difficulty when it was alleged that on the death of her first husband, Katherine had become a 'King's widow', i.e. a ward of the Crown, and that Dwnn had married her without obtaining a Royal License to enable him to do so legally. He hotly denied that she had been a 'King's widow,' and on 27 November 1438 a Commission was appointed to enquire into the matter. The outcome is not recorded, but clearly it was in Dwnn's favour, for the couple continued to live together at Picton Castle and to enjoy the estates.

Owain Dwnn of Picton Castle died about 1460, leaving an only son, Henry, who succeeded to the estates of both parents. He married a kinswoman, Margaret daughter of Sir Henry Wogan of Wiston, by Margaret daughter of Sir William Thomas of Raglan, Mon., from whom the Herbert family descends.

Henry Dwnn took part in local affairs, and, during the Wars of the Roses as an active Yorkist, with fatal results. He fell at the Battle of Edgecote near Banbury on 25 July 1469, leaving a widow with three small children. His Inquisition Post Mortem, held at Carmarthen on Monday before the Feast of the Holy Trinity 1470, recorded that on the day of his death, 'Henry Dwnn formerly of Pikton, Esquire,' held the following properties as of fee:

The manors Llanddowror and Llandeilo (Abercywyn) in capite by service of one kinght's fee, of the yearly value of £10. Four messuages and 120 acres of land and wood in Castell Toch, held of Philip Dun by fealty and suit of court at Lagham, or yearly value of 26s. 8d. Four messuages and 100 acres in Court Robert held of William, Earl of Pembroke, at rent of one penny, suit of court at Trayne Clynton, of yearly value at 20s. Two messuages and 20 acres in Llanstephan, held of William Harbard, Earl of Pembroke, by fealty and 12d., of yearly value of 6s. Three messuages and 30 acres in Le Knapp, of free burgage, of yearly value of 6s.8d.

One hundred acres of land and 20 acres of wood in Clogvrain, held of David Philip Thomas by fealty and yearly rent of 12d, and of total yearly value of 10s. Three messuages and 100 acres in Llay the, held of the said Earl of Pembroke at yearly rent of 2s, and suit of court in the lordship of Llanstephan, of yearly value of 20s.

The said Henry Dun died on Monday in the Vigil of St. James the Apostle 9 Edward IV [25 July 1469.

His next son and heir is William Dun aged 5 years on the day of this Inquisition.

This is all the land deceased held in county Carmarthen.

It should be noted that the medieval 'county Carmarthen' was limited to the general area of the town, with certain adjacent lordships and commotes as shown on Dr. Rees's map, *South Wales and the Border in the XIVth Century;* the lordship of Kidwelly within which Mudlescwm and other Dwnn properties lay, was beyond Carmarthen's jurisdiction.

From 'A Tale of Two Mansions'

BETWEEN farm and *plas* was the "drive", now a cart track, and the chestnut trees mentioned by Mr. Green have largely disappeared. During the first half of this century Mr. E. T. Davies who spent all his earlier life here, confirms the former existence of the trees, beech as well as chestnut, and tells me they had been mostly uprooted during severe gales, and in addition to those lining the former drive, others grew around both *plas* and farm, particularly near the coachhouse. Staples and bolts had been driven into the trunks of several, and from them carcasses and hunks of meat were hung, to be devoured by the fox-hounds kept at Ffrwd during the days of gentry. Enthusiastic sportsmen, they cultivated woodlands and plantations, many of the latter growing in corners of fields, to encourage game birds, particularly pheasants. Hazards of the cockpit were also to the family taste, the fighting cocks of Ffrwd were famous in their day, the feathered contests taking place in a wooded corner of Cae Eithin.

Henry Vaughan of Derwydd

HENRY VAUGHAN OF DERWYDD – A ROBUST CAVALIER

HENRY VAUGHAN had been born about 1587, and so was very young when he married in 1602-3 Sage daughter of John Gwyn Williams and Elizabeth heiress of Derwydd, daughter of Rhydderch ap Hywel ap Redo, a not unusual feature of those, and indeed, much later days. He settled at Derwydd in the right of his wife, and added considerably to the estate by numerous purchases. In 1610 he bought lands in Llanfihangel Aberbythych parish; in 1611 Morgan Penry of Llandebie, gentleman, released to him parcels of land called y Kae kenol, yr Anhereg, kae Davydd Lloyd, kae'r lloi, and Anhereg yskallog, at Glan Gwyddvaen in Llandybie parish; in 1613 Ynys Gwythfaetu in Llandybie parish from Morgan Penry, gentleman: in 1615 a moiety of Derwydd issa from David Howel, for £20; in 1616 his brother William Vaughan of Torycoed (and Anne his wife) conveyed five messuages in Llandybie, Llandeilo Fawr, and Betws, to him for £80; in 1618 he bought a messuage in Llandybie parish from Griffith Penry of Swansea; in 1628 three messuages in Llandeilo Fawr parish from Thomas John Howel and Maud his wife, and Gwalter John Walter and Elizabeth his wife. On 29 September, 1632 Thomas Griffith Lloyd of "Keven Trawakood in Llandeilo Fawr, gentleman", mortgaged messuages and lands at Innys Rose Mayne, a messuage called Kae Newyth, and other messuages on the south side of the highway from Y Castell Rhyth to the mill ditch of Rose Mayne, in Llandeilo Fawr parish, in the sum of £200 to Henry Vaughan. The mortgage was not redeemed, and on 28 September 1638, Thomas Griffith Lloyd covenanted to deliver all the deeds and papers to him, and to levy a fine in respect of the properties.

No record exists to show that Henry alienated any property. Probably the marriage settlement limited his power in that respect, although it would have been possible for him to sell lands he had acquired or were outside any settlement or entail. He could of course make leases. Thus on 8 April 1630 he granted a lease for 99 years to John Griffith Harry of

Llanfihangel Aberbythych, gentleman, of a messuage called Cae Llwyn, for 13s. 4d. per annum, the carriage of a load of lime yearly, and a heriot on the death of a tenant.

The Vaughans showed a high sense of family solidarity, and a readiness to further the interests of kinsfolk. This was particularly true of their association with the borough of Carmarthen where their public and voluntary services were not so altruistic as might appear on first sight. Thus on 24 November 1632 Lewis Walton of Gloucester, saddler, and Anne his wife, granted to Richard, Lord Vaughan of Golden Grove, "all that scite and precineks of the late dissolved monastery and a howse called by the name of graye ffryers sett, layinge and beinge in att or neare a streete called Gellstreets alias Ge Street alias Lamas streete", and adjacent closes called the greate parke, the park hill, Park y Clomendy, and "the little park alias the ffryers Parke". To increase the influence of a younger branch in the borough, the grantee immediately afterwards assigned the property to his uncle Henry Vaughan of Derwydd. On 18 February 1634-5 Henry was party to the marriage settlement of Hugh Phillips of Merthyr, Carmarthenshire, and Katherine Gwyn of Llangadog, widow (half sister to Vaughan's wife), and in a deed dated 24 November 1642, Vaughan describes Hugh Phillips, then of Llangadog, as "my trustie and wellbeloved Friend and Brother in Lawe".

He also acquired some leases. On 10 January 1638-9, Henry and Richard Thomas of Carmarthen, and Robert Toye of Llether Cadvan, in consideration of £100, assigned to Henry Vaughan the remainder of a lease for 99 years (granted on 12 May 1635) of four messuages and parcels of land in Llandeilo Fawr parish; and took a lease of six south Carmarthenshire livings from Lord Henry Percy, younger son of the ninth Earl of Northumberland, for the large yearly rent of £750. In 1637 he gave to his sister Anne Vaughan a lease of the glebe lands and houses then in her occupation, and all the glebe in Llanelli (except the part held by the Revd. Rees Lloyd) for £12 a year. However, Anne proved a tardy payer, and in the following year Henry had to write requesting her to pay the moneys she owed to him.

These purchases and leases indicate that Henry Vaughan must have had a good deal of ready cash available. Like all his family, he seems to have been of an acquisitive nature, if we may judge from a survey of the lordship of Kidwelly made in 1609, which recorded that Henry Vaughan had enclosed, for his own purpose, part of the common on the side of Allt Canatha above Kidwelly.

He took an active part in public life, being a Justice of the Peace and Quorum, High Sheriff for Carmarthenshire in 1619-20, senior sheriff of Carmarthen in 1619, and mayor in 1632. He sat as Member of Parliament for the borough of Carmarthen for the years 1621-29, except for a short time in 1625 when he was unseated after a double return, the challenger being Sir Francis Annesley who had married Dorothy Philipps of Picton Castle. He was elected member for the county in 1640 and held the seat until 1646. Parliamentary records reveal that he could speak the native tongue. In 1641, on a motion by Sir Symonds d'Ewes, two Welsh-speaking members, namely, Sir Harry Vaughan (Carmarthenshire) and Pryse (Cardiganshire) were added to a committee of the House of Commons, to cope with monoglot witnesses from Wales who were being examined in connection with a disputed return for Caernarvonshire.

He was an alderman of Carmarthen, and with his brother-in-law, John Protheroe of Nantyrhebog, another alderman, was among the trustees of the charity established in the borough by Arthur, Lord Chichester, on 16 March 1621. He held several appointments some of them offices of profit. In the reign of James I, Henry Vaughan and Thomas Aylesbury, held the *raglorship* of Caeo, Cethinog, Maenordeilo, and Mallaen, and he was deputy coroner of Kidwelly (Cedweli) under his brother Sir John Vaughan of Golden Grove. On 25 October 1630 Henry, his brother Walter Vaughan of Llanelli, and one David Morris, sat as commissioners in Carmarthen castle, where they received the presentment of the jurors of the lordships of Gwidigada and Elfed, which stated that the castle did not lie in the parish of St. Peter, but "within the lordship of Elvett". He was a Deputy Lieutenant for Carmarthenshire before 1639. The base of the chalice of Llandeilo Fawr church is inscribed "Bought by Henry Vaughan, Esq, Church-Warden", and J. T. Evans is probably right in identifying him with the squire of Derwydd. The stamp shows that it was made in 1631.

Holding such position in Carmarthenshire it was natural that he should have come to the fore during the Civil War. Like all his family he declared for the King, and proved himself the most zealous and steadfast of royalists. On 1 January 1642-3 he was knighted at Oxford, being then a lieutenant-colonel under his nephew, the Earl of Carbery the commander of the King's forces in south west Wales. On 26 October 1643 the king appointed him Sergeant Major-Generall. His commission, signed by the monarch, is preserved in the Cawdor muniments, now in the Carmarthenshire Record Office, and as few such documents of this period have survived, it is well to print it in full:

"(signed) Charles R. Charles by the grace of God King of Great Britaine France and Ireland Defender of the faith, &c. To Our trusty and wellbeloved Sir Henry Vaughan, Knight, Greeting. Whereas a great and Rebellious Army hath beene raysed against Us under the Comand of Robert Earle of Essex which Army hath not onely severall times endeavoured to take Our life from Us in sett Battailes, but the same and other Forces raysed by divers Trayterous and seditious Persons under the name of King & Parliament and cherished and mayneteyned by the disloyall and Rebellious Citty of London and other parts of the Kingdome have Comitted all the Arts of Outrage, Robbery, and Murther upon Our good Subjects throughout the Kingdome, and doe still continue the same, and thereby endeavour to effect their damnable designe to destroy Us and Our Posterity and to change the present Government both of Church and State into Anarchy, Tyranny, and Confusion. For prevention whereof and for the defence of Our Royall Person and Posterity, the true reformed Protestant Religion the Lawes of the Land, the Liberty and propriety of Our Subjects, and the just Priviledges of Parliament. Wee being enforced to have in redynes divers Forces of Horse, Foote and Dragoons well armed and furnished with all things necessary for Our Service to be employed therein as Wee shall direct, Wee therefore reposing especiall trust and confidence in your fidelity diligence and dexterity in such affaires Doe by these presents Constitute and appoint you Sergeant Maior Generall of all such Forces either of the Trayned Bands or other Voluntiers raysed or to be raysed in any our Counties of Carmarthen, Cardigan & Pembrooke, and in the Counties of the Townes of Carmarthen and Haverford West now under the Command of Our right trusty and right welbeloved Cosen Richard Earle of Carbury Our Lieutenant Generall in those Counties by virtue of Our Commission to him granted for the same, And the same Forces so raysed or to be raysed you are upon all occasions to leade, Conduct, and Command as Sergeant Major Generall thereof against all or any persons Rebelliously taking up Armes without Our Authority, or against Our Royall Commands, And them to chase, pursue, kill & slay as Traytors and Rebells Commanding all subordinate Officers and Souldiers of the said Forces you to obey and observe as their Sergeant Major Generall for Our service according to this Our Commission hereby given unto you. And you your selfe diligently to execute and performe all such Orders and Commands as you shall receive from time to time from Our selfe or Our said Lieutenant Generall according to occasion and the discipline or warr, And in all things to governe your selfe as unto your duty and place of Sergeant Major Generall doth of right apperteyne and belong. And Wee doe hereby Command all Our Commissioners of Array, Justices of the Peace, Mayors, Baylifies, Constables, and all other Our Ministers and loving Subiects to be ayding and assisting to you and to obey such Commands as you shall from time to time give unto them for Our service. Given under Our Signe Manuall at Our Court at Oxford this 26th of October In the Ninteenth yeare of Our Raigne".

His critics alleged that Sir Henry had been "the instrument of much mischief' in south-west Wales and had treated opponents with severity. He was a commissioner of array under the Great Seal at Oxford, and raised money for the King's occasions, and himself contributed money, horses, and men. Initially, the royalists were successful, particularly in Pembrokeshire where the English element had stood stoutly for Parliament. Sir Henry commanded the forces in person, with headquarters at Haverfordwest, but was obliged to retire from the town in March 1643-4, before the threat of Rowland Laugharne's superior force, and fell back on Carmarthen castle but that stronghold too was forced to capitulate.

Sir Henry's influence in west Wales and his uncompromising character could not be overlooked by his triumphant adversaries, and on 27 April 1644 the Committee for Compounding ordered him to pay £160, and on 20 August 1645 he was assessed at £500, his estate being then valued at £600 per annum. Among near kinsmen and neighbours who had served under his command, were his sons Lieutenant-Colonel Henry Vaughan and Walter Vaughan, his son-in-law Ensign Morgan Owen of Glasallt, Ensign Rice Prichard of Llandovery, and Francis Jones of Tregib near Llandeilo.

On 5 February 1643-4 he had been disabled from holding a seat in Parliament. In addition to political charges, other accusations were made in order to embarrass him further. Although a member of the Committee for Examining Scandalous Ministers, he was accused in 1644 with employing unsuitable clerics – "six scandalous ministers, no preachers", to whom he paid a mere pittance, in the six Carmarthenshire rectories and chapels of which

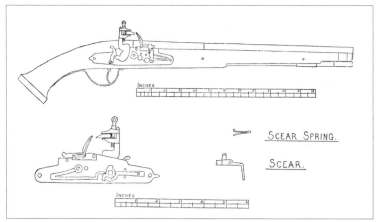

English Drag-lock pistol, c. 1620

he was patron by demise from Lord Henry Percy, which I have mentioned earlier. It was also suggested that he sheltered papists. These charges were outlined in a petition to the House, from a disagreeable person called Hugh Grundy of Llangyndeyrn parish, a man with a chip on his shoulder, and who bridled at the very name of Vaughan. Indeed the Vaughans had proceeded against him in the Court of Star Chamber, and now came an opportunity to pay off the old score. He was, of course, a Parliamentarian, like his son, Ralph. who spied on Carmarthenshire royalists and reported them to Parliament for concealing assets and avoiding punitive interdictions. Whatever may have been the truth of the charges against Sir Henry, it is clear from accounts and other documents in the Derwydd muniments that he had discharged many of his duties towards the church livings he held in lease. From 1630 onwards he and Walter Vaughan paid several sums towards repairing chancels and towards the stipends of curates, and Sir Henry was still doing so in 1652.

Unlike his nephew, Lord Carbery, Sir Henry continued to support the King after the royalist eclipse in west Wales in 1644. He joined the royal forces in England, and fought at Naseby on 14 June 1645 where he was taken prisoner. Once in their hands, the Parliamentarians took care that opportunities for further "mischief' were denied him, and four days after his capture he was brought before the House, and committed to the Tower. His disbursements in the royal cause, from his own pocket, and the fines imposed by the victors, caused him acute embarrassment. Seeking some relief from his predicament he appealed for clemency and submitted a list of his debts, amounting to the sum of £3,603 10s. This included £35 owing to the Serjeant at Arms, and £20 for "keep for lodging and diett of the Tower". He added, "the house and demanes where I live was my wifes, and the best part of my estate was my wifes inheritance . . . I have nine children's mouthes to feed . . if you extend your favours by ymposing this fine, then I hope you will, by all honourable means, signifie my present condicions and extreams". His two sons, Henry and Walter, were prisoners in other castles.

He languished in the Tower until 1 October 1647 when he was removed to the Fleet, where he still lay in July 1648, "like to be in a starvinge condicion", according to a letter he addressed to his wife. This letter is included in a privately printed work, *Some Notices of the Stepney Family* by Robert Harrison (1870), but as the work is not generally available, I feel it worthwhile reproducing it here:

"Dear Wife, I am informed that your son Harry is prisoner in Denby Castle. This is a trial of your patience. And your son Walter is prisoner committed by a Committee of Derby Howse. Your husband in the Fleet, and like to be in a starvinge condicion. These are the usages of these tymes. I pitty them that are our tormentors more than they doe any of us whom they had thus oppressed, and I hope God will never suffer me, if I have any part of such power as they have over us, to be soe unmercifull as they have been to either of us.

"I write not this to mak you sad or to tak any grif, but to comfort you, and that you may thank God that your husband and children's sufferinge is neither for oppression, or any such pticular charge put against them other than being loyall and good subjects, such as will never doe any act to prejudice any other; let this comfort you, that God will never forsake us. These are but trials. Doe not doubt, though we are deprived of lands and wordly goods, but God can restore the increase as to Job.

"I shall give you now an account of Mr. Boyes resolution, that if you do not speedily send to give him satisfaction for your friends engagement, he intends to put their lands in suit. I did much adiure they would alter the former days of payment, being the 20th of November. I did conseve that Viccar's stypende and all other taxations was to be deducted out of the £400. I am since my last letters in formed you have been allowed for use for the year past. That bargain begines for the next year, if you perform the payment of the £400. This must be suddenly donne, or els Mr. Bowes *(sic)* will not seal the leas and stand to Mr. 'Mason's agreement. I have not heard one word from you this six weeks, though I have *writt* severall letters to you. I have expressed therein my lowe condicion and poverty. Doe what you can; at the present my credit is at the stak. Be assured by God's grace you shall not be put to the lik trouble and miserable perplexity hereafter. The next I shall writ I hope not long after, but I shall have the comfort of seinge you. In the mean tyme be of good corage. I tak leave and rest / Your loving Husband / Henry Vaughan. Dated this 29th July 1648."

Sir Henry resolutely declined to compromise or come to terms with the government and his steadfast conduct was acknowledged in a Cavalier ditty of 1647, which ran:

> *"Sir Harry Vaughan looks as grave*
> *As any beard can make him,*
> *Those (who) came poore prisoners to see*
> *Do for our Patriarke take him,*
> *Old Harry is a right true blue,*
> *As valiant as Pendraggon,*
> *And would be loyall to his king*
> *Had King Charles ne'er a rag on.*

Parliament, more practical than poetical, excluded him from the general pardon of 13 October 1648, and he remained a prisoner until 1659 when he was released, perhaps through the influence of Colonel Philip Jones of Fonmon who had already shown much of the quality of mercy in favour of the house of Golden Grove.

Although restricted by prison walls he was able to participate in the affairs of his estate. On 29 September 1655 he mortgaged lands called 'Yr Ynys ar Lan Kennen" in Llandybie parish, in £25, to John William Lewis of Llandeilo Is Cennen, gentleman; on 18 April 1657, Sir Henry and his sons Henry and Walter, were parties to the post-nuptial settlement of William Awbrey of Llandeilo Fawr, and Rebecca his wife; on 4 May 1657 Bridget Lloyd of "Keven Treskoed", widow of Jenkin Lloyd of Kidwelly, gentleman, conveyed "Keven Treskoed" and five adjoining closes, three messuages called "Kae Banall, Tyr Castell Rydd, and Owaun Isbarivirick", in Llandeilo Fawr parish, also a house lately inhabited by grantor, a close and two parcels of land in the town of Kidwelly, and two messuages and lands in Llangyndeyrn parish, to Sir Henry, and in the November following Sir Henry leased Cefn Triscoed to Griffith Lloyd and Catherine Lloyd, widow, who were both living there at the time.

His simple faith, that "God can restore the increase as to Job" as expressed in the letter to his wife in 1648, was justified. He lived to see his own and his king's restoration, but was not destined to remain more than a few months at the home from which he had been excluded for so long. He made his will on 27 November 1660 and died before 5 January following when an inventory of his goods at the White House and Derwydd were compiled. In his will, proved at Carmarthen on 22 January 1660-1, he named nine of his children, gave power to Lord Carbery to work minerals on the Derwydd estate, made bequests to his servants, and gave a legacy of £5 to the poor of Llandybie. His wife, Sage, had predeceased him. A portrait of Sir Henry, painted in 1644, hung in Derwydd house until the sale in 1998.

John Vaughan – the last Vaughan of Golden Grove

Chapter VI

HEALTH, WEALTH AND FASHION

Carmarthen and the Doctors

IT SEEMS STRANGE that no book has been written on the history of the medical practitioners of Carmarthenshire. Apart from a few brief and inadequate biographical studies of one or two doctors, no comprehensive study has been attempted, and not even a list of the bygone practitioners of this county is available. Nevertheless, Carmarthenshire, has a long and distinguished association with the medical profession, and perhaps I may be allowed to review, briefly, the background of a subject that I consider deserves the attention of serious scholarship.

The earliest references to Welsh doctors occur in a book that owed its origin to a Carmarthenshire man, namely Hywel Dda, sometime ruler of this territory. Compiled at Whitland in the early part of the 10th century, the justly famous Laws of Hywel Dda show that the doctor occupied an honourable position in Welsh society. The royal physician sat near the king, and shared the quarters of the commander of the Household Troops. For his services he received grants of land, his maintenance and apparel. His privileges were carefully described, as well as his fees for services outside the Household. Some of these may look ridiculously small today, for instance he was paid fourpence for blood-letting, and a further fourpence for applying herbs to afflicted parts – but one must remember that the monetary values of those days differ greatly from ours.

Outside the royal court and the noble households, doctors were rare birds. The founding of monasteries gave a fillip to the study and practice of medicine, and up to the middle of the 12th century the monks and churchmen combined the practice of medicine and surgery with their spiritual duties. The monks of Whitland, Talley, Kidwelly, the priests of The Friary and Priory in this town, brought medical as well as spiritual solace to their flocks. When the Pope ordered the clergy in 1163 to confine their ministrations to ecclesiastical matters, medicine became a secular concern. But the Churchmen were not wholly divorced from the art of healing, and the herbal gardens of the religious houses continued to flourish throughout the Middle Ages. Even today, one occasionally finds a rare herb growing among the ruins of the old monasteries.

Medieval manuscripts contain numerous references to doctors, and a study of early Welsh pedigrees reveals the names of many men who followed the calling of "Meddyg" (doctor). Perhaps the best-known of these are the Physicians of Myddffai, Meddygon Myddfai, whose fabled origin provides Welsh folklore with one of its most attractive legends. You are all familiar with the story that a water maiden from Llyn y Fan Fach married a local farmer by whom she had a family. She bestowed on her eldest son, Rhiwallon, the gift of healing. Rhiwallon afterwards became physician to the prince Rhys Gryg (d. 1234) and was assisted by his three sons, Cadwgan, Griffith and Eynon, all doctors. The water maiden element may be a myth, but sufficient evidence exists to show that a long and vigorous medical tradition flourished in Myddfai parish. Records recently deposited in the Carmarthen Record Office by Lord Emlyn reveal that during the Middle Ages the freeholders of Myddfai were obliged to furnish the lord of that manor with a doctor to accompany him whenever he travelled in Carmarthenshire and elsewhere in Wales.

The family, which finally took the surnames of Jones and Williams, produced many able doctors and surgeons. The tombstones of two of them, David Jones (died 1719) and his son John Jones (died 1739), both surgeons, may still be seen in Myddfai churchyard.

Among the last of the male line was Dr. Rhys Williams M.D., who died in 1842.

One descendent of the Physicians of Myddfai became Bishop of Llandaff, namely Dr. Owen of Glassalt, who died in 1645. Another of their descendants was the late Major J. W. Bishop of Llandeilo.

Equally familiar is the manuscript of medical recipes called *The Book of the Physicians of Myddfai* – the earliest treatise on medicine produced in Wales. Although many of the recipes are strange and grotesque, based on charms and superstitions, yet many of them, I am told, are still effective. One, based on a very practical basis, advocates the slow burning of herbs, like wormwood and camomile, on hearths to produce smoke to kill harmful germs – an early form of fumigation. The cures cover a wide range of ills –gout, freckles, fractured bones, failing eyesight, insomnia, warts, carbuncles, chilblains, toothache, the itch, and the plague, to name but a few from the calendar of human anguish.

Wormwood

Let us look at some of the recipes.

If a man was inclined to speak in his sleep, sometimes a dangerous form of eloquence, the doctors of Myddfai were ready with a sovereign panacea – "Take the seeds of rue, pound them with vinager, till they form a paste, mix it well with old ale, strain through a clean linen, and drink same."

If gout was the enemy they told the sufferer to "Take wood sage, pellitory of the wall, wheat bran, cow's dung, and salt, boil together in wine or cider vinegar, and apply as a plaster".

If haemorrhoids troubled, all one had to do was to "Take smoke dried goat's flesh, desicate completely, and reduce to as fine a powder as you can: lay some thereof on live coals in a fire-proof utensil, and put same in a commode (cadair gist) and sit thereon".

Toothache? Well then, "Take holly leaves and boil in spring water, till they are tough, remove the pot from the fire, put a cloth about your head, and hold your mouth over the pot to inhale the vapour. It will cure you."

Balding? Not to worry. "Take two spoonfuls of olive oil, two spoonfuls of new honey, and an onion as large as a pigeon's egg, pound them together till it becomes an ointment, and anoint your head with it night and morning. Wear a leathern cap till the hair is grown. It is best to pound the onion well before it is added to the ointment."

How to be the life and soul of the party, and yet keep Bacchus in check? Here too, our doctors had sage advice to offer, "Take a handful of betony, bruise well, mix with spring water, strain carefully: drink this and you will not get drunk that day".

If one forgot this advice, and awoke with a hangover, the good doctor can still offer solace, "Take three spoonfuls of the juice of betony, and tickle your nostrils with a hen's feather."

Doubtless many a star of bacchanalian routs blessed the name of Myddfai.

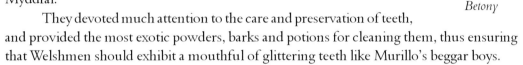

Betony

They devoted much attention to the care and preservation of teeth, and provided the most exotic powders, barks and potions for cleaning them, thus ensuring that Welshmen should exhibit a mouthful of glittering teeth like Murillo's beggar boys.

These might appear to be somewhat light-hearted examples, but they do indicate the catholicity of the practice of the medieval doctors. They emphasised cleanliness, washing in pure spring water, and plenty of exercise. One piece of advice offered – "never sleep during day time" – seems directed against Civil Servants. They produced a formidable list of "Gluttony, drunkenness, late eating, much sleeping after meals, tainted air, anger, depressed spirits, much standing bare-headed, eating hastily, too much warmth, excessive watching, too much cold curds, all kinds of nuts, too frequent bathing, onions, garlick, yawning, smelling a white rose, excess of fornication, too much music, singing and reading, strong drink before sleeping, restless sleep, too much fasting, and frequent wet feet".

Their remarks concerning surgery often refer to wounds on the battlefield, and they state how experience had confirmed what was the most efficacious treatment in such cases. War, then as now, gave a great impetus to the art of surgery.

From the Tudor period onwards the picture is clearer. There were still few doctors, and most laymen acquired a smattering of knowledge about herbal medicines on the "do-it-yourself" principle. Gardens of humble cottagers, working farmers, and country squires, all contained a bed of useful herbs. War, pestilence and famine, always the chief executioners of the human race, stimulated medical research. The advance of science has eliminated many of the horrors that assailed and depressed our ancestors. Diseases common enough even only half a century ago are today as rare as "penny blacks". Take for instance the Pestilence, which decimated the population of certain areas from time to time. A precaution against this dread visitant is included in an early *Welsh Book of Medicine* written by Ellis Griffith. It reads: "Take a handful of sage, of rosemary, of wormwood, and federfoy, half a handful of rue, half a handful of tansy, wash them clean, and place in a glass of Malmsey wine, and drink a silver teaspoonful whenever you feel ill, and that drink is bitter as gall, yet you will never sicken of the Pestilence."

Welsh doctors soon became recognised outside the confines of the Principality. Hugh Morgan became Queen Elizabeth's secretary. Another of her friends was Dr. John Dee, a doctor, alchemist, astronomer of Welsh extraction, who incidentally was the first man ever to use the term "British Empire" – which in our degenerate days has become almost a "dirty word". Dr. Matthew Gwynne, also friend of the Queen and of King James, became the first Gresham Professor of Physic. In the next century, Dr. John Morgan (born 1725) founded the first Medical school in the United States of America, and was Physician-in-Chief to the U.S. army.

Tansy

The skill of Welsh doctors brought them to the notice of the Crown. Dr. Noah Thomas of Neath was appointed Physician to William IV: Dr. David Daniel Davies (his surname was originally David by the way) of Llandefaelog attended members of the Royal Family, was present on the occasion of the birth of Queen Victoria, and became Professor of Midwifery at University College Hospital. Nearer our own day, the distinguished Sir John Williams of Plas Llanstephan, born at Gwinfe (not very far from Myddfai) became a court physician.

I would like to add the name of another Carmarthenshire man to the list of royal doctors. Going through some old papers the other day, I discovered that a doctor had lived at Glanrhydw called Doctor Richard Price, son of Lewis Price, a Carmarthenshire landowner, related to the Vaughans of Glanrhydw and Plas Gwyn. He became Physician and Accountant to King George II, and was the first Carmarthenshire doctor to hold a Court appointment. It is interesting to note that Llandefaelog parish has produced two Royal physicians.

Some Welsh doctors achieved fame in other ways. For instance, Dr. William Price (1800-1893) who after serving an apprenticeship with a Monmouthshire doctor, entered the Royal College of Surgeons and qualified in 1821. I shall not be accused of exaggerating if I venture to call him eccentric. In addition to his medical qualifications, which were of the highest, he claimed to be an Arch-druid and performed ancient rites on Glamorganshire cromlechs. He usually wore a white tunic, scarlet waistcoat, and green trousers. He practised free love, advocated cremation, was a vegetarian, scorned orthodox religion, despised the law, and was a chartist leader. After the riots of 1839 he escaped to France disguised as a woman (shades of Mr Vassall!) As a result of a lawsuit in 1844, in which he was the central figure, the legality of cremation in Britain was finally established. An interesting point is that a medical notebook of this mercurial medico, containing recipes in his own handwriting, has recently been found and is now in the safety of our own Record Office in Carmarthen.

Carmarthen has not been lacking in its contributions to the arts of healing. For many centuries it was the largest town in West Wales, the centre of most of our County's activities, the seat of administration, with flourishing markets and a brisk sea trade. Generations of skilful doctors have ministered to the wants of its burgesses. Indeed Dr. Webb's house in Spilman Street has been a doctor's house for nearly a century and a half, and the presence of such places gives a depth to our historical consciousness. Take another example, the Infirmary.

The pioneer of this enterprise was Dr. Henry Lawrence (when young, he accidentally knocked out "Patch" Philipps' eye when playing bows and arrows) who attempted to set up a dispensary in the town. In 1846 a strong committee was formed to establish the Infirmary. Among the most active of the promoters being Lord Dynevor, Sir John Mansel, Bishop Thirlwall, Thomas Charles Morris, and, of course, Dr. Lawrence. Finding a suitable building proved most difficult. The Drill Hall had been promised but the negotiations broke down. Nothing daunted, the Committee went ahead and before long found a temporary building to suit their purpose – the old gaol of the Borough at Carmarthen.

Eventually they acquired a piece of ground in Priory Street, namely the site of the old Grammar School. There they built their hospital, and there it still stands today, a monument to the voluntary efforts and the determination of our predecessors. It was officially opened in 1858, and you may be interested to learn that the total cost of the building, including the purchase of the site and all legal charges, amounted to £4,495 10s. 7d. The medical staff consisted of one physician and four surgeons. There is a feel of history in the fact that the building stands between St. Peter's church and the site of the Old Priory, whose medieval clergy, as I mentioned earlier, had also practised the healing arts of the doctor. While we salute and welcome the fine modern hospital that is the pride of west Wales, let us not forget those valiant pioneers who gave us the Infirmary – "The County and Borough of Carmarthen Infirmary" to give it its old title.

The other day I looked through the book of rules governing the Infirmary published in 1857. There are a few comments that I would like to make on the contents.

The Rules and Regulations were detailed and precise. The Resident Medical Officer was to receive a salary of £100 plus lodgings, coal, and candles. Each Surgeon was allowed to have two pupils who were charged not to conduct themselves disrespectfully or improperly to the matron, not to enter the women's ward unaccompanied, and were to be dismissed instantly if they appeared in the building in a state of intoxication. The Matron was to be a pearl beyond price, unmarried, between the age of 30 and 60, with a myriad of duties, in the execution of which she was to be helped by nurses and maid servants. The patients were to behave properly, not to swear or give abusive language, not to play at cards or dice, not to smoke in the wards, and not to be out of bed after 8 p.m. Everyone was to make as little noise as possible, to speak quietly, in an earnest conspiratorial manner like people in the Reading Room of the British Museum.

The history of the medical profession in Carmarthenshire is a subject that merits closer investigation, and the results placed on permanent record. This can be done by research among the archives that exist in the county, that is by consulting primary evidence. It would be a splendid achievement if a Medical Historical Committee were formed in Carmarthenshire to work towards this end, to collect old medical diaries, journals, recipes, letters, and other papers that doctors no longer require for current work. In another 15 or 20 years it may be too late. I am informed that a great deal of such material does exist, so that Carmarthenshire doctors can face the task of collecting and recording the evidence with every confidence. I would like to think that the time is not too far distant when I can add to my bookshelves a worthy history of Carmarthenshire doctors.

DIARIES OF A DOCTOR'S WIFE 1807-9, 1818

FEW SOURCES bring more satisfaction to the historian, particularly one engaged in compiling family and social chronicles, than diaries and journals of bygone days. In essence they were private records, often containing memoranda, verdicts and observations, not intended for public consumption, and would have been withheld or couched in more diplomatic and discreet language if delivered before an audience. Not that all such records are characterised by refreshing or explosive frankness. Indeed most are little more than prosaic day-to-day reports presented in abridged, or précised form, acquainting the reader with the diarist's progress through life. Whatever the contents, all are welcome, for they provide us with useful revealing information, confirming, modifying, or contradicting preconceived views and prejudices we may have held on certain subjects. All is grist to the historian's mill. Robert Browning neatly summed up what our attitude should be to such evidences, when he wrote:

"Every joy is gain,
And gain is gain, however small".

Among diaries preserved in the Dyfed Record Office at Carmarthen are two for the periods 1807-9 and 1818 compiled by the English wife of a Welsh doctor who, by a turn of fortune's wheel found himself, midway through his career, transformed into a country gentleman presiding over a fair estate. Somewhat tattered and in parts not easily deciphered, the volumes are the sole survivors of a series, and it is regrettable that more have not come to light. Not that the diaries are spectacular, indeed they are sober records couched in a minor key, seemingly trivial to us today, yet they expand our knowledge of the daily life of a class that formed, at one time, a significant segment of the Welsh community.

The diarist came to Carmarthenshire by marriage to a man who bore two surnames. He was Evan Jones, descended from a landowning family seated at Penyrallt in Llangoedmor near Cardigan. The father, David Jones, High Sheriff of his native county in 1748, had died in 1763, aged 49, leaving eight sons and five daughters, and it is the seventh son, Evan, born in 1758 who now commands our attention. Educated for the medical profession, Evan Jones qualified as a doctor in the early 1780s and is described in contemporary papers as "M.D. and surgeon". He settled in the county town of Carmarthen, soon acquired a high reputation, and is often mentioned in the muniments of west Wales county families. What is important to note is that Evan's sister, Elizabeth Jones, born in 1736 had married one

Evan Protheroe, owner of the Dolwilym estate in Llanglydwen parish in West Carmarthenshire.

I now turn to the doctor's brother-in-law Evan Protheroe, squire of Dolwilym, an estate owned by the family since Elizabethan days. His father, James Protheroe of Llwyn Huke farm, a younger son, succeeded to Dolwilym when his elder brother John died unmarried in 1720. But James only lived to enjoy the estate for ten years and was buried at Llanglydwen in 1730, leaving by his wife, Rebecca Eynon of Llandisilio, an only child, Evan, who found himself owner of Dolwilym. Born in 1715, Evan Protheroe married at the age of 32 to Mary Griffith of Llangolman in north Pembrokeshire. She died in 1765 and in the following year the widower married Elizabeth Jones of Penyrallt, an elder sister of the doctor. Much older than either of his wives, Evan Protheroe took a prominent part in public life, was a Commissioner of Taxes, a Justice of the Peace, and in 1779 High Sheriff of Carmarthenshire. On 17 December 1795, then in his 80th year, he died and was buried with his forebears in Llanglydwen church. And so with his death, the main male line at Dolwilym became extinct.

Evan Protheroe left no issue, and although he had several first cousins, (children of his father's sisters, viz. the Lewises of Fron in Llanddewi Velfrey and Lewises of Cilhernin in Llanboidy), he devised the Dolwilym estate by will dated 16 November 1795, to his wife Elizabeth for life, afterwards to her brother Dr. Evan Jones and his heirs for ever, provided that the doctor and his heirs

Dolwilym

resided at Dolwilym and took "the sirename Protheroe and called themselves by no other sirename". The widow remained at Dolwilym until her death on 16 July 1813 when in her 77th year, and then her brother Dr. Evan Jones became Dr. Evan Protheroe as inheritor of the estate.

As in many cases of this nature, speculation arose concerning reasons for the disposal of the estate away from those who had every right to consider themselves to be testator's heirs at law. However, there can be no doubt that Evan Protheroe had every right to dispose of the property in any manner he thought fit. The Lewises considered themselves unfairly disinherited and held the view that Evan's second wife's family had influenced him to bequeath the property to them, and had even persuaded the lawyers to withhold deeds and legal documents from scrutiny by the claimants. A note in the Carmarthenshire Antiquarian Transactions Vol. IV (1908-9) p. 85, contains some local gossip inspired by the subject, and the reason for the testamentary arrangement as follows – one of the Lewises having heard that old Evan had died, sent out invitations to friends to attend a feast and dance to celebrate his succession to Dolwilym as heir and next of kin; whereas in fact Evan was still very much alive and, hearing of the intending celebrations felt so deeply incensed that he left the property to a member of his wife's family.

Emma Protheroe

In 1797 Dr. Jones as he then was, married a widow, Mrs. Emma Garrick, a daughter and co-heiress of Perceval Hert, a wealthy malt-distiller of Brentford, Middlesex. She had married in 1778 David Garrick, a captain of the 1st Dragoon Guards, who lived at Hampton, descendant of a Huguenot who had found refuge in London during the late 17th century. His father, George Garrick, was brother to the distinguished actor David Garrick, (1717-1779) for whom he worked as business manager in Drury Lane, and is remembered largely for fighting a duel in Hyde Park on 6 March 1770. His mother was Elizabeth, daughter of Nathaniel Carrington, King's Messenger, who lived in Somerset House off The Strand. The captain of dragoons died in 1795 without surviving issue, and two years later the widowed Emma married Dr. Jones, and thus commenced the Garrick connection with west Wales. Not that all the Garrick visitations were as felicitous, for when Emma's cousin, Nathaniel Garrick, who bore a striking resemblance to a foreign potentate then hostile to England, came on a sightseeing trip in 1803, he was arrested in Pembrokeshire under the belief that he was none less than Napoleon Buonaparte in disguise, and was only allowed to return to England by way of Tenby under a pass from the Mayor of Haverfordwest, having been vouched for by Dr. Jones and Emma.

After the wedding they lived for a little while as tenants at Westmead, a large old residence near Pendine, and about 1800 they secured a lease of Gellidywyll, a hill-top mansion in the parish of Cenarth, near Newcastle Emlyn, a property owned by the Brigstocke family whose main residence was then at Blaenpant in south Cardiganshire. On 26 March 1808, Dr. Jones obtained a renewal of the lease for a further five years. By her Welsh husband Emma had two children – Evan Jones born on 1 June 1800, died on 1 November following and buried at Churchill, Somerset, and Emma Hart Jones born on 26 April 1802, privately baptised at Gellidywyll on 9 July following by her father's brother, the Revd. David Jones of Bath. They remained at Gellidywyll until 1813 when, on the death of Mrs. Elizabeth Protheroe of Dolwilym, the family moved to dwell at that house, and thereafter the doctor and his wife and daughter were known by the surname Protheroe. In contrast with their former home, a hilltop Pharos, the house of Dolwilym stands in a green glade deep in the valley bottom, on the banks of the river Taf, sheltered by steep wooded hillsides, a sylvan hermitage aptly christened "The Happy Valley" by its new mistress.

The earliest of her surviving journals, covering the period 1807-9 was written when she was Mrs. Jones of Gellidywyll, and the later, the 1818, when she was Mrs. Protheroe of Dolwilym. Ill-health clouded her later years, and the diaries contain several references to her sufferings, such as the entry of 1 May 1818 which shows she had been confined to the house for seven months, and the *cri de cœur* of the following, 30 August, "I have been a sad cripple for two years and 1 month to this day". Particularly pious, her journals bear ample witness to her religious attachments, as well as containing worldly information about social conditions and fashions of the time. She died on 5 February 1826 aged 64, and Dr. Protheroe on 22 February 1841, aged 83. Both were buried at Llanglydwen.

Both parents were devoted to their only child, Emma Hart Protheroe. She received her early education in Mrs. Thomas's boarding school for young ladies at Haverfordwest. On 3 June 1819 when only 17 years of age she married the 34 years old Captain William Garrick Brydges Schaw of the 46th Regiment, second son of Colonel Frederick Brydges Schaw of Weston Park, Surrey by Arabella Garrick, sister of the aforementioned Captain David Garrick of the 1st Dragoon Guards. Schaw who had seen foreign service, returned to England in January 1818, and came to Dolwilym for the first time on 10 June of that year. From the entries in the diary, the captain and young Emma spent much time together, and it is clear that her mother, delighted by the turn of events, was not to be disappointed by the result.

On their marriage Captain Schaw took the surname Protheroe, and with his wife settled at Colby Lodge, a neat Georgian residence near Amroth, but by 1839 they had moved to a small country house belonging to the Dolwilym estate, called Glyntaf, pleasantly situated on the breast of a hill above Dolwilym, where they continued until Dr. Protheroe's death in 1841, when they moved to their final home in the sheltered vale below. It was their great-grandson, the late Mr. G. F. Protheroe-Beynon, O.B.E., of Trewern, afterwards of Hurst House, Laugharne, who placed the family archives in the Carmarthen Record Office, among them the diaries which we shall now examine.

Commencing on 25 September 1807, ending on 27 September 1809, the first volume concerns life at Gellidywyll, events in northeast Carmarthenshire and the Tivyside generally; the other volume, written when Mrs. Protheroe was in ill-health and more or less confined to the house, includes the whole year 1818 and describes life at Dolwilym and the surrounding district.

A perusal of the journals provide revealing, if fleeting, glimpses of Welsh country life, during the early 19th century. One is impressed by the large number of callers (including some casual "droppers-in"), and the frequency of visits. Guests were entertained to dinner – as many as 18 sat around the Dolwilym dining table, most were lodged overnight, some stayed for several days. Family friends came to indulge in fishing, shooting, coursing, particularly fox-hunting, often attended by their own servants, some even brought their own packs of hounds, all of whom were accommodated with food and lodging, so that the mansion, stables and kennels were as full as one of David Garrick's "first night's" at Drury Lane.

Visitors were by no means limited to sporting gentlemen and their wives, and we find artists like Henry Haverfield staying for several days during which he executed portraits of members of his host's family. The Protheroes were similarly entertained on return visits. Not only did carriages and horses carry guests to dinner, but even to breakfast, once a popular convention of genteel society. They included kinsfolk and local gentry as well as friends from further afield – London, Bath, Cheltenham and the English shires, while a few arrived from France. Race-meetings, militia reviews, balls and routs contributed to the delights of rural life. Mrs. Protheroe was by no means divorced from contact with

Cromlech at Dolwilym

"ordinary" people, as shewn by her interest in marriage biddings of servants, while the indoor and outdoor staff and tenants were sumptuously regaled to meals at certain festivals such as Christmastide – for instance on 5 January 1818, "the poor people came for barley and the children for Christmas gifts, and a party of about forty dined in our kitchen". This hospitality was typical of the countryside. Neither were visits confined to residences and the diarist mentions outings to the Preseli hills, Cardiganshire beaches and to country fairs.

Dr. Protheroe was continually on the trot viewing properties on his estate, attending meetings of the Justices of the Peace, Grand Jury Service, manorial Courts Leet, and, as medical officer of militia, attended annual camps of the local battalion – all in addition to professional visits to patients, with whom he was very popular.

Such a life-style often led to mansions being enlarged and rebuilt, and we hear of rebuilding at Dolwilym in 1818. Lewis, compiler of the *Topographical Dictionary of Wales,* noted in 1835, 'Dolwilym the seat of Evan Protheroe, Esq., M.D., is a handsome modernized mansion, romantically situated in a deep vale', adding that the parish church was 'repaired and beautified some years since' at the expense of the Dolwilym family. Among the first things that the doctor's daughter and her husband did on inheriting the estate in 1841, was to completely demolish the old mansion and to erect a new one on the site. Expenses of the rebuilding from February 1842 to 1845 amounted to £216 14s. 9d. A view of this mansion occurs in Thomas Nicholas's *County Families,* (1872) from a photograph taken by C. S. Allen of Tenby (c. 1870). A tablet in an outhouse stating it was built by Evan Protheroe in 1788 is the only relic of the original; and another stone is inscribed "This house was built by W. G. B. Protheroe in 1843". About 1908 the second mansion was burnt down and a third mansion was built, but the family abandoned it and moved to nearby Glyntaf. Dinners for tenants were sometimes held there afterwards. During the 1st World War the mansion was occupied by German prisoners of war. After this it deteriorated and by today is a complete ruin, roofless, with skeletal grey walls, reminding us of Byron's melancholy line in Childe Harold "Man marks the earth with ruin".

The diaries are charged with instances of the giving and receiving of presents which brought pleasure into people's lives. But what happened to all these presents? Doubtless the great majority were enjoyed by those for which they were intended. Mrs. Jones, as she then was, allows us to peer through a little gap in the curtain on 14 May 1809 and the revelation may not surprise everyone. "Mr. Lloyd of Bronwydd sent us a turbot, which we sent on to Clynfew. I wrote to thank Mr. Lloyd".

Letter writing was almost an employment. Local letters were often delivered by friends and callers, the parson, the butcher, servants, on foot and on horseback, while letters directed to English relations and friends usually went by way of the National Postal Service. The countryside was never so isolated in bygone days as we are sometimes led to believe. Whatever the distances, people were constantly "in touch".

Jollifications dictated by conventions of the time reveal only one facet of her behaviour. Emma was deeply pious as revealed by numerous references to her religious attachments and observances which form a notable feature of the entries. Services for the family and household staff, usually conducted by herself, were held in the home on the Sabbath, occasionally helped by clergymen such as the Rev. Mr. Morse (who also ran a small "prep" school in Clydey parish). When her health permitted she attended the parish church, was on friendly terms with parsons, and with evangelically inclined neighbours such as the Lloyds of Bronwydd and Bowens of Llwyngwair whose parlours often resounded with Biblical verse, prayer and hymn. Among her correspondents was the famed religious writer Hannah More, a close friend of the Garricks, especially of the illustrious actor whose death in 1779 deeply affected her. To miss Sunday observance whether at home or church was an unhappy experience for the diarist as her entry on Sunday 11 October 1807 reveals – "A Black Day as it was not spent in the service of the Lord". At the end of a year she rounded off her diary with fervent thanks to the Lord for this manifold blessings.

Mrs. Protheroe was not wholly divorced from worldly vanities by any means, and like other English ladies who had found partners in the west, succumbed to the seductions of the Welsh penchant for genealogy, to become enmeshed in the spidery webs that connected her new found relations not only to Cadwaladr and Cunedda, but beyond them to the heroes of the Mabinogi and the warlike kings of the mountain crags. Although her researches were not as ambitious or as spectacular, nevertheless they were of the true stuff of genealogy as shown by her entry of 13 March 1809: "Left Dolwilym and came back to Gellydoweill; obliged to walk the mare home as she had hurt her leg in the stable – We were five hours in coming home and starved with cold". Mrs. Protheroe says that Doctor John Jones of Haverfordwest and Mr. David Jones of Penrallt were two sisters' children, so that "Mr. Lloyd of Bronwidd and my husband are second cousins". Also that "Mr. James Lewis of Dolehaidd, (father of the present Colonel Lloyd of Dolehaidd) and Mr. Jones of Penrallt were second cousins. Miss Hensley of Panteague who married Captain Alleyne of Cresselly and Miss Philpin of Ethenduon who married Mr. David Jones of Penrallt were second cousins . . . The first cup of tea ever made in the parish of Llangoedmor was made in the house at Penrallt".

Llansteffan Castle, guardian of the estuary bay

FLORENCE NIGHTINGALE REGRETS . . .

AMONG THE SOLDIERS who took part in the Crimean War was Howell Evans, the son of one of the tenants of the Glaspant estate in northwest Carmarthenshire. The date of his enlistment is not known, but the letter printed below shows that he was a Gunner and Driver in No. 1 Company, 12th Battalion, Royal Artillery. In June 1855 he was posted as "missing". His parents were alarmed at receiving no news of their son and finally asked their landlady, Mrs. Howell of Glaspant, to assist them. Accordingly, Mrs. Howell wrote direct to Florence Nightingale as it was possible that Howell was in a hospital, or had come to her attention in some way. It is clear that Miss Nightingale went to some trouble in the matter and her reply, written in her own hand, indicates the extent of her humanity and concern. I am grateful to Mr. Harry Howell, J.A., of Glaspant, Newcastle Emlyn, for permission to reproduce the letter.

General Hospital,
Balaclava.
May 20/56

Madam,
It is with very sincere sorrow that I am obliged to confirm the fears of the father of the late Howell Evans about his poor son.

I grieve to say that Gunner & Driver Howell Evans, of No 1 Company, 12th Battalion, Royal Artillery, was struck off the strength of this Army, June 29/55, as having been "missing since February 6/55".

His Company was in the Siege Train and went home in February/56. It is now at Woolwich. His father had better apply at the Office of the 12th Battalion. No trace of the missing man being obtainable here.

To you, Madam, I will say that, after the most diligent inquiry, it appears to the Commanding Officer of the unfortunate man & to myself, from the evidence, to be feared that Howell Evans is a deserter.

To the father, I would say, (if on enquiry at the above address it appears that nothing more is to be learnt), that I regret very much that I am unable to send him any of those particulars concerning his son which it is natural that he should wish to hear, but though I have made every enquiry in my power, I am unable to do more than send him the sad certainty of his death, (for I would fain put it so).

Although it be impossible to us to retain particulars of the deaths of all those brave soldiers, who have died in the service of their country, during that fearful winter, it is a comfort to me, who have seen so much of their patient suffering, to remember that no one is forgotten by the Father of us all, I trust it will be a comfort to the father to remember that all are in His "hands". I doubt not he has suffered much from painful uncertainty concerning his poor son. Let him (if no further news is to be obtained), know that he now is at rest from all cares & sorrows of this world. May he be supported to bear them, till it please God that those who have been separated by death shall meet again in the better life to come.

I have never had so painful & unsatisfactory a letter to write.

I beg to remain, Madam,
Your obedt servt
Florence Nightingale

Gellideg in its days of Edwardian grandeur

DIARY OF A YOUNG LADY OF FASHION 1865-71

THE DIARIES of Miss Hermione Jennings of Gellideg for the years 1865-71, provide a vivid picture of the life of a young lady of fashion, containing descriptions of assemblies and routs in Carmarthenshire, her presentation at Court, her first London season, visits to country-houses and watering places, archery meetings at Llandeilo, dinners and house parties in West Wales. She was observant, pert, articulate, and her writing is like good conversation of some vivacious hostess out of Madam de Sevigny or Proust, who has known courts and men. Later she married Captain Barclay of the 63rd Regiment of Foot.

Attractive features of country house life in Victorian days are revealed in her pages. One is the scale of entertainment. It was by no means unusual to find as many as 20 or 30 guests, complete with maids and valets, arriving and staying three or four days. There was no wireless or TV or canned music in those days, and so impromptu concerts, charades, and plays were produced and the parts acted by the guests and their hosts, visits were made to places of interest, old castles, and churches, Twm Shon Catti's cave, and so on. These were the creative activities of people relying on their own abilities, the important art of self-help and self-reliance.

Visit to the Gulstons

On Tuesday July the 31st, Mamma and I went to stay at Dirleton, the Gulston's place. When Mamma first got up she was not at all well and thought she would not be able to go, but however she got better and we started from here with Wakeford at 10½ and drove to Carmarthen where we did some shopping. We met Mr. Goring Thomas at Bagnall Davies's, and talked to him some time. We then went on to Carmarthen Station and went by the 2.20 train to Llandeilo where we changed trains for Llangadock. Mr. C. Bishop got into our carriage at Llandeilo. We found a close carriage awaiting us at Llangadock which took us up to Dirleton in a very short time as it is only a mile from the station. We were shown into the drawing room where we found Mrs. and Miss Gulston, and soon Lizzie Gulston came in and Harry and May Gavine (Giveen) (Mrs. Gulston's nephew and niece). After talking a little time we had lunch and were then shown our rooms, after which Mrs. Gulston took us all over the house which took nearly an hour as it is an enormous place with long rambling passages and heaps of rooms not half furnished. At 4 o'clock Mamma and I went with Mr. and Miss Gulston in the sociable for a very pretty drive, with lovely views. Harry went on the box, and went one way along the turnpike road and came back another. We got home about 7¼. We had dinner at 8 in the old dining room. There was no party, only themselves who consisted of Mr., Mrs. and the two Miss Gulstons, Stepney, Frank, and Arthur Gulston, and Harry and Robert Gavine. I went in to dinner with Stepney Gulston. The governess, Miss Young, appeared in the evening when we all sang Chrysty's Minstrells.

Wednesday. We got up and came down to breakfast at 10. Miss Gulston did not get up till about 11, so we had breakfast alone with Mrs. Gulston as all the others had breakfasted early. At 12½ Mrs. and Miss Gulston, Mamma, and I went in the brougham to Llandeilo for the archery meeting. We first stopped at the Cawdor Arms and went upstairs to look at the prizes, which were none of them very pretty. We then went on to the archery ground where after a little waiting about we began shooting. Mr. T. Jones was the captain of our target which Miss Gulston and I had to ourselves. It was a grey sort of day with no sun, but a good deal of wind, and before we had finished shooting at 60 it came in to rain. However we finished 4 dozen arrows before we went into the tent. The shooting began at 11 and we had

luncheon in the tent at 3, during which time it rained in torrents. Amongst those whom we knew were Mrs. and Miss Cross and Alaric Cross (Richie came with them) Mr. Alboy Pryce, Mrs. Harries of Aberglasney and her niece Miss Pugh Pryce, D. Jones M.P. and his daughters and Miss Johns, Mr. Long Price and two of his sisters, the Jones' of Velindre, the Lloyds of Glensevin, etc, etc. Miss Gulston and I kept close together in scores all the way through and when we left off shooting at 60 she was one ahead of me. After luncheon we only had time to shoot 6 arrows before the rain came down so heavily that we were obliged to leave off and after waiting in the tent half an hour the prizes were distributed as there seemed no chance of the rain leaving off. During the last 6 arrows I had got two whites while Miss Gulston got nothing, so I was now just one ahead of her, and got the second prize in consequence, viz. a double scent bottle with gold tops. Miss C. Lloyd got the first prize, a scent bottle like mine only red glass. The gentlemen who got prizes were Mr. T. Jones and Mr. Phillips. The other ladies who shot were Mrs. T. Jones, Miss Neville, and Miss Hughes. After the distribution of prizes we all went to the Cawdor Arms and had tea, after which we drove home, taking Richie back with us on the dickey behind with Harry Gavine. Had dinner at 8 in the small dining room. No party. Had singing in the evening, "Long live the merry merry heart", etc.

Thursday. Showery. Went about the grounds with Miss Gulston, Mamma, and Richie. Then we went in the boat on the river, and I went a little way in the coracle with Stepney Gulston. When we came in, I played at a game with bags of peas with Arthur Gulston. After luncheon which was at 2, Mamma, Richie, and I went with Miss Gulston and her eldest brother in the sociable to Llandovery, where we called on Mrs. Jones of Velindre to ask her to come that evening to the dance at Dirleton. I talked to the two Miss Nevills who were staying there, one of whom stammered very much. We tried at several shops to get Richie a pair of white kid gloves, but in vain, such articles were unknown in these regions. We came back a different way and called at Cilgwyn (Mr. Gwinne Holford's) to see old Martin who showed us over the house and was affected to tears. We were 14 at dinner. The Peels of Taliaris came, a party of 5, Mr. and Mrs. Peel, Mr. Herbert Peel, and two daughters. I went in to dinner with Mr. Jones of Velindre. During dinner S. Gulston who sat on my right hand, passed my fan round the table, which at last came back to me on the other side. After dinner there was a dance in the dining room which was kept up till 1. Mrs. Jones of Velindre and two Miss Nevilles came. Alaric Cross arrived at 3 in the evening.

Friday. Very showery. I played croquet on the new ground with Lizzie Gulston and her brothers and Harry. Miss Gulston and Alaric Cross looked on. It came on to rain several times very hard but we went on playing all the same with cloaks and umbrellas. We had luncheon soon after 1, and left Dirleton at 2. A. Gulston went with us to the station, and ran back to fetch my archery box which I found I had left behind when half way to the station. A. Crosse went back with us to Carmarthen station. Did some shopping at Carmarthen and then came home where we arrived at 6.

Croquet Party and Dance at Aberglasney and Visit to Dirleton

On Thursday the 7th of August, Arthur and I went to Carmarthen station by the 1.15 train accompanied by Guilietta Crosse who joined us at Carmarthen station and who was also going to Aberglasney. At Golden Grove station she was met by her brother and Mr. Peel whom he had been staying with and who had driven him over to the station. As the Aberglasney carriage was not there to meet us, Mr. Peel offered to take us over to Aberglasney in his carriage, which we accordingly did. But after proceeding about half way we met Mrs. Barnes's carriage coming for us, so we changed and arrived at Aberglasney (a curious old fashioned looking place) in about a quarter of an hour. Mrs. Harries and her father Mr. Phillips received us at the door, and taking us in to the drawing room, and from thence to a small room beyond, where a cold lunch was prepared. We sat down to an elegant cold collation which Miss Pugh Pryce, Mrs. Harries's niece, soon came down to, and a Mr. and Mrs. Alexander who were staying in the house, the latter a very eccentric vulgar person of about 30.

About an hour after lunch the Gulston party arrived whom it had been arranged I was to go back with, while Arthur remained at Aberglasney until the following day, and was then to join me at Dirleton, and as Mrs. Gulston particularly wished us to remain with them till Saturday instead of returning the following day; Arthur was to telegraph home the next morning to tell them so. The Gulston party consisted of Mrs. and the two Miss Gulstons, Stepney and Arthur Gulston and Mr. Gavine, Mrs. Gulston's brother.

We played croquet all the afternoon on the lawn. There were three sets, and people came dropping in all the afternoon. Those playing in our set were Horatio and Stepney Gulston, Mr. Gavine, Mother Gamp alias Mrs. Harries, Guilietta Crosse, and Miss Alexander. At 7 we left off playing and got ready for dinner. The Gulstons, G. Crosse, and I all had the same room. We all wore high white muslin dresses and wore natural flowers in our hair. We had dinner at about a quarter to eight. I went in with Stepney Gulston. We were about 24 altogether. There were 18 at the principal table and 6 at the side table. In addition to those I have before named there were Captain Lloyd and two Miss Lloyds and young Lloyd, a young man staying with Mrs. Harries and Mrs. H's ward, a boy of about 14, Mrs. Phillips, Mrs. Barnes's sister, etc, etc. Guiletta sat at the side table and made a great noise laughing and shrieking. After dinner we had dancing in the hall which was oak, but we were obliged to dance round the billiard table which was too heavy to be moved. We left Aberglasney at 12 and reached Dirleton at about 1½.

Friday. Had breakfast at 11 and was introduced to Mr. Mrs., and Miss Foley and two gentlemen staying in the house. At 12 we played croquet till 2, the players being Mrs. and Miss Foley and myself, Stepney and Arthur Gulston, Lizzie Gulston, and Mrs. Gavine. After luncheon Arthur and I went in the boat with Mr. Gavine, Stepney Gulston and Robert,

down the river to Llandeilo, about 7 or 8 miles. Arthur rowed us all the way. We got to Llandeilo in about two hours, and, leaving the boat at the railway station, we came back to Llangadock by the train which arrived in about a quarter of an hour, and in which Mr. and Mrs. Biddulph were coming to stay at Dirleton. We got into the same carriage with them and Mr. C. Bishop, and got out at Llangadock where the poney (*sic*) carriage was waiting for the Biddulphs who went up to Dirleton in it while we all walked back. There was no one else to dinner but those staying in the house. The French maid did my hair, and I wore my high white dress. I went in to dinner with Mr. Gavine. The Aberglasney party came in the evening, when we had dancing in the new drawing room, which we wound up by a cotillon which I danced with Stepney Gulston who led it. We went to bed about 4.

Saturday. Had breakfast soon after 11. Then played croquet till 1½, after which we got ready to leave and took our departure at 2, Mr. Gavine driving us in the poney [*sic*] carriage to the station. A. Gulston went as far as Llandeilo.

Third Visit to Dirleton

On Monday, the 3rd of September, Mamma and I with Wakeford and Lewis went to stay with the Gulstons for the archery meeting. Went from Carmarthen by the 1.15 train, and got to Llangadock at 2.30. Baron de Rutzen got into our carriage at Carmarthen and went with us, as he was also going to stay at Dirleton. When we arrived we had luncheon after which we played croquet till 6½. Those in our game were Arthur and Lizzie Gulston, Miss Young, Miss Pollzac, Baron de R and myself. Afterwards Miss Gulston took Lizzie's ball. Mr. and Mrs. and two Miss Llewellins and Mr. Somerset and his brother arrived by the 6½ train. I went in to dinner with Mr. Somerset senior. We had singing in the evening.

Tuesday. Wet nearly all day. We drove in the van into Llandeilo in hopes of it clearing for the archery meeting. Mrs. and Miss Gulston, Stepney Gulston, and Mr. and Miss Llewellin went in the van, the others were to come afterwards. We got to the Cawdor Arms soon after 1, and found no one there but the Bishops. As it was still raining with no hopes of clearing up, Mrs. Gulston and Mr. C. Bishop sent messages and telegrams to all the members of the club, saying that the meeting was postponed till tomorrow, but the dance would be tonight. We then had luncheon and waited in the room at the Cawdor Arms all the afternoon where the Lloyds of Glansevin and the Smiths and others came afterwards. The rest of our party arrived about 4 and then we played games, and acted charades in the ball room till 5½. Then we dressed in the bedroom putting on muslin garribaldis etc, and then had tea. Several more people arrived, the Miss Joneses of Pantglas, the Miss Pryces of Talley, etc. Dancing commenced at 7 and was kept up till 11½. There was a supper provided at 10½. The band was from Swansea. We arrived at Dirleton about 1 where a cold supper was provided.

Wednesday. Very showery day, doubt as to whether the meeting would take place or not. Young Lloyd (of Glansevin) rode over at 12 to ask if we were going or not. Mrs. G. sent him to telegraph to C. Bishop to ask if the meeting was to take place or not. The answer came that it was. At 2½ Mrs. G., Miss G., Mr. and Miss Llewellin and I started in the covered sociable for Llandeilo. It rained nearly the whole way, and when we got to the Cawdor Arms, Mrs. G. had out Mr. C. Bishop and arranged with him that the meeting should be put off till the first Wednesday in October. We met young Jones of Pantglas on our way and took him with us back to Dirleton where on our return we found young Lewis of Stradey had arrived. We played at games in doors till it was time to dress for dinner. The Peels, and the two Mr. Gwinne Holfords came to dine. I went in with Mr. Somerset. A large party arrived in the evening for the dance that was to take place. Those whom I knew were Mrs. Harries and Miss Pugh Pryse, the Pryses of Talley, the Lloyds of Glansevin, Mr. Phillips, Captain Lewes, the Miss Jones of Pantglas and Mr. Jones of Blanos, the Jones of Velindre, the Tom Jones, ete, etc. We danced in the dining room and the band came over that played at the Cawdor Arms the night before. The dancing was kept up till nearly 3 and ended with a cotillon which I danced with Mansel Lewis. The supper was in the old dining room, and the refreshments in a little place in the hall. *Thursday.* Wet all day. Had breakfast at 11½ after which we played games in the hall till luncheon time. We left Dirleton

Dirleton

at 1.40 and went with the Llewellins and Baron de Rutzen by the 2 o'clock train. We parted from the Llewellins at Llandeilo, but Baron de Rutzen went with us as far as Carmarthen. I bought a sailor's hat, black leather, at Bagnall & Davies, and also a buckle, price 8 shillings. Reached home a little before 6.

Dinner Party at the Crosses [Iscoed]

On Thursday the 23 of August, Mamma, Richie, Arthur, and I dined at the Crosses, a party of 12. Met Sir J. and Lady Hamilton and Mr. O. Jones, and old Miss Crosse. I went in with Alaric, King of the Goths. Had singing in the evening and a game of Pope Joan.

Luncheon Party at the Prices [Oaklands]

On Tuesday the 21st of August, Mamma, Richie, Arthur, and I went to lunch with the Pryces of Oaklands. We met Mrs. Crosse, young Crosse, and Guilietta, Mr. F. Bishop and Miss J. Bishop, Miss Andrews, and a cousin of Mr. Pryce's. After luncheon we played croquet. We played a game, Gellydeg v Iscoed. Richie, Arthur and I playing on the side of Gellydeg, and beating young Crosse, Miss Crosse, and Mr. E. Bishop.

Dinner Party at Mrs. H. Williams [Edwinsford]

On Friday the 21st of September, Mamma, Richie, and I dined with Mrs. H. Williams, a party of 10. Met 3 of the Crosses, Lady Hanbury, Mr. O. Jones, and Mr. Davies the curate. The latter I went in to dinner with, Richie took in Guilietta. In the morning we played vingt-un. I won 3s. 3d.

2nd Dinner Party at Mrs. H. Williams

On Wednesday the 17th of October, Mamma and I dined at Mrs. Hamlyn Williams'. Papa was to have gone but he came back from a meeting at Carmarthen feeling not very well, and therefore sent an excuse. The party consisted of only the Goring Thomases and ourselves. We played vingt-un after dinner and I gained 1 shilling.

Fourth Visit to Dirleton for the Archery Meeting

On Thursday the 24th of October I went to stay with the Gulstons taking Wakeford with me. We started from home at 3 and reached Carmarthen station at 4.40, thinking we had half an hour to wait. But finding the trains had been altered we had only just time to get into the train before it started. On reaching Llandeilo station we found we had half an hour to wait there, so we took a walk through the town. On returning to the station we fell in with Little C. Bishop who got into our carriage and went with us as far as Llangadock. On reaching that station we found that my box had been left behind. So I telegraphed to Llandeilo telling them to send it on by the first train tomorrow. There was no one else at Dirleton but the Gulston party who had only that day returned from their visits in England after coming back from the wedding in London. The sons at home were Stepney and George. We had singing in the evening. Miss Gulston lent me things to wear.

Friday. A grey day, without rain or sun, very good for the new archery meeting. At 12½ Mrs. and Miss G. and George G. and I started in the brougham (after many botherations) for Llandeilo. We reached the archery ground after everybody had assembled, and after putting on our things and speaking to different people, we proceeded to our targets. Horatia and I were at the same target, the furthest from the tent; the only others at our targets were G. Gulston and the Captain, Mr. Tom Jones. It was a very good meeting and there were a good number shooting and several strangers. Miss L. Jones of Pantglas shot, and Miss C. Lloyd of Glansevin, two Miss Bishops, and three Miss Hughes, etc., etc., and several more, also a good many gentlemen. After shooting at 60 at which I scored 60 we went into the tent and had luncheon after which we went on with the shooting for an hour, more shooting 2 dozen at 50. On leaving off I scored altogether 111. After waiting about half an hour while the scores were being added up, we all went into the tent where the successful shooters were named by the Hon Sec. C. Bishop, and the prizes awarded. The first prize was given to Miss C. Loyd by D. Pugh Esq. M.P. who made her a speech. The prize was a pair of earrings. The second prize given by D. Jones, M.P., he presented to me with a flowery and complimentary speech ending with "that he was very glad to award the prize to so *fair* and lovely a damsel". The prize was a very pretty gold locket with 3 corral berries and green enamel leaves and a small diamond on each berry. I also had my choice of a pair of marble candlesticks but of course I chose the locket. The other prizes were won by Mrs. T. Jones, Miss Gulston (for best gold) and Miss Neville. Miss Snead got the strangers' prize. There were three gentlemen's prizes but who got them I forget. There was a dance afterwards at the Cawdor Arms from 7 till 11. We reached Dirleton at 1.

Saturday. Beautiful bright day. I was to have gone home but Mrs. Gulston had pressed me to stay till Monday and had written to tell Mamma so. I wrote after breakfast to Mama giving an account of the archery meeting and then practiced my singing. At 1 Horatia, George Gulston, and I went in the pony carriage to call on the Peels of Taliaris. Horatia drove and George and I sat behind. We saw Mrs. Peel, Mr. Herbert Peel, and an odd child. We returned to Dirleton about 5. Mrs. G. received a telegram from the Jones' of Pantglas (whom they had expected to come and stay till Monday at Dirleton) saying they were too knocked up by the festivities of yesterday to be able to come. Mr. Somerset arrived; we had singing in the evening.

Sunday. Fine. We all went to Llangadock church in the morning. The service was half English and half Welch. Horatia and Mr. Somerset behaved very badly, laughing, etc. She gave him the marriage service to read and a hymn on matrimony to learn by heart. After church we went to call on the Lloyds of Danyrallt in the town, but on finding the children there had the whooping cough we all left except Mrs. Gulston who stayed there for luncheon. At 3½ we all went on the river in corracles. Horatia, Mr. Somerset, G., and I each in four separate corracles. Mr. Somerset bringing his very near Horatia's, she upset him. While he went in

Danyrallt

to change his things, S. Gulston took his corracle and we all went down the rapids. We then took the corracles in, and Mr. Somerset having returned we five went for a walk in the meadow by the river, where Mr. Somerset did the *excessively* agreeable to Horatia. We returned about 6, and had dinner at 7½. We looked over photos, etc., in the evening.

Monday. Fine bright day. I left Dirleton at 11 and drove to Llandeilo Station with Horatia, in the sociable. Got to Carmarthen about 3, did some shopping, went to the Junction Station to fetch Richie's portmanteau which he left there on Saturday on his return from staying at the Colbys. Saw the partial eclipse of the sun very well. Reached home a little before 6.

Third Dinner Party at Mrs. Hamlyn Williams

On Thursday, November 1st, Papa, Mamma, and I dined at Mrs. H. Williams who had asked me to stay there till Saturday. Mrs. Price, Oaklands, had asked us to dine with her on the same day which we had declined. I went in a high white garibaldi (because my neck was covered in flea bites) and wore coral ornaments, with holly in my hair. We were 11 at dinner and met Mr. and Mrs. Lloyd Phillips, Captain, Mrs., and Miss Crosse, and Mr. Owen Jones. At dinner I sat between Mrs. H. Williams and Captain Crosse. In the evening we had riddles and puzzles to amuse us. Papa and Mamma went at 11, and I was left. Soon afterwards I was shown to my room which led out of the drawing room and looked out on the garden. Mrs. H. Williams's maid did my hair, an old woman who had lived with the Stracys and knew the Arkwrights.

Friday. We had breakfast about 10. It was misty nearly all the morning and we stayed indoors and worked and talked. I played frogs and toads with Mrs. H. Williams. Luncheon at 1, after which we drove to Iscoed where we met a Major and Mrs. Hill, awfully vulgar people. We walked over the garden at Iscoed and returned to Ferryside about 4½, when Mrs. Phillips and I walked about the grounds. No one else to dinner but ourselves; in the evening had puzzles and whist. To bed at 10½.

Saturday. After breakfast played frogs and toads till the carriage came for me at 11. I returned home. Lady Hanbury gave me a puzzle.

Fourth Dinner at Mrs. H. Williams's

On Thursday the 8th of November, Papa, Mamma, and I dined again with Mrs. H. Williams. We had been asked by her to call for Mrs. Phillips, Undercliff, on our way and bring her up with us. This we did, though not knowing her then it was rather awkward. Her husband walked up. We met, besides the Phillips's, Mr. and Mrs. Goring Thomas, and Mrs. Harries (Aberglasney) who were staying in the house. I went down to dinner with Mrs. Harries who burnt her mouth at dinner. We played vingt-un in the evening. On our way home we set down Mrs. Phillips.

Our Magic Lantern Party

On Monday, December 17, we had an exhibition of the magic lantern to all the gentry of the neighbourhood. The performance began at 3 and lasted an hour and a half. I exhibited the tragic parts and Louy [*sic*] the comic. Those who came were Mrs. H. Williams, Lady Hanbury, Mr. and Miss Crosse, two of the Miss Stoakes, Mrs. Stevens and their son David, Mr. and Mrs. Price and two of their children, and the little girl the ward of the Andrews. We had asked besides the Owen Jones', the Phillips', the Andrews, and Mr. Malephant, but they disappointed us at the last. The exhibition was in the hall after which they had tea in the drawing room which was helped by Wakeford and Elizabeth behind a long table.

Our Visit to Mrs. Biddulph

On Wednesday, December 19, Mamma, Richie, and I went to stay at Dirwin for a day or two. We went from Kidwelly station about 1, taking with us Lewis and Wakeford. Arthur walked to the station to see us off. We changed at Llandore for Swansea where we arrived about 2½. Mama and Wakeford did shopping while Richie and I walked about the town and were photographed at Andrews'. We returned to the station about 5 where we met the others, and, hiring a fly with half tipsy driver proceeded to Dirwin, a distance of about 3 miles. On arriving we were shown upstairs to the tea room, where we found Mr. and Mrs. Biddulph, Miss Gulston, young Jones, and a Miss Foley. Soon afterwards Frank Gulston arrived from London. Then we proceeded up stairs to dress for dinner. We had the same rooms as last year. I wore my blue dress with blue wreath. On going down to the drawing room, young Jones began showing us conjuring tricks. Soon afterwards Mrs. Gulston made her appearance, and then Miss Chambers. Mr. and Miss Wilmott and Mrs. Morrice dined there, whom we met last year, and some others besides. I went in to dinner with a Mr. Smith who came with Mrs. Morrice. After dinner the Sketty bell ringers came and played several tunes in the hall on their bells, which was very pretty. We had singing afterwards, then a game of poole [*sic*], and then a little dancing round the billiard table till 12 o'clock.

Thursday. Fine and cold. Came down to breakfast at 10½. Miss Gulston as usual not down. Pottered about in the drawing room in the morning. Some played billiards and Poole, and some sang. Young Jones imitated Miss Gulston singing "I cannot sing the old songs". Miss Chambers drove Richie and me out in a pony carriage in the afternoon. She payed a short visit while we drove on and then came back for her. Drove back to Dirwin through Sketty, a very pretty village. On our return we found Mama in the little boudoir reading (staying at home for her cold) and Miss Foley down in the drawing room. Miss Chambers, Richie, and I then walked down to the sands where we had to climb some wire fences to get to the sea. I lost my bunch of charms. After looking for them in vain we returned home. We had tea and then Arthur Gulston made his appearance, just returned from his holidays. Several people came to dinner, amongst them Mr. and Mrs. Wilmott and another Miss Wilmott, Mr. Smith again, and others. I was taken in to dinner by a naval gentleman and had A. Gulston on the other side, had great fun chaffing him. Had a regular dance in the evening, kept it up till one, ended it with a country dance and Sir Roger de Coverley. A lady came who sang splendidly.

Friday. Came down soon after 10, just in time to see Miss Chambers off. Then we had breakfast. I played billiards and poole with the young Gulstons and young Jones. Then I put up my things. Richie and I took leave of Mrs. Biddulph and proceeded to the sands to look for my charms, but could not find them. We then walked on to Swansea and went to see our photos at Andrews'. I was done again. We bought a bunch of mistletoe and then went to the station where we joined Mamma and the Gulstons who had just arrived, the latter with their 36 parcels and their attendant slave, young Jones. We started soon after 4 in the same carriage as far as Landore, where we had to wait an immense time for the train. We then got into different carriages, and went on to Llanelli where the Gulstons got out, also Mr. Lewis of Stradey who was in our carriage. We got home a little before 7.

Précis of Miss Jennings account of a visit to Pantglas, near Llanfynydd, in January 1867

Wednesday Jan 23, "Mamma and I went to stay for three days with the Joneses of Pantglas". They were welcomed at the door by Mr. and Mrs. Jones, Miss Jones, and, she writes, "the youngest boy little Gerwyn Jones, who was about 10, a good looking child with large prominent teeth". There were 18 guests, including 6 of the Stepney-Gulstons, Mr. Crawshay, Mr. and Mrs. Drummond, Mr. Somerset, and Miss Boultbee. After dinner they all went to a private ball at Aberglasney, where they danced until 5 a.m. They returned with the dawn to Pantglas where the party had another supper before going to bed.

Thursday. "At 12 o'clock I came down to breakfast." During the afternoon she helped to arrange charades; looked through a cutting book of heraldic crests; singing in the drawing room where Alfred Jones sang "Champagne Charles" and "Paddle your own Canoe", and "joined in the chorus". In the evening they played a charade in the hall, those taking part being dressed in a variety of costumes, old uniforms, hunting coats, and so on. Stepney Gulston read a prologue which he had written himself. In one scene, young Gerwyn Jones, the lad with the prominent teeth, appeared, dressed up as a baby in a pram complete with rattle and bottle. He seems to have entered into the part with immense zest, for Miss Jennings says – "This scene was spoiled by Gerwyn Jones' hideous howling so that not a word could be heard." After this they danced until 2 a.m.

Friday. Came down to breakfast at 11.30. In the afternoon they went in carriages to Aberglasney, then Llandeilo "where the gentlemen bought us lemonade and goodies". In the evening they danced at Pantglas, which ended at 6 o'clock on Saturday morning.

Saturday. Came down to breakfast at 12, after which all the guests prepared to go their different ways. It was then that a quaint incident occurred. Miss Jennings writes as follows – "Mr. Somerset got into a carriage *alone* with Miss Boultbee to go to Carmarthen. Mrs. Gulston was angry at this and insisted on a maid going inside as well and travelling with them. They waved goodbye and drove down the drive, but we afterwards found out that as soon as they were out of sight they turned the maid out again. Mrs. Gulston was *very* angry with Miss Boultbee about it and abused her very much."

A swarm is a sign of good luck

NOTES ON BEES

IN THE OLD DAYS honey formed an important article of food and also of medicine. Until the introduction of sugar, honey was the only form of sweetener. The Ancient Britons kept swarms of bees before the coming of the Romans.

Bees were sufficiently important to be included in the Laws of Hywel Dda (codified at Whitland in the period 900-930 A.D.).

Here are some of the Laws relating to them:

1. For a wing-swarm of bees, 4d. is to be paid without augmentation.

2. On whatever boundary a wild swarm of bees is found, the Law says that it is right for the owners to hew the tree on each side alternatively, and he on whose land the tree fell, was to have the swarm.

3. If bees come to another person's skep, and eat the honey, and the owner of the honey is willing to be compensated by the owner of the bees who devoured it, the Law says that he is not to swear to them without a skep as they cannot be distinguished, and he cannot recover them from the owner of the skep, for he did nothing illegal with them, and their annoyance was not less than their benefit.

4. Among the goods of the bondsmen, the lord is entitled to honey.

5. A bondsman cannot sell honey without the lord's permission.

6. The Princes of Dynevor are to pay the following dues to the Princes of Gwynedd – 4 tuns of honey, each tun containing 4 "mu", each "mu" containing 2 "gren", each "gren" being a load for 2 men on a pole carried between them.

Bees were valued by the swarm from 4d. to 24d., according to the size of the swarm. They were of great importance in the Middle Ages, as honey took the place of sugar, and mead made from it was a national drink in Wales.

The Gwentian Code in the Laws of Hywel Dda, says that bees originated in Paradise, but when Adam sinned in Eden the bees fled with the blessing of God upon them, and this blessing made it necessary for candles to be made of beeswax to be used whenever Mass was sung in the churches.

Honey was a basis for several medicines. Still used in the countryside as a cure for sore throats.

Honey was the chief drink and food of the Druids.

Folklore beliefs

If the Queen bee flew to a child when he was asleep, it meant that he would enjoy good luck throughout his life.

If you do not confide your joys and sorrows to the bees, all your hives will waste away within a year.

A hive given as a present to a person will bring good luck to the home; but a hive of bees bought will not thrive so well – Bees should be paid for in kind.

Sunday is considered a lucky day for swarming bees.

A strange swarm settling on a house or entering a garden is a sign of prosperity and good luck.

Bees and crickets bring blessings to a house and it is unlucky to kill them.

In some parts of Wales, when a husband died, the widow would go to the garden, knock softly on the hive, and say, "He's gone, he's gone." If she heard a humming it meant that the bees would remain, but if not the bees would quit the place shortly.

Thought to be unlucky to remove hives except on Good Friday. The honey of wild bees in the woodland and elsewhere, were collected by the Welsh.

So plentiful were bees in Carmarthenshire in the seventeenth and eighteenth centuries that honey and beeswax, were exported in ships from Carmarthen Quay.
In August it was custom in Carmarthenshire, and still is, to take the hives up to heather-growing areas, such as Trelech, so that the bees might suck from the ling heather, which imparts a delicious taste to the honey.

> "A swarm of bees in May is worth a load of hay.
> A swarm of bees in June is worth a silver spoon.
> A swarm of bees in July is hardly worth a fly." – *Old saying*

On 1 January 1827, "The Bee Hive Society" (Cymdeithas Gyfeillgar y Cwch Gwenyn) was formed at Tregaron, and held its meetings at the Talbot Hotel. Its object was to raise a fund to support members in their old age and towards the burial of members and their wives. This society remained in being until the coming of the Old Age Pensions Scheme.

Bees were kept by the Celts, Romans, Egyptians.

Jupiter the Roman god was said to have been fed by bees in his infancy.

Of Plato the philosopher it is said that bees settled on his lips when a child, indicating that he would become famous by his honeyed words: "bees, the little almsmen of Spring bowers . . ." – *Keats (Isabella, XIII)*

Bees in Coats of Arms

Bees symbolise industry and are often included in heraldic devices.

The coat-of-arms of Trahaearn of Newcastle Emlyn, a medieval Welsh chieftain, bore six bees. The coat-of-arms of Lord Merthyr contains three bees in flight, and on the shoulder of the two lions supporting his shield is a similar bee.

The bee has given the language one of its most delightful words, namely "honeymoon".

"Marriage, like the useful bee, builds a house and gathers sweetness from every flower, and labours, and unites into societies and republics" – *J. Taylor.*

The bee has given another word to the language, namely "beeline". When the bee prepares to return to its hive it flies on a fixed line and is guaranteed to arrive there safely by the shortest route. It is dangerous to move a hive when the bees are out, as they may not find it again.

One of the finest books written in modern times is Maeterlinck's book on *The Bee*.

"Alas, poor Bonzo"

DOG GRAVES

Cemetery in Grounds in Cilymaenllwyd House, in a wood just west of the house, near the old Tennis Court and Summer House

Tombstones

1. *Sweep,* Died April 1936.
2. In memory of *Polly,* born at Luttabund in Afghanistan 1879. Died at Llanerch September 1892. Ci Ffyddlon.
    Also *Napoleon* (Pol), found at Waterloo 1903. Died at Llanelly 1912.
    Also of *Napoleon* (Popol the Puppy), born 1922. Died 1923.
3. *Queen Dalvia.* Born 1930. Died 1938.
4. Dear Little *Sospan Snow White,* born 1936. Died 1941.
5. *Bingo Lewis* son of Josephine. 1939.
6. In memory of our pet *Shirley Mackay.* Died March 1 1950
7. Gallant Little *Nell,* born June 1934. Died by enemy action while with the 2nd Bn Coldstream Guards, March 1941 (a terrier Jack Russell, bomb fell in England & killed the dog).
8. Dear Little *Josephine,* aged 11 years, a Quaint Funny Little Friend Greatly Beloved. 1937-1948.
9. *Ferdinand.* Born 1929. Died 1941. Brother of *Franz Joseph.*
10. *Sweep.* Died Aug 1936.
11. *Feeble Utterance* (Hissock) Born 1932. The Father of the Cilymaenllwyd Racers, who died after many victories August 1942.

12. *Titipu* the wise and wonderful Woozle. 1941-1958.

13. Beautiful *Phil* wife of Max, kind, considerate, unselfish. Died aged 15 years. 'J'attendrai." 1931-1946.

14. Two little Black Brothers, *Wuffie* and *Misery,* who lived happily with us for 15 years. Faithful Wuffie. Poor Little Mizz. 1932-1947.

15. Tread lightly, lightly tread, for here rests Cherie, a faithful guard and companion for fifteen years. January 13, 1863.

> *Poor little Cherie thy course is run*
> *Three lustrums now exhausted*
> *But oh! too short thy fate is spun*
> *Too soon thy dear life ended.*
>
> (on an oval tablet)

All the above are in a small grove, surrounded by yew trees, and protected on the outside by a ha-ha that surrounds the grounds of the site of old Stradey house and curtilage. It is at the SE end of the wooded curtilage. On the west runs the Afon Dulais, beneath an old arched bridge near the pillared entrance of the old vanished mansion. Across the river is the walled flower garden, the wall being 10 feet high. Below the bridge, a few yards, are the remains of a weir. There are box trees, camelia bushes, ilex, etc. It is the remains of an ornamental garden around the old house. There are also traces of a rose garden, with iron arches. Also the remains of stone dolphins, three of them entwined, once forming part of a fountain.

Dog Cemetery at Stradey Castle, Llanelly

1. A pediment supporting an urn, over all about 5 ft. high. Urn now broken. The inscription on a marble panel let into the side of the pediment.

> *Fond memory rears these tablet stones,*
> *O'er a lost setter's mould'ring bones,*
> *And yearns to dwell on canine worth,*
> *Now bedded 'neath these clods of earth,*
> *Form and beauty yet untold,*
> *Cast in Nature's purest mould –*
> *Instinct, oh! call it reason,*
> *Matchless in shooting season –*
> *Fidelity unbounded,*
> *On love to master grounded*
> *Courage that might grace a hero*
> *All these once were thine, Poor Pero.*
>
> (n.d. but belonging to D.C.M.-L. grandfather)

2.   An oval White marble tablet.

May

Ten years and more of faithful service ended,
Thy bones, poor "Dash", with "Pero's now are blended –
Those long silky, pendant ears – those sparkling eyes –
That beauteous coat – all, alas! Death's gloomy prize:
In health and strength, no spaniel of thy class,
Could thee in covert or in brake surpass
To rouse the winged quarry, for the sportsman's aim,
Or track more surely the four-footed game –
At home – thy social bearing, winning ways,
With playful, easy temper, earn'd all praise –
At once the companion, and thy master's friend,
What joy to these, his footsteps to attend;
But when from home perchance thy master went,
Who but "Dash" to guard his house! thereon intent
Th' hall door mat then thy post, with watchful bark;
And who but "Dash" – the foremost his return to mark!
What more could vaunted reason! – stern morality
Ponder this, O Man! and learn humility. 1868

3.   In Fond Memory of Job Trotter, obit Feby 3, 1888, "Treu und fest."
Also (to a minor degree) of "Phiz" alias "Dumpling" obit Jany 2, 1888.

Her manners were beastly.
Fast friends in life;
in Death they were scarce divided.
Plus j'ai connu les hommes, mieux j'ai arnie lee chiens

(A gothic type stone shaped like a gothic window).

4.   Peter. Semper Fidelis. 1942.

To Serpent, the property of Lady Stepney

TAKEN FROM THE SQUIRES OF HAWKSBROOK

Legal Matters

In 44 Elizabeth (1601-2), James Prydderch of Hawksbrook, J.P., late deputy-steward of the Crown Lordship of Llanstephan, brought an action in the Court of Star Chamber against Rice Lloyd gentlemen, David Barrett and others, for an assault on the plaintiff at St. Keets in the Lordship of Laugharne, caused, it "was alleged, by the ill-will they bore him on account of fines and amercements at a Court Baron and for terrifying the officers of the county so that they dare not arrest the defendants on a conviction at the Carmarthen Sessions and for rescuing men pressed by the deputy lieutenant for service in Ireland".

The Star Gazer of Hawksbrook

A FAMOUS Cornish scholar, Sir William Lower (knighted 1603) married Penelope, daughter of Sir Thomas Perrott who owned estates in Carmarthenshire. Sir William came to live at Trefenty, two miles north of Laugharne where he spent his time in the study of the heavens. He worked closely with Thomas Harriott, another famous astronomer, and they were both assisted by John Protheroe of Hawksbrook

It was a time of great discoveries. In 1608 the telescope was invented by a Dutchman and in the following year telescopes were made by Galileo in Italy and Harriott in England. In 1609, Lower observed the moon very carefully and made a rough map of its surface. In January, 1610, Lower and Protheroe observed the moon together in Carmarthenshire, and

on 6 February, the former wrote to Harriott, stating that he had studied the moon with the help of a small Dutch telescope sent to him by Harriott. He says that he can see certain features on the moon, but "I must confess I can see none of this without my cylinder. Yet an ingenious younge man that accompanies me here often and loves you and these studies much, sees manie of these things even without the helpe of the instrument,

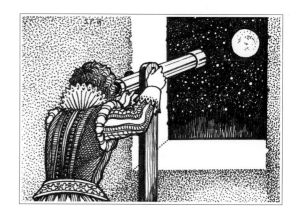

but with it sees them most plainielie; I mean the younge Mr. Protheroe". In November, 1610, Galileo discovered the spots on the sun, and in the following month Harriott did the same thing independently. On 12 April, 1615, Sir William Lower died at Trefenty, leaving a son and a daughter Elizabeth (Drummond), eventual heir of Trefenty. John Protheroe kept up his friendship with Harriott, and on the death of the latter in 1621, Protheroe was one of the executors of his will. It must be a source of pride to all Welshmen, and especially to Carmarthenshire people, that John Protheroe assisted these eminent men of science in their discoveries. For centuries however, he has been totally ignored by his countrymen, who, taken up with literature and music, seem to be unable to appreciate anything of a scientific nature.

I have had the good fortune to find an epitaph written to John Protheroe, the astronomer, of Hawksbrook. It is contained in NLW MS. No. 5390D, a manuscript written in the second quarter of the 17th century.

Deplora plora & (dum spiras) ora:
Clauditur hoc tumulo vir præstantissimus: Ecce
Inclita præclarum percupit vrbs hominem
(Proh dolor ipse bonus, nemini virtute secundus,
Prædoctus, Justus, Magnanimuque fuit:
Singula (quis nescit) mortalia pulchra vanescunt
Et modo quem tullus, nunc Paradisus habet:
Astra petit virus: proprim sic singula centrum,
Terra caro terram, mens colit alta polum.

See and be sadde: For heere doth lye
As great perfection as could dye,

All the prime artes and choicest vertues straue
Wch of them all the Soueraigne rule should haue
Of this clay'd corps, (while ear'st Greate heavens maker
Lent it a soule to be this mowlds partaker)
But (o the greife) amidst this strife comes death
And parts this body from the liueinge breath,
Who well assur'd that he another daye
Should rise with Christ, with death heere downe he laye:
Thus Merlyns countrymen (alas the woe)
Have ever lost theire peerelesse Protheroe:
His worth still liues, his fame shall neuer dye
Death lays him lowe, But why? To raise him high:
For though his bodye heere interred lyes,
His soule with angells ayde hath clymb'd the skyes:
Wheare with Jehovah's glorious hoaste he singes
Still Allelhuya to the king of kings,
In fine, the arts, the heavens, and the grave
His endless fame, his soule, his body haue.

James Hayward

CHAPTER VII

AMBITION, GREED AND DECAY

CASTELL GORFOD – A GHOSTLY EXPERIENCE

AT ABOUT 5 p.m. on 30th August, the Pembrokeshire and Carmarthenshire Otter Hounds, completed a day's hunting at Castlemorris Bridge over the Western Cleddau. Colonel Buckley had another call to make in Pembrokeshire before returning to Castell Gorfod, and he handed the key of the house to Kemmis Buckley, and explained in detail where keys to various locked doors might be found. It is the Colonel's custom to lock, not only the outer doors of the plâs, but certain inner doors as well.

Major Buckley and I departed, drove through the Precelly hills and finally reached Castell Gorfod, at about "sevenish". It was a beautiful evening and a slanting sunlight made the valley before the house a very attractive picture. We disturbed a contemplative buzzard perched on a post at the side of the rear drive, and commented on the flights of crows and rooks wheeling over the tall trees around the house. Otherwise the whole place was perfectly peaceful and we saw no other living creature.

Major Buckley opened the front door and we entered the reception room on the right hand side of the entrance hallway. He then produced two drinks and went to the writing table in the inner part of this room, where he jotted down notes to help me with a TV programme for the BBC, which I was preparing. While he was so engaged I sat at the round table looking through an old commonplace cutting book which he produced for me. It was completely quiet. We were the only people in the house. Major Buckley was writing, I was turning the pages, when I distinctly heard *footsteps*, and *then heard a door being opened,* which I presumed was at the door leading into the dining room from the kitchen. The footsteps then were then heard in the passageway where they seemed to shuffle a little. The floor of the dining room is tiled. They were distinct and clear, and seemed to me that they were made by nailed boots.

Without moving from my place I looked up towards the doorway where I expected the visitor to appear, but saw no one. I thought to myself – This must be a servant, or perhaps the Colonel has returned and let himself in through the back door. Major Buckley then said, "Someone is walking about in the back, I wonder whether father has returned," and then cried out "Hello there Colonel." There was no reply. I heard the footsteps again as if moving and they ceased after 3 or 4 paces. I called out "Hello Colonel." Again, no response. I did not hear the footsteps after this.

Major Buckley got up, and said, "I'm sure someone is 'scrabbling' about in the dining room or somewhere. Someone has come in. It can't be Father as he uses the front door."

I said, "Perhaps some servant man."

He replied "no, there is no servant in the house at all."

He walked briskly into the hall, and went to the rear of the house, while I peeped into the next room and the front hall. Major Buckley returned and said, "the doors are still locked as Father told us," and he looked around again.

Just before I heard the footsteps

Castell Gorfod

for the first time, I had become conscious of a light *breathing,* which broke out into a little snore and then a longish sighing noise. It sounded to me as if it might be a sleeping dog, for the noise came from floor level between my table and the window. I knew there was a dog at Castell Gorfod, and I looked around casually under the table and beyond but saw nothing, and thought no more of it. After the episode of the footsteps, this breathing broke out again, quite strongly, and I said to Major Buckley, "the dog is here somewhere having a snooze." I then looked more carefully, into the dining room again but saw nothing. I was rather puzzled and had another look between the round table and the window, and beneath the window seat. Looking out through the window I noticed the little dog on the veranda, poised and alert, gazing at the entrance door as if it wished to enter. I told Major Buckley, and we both went into the passage. I opened the front door and the dog came in at a run.

I can only say that the breathing sounded "dog-like" to me, being very much like the sleeping noises made by my own dog. On the other hand of course, it may well have been human breathing. When we left shortly afterwards, Colonel Buckley had still not arrived.

At this time I *had never heard* of any 'ghost' or supernatural visitant connected with Castell Gorfod, and had never been given any suggestions or hint of anything that might have inclined my thoughts in that direction.

The weather was fine. The sun was still shining. The temperature was cool. The house was perfectly quiet within, apart from the noises described above.

FROM ARTICLE "YSTRAD CORRWG AND GLANGWILI"

The Serpent of Glangwili

Serpent about to get the point

An elderly farmer who had been brought up near Glangwili, told me the following legend he had heard in boyhood. Long ago a winged serpent (*wiber*) plagued the inhabitants of this otherwise peaceful vale by lying in wait amongst the hillside groves, pouncing on passers-by, and when surfeited by these depredations, it returned to roost in the glade still known as Allt-y-Wiber. To combat the hideous visitant, the parishioners erected a scarecrow *(bwbach)* in the woodland afterwards called Allt-y-Bwbach, and filled the figure with sharp iron spikes. In due course the serpent came by, immediately made a furious onslaught on the figure, resulting in fatal wounds, then fluttered feebly away to Cwm Coch (so called from the effusion of its blood), there expired and was buried in a deep pit.

Also from the same article

Of the seventeen children of the marriage of Griffith Lloyd of Ystrad Corrwg and Lleucu, daughter of Thomas ap David ap Llewelyn ap Howel, only one, David, left issue. Of the eight sons, only two, Morris the eldest and David the seventh son grew to maturity, and of the nine daughters four married but none had children. Morris was still living in 1597 but predeceased his brother David who succeeded to the estate.   He had four sons and eight daughters by his second wife, Jane daughter of Sir Christopher Turbervill of Penlline, Glamorgan.

David Lloyd of Glangwili endeavoured to secure the succession to the coronership for one of his friends, he arranged with Walter Vaughan of Golden Grove in 1600 to "fix" the appointment, but rumours of their manoeuvres reached the ears of Sir Thomas Jones of Abermarlais who thereupon mustered his adherents to defeat the intentions of Lloyd and Vaughan. When the day of election came, David Lloyd and his supporters, noticing Carmarthen's shire hall to be packed with Sir Thomas's faction, withdrew quietly to the nearby castle and there elected as coroner, one Harry Lloyd, later described by his opponents as "a man unlearned, unskilful, and one of small ability and worth".

(PRO Star Chamber Proceedings 5.52.17).

THE LEGEND OF CADIFOR'S COURT

In solitary uplands far away
betwixt the blossoms of a rosy spray,
dreaming upon the wonderful sweet face
of nature, in a wild and pathless place.

THESE LINES from a sonnet came to mind on the heights of Cefen Trelech, just above Blaen Cych, source of the river whose course for over eight wooded meandering miles forms the boundary between Carmarthenshire and Pembrokeshire. There must be few rivers in Wales which are unspoilt from source to estuary. This we can truly say of the Cych, for throughout its course, until it pours into the Teifi at Abercych, no work by the hand of man has intruded a single blemish to mar the beauty of the gorge through which it flows, while the "wonderful sweet face" of the flanking uplands remains equally free of any such intrusions.

The "romantic mountain stream" as Fenton calls the Cych, flows northwards through a deep vale, while a dozen headlong brooks contribute to its depth and power. From the Carmarthenshire side pour the Sylgen, Ymerson, Barddu, Mamog, Dwrog, Nant Lwyd; from Pembrokeshire side, the Pibydd, Pedran, Cneifa, Dulas, Seli and Morw. History laden names along the shoulders of the glen contain echoes which set the fancy aglow, Cnwc y beili, Ffwrn Cadifor, Efynnon Wenfflwch, Plas yr hafod, Morlogws, Pant Lleucu, Hendre Cymry, Park Nest, Llwyn Finion, Llain Wallter, and Babiog; some remind us of early religious life – Capel Tanglwst, Capel Iwan, Cil Frychan, Cnwc y lleian, Cnwc y bettws, Park y bettws on Glas-pant, Llannerch y Meudwy, Clyn Mynach, Gwar y clas, and Parc y person gwyn, and Eglwys Cilrhedyn which keeps tranquil guard over the rolling acres; others resound with clash of battle and skirmish – Parc y fyddin on Penbryn Garadog, Parc y frwydr, Penrhiw'r cyrff, Castell Gilfach Garn, Hen Gaerau, Dan y gaer, Rhiw castell, while Pant yr heddwch marks the place where a truce was made between contending warriors and from the high places at Crug Iwan, Crug Ieuan, Crug Llwyd, and Crug y gorllwyn, Celtic chieftains still watch us from their graves.

Land of Enchantment

The vale of Cych is a splendid dream, a haunted glen, a land of enchantment, spell-weaving. We owe a debt to Dyfed for the gift of Glyn Cych, for out of it sprang the tale of Pwyll Pendefig, lord of the Seven Cantrefs, one of the most enduring romances of the early literature of the Welsh. Here Pwyll "let loose the hounds in the woods, sounded the horn, and began the chase". Having lost his companions he came to a glade where a strange pack – "brilliant shining white and their ears were red" – had brought a stag to bay. He whipped them off and set his own hounds on the quarry. Then Arawn, owner of the balked pack arrived, justly aggrieved, resentful, and to atone for his conduct Pwyll undertook to impersonate Arawn for a year, and in that guise to slay one Hafgan. At the end of the term, his mission accomplished, he returned to Glyn Cych and all was well. And so opens the first branch of the *Mabinogion*. The Triads inform us further that Pwyll's young son, Pryderi, also wandered through this magic vale, guarding an immense herd of swine belonging to his foster-father Pendaran Dyfed.

But the history is not confined to poetry and romance. The river has been a political boundary from early times. It divided the comote of Emlyn into Uwch Cych (on the eastern or Carmarthenshire side) and Is Cych (on the western or Pembrokeshire side). The comote formed part of the old kingdom of Dyfed, whose heiress, Elen, brought it early in the 10th century to her husband Hywel Dda ruler of Deheubarth. Shortly after their appearance in west Wales, the Normans built a motte and bailey castle at Cenarth Mawr, a mile or so to the east of Cych, which became the scene of an exciting affair in the year 1109, namely the abduction of the alluring Nest, wife of the Norman Gerald de Windsor, by Cadwgan a younger son of the royal house of Powys. During the next century and a half, Emlyn was held at different times by Welsh princes and Norman barons, until finally in 1284 Uwch Cych became a Crown possession and Is Cych was incorporated into the feudal lordship of Cilgerran. The arrangement lasted until the Act of Union in 1536 by which Wales was divided into shire ground following the English pattern. The river continued to serve as a political boundary, the riparian parishes of Cenarth and East Cilrhedyn remaining in Carmarthenshire, and those of West Cilrhedyn, Clydey and Manordeifi, in Pembrokeshire. These territorial divisions remained undisturbed until 1935 when the parish of East Cilrhedyn was absorbed into Cenarth.

On Cefen Trelech, over 800 feet above sea level, the eye dwells with long delight on a panorama of undulating upland. We gaze upon a purely rural landscape dotted with whitewashed farm buildings among groves on broad bosomed hills, lone cots crouched among the heather, farmlets and tiny homesteads encompassed by hayfields and stone enclosures, evidences of the determination of generations of hill farmers to wrest the soil from encroaching gorse and bracken. It is a land of scattered dwellings, and we are reminded of Giraldus' word's when he wrote of the Welsh in 1188, "They neither inhabit towns, villages, nor castles, but lead a solitary life in the woods . . .".

Nest's abduction

The woodlands have long been tamed but the old way of life survives. The people may be solitary, but are not lonely. When I asked a farmer's wife who lived in a secluded nook near the river's source, whether she felt lonely, she replied, "Never. Apart from the farm work, I fish a great deal and my husband and I often go out with the gun; we are sheltered from the winter storms, and in summer the air is full of song and the fields and hedgerows ablaze with flowers." No sane person could be unhappy in these sylvan solitudes. Practically every farm shelters Welsh speaking families, mostly freeholders, people with a lively sense of lineage, sturdy, independent, courteous, heirs of age old traditions and legends that enwreath people and places in these remote parts. There is a society of upland folk, their national identity belonging to a rural, pre-industrial past, as unchanged as their beautiful surroundings.

Notable men

The parishes bordering on the Cych contained a large number of gentle families of high antiquity, whose ancestors were local leaders in the days of the Welsh princes, and who survived the vicissitudes of the medieval centuries and the political and economic changes of Tudor and post-Tudor times. Generally, their estates were small, and the families owe their survival largely to the fact that they were resident squires who personally administered their estates; participated in farming and other productive activities, living on an easy footing among their tenants, often in a sort of patriarchal simplicity. Among those on the Carmarthenshire side, all in Cenarth parish, were Lewes of Gellidywyll, descended from Ednywain ap Bradwen Morgan of Pengwern, descended from Cadifor Fawr of Blaen Cych, followed there by the James family descended from Gwynfardd Dyfed; Howell of Glaspant, descended matrilineally from the Lloyds of Bronwydd; Lloyd and Morgan of Cenarth and Saunders of Clynfelin fawr who established a woollen manufactory on the banks of Cych, the last of whom, William Saunders, died in 1799 at the advanced age of 89 and was buried in Cilrhedyn church. On the Pembrokeshire side, in Clydey parish, were Lloyd of Dolau Llannerch and Penalltyllyn; Morgan of Blaenbylan and Coedllwyd; Morris of Nantylladron; Harries of Werngoy; Lloyd and, later, Lewis-Bowen of Clynfyw, and Davies of Lancych followed there by Jones-Lloyd matrilineally descended from the family of Castell Hywel.

Of this network of gentry families, all connected by common ancestry or intermarriage, only a few remain today Jones-Lloyd of Lancych, Lewis-Bowen of Clynfyw, and Howell of Glaspant.

Notable men have been reared in these parishes, twenty-nine of them sufficiently important to be included in *The Dictionary of Welsh Biography* – parsons, ministers of the gospel, musicians, surgeons, poets, authors, antiquaries, a sculptor, and an admiral.

Among these notables are David Marks (1788-1871) of Cilrhedyn, musician; Revd. Erasmus Saunders, D.D. (1670-1724) of the Clynfelin family, an eminent divine, author of *The State of Religion in the Diocese of St. Davids* (1721), and father of Dr. Erasmus Saunders, Canon of Windsor; James Morgan Gibbon of Pontseli (1855-1932), Independent Minister; John Milo Griffith (1843-97) of Pontseli, sculptor; Dr. Thomas Rocyn Jones (1822-77) of Manordeifi, surgeon; John Jones, "Mathetes" (1821-78) of Cilrhedyn, Baptist Minister and author of literary works; Maurice Morgan of Blaenbylan (1725-1802) Shakespearean commentator and political writer, who became an Under-Secretary of State in 1782.

Not included in that "Golden Book", but equally worthy of remembrance, are Josiah and Jonah Evans of Pontseli, famous 19th century smiths, inventors and manufacturers of an improved plough, "arad Pontseli," and old Dafydd ap Hywel of Morlogws [sic], a versewright of the homely kind, grandfather of the Revd. George Enoch, sometime vicar of Clydey, and of Captain John Enoch of the 23rd Foot who fought at Waterloo.

I might add that the forebears of Sir Ben Bowen Thomas, sometime Permanent Secretary to the Welsh Department, Ministry of Education, and happily still with us, came from the parish of Clydey.

Lord of the Seven Royal Courts

But it was another and much earlier worthy that had drawn me to the district, one whose actions were sufficiently significant for inclusion in the historical chronicles of medieval Wales. To the compiler of the *bruts* he was Cadifor ap Gollwyn, to the genealogists and bards he was Cadifor Fawr, Lord of Blaen Cych and of the Seven Royal Courts of Dyfed. His memory lives after the passage of over eight centuries, while his name is commemorated in Ffwrn Cadifor, a mysterious construction set in an overhanging cliff in the defile a few hundred yards from Blaen Cych itself.

The source of the Cych is hidden in a heavily wooded ravine. A few steep yards above it stands a tiny roadside chapel belonging to the Independents, built at the end of the last century as a branch of the flourishing Capel y Graig, Trelech. About a quarter of a mile westwards along the road is the farm formerly called Plas Llwyni – still so called by the people of the district – but christened Cadifor Hall in the latter part of Victoria's reign, which remains its "official" designation to this day. I have been unable to discover who was responsible for the introduction of the later name, but I suspect it to have been inspired by antiquarian considerations, for the memory of Cadifor has always lingered hereabouts. Religious meetings were held in the parlour of Plas Llwyni before the little chapel was built.

No traces of early human settlement exist in the immediate vicinity of the source of the Cych, but there can be no doubt that Cadifor lived somewhere in this area of which he was overlord.

A few hundred yards to the north-west is the farmhouse of Gilfach Garn alongside the remains of a once powerful fort.

Originally, the farmhouse stood on the eastern side of the old castell. An inscribed stone in the courtyard wall states that an earlier Gilfach Garn had been built in 1769 by one William Jones, and a tablet set high in the front wall of the house describes its fate – "the old house which was built about 200 feet to the north-east from this spot took fire from the back parlour flue and burnt down at night on August the 8th 1831." Would that all house-holders raised such memorials so that he who reads might be instructed.

In the field below the farmyard I came upon Castell Gilfach Garn, a green arrowhead of land above the junction of the Pibydd and the Cych. The ground falls abruptly about 50 to 60 feet to the bed of the ravine, providing a natural defence against attacks from the north, east, and west. Traces of two ramparts raised to protect the vulnerable south side, are still to be seen, one of which now does duty as a hedge; these ramparts run along the "neck" of the promontory, something over 200 feet long, the enclosed area containing about half an acre. The fairly even surface slopes gently towards the point of the promontory, and there are traces of defences at the top of the steep sides. The entrance was near the ruins of the old farmhouse of Gilfach Garn.

According to Mr. Thomas, the owner-occupier of the farm, here was the castell of Cadifor Fawr whose pages lived at Gilfach y Gweision, another farmhouse about a hundred yards away, and the local people speak of cellars and dungeons below the fort, connected by a secret tunnel to Gilfach y Gweision. Not far from the last named farm is Gilfach Ymerson (rendered as Ymryson on O.S. maps), also associated with the lord of the castell. Tradition states that Cadifor's dwelling was in the ravine itself, a massive structure built in the form of a bridge across the stream, sufficiently near to the fort to which he could retire when danger threatened. Cadifor and twelve of his warriors, clad in full armour, are said to lie sleeping in a cavern in the glen below, awaiting the call to return to "liberate" their fellow countrymen.

Trek to an Oven

I was anxious to see Ffwrn Cadifor, and Mrs. Thomas very kindly offered to lead me there. She led the way down the break-neck side of the promontory, at the foot of which the brawling Pibydd meets the Cych. We crossed the water and wound our way along the floor of the deep dank ravine, clambering over fallen trees, hacking our way through thicket, fern, and bramble, the stream dancing merrily below us. At one time a cart track ran parallel to the bank leading from Gilfach y Gweision towards a corn mill beyond Morlogws, but this had been strangled by brambles and undergrowth, although parts of it are clearly defined, The trees enclosed us like a guard of honour of tall guardsmen, and through the leafy canopy I could occasionally catch glimpses of the blue sky above. We lost all trace and sound of human life, the workaday world seemed far away, and I felt a sense of guilt that I was trespassing on a secret place of age-old peace, where the vixen and her brood gambol, where the badger rolls at ease, and the otter glides gaily beneath the sheltering bank.

Eventually we arrived. Ffwrn Cadifor is near the bank of the Cych, in the parish of West Cilrhedyn. Here, say the cognoscenti was the oven of Cadifor, where bread was baked for his household. The site is not easily found, and I doubt whether I would have come across it without the good offices of my guide. It lies in a natural declivity in the rocky side of the glen, on the 400 foot contour line, about a hundred yards south of the confluence of the Cych and the Sylgen.[1]

The Ffwrn consists of a curved stone bench, around the back of which are well preserved remains of a stone wall, curved in such a way as to suggest that it originally formed a cell about six feet high, something like a beehive in appearance. Above, hangs a cliff of shale and rock, capped by trees and bushes. It was high noon when I saw the place, and spots of sunlight filtered through the branches, falling like little golden dimples on the bench.

Across the river, opposite the Ffwrn, are traces of an old water trench – "pownd dwr" as Mrs. Thomas called it – to carry water to a mill further down the valley. This seemed hardly feasible to me, but the indisputable fact remains that a man made conduit has certainly existed there.

Who was Ffwrn Cadifor? The chieftain's oven I was told, and to support the assertion my attention was directed to reddish marks on the stones, alleged to have been caused by fire, but on examination I could see quite clearly that the discolouring had resulted from the action of water percolating through the side of the bank. One finds it difficult to believe that a domestic arrangement of any kind should have been constructed in so remote a spot, far from human habitation, and particularly difficult, indeed often dangerous to approach, unless, of course, some building had stood alongside, but it is topographically impossible for a house to have been built near the Ffwrn, for the valley is narrow and steep at this spot. However, there is an earlier tradition, which if true, provides an example of the ingenuity of our ancestors, and supports the view that the Ffwrn could have formed part of a dwelling.

The earliest written reference to Ffwrn Cadifor occurs in the *Historical Tour of Pembrokeshire* by Richard Fenton who visited it about the year 1800. The Ordnance Survey map of 1831, prepared by a local man, Thomas Colby, then a lieutenant in the Royal Engineers, shows a cottage called Cadifor above this spot, whose ruins are to be seen in the field, now part of Blaen Pibydd farm. Neither the Ffwrn nor the cottage is included on the 25 inch map in 1890, but on the 6 inch map published in the following year the little nook is marked as "The Oven".

Let us turn to what Richard Fenton had to say. Having crossed the Pibydd, he entered the valley, and recorded his impressions in these words:

"Here the channel of the river occupies the whole of the narrow space from one hill to the other, admitting only of a dangerous path worn through the rock on one side, and difficult for foot passengers, so that I was forced to ride along the rocky bed of the river, and follow its windings till I came to an interruption of its course by the fall of another stream into it from the left, when I found myself in sight of the spot I was in quest of, shewn me by my guide, and called by the country people Fwrm Cadivor, the Oven (figuratively, *pars pro toto,* for the whole house) of Cadivor Vawr, or the great. At the mouth of the continuation of the vale through which the Cych is poured, tradition says, that this powerful chieftain had his palace built across this barrier river on arches from hill to hill, with the roots of its foundation in both the counties of Carmarthenshire and Pembrokeshire, over which a great part of his possessions extended . . . From what here appears, it required a very creative imagination to furnish an idea of the structures said to have occupied so singular a site, for there is no trace to assist conjecture, except what is called the Oven, a slight excavation in the rock on one side, scarcely deep enough to shelter the shepherd from a shower, and a small channel in the slatey rock; on the other an old aqueduct, which seemingly, must have been for conveying water to the level of such a building, whatever it might have been that was perched above the narrow pass. Cadivor Vawr is always styled Lord of Blaen Cych, that is of the region round the source, and probably might have had his abode somewhere hereabouts at the head of his territories in the midst of vastnesses where enemies could not easily attack him, and in a spot highly favourable to the chase, and the predatory sort of warfare which characterised that barbarous age."

Riddle of the Pass

If this has a basis of truth, then it might well explain the existence of the Ffwrn and of the water trench. That no trace of such a structure has been found may be due to the fact that it was made of wood, for we know that the Welsh of those days did build their dwellings of that material. When the house was abandoned, decay would have set in, and it is not unlikely that the materials were removed by local people. We know too that Cadifor Fawr left this district to settle at his wife's home, Cilsant, some six miles to the south, which became the chief residence of his descendants.

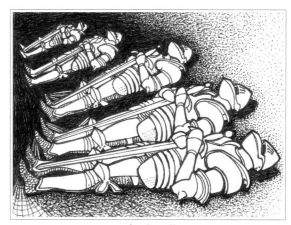

Waiting for the call to arms

What can we make of these traditions? The story of the chieftain and his warriors sleeping in a cavern awaiting a summons to lead his countrymen to victory is common form throughout Europe, the best known example being the tale concerning Frederick Barbarossa. That it was applied at all to Cadifor is evidence of the impression he had made on his countrymen, which is in harmony with the testimony of the historical chronicles. The story of the house bridging the pass is more individual and I have not found another example of it in Wales. however I did find an extension of it further down the valley. Just above Pont Cych where the road from Cilrhedyn church enters into Cwm Cych, is a steep bluff called Castell on which stands a promontory fort similar to that of Gilfach Garn. I was told by a cottager that it was the castell of Pwyll of the Mabinogion who had a great hall built in the form of a bridge across the Cych; this I consider to be an adaptation of the Cadifor tradition. Of course both this castell and that of Gilfach Garn, are clearly much older than Cadifor's time, perhaps dating from the Iron Age, but there are numerous examples of such forts being used many centuries later by those who lived in their vicinity. It is by no means impossible that Cadifor did in fact dwell in such a structure, hidden from marauders and enemies, and sufficiently near to a castell to which he could retire as and when prudence dictated.

Such are the traditions and legends about the home of Cadifor. What about the man himself? Fortunately we have a reputable source of information to enable us to form a reliable picture of him, also providing us with reliable milestones in the form of dates.

According to the various genealogies, Cadifor came of royal stock, and they agree on the lineage back to his great-great-grandfather as follows Cadifor ap Gollwyn ap Gwyn ap Rydderch ap Elgan Weflhwch. As Cadifor died in 1091, it is reasonable to assume that the great-great-grandfather lived in the first half of the 10th century, in the reign of Hywel Dda. The name Elgan was known in west Carmarthenshire – Keven Legh Elgan near Whitland (1199-1216) and Trallwn Elgan in Talyllychau (1327-1377). The soubriquet 'weflhwch' means 'sow-lip' and may refer to some physical attribute. Several manuscripts take the pedigree back far beyond Elgan Weflhwch to Owain Fraisg, a king of the royal family of Dyfed who lived in the 5th century, but these lack chronological stability and it is impossible to accept the lineage in the form it has been recorded. However, the ancestry may be accepted with confidence so far back as Elgan, and an ancestor who lived in the first half of the 10th century should satisfy the most pedigree proud amongst us.

Founder of a Clan

Without doubt, Cadifor is the most important figure in the family tree. He is the real founder of the clan, the hero ancestor. The Golden Grove MS devotes nearly a hundred folios to his descendants and the compiler found it sufficient to start the series with "Kadifor Vawr of Blaenkych, Lord of Dyvett". His stature was such that it was considered unnecessary to look beyond him. Apparently there were no heroes before this Agamemnon.

The historical chronicles contain several references to him and his family, and he is described as having been the ruler of the whole of Dyfed at one time.[2] The age in which

Gruffyd falls

he lived was one of great turbulence, particularly in west Wales, and it is quite possible that Cadifor had been able to acquire sovereignty during those confused years. He was sufficiently important for his obituary to be recorded in the *Brut* under the year 1089 (1091) – "ac y bu varw Kedivor vab Gollwyn". Even after his death the family was powerful enough to attempt a coup d'etat in the kingdom of Deheubarth. Dissatisfied with the rule of Rhys ap Tewdwr of Dynevor, the sons of Cadifor invited Gruffydd ap Maredudd ap Owain, an exiled prince of Deheubarth (who had lived in Herefordshire since 1072 on estates bestowed on him by William the Conqueror) to join them in ousting the ruling sovereign. Gruffydd accepted their embassy, and arrived with a force in west Wales where he was joined by the Sons of Cadifor and their warbands. The challengers met Rhys near St. Dogmaels where a severe battle resulted in the death of Gruffydd and the total overthrow of his army. Llywelyn ap Cadifor and his brothers managed to escape, and returned to their mountain fastness to lick their wounds. And so, Sir John Lloyd says, "the attempt to set up a puppet king under the protection of a powerful clan came to nothing".[3] Rhys ap Tewdwr did not live long after his victory, and during Easter week of the following year fell in battle against the Normans in Breconshire.

Despite the setback at St. Dogmaels the sons of Cadifor were able to retain an enormous territory in west Carmarthenshire, probably due to the preoccupation of Rhys with the Norman pressure that threatened his eastern borders.

Another member of the family also became involved with royalty but in less disastrous manner. The *Brut* records that one of Cadifor's daughters married prince Cadwgan of Powys (died 1111) son of the great Bleddyn ap Cynfyn, by whom he had a daughter named Elliw ("Oellyl o verch gedivor ap gollwyn y gwr a vu bendevic ar holl dyved" – Elliw by a daughter of Cadifor ap Gollwyn the man who was overlord of all Dyfed).[4] This union with a prince of the dominant house of Powys indicates the status of Cadifor and shows that he was known far beyond the confines of his native Dyfed.

Cadifor Fawr married Elen daughter and heiress of Llwch Llawen Fawr, lord of Cilsant, "o lin y 'brenhinoedd", of the lineage of kings, according to the deputy-herald Lewys Dwnn. After the marriage, Cadifor left his stronghold in the vale of Cych and settled at his wife's home which was sited more or less in the centre of his vast possessions. Cilsant in the parish of Llanwinio, stands on a promontory hill fort on a steep bluff above the river Cynnin.

Black Lion and White Boar
Although Cadifor lived in pre-heraldic days, later genealogists credited him with having borne as his ensigns "the black lion, and in right of the old castle of Dyfed, the white boar",[5] the latter animal being the arms assigned to his father-in-law. The reference to the boar is obscure, but it may be connected with the legend that Llwch hunted a monstrous red-headed boar that had long terrorised the land, finally cornered it, and tied it to a tree at Llain y badd ("The 'Slang of the Boar") on the hills to the east of Cilsant.

We do not know where Cadifor was buried. Perhaps at Cilrhedyn, for he is said to have founded and endowed that church.[6] As we have seen, his name is commemorated in Ffwrn Cadifor near his old main fastness, and it occurs in several places in Dyfed, such as Craig Cydifor in Ciffig parish, Llodre Cadevor somewhere in west Carmarthenshire, and Tre Cadifor near Dinas in Pembrokeshire. It is interesting to find that in the parish of Llanwinio, where Cilsant is situated, there was a Crug Cadifor (The Sepulchre of Cadifor) mentioned in a deed dated 14 September 1854, which states that the farm of Penyrallt "formerly comprised three several messuages, tenements, farms, and lands called respectively Pantyeirew, Crugcadivor, and Gwilod y Cyrn".[7] Crugcadifor is now called Crog, half a mile to the north of Penyrallt. In 1331 a stream flowing into the Teifi from the Cardiganshire side, between the Cerdin and Clettwr, was called Nant Kedivor. I do not suggest that all these places were named after our hero, but it seems significant that the name was popular in the area where he had lived. Not only has his name survived but his family, the wide-branching house of Philipps, remained for centuries one of the leading stocks in west Wales, and is represented today by the owners of Picton Castle in Pembrokeshire and Cwmgwili in Carmarthenshire.

As I returned along the labyrinthine way from the Ffwrn, ghosts of earlier wayfarers whirled around me, eager, grey-clad Pwyll and his questing hounds, golden tongued Cadifor Fawr with his bodyguard of light-armed youths, warrior-farmers bearing bow, bill, and lance, Caradog of Penbryn, Einion of Llwyn, Iwan of Capel, Gwallter of Llain, and Gwilym of the Hendre. We exchanged no words, for the way was hard, the climb steep and arduous. I laboured up the slope, the murmur of the Cych still in my ears, till suddenly I stood on open ground. I had left the Middle Ages and the magic of the glen. Pwyll and his pack, Cadifor and his retinue, all melted away into the woodland twilight of Glyn Cych. Before me stood Mr. and Mrs. Thomas. Together we crossed the green sward of the castell and came to the farmyard of Gilfach Garn to be greeted by an old sheepdog barking with frantic joy at the return of his master.

(Postscript. I wrote this account shortly after my visit in 1964. Since then, alas, my hospitable host Mr. Thomas has passed on, and a new family now lives at Gilfach Garn.)

References

[1] Its grid reference is 293335 (O.S. Map SN 23).
[2] *Brut y Tywysogion.* Peniarth MS, 20. Ed., Prof. Thomas Jones. Pp. 256, 75a.
[3] History of Carmarthenshire, ed. J. E. Lloyd, i, 218.
[4] *Brut* v Tywysogion, cited above.
[5] "Kydivor o vlaen kych, y llew dy, ag o hen gastell dyfed y baedd gwyn" –Llanstephan MS 12. fo 99. Cadifor's arms are usually blasoned *argent* a lion rampant guardant *sable;* those of Llwch Llawen Fawr (Happy Llwch the Great) *argent* a boar statant proper, head *gules,* standing beneath an oak tree also proper.
[6] Fenton, *Tour,* p 267.
[7] Deeds in Carmarthenshire County Record Office.

CYSTANOG – THE HOUSE AMONG THE TREES

IT ALL STARTED with a faded letter, written in 1791, from Mrs. Philipps of Cwmgwili to her husband, John George Philipps, Member of Parliament for the Borough of Carmarthen.

Among other items of local news was this sentence "I visited Mrs. Thomas of Cystanog House and spent two nights there". Now, it is the duty of an archivist to interpret all references that appear in his documents. I had not heard of Cystanog house before and so carried out some initial searches. In the Sheriff's Roll I found that a Richard Thomas of Cystanog had been High Sheriff in 1788, and among lists of Justices of the Peace in Session Records; I traced him to 1833 when he died.

I then decided to locate the house. Remember, I was looking for an old residence, or at least a substantial house that had been in former times the seat of a country gentleman. After a study of the ordnance map I found the name easily enough. It marked what appeared to be a cottage on the banks of the Towy not far from the hamlet of Abergwilli. One day I visited it. There, in a water meadow, I found an insignificant ruin, the straggling wall of a little garden, over which two tall trees towered. This spot, I reflected, marked the remains of the former mansion which like the family, had departed leaving this sparse remnant as the inadequate memorial to its former existence.

Some weeks afterwards, I found among our records a copy of the will, dated 1762, of one Thomas Vaughan, of Cystanog, esquire and Justice of the Peace, which showed that he owned an extensive estate. A bachelor, he left the property to his kinsman who was the Richard Thomas I have named earlier, I had no difficulty in tracing in the Golden Grove manuscripts the pedigree of the Vaughans of Cystanog, descendants of Welsh princes and medieval nobles. The genealogical evidence, certainly, was clear enough. So too the site of the residence, or so it seemed.

Then came the first cloud into the blue sky of my contentment. I had visited a lively octogenarian lady living near Carmarthen to collect some old documents for my Record Office. In the course of conversation I asked whether she knew anything about Cystanog, and told her that I had already visited the ruins. "Oh no", She replied, "what you saw was Cystanog Fach, a cottage. The mansion was much further away, near the Bishop's Palace at Abergwili. I don't remember it, but my father often told me about it – a great house among the trees".

Armed with a map I went to the area again. I found no sign of a grove which would have sheltered a great house, or a single stone to indicate where it might have stood. The whole area consisted of low lying fertile meadows given over entirely to nature. Yet, if there had been a Cystanog Fach, surely at one time there must have been a Cystanog Fawr. But where? Within a few months a happy form of serendipity, led my footsteps to the spot that had eluded me for so long. While clearing the cellars of a Carmarthenshire auctioneers I discovered an old plan that had been prepared in connection with the coming of the railway in 1852. On it was marked the mansion house of Cystanog, its garden, courtyard, and drive, the coachhouse, stables and other adjuncts of the residence, so that I now knew exactly where, it had stood.

I then consulted the aerial photographs of the area in possession of my colleague the County Planning Officer. The markings, colourings and shades showed the site as clearly as if the mansion and its outhouses were still there, and fitted perfectly into the plan that I had found in the auctioneer's cellar. Here then, had stood "the great house among the trees" its fame a lingering chord in the memory of aged folk, its memorial the lush pastures and wild flowers that carpet the floor of the vale of Tyvi. About a year went by, and then came a small parcel of documents from a gentleman living in Kent. They revealed a dramatic tale.

On a quiet Thursday evening, 6th of May 1777, an aged widow lay dying in an old mansion called Cystanog in a meadow between the Bishop's Palace at Abergwili and the bend of the river. She was Mrs. Margaret Pardo whose husband, the Rev. John Pardo, Rector and Prebendary of Aberarth in Cardiganshire, had died during the previous year. The widow, had inherited the mansion and estate as the heir of her maternal uncle, Thomas Vaughan who had held the property under the settlement in tail of his ancestor another Thomas Vaughan who had died in 1651. The Vaughans of Cystanog were a junior branch of Vaughans of Plas Gwyn in Llandyfaelog parish who traced in, the main line, to the Princes of Powys and through female line to those of Gwynedd and Deheubarth, and also to Norman barons and other medieval magnates. Mrs. Pardo had no children. She made a careful will, and named several relations who were to be her beneficiaries. The solicitors found that the relations so named were already dead, except a distant cousin called Richard Thomas of whom little was known except that he lived at Chatham. Mrs. Pardo's will stipulated that the estate was to be held by this Richard Thomas for life, then by his children in seniority, and if he left no children, it was to revert to the right heirs

Relations, relations

of the Vaughans of Cystanog. In this context the words "the right heirs" were to be of vital importance.

After Mrs. Pardo's funeral, her solicitor, accompanied by his clerk, set out on the long journey to find Richard Thomas. On reaching London they found his brother, a humble pastrycook in a hotel. From him they obtained the elder brother's address. They rode on to the dockyard at Chatham, and after some enquiries found Richard knee deep in shavings and sawdust, earning his daily bread as a carpenter. On hearing the good tidings he left his laborious toil, came to Cystanog and set up as a country gentleman. A year later he was appointed Justice of the Peace, and in 1788 served as High Sheriff of Carmarthenshire. He lived in great style at Cystanog where he entertained lavishly and bought an additional country house at Hollingbourne, Kent. Although uneducated in the formal sense, he was intelligent and prudent and made the transition from carpenter's shop to country mansion with little difficulty and bore his newly acquired honours with a modest dignity.

Richard Thomas died in 1833, having enjoyed the inheritances for over 50 years. He left no children, and so the time had come when the Cystanog estate should pass to the right heirs of the Vaughans, under the limitation created in the will of Mrs. Pardo. This meant, the nearest blood relations of Thomas Vaughan of Cystanog who had died in 1767. But who were the right heirs? At that time, there lived in Spilman Street, Carmarthen, one Captain Henry Vaughan, a retired naval officer who had served with distinction in Nelson's ships. His family had lived for many centuries at Plas Gwyn in Llandyfaelog, but crippling mortgages had obliged him to sell the estate in 1795, and now he was passing the evening of life supported by prize money that had come his way in the Service and the half pay which the Admiralty allowed him. He consulted his pedigree which proved beyond any doubt that he was a kinsman of Thomas Vaughan, and was accepted as the right heir, entitled to the estate of Cystanog. The old seadog was delighted that his branch of the family had returned once more to the fold of Carmarthenshire's squirearchy, and looked forward to enjoying the fertile acres that lay in the valley between Abergwili and Llangunnor. Alas, before he had finished answering congratulatory letters, he received a rude shock. One fine morning, a few months after he had taken possession, a knock came at his door, and Captain Vaughan found on the threshold a strange bevy of men, women, and children.

They were humble folk from the locality rejoicing in the names of Jones, Thomas and Morris. He asked what they wanted, and one, who seemed to be the spokesman, replied "We are the right heirs of the Vaughans of Cystanog". The astonished captain gazed at them in horror and disbelief, and mastering his emotions told them quietly to go away to their homes, and closed the door.

They did go away, but not to their homes. They trooped down Spilman Street until they came to the office of Mr. Hughes, the solicitor, in Guildhall Square. With unrestrained eloquence they stated their case. One told of a tradition heard from his father, another a tale his grandmother had oft times recited, and another produced some tattered scraps of paper from his breeches pocket. Mr. Hughes listened patiently, and after questioning them, agreed to look into their claims. Apart from the traditions handed down to them that their ancestors had been the gentlefolk of Cystanog, his clients had no deeds and documents to support their claim. Hughes set to work, and the evidence and papers he amassed have survived. He made extracts from parish registers, copied inscriptions from tombstones and monuments, transcribed wills in the Probate Office, consulted records of the Great Sessions, interrogated many people. From the evidence he was able to trace the pedigree of his ragged clients back for some 200 years to a Miss Elen Vaughan of Cystanog. Around 1640, Elen had married a tenant-farmer, an event viewed with deep displeasure by her aristocratic family. Her descendants gradually sank in the social scale to become smallholders, pig dealers, carpenters, coachmen, and labourers. Nevertheless, they were the nearest heirs in blood to the Vaughans of Cystanog, and they now claimed their heritage.

In 1833 they instituted an action in the High Court of Chancery. Captain Vaughan contested it, but died suddenly in July of that year, and his son Captain Herbert Henry Vaughan of the 67th Regiment of Foot then became defendant. In the following year the verdict was given in favour of the claimants who were declared to be the right heirs. The case cost them £382, a trifling sum for an estate then valued at £36,000.

What became of these descendants of the patrician house of Vaughan, descendants of Welsh princes and Norman barons? Regrettably they proved unable to elevate themselves to the position once held by their forebears or to re-establish and further the fortunes of their house. They were numerous, so the shares were comparatively small. By 1878 there were 41 descendants, and in that year they broke the entail, sold the property, and divided the proceeds. The mansion, then in decay, was taken down in the 1890s, and the materials sold. You can still walk along the remains of the drive, but it ends in a field of pasture, and where Cystanog stood, not a single stone is left to indicate its site. It has literally disappeared from the face of the earth.

The descendants remain with us. I have known several of them, a postman in Carmarthen, a clerk in a local authority office, a miner in Ammanford, and a schoolteacher at Maesteg. You will not know them. But most, if not all of you will have heard of one of the descendants of the heirs of Cystanog. She enjoys an international reputation as a fashion designer, no less than Miss Mary Quant, O.B.E. From coronets to high couture.

Cystanog

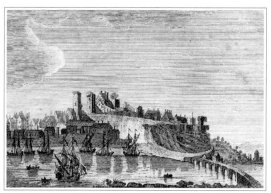

Carmarthen Castle

JACOBUS – A SHORT STORY

AFTER NEARLY twenty years I decided to return to Wales. I looked forward to renewing old friendships and forming new ones, for at the age of fifty I felt still sufficiently active and receptive to enable myself to adapt to new or changed conditions. My choice fell on a west Wales county town, formerly the administrative capital of a wide area, continuing to enjoy some eminence among the towns to the west of Cardiff.

My first problem was to find somewhere to live. I had almost despaired of obtaining a place when a stroke of luck put an end to my worries. An empty house lay tucked away within the ruined walls of the ancient castle, and through the good offices of friends I obtained a temporary tenancy of it.

First built in the reign of the Red King, the castle stood on a knoll overlooking a rivercrossing that possessed a strategic significance. More than once it had fallen to Welsh attacks led by the warlike princes of Dynevor, only to be recovered by the Anglo-Normans who could ill afford to allow their position to be weakened by the loss of so important a base. Three English kings had rested within its walls; on two occasions the standard of Glyndwr had fluttered from its ramparts. Welsh archers had mustered there, before departing for the field of Agincourt; the Royal Justiciars had held courts there, and the Chamberlains, who received taxes from unwilling hands, cast up their accounts within the safety of its towers.

An engraving made during the reign of George II showed that it had become a mere shell. In the year the French stormed the Bastille a prison rose on the site of this Welsh castle, and during Victoria's reign the police were also established there. All these, in turn, departed, and on the foundations of the demolished prison, a block of offices rose just before the second World War. A high wall cut off the medieval part, still an imposing fragment, from the modern buildings.

Thrilling tales told of secret passages along which bygone burgesses escaped to the safety of the vaults beneath the castle, also used by enterprising smugglers who carried kegs of brandy and rum from boats which came with the flow-tide after dark.

Immediately inside the impressive medieval gateway, flanked by two well preserved towers, and between the high walls, stood the house, and there my wife and I came to live. It faced south, and beyond it stretched a garden which ended at a ruined drum-tower.

Quiet, secluded, it suited us admirably, and we felt something of a thrill to be surrounded by over eight hundred years of history, and an exciting history at that. We shared this sanctuary with pigeons which we tamed so that they ate out of our hands, a cloud of chattering sparrows of amazing voracity, bats that darted like black lightening in the twilight, and a solemn owl who lived in a cavity behind the house maintaining a standoffish attitude despite all our efforts to befriend him.

We came there early in the year, and the flowers we planted in tubs and boxes made a colourful picture when summer came, giving pleasure to ourselves and sustenance to the bees who quickly found them. Here we dwelt in a cloister of peace and rest.

The house, as I have said, faced south. At the back were the bedrooms whose windows looked out on the great wall of the keep, at its foot a small courtyard, the sole access to which lay through a long passage running through the house. Nothing grew on the lower half of the wall; a heavy creeper, home of a myriad thrushes, covered the upper half.

The distance across the courtyard, from the rear of the house to the wall of the keep, was about twelve feet. The morning sun warmed this hidden nook, but the most attractive sight came at night when the moonbeams thrust into the shaft so that the grey stones shone and the leaves glistened as if they had been dipped in silver. My bed faced the window, and it became one of my simple pleasures to gaze out on this fairyland of silvery peace before dropping off to sleep.

I had gone late to bed on the evening of a Sunday in May. Well past midnight, the moon was shining so that I required no other light to guide me. I soon fell asleep.

How long I lay asleep I don't know before I found myself gazing through the window. The moonlight still bathed the walls: I saw everything clearly, and recall noticing a crevice from which a solitary wallflower curved upwards. I raised my eyes to the top of the window, and saw beyond, the twigs and leaves of the thick creeper like some giant's beard, still and glistening. Complete silence. Not a breath of wind.

Suddenly the leaves and branches shuddered convulsively, and a long thin object, resembling a snake seemed to glide down the wall. It hung still for a moment, a dark line against the whitened stones. It moved again, and looking up I discerned further rustling movements among the growth in the upper part of the wall.

Slowly, a pair of white shoes came into sight, then legs encased in red stockings, then a cloak of the same colour surmounted by a wide floppy hat adorned with a long feather, and I watched a man descending until he disappeared into the courtyard below.

I was greatly alarmed. Was it a burglar? Before I could move, the rope wriggled once more, and a second figure, similarly clad, came swarming down.

Curiously enough, the appearance of the second man, dispelled my anxiety, and I no longer thought of burglars. Instead an overwhelming curiosity to learn more about my unconventional nocturnal callers consumed me. For both men were attired in clothes of the 17th century. I had not glimpsed their faces as their backs were towards me when they slid down the rope.

I went to the window to see what was going on. The distance to the bottom of the courtyard was about fourteen feet or so, and I peered cautiously round the curtains which we never drew, so that those below would not spot me. There, in the bright moonlight I saw them; crouched low at the foot of the keep. The long feathers in their hats tossing as they moved.

As they were close against the masonry and their movements concealed by the cloaks, I could not see what they were doing. I noticed one on his knees, who seemed to be trying to dislodge a stone at the base of the wall. They worked silently, quickly, with the utmost concentration. I watched fascinated, I suppose for about five minutes. Whatever they were after they knew exactly where to look, I became even more curious about their motives.

Then one of the crouching figures stood back. The other, still kneeling, plunged an arm into a cavity and drew out something which he hid in his cloak. Together they then pushed back a great stone which fitted exactly into the hole. This accomplished, they stood up and turned towards the dangling rope.

To avoid being detected I stepped back into the room, and waited. Only the even breath of my sleeping wife broke the silence. Slowly a man came into sight, climbing laboriously, encumbered by something he carried. Deliberately he continued upwards, and I could see the toes of his buckled shoes taking advantage of every cranny and ledge that scarred the wall. With the help of these footholds and the rope he reached the top and disappeared.

The second man then came into view; he moved much more quickly, even hurriedly. I noticed he had wound the rope around his body in the manner of mountaineers. He climbed hand over fist at a fine rate. As I watched him disappearing, there was a sudden jerk. His body hurtled down and hung twitching against the wall. The rope was no longer around his shoulders, but around his neck. He hung there for some seconds. Then the body swung round to face right into my bedroom, I gazed in intense horror, for he had no face – only a white blank, as white as the moonlight that lit the grotesque scene. The body swung slowly, horridly.

The shock was so great that I staggered back overcome with a feeling of nausea. Somehow I managed to climb onto the bed where mercifully I passed out.

In the morning my wife woke me with a concerned chiding for having slept outside the blankets, thus risking a cold. Feeling tired and chilled, I got up. After a few minutes the memory of the night's events came flooding into my mind. I rushed to the window but saw nothing unusual. A thrush warbled on the rampart, the flowers drank in the morning sun, and I could see no signs of disturbance at the foot of the wall. I stood there thoughtfully, and decided to dismiss it all as a ridiculous though highly unpleasant dream, not worth mentioning to my wife whose practical personality rarely welcomed such fantasies.

Now, I must tell you that every morning I walk to a tobacconist's shop, situated about twenty paces from the barbican. Shortly after nine o'clock I went to get my customary cigarettes, but found that the shopkeeper had not arrived. Rather than wait, I walked to another shop. The woman who served me said "Excuse me sir, as you are fond of old things, can you tell me what this

The Gatehouse, Carmarthen Castle

is?" handing me a coin. I recognized it at once as a Jacobus, a coin of the reign of James the First. "Where did you find this?" I asked. She replied, "Shortly after we opened this morning a stranger came in and ordered some tobacco. He gave me this and left immediately. At first I thought it might be an Irish coin, we get lots of them here, and I went after him, but he had gone." I explained to her the value of her acquisition, adding that if she ever felt like selling it, I would be obliged if I were given the first offer. She said she would do that and put the coin away on a shelf behind her.

As I walked back to the house, the coincidence struck me like a thunderclap. A Jacobus! Two men in 17th century clothes! What had they been after at the foot of the wall? I hurried home and told my wife the whole story. After I had finished, she said, "Well let's go and see whether the wall has been disturbed."

We passed through the dark cobwebbed passage, the heavy door creaked open on rusty hinges, and we stepped into the tiny courtyard carpeted with leaves which, summer and winter, fall onto its stone floor. There were no marks, not a solitary scratch on the wall where I had seen the two men so busily at work. The stones fitted perfectly, the mortar appeared firm, the leaves lying around had not been disturbed.

"That's that", I said, "Just a silly dream to teach me to go to bed earlier in future." As I made to go, my wife who had turned to take a closer look, clutched my sleeve, and pointed in silence. I bent down. There, close to the wall, glinting among the fallen leaves, lay a solitary Jacobus.

N.B. Major Francis Jones was Carmarthenshire County Archivist, he, and his wife Ethel, once lived in a house virtually part of ancient Carmarthen Castle, a few yards from his County Hall offices. This short story was written there; it exhibits his versatile imagination and pen. *H.C-J.*

FROM PEMBREY COURT
AN OLD CARMARTHENSHIRE MANOR HOUSE
Wreckers and Maritime

IN THE BAY we can see the hazardous sands of Cefn Sidan, scene of numerous shipwrecks in the days of sail, tragedies all too frequently attended by predatory 'gentlemen in waiting' known locally as *Gwyr y Bwelli Bach* (Men of the Little Hatchets), a soubriquet indicating the sinister nature of their reprehensible activities. For me, Cefn Sidan contains a mournful memory that has chimed in my mind from boyhood when I learned that it had been the graveyard of a small sailing vessel carrying grain from Pembrokeshire, captained by my great-great grandfather, when, during a sudden and violent tempest the hapless craft was cast upon this devouring shoal, captain and crew swept out to the "vasty deep", their bodies never recovered.

It was agreed that the manor of Pembrey belonged to Lord Ashburnham and that it bordered on the sea. The lands called Caldecott extend also to the sea and adjoin to the manor of Pembrey: on all other points both Pembrey and Caldecott are abounded or surrounded by the manor of Kidwelly. The residents of the manor of Caldecott have been summoned, it is believed, to the Court Baron of the Lordship of Kidwelly. There are also Courts Baron and Leets held by Lord Ashburnham's steward for the manor of Pembrey and fee farm of Caldecott. Lord Ashburnham and his ancestors have immemorially named a Water Bailiff who has usually been resident at the Court House, who, with the assistance of Lord Ashburnham's tenants have exercised a right of taking goods and merchandise cast on shore on the manors of Pembrey and Caldicott, claiming them for the Lord's use. These effects were uniformly carried to one of Lord Ashburnham's farms, and when the property was claimed it was returned to the owners on payment of salvage to Ashburnham's agent.

An echo of "*Gwyr y Bwelli bach*" is contained in the next entry which reads: "The right of wreck upon this immediate part of the coast (Caldecott) seems not to have been distinctly exercised within the memory of man, but whenever a ship has been stranded large parties came down from the Country, some joining the tenantry of Lord Ashburnham, and others the tenantry of Lord Cawdor, and whichever proved the stronger party took the greater share of the Prey – this appears to have repeatedly happened though without the knowledge of the respective Proprietors." Lord Cawdor contends "that the Lordship of Kidwelly is a liberty and has the return of all Writs issuing into it, except *non omittas* processes, and that the Lord always approached his own Coroner for that district who is paid out of the County

"Perks"

rates, and the sheriff and coroners for the County do not enter into that Liberty . . . There are some small manors within the Lordship of Kidwelly exclusive of the manor of Pembrey, but the Coroner and Bailiff of the Liberty of Kidwelly always enter those manors to hold Inquisitions and execute all process, and the inhabitants of such manors are impleaded in the Courts Baron of the Lord of the manor of Kidwelly". Lord Cawdor claimed that he and his predecessors immemorially seized goods cast on shore on Caldecott lands "but this had only happened when the Water Bailiff and Tenantry of Lord Cawdor were too strong for the Water Bailiff and Tenantry of Lord Ashburnham". There was nothing concerning wreck in the grant of 1630, from which Caldecott was also excluded.

Lord Ashburnham co-operated with the research, and allowed his agents' books and records to be scrutinized. Among entries relating to salvaged wreck, are:

1763   Received balance left unpaid of Wine (salvaged) sold this year, 8s. 10d. For salvage of the tobacco ship that came ashore at Pembrey, 5 gns. For timber that came ashore at Pembrey, £1 10s.

1764   For 'ulledge' cask with a small supply of rum in it that came on shore, £4 10s.

1766   Caldecott: received for a boat taken up at Towin (in Caldecott) afterwards claimed on oath by Capt. Jones of Carmarthen, 1d.

1768   Caldecoet: received the profit of 4 casks of wine (sold by auction at Towin on 15 March 1768), £17 4s.

1770   Received for the salvage of a Dutch vessel stranded on the fee farm of Caldecott, 5 gns. Received for a hogshead of claret, £4 18s. but deducted 5s. for carriage of it from the sand of Towin.

1776   Received of Mr. Griffith the Collector of Customs at Llanelly the produce of the tobacco of the ship *Pompey* thrown on Pembrey manor in February 1773, £83 4s. (The agent also sold staves and rigging of the *Pompey*.)

The Churchyard of St. Illtud's church at Pembrey contains the grave of Colonel Coquelin and his daughter Adeline, "niece to Josephine, consort to that renowned individual Napoleon Bonaparte, travellers on the *Jeune Emma*, shipwrecked on the Sidan Sands, December 21 1828". In 1983 the skeleton of the wreck could still be seen.

Llechdwnni

From Llechdwnni Revisited

RHYS LIVED AT CRUG, tracing his lineage to Urien Rheged whose armorial ensigns depicting three ravens are still proudly borne by his descendants. During the years 1300-50 it was home of Sir Elidyr ddu whose pilgrimage to the shrine of our Lord in Jerusalem brought him the title of Knight of the Holy Sepulchre. By his wife Elsbeth, descended from the Breconshire chieftain Moreiddig Warwyn, Sir Elidyr had a son and heir, Philip (*vivens* 1362-87) who married Gwladys a daughter of Dafydd Freis. He, in turn, was succeeded by a son, Nicholas ap Philip who 'dwelled at Crug, a simple howse in the parish of Llandilo' as noted by an Elizabethan antiquary. His marriage to Janet, daughter of Gruffydd, son of Llywelyn Foethus (*vivens* 1330-50) an important landowner and office-holder, was attended by an unusual, even tragic, circumstance which has served to keep his memory green. As recorded by an Elizabethan antiquary, Nicholas 'haveing received a dangerous wound on his wedding day, being told by his physicians that in case he refrained from his wife's bed for a few days, he should recover, or els assuredly dye; he, however, would not abstain from his wife's society on his nuptiall night, thereby hastening his death, for soone after, he dyed, leaving his wife with child of a son'. According to NLW MS 1602, the fatal wound was delivered 'by his owne kinsman', and the posthumous son styled '*mab y dyn marw*', son of the dead man.

In due course the young widow gave birth to a son Gruffydd ap Nicholas, *mab y dyn marw*, who grew up to become a leading figure in west Wales, and laid the foundations of the family's future success.

Llechdwnni Records
A Catalogue of ye bookes in the Study etc. 1688

Folio – Heylen's Cosmography. Lloyd's Archaeologi Britt. A manuscript folio. Dr Tillotson's Sermons. An old law booke. Dalton's County Justice. Military Art by Elton. History of ye Caribe Isles. A manuscript folio. *Quarto* – Fuller's Pharma Estempr. Kilburn's Justice. Kitchen's Court Leets. Clerk's Guide. Misteries of Clerk. Wingate's Abridgements.

Explanatory Law Terms. Dr. Taylor's Holy Living etc. Xenophon. Dr Hammond Practical Catechism. Art of Contentment. Whole Duty of Man. Collect: form of Prayers. Lady's Calling. Unfortunate Queen. *Octavo and Duodecimo* – Sicilian Tyrant. Chambn: Comp: Justice. Kilburn's Presidence. England's Military Discipline. Play Book. Doctrine of ye Bible. Beveridge's Private Thoughts. Military Offices. Clark's Description of the World. Reign of King Charles II. Wars of England. Ovid Metamorphosis. Landlord's Law. Guide to Constables. Hakewell on Parliaments. Remedy of Prophanes. Grove of Beatitudes. Erasmus. Culpeper's Herball. Lacini Opera. Speed's History of England and Wales. Playford's Vade Mecum. Treatise of Law maxims. Niesina, a Romance. Proceedings in Court Wales. Learning's foundation. 4 Bibles. 2 Common Prayer Books. Prep: Lord's Supper. Lake. Companion to the Alter. Cry to God. Weeks' Preparations. Mirrors that Flatter. Gentleman's Companion. Golden Grove (by Jeremy Taylor). Psalm Book. Private Manuel Devotion. Armst: Lord's Supper. A Saint Indeed. Prep: off. to ye Holy Communion. Little Handful of Comforts. Crucified Saviour. Smith's Lives of Blessed Christians. Dr Taylor's Golden Chain. Paraphrase on ye Song of Solomon. Doctrine of the Bible. Glanville's Invit: Sacra Prophet, Prayers, King Charles. Gibb's Divine Treatise. Hall's manual of Devotion. State of London in 1661. Principle of Law.

Farming Matters

Agreement with Servants – Taken from the personal papers of Owen Brigstocke of Llechdwnni, 1667-73

1667 My agreement with Mary Morgan for hearding my cattle at William Harry David's land from this day till All Saints day next. He is to heard all such cattle as I shall send thither and to keep them from trespassing on my demaynes of Llechdonny and every other neybour. He is to keepe the cattle at night where I shall appoynt and if I order him to bring them to Llechdonny fould he is to doe soe. If any strange cattle comes to the land he is to send them to the pound.

1670 I am to pay Gwenllyan for hearding 10s. Paid in wheat 5s. Paid in cheese 1 stone, 5s. 3 pecks of barley, 6s. In money, 5s. 1 peck of barley 2s. 1 stone of cheese. 1 quarter of a stone of wool 3s. 6d.

1673 Gwenllyan is to herd my cattle and fodder them summer and winter. She is to make and keep up the fences and to keep the hay ground from being grazed, to drive out all trespassing cattle to the pound, to keep the sheep on the mountain. She is to have 30s. in money, half the Michaelmas wool, and half a bushel of barley and the wheaten stubble to sow barley in it.

CHAPTER VIII

HISTORIC CARMARTHENSHIRE HOMES AND THEIR FAMILIES

ABERGLASNEY

IN 1998 I found myself unexpectedly commissioned to write a book about Aberglasney. Publication was timed to coincide with the opening of the restored garden in summer 1999 and the transmission of the BBC television series *A Garden Lost in Time*. The deadline was alarming, but happily the Aberglasney Restoration Trust was able to hand me a bundle of documentation that they had assembled in order to secure funding. Among this research was the delightful article "Aberglasney and its Families" that follows.

This was my first encounter with the work of Major Francis Jones, and I was enthralled. His account in the forbidding-sounding *National Library of Wales Journal* proved to be a ripping yarn, told in a lively way. There was pathos and drama in the lives of the people who had lived at Aberglasney. Each successive dynasty arrived with panache but subsequently "staggered among the thornbushes of debt" or died away heirless. I could not have wished for a better introduction to my subject. If this article was my Bible, his *Historic Carmarthenshire Homes* became my Baedeker, providing a gazetteer of the houses that proved to be connected with generations of Aberglasney owners through purchase or marriage.

In due course I found Major Jones's name cropping up time and again as I followed various scents to find out more about Aberglasney's neighbours, relatives and connections. Through other articles I made the acquaintance of John Walters Philipps's aunts, the slightly dotty Jane and Frances Walters of Perthcereint, Cardiganshire, and of Hermione Jennings, the "Young Lady of Fashion" who competed at archery contests with the future Mrs. Mayhew

Photo: Grenville Barrett, L.R.P.S.

and danced at Aberglasney around the billiard table, which was too heavy to be moved.

A poignant moment in the following article occurs when on a visit in 1968 Major Jones finds that the painted window displaying John Walters Philipps's blazon had been smashed to fragments by hooligans. The property was even more deeply in decline when I first saw it some twenty years later. How amazed he would surely have

John Dyer, poet

been to find its fortunes reversed – and particularly to learn that the house was saved because of the survival of its unique terraced garden, that "unusual and attractive architectural feature".

An unexpected chapter has been added to the story of Aberglasney, bringing new faces and a new "family" of custodians and visitors. Some of them add footnotes to the information available to Major Jones. We knew there to be descendants of the poet John Dyer, and I have met some of them. His brother Thomas was thought to have no issue by his wife, née Dorothy De La Place, but two descendants have independently written to me recently. Other jigsaw pieces turn up from time to time, including a host of tall stories and red herrings!

I am sure Francis Jones would have relished them all.

Penny David, Lampeter, September 2002

Letter dated 6 February 1769 from Francis Parry, *Boreas*, Spithead, to Wm. Dyer Esq., at Court Henry near Cross Inn, Carmarthenshire regarding the death of Robert Herbert Dyer, died 29 November 1768. He was baptized 21 August 1748 and was still a minor at his death. He was the son of Robert Archer Dyer and Elizabeth (Herbert) his wife.

'It's a most disagreeable subject to write of ill news, and that office generally is ye lot of a friend which is now ye case, undoubtedly you are now much alarm'd at receiving a letter from ye *Boreas* from a new correspondent, and at not hearing from your amiable brother; but as ye strokes of Providence are certainly for some greater ends than we have penetration to dive into, don't doubt but you will submit to this stroke with a Christian resolution; and I must now tell you that you have lost a most worthy Brother, and I a generous, good friend. I thought it a duty incumbent on me (not only from ye recommendation I had from Captain Lloyd)as a friend to have him decently interr'd which was done at Lisbon. Ye only extra-ordinary expenses were a dozen pair of gloves to ye Midshipmen. The unfortunate accident happen'd ye 29th of Nov. 68; at 10 at night we were walking together and a block fell on his head and kill'd him on ye spot. I have his cloathes in my care which are not very considerable, ye money I had lent him and ye burial are about £13 5. 0., we are now at Spithead waiting for orders, so beg your direction for fear we should sail: beg my compliments to Captain Lloyd, and am/Sir/ your obedt Servt/ Frances Parry'.

Rudd tomb at Llangathen

ABERGLASNEY AND ITS FAMILIES

ABERGLASNEY is an historic mansion that has been a part of the Carmarthenshire landscape for over five centuries, the home of notable men, some of whom became figures of national consequence. During the later Middle Ages it was the seat of an important family who eventually took the surname Thomas, and may have been the home of their ancestors who lived during the early 14th century.

Before the end of Elizabeth's reign, the descendants of its medieval possessors had left Carmarthenshire and sold the mansion to Anthony Rudd, Bishop of St. Davids from 1594 to 1615. The precise date of the purchase is not known, but it probably took place shortly after his elevation to the See, and Archdeacon Yardley tells us that the Bishop "built a hansome seat (with a very decent chapel, with a curious pulpit, ornamented with painted glass) called Aberglasney" *(Menevia Sacra, p. 103).*

No trace remains of the earlier mansion, and doubtless it was demolished when the Bishop built the new palace. His descendants continued at Aberglasney until 1710 when Sir Anthony Rudd's mortgagee sold the place to Robert Dyer, an attorney at law, whose descendants remained there for nearly a hundred years.

We do not know what changes were made to the house that the Bishop built, but it is abundantly clear that the present house contains no features of late Elizabethan or early Jacobean architecture. It has been much changed, doubtless remodelled, suggests the 18th century in style and plan, and is likely to have been largely the work of the Dyers. On the other hand, the construction and design of a gateway, still standing a short distance to the left and front of the house, may be a relic of the Bishop's period.

In 1783 Joseph Gulston called at Aberglasney, describing it as "an old house with a large Hall. In the center is a Staircase which carry's you to a Chapel of which nothing now is remaining but the Pulpit which is old and curious. There is a terras round the court built on Stone Arches . . .". The pulpit has gone, but the terrace built on stone arches that took Gulston's eye, has survived, and its location as well as its construction, provides an unusual and attractive architectural feature. Gulston went on to mention some of the pictures he saw there, namely, a portrait of John Dyer (the poet, 1701-58) "painted by himself, in blue velvet, hand rests on a table, brown wig, very indifferent"; Robert Dyer (brother of the poet) "down to the knees in a blue velvet coat, neckloth twisted through the button hole"; Mrs. Dyer (*née* Croft, wife of Robert) "sitting, a most beautiful woman . . . the head is painted by Sir Godfrey Kneller, but the neck, hand, and Drapery are bad, by some of his people"; four children of the foregoing, "small, whole length, with a Dog"; two portraits of Mr. and Mrs. Dyer (grandparents of Robert) "two postures, common, very indifferent"; Sir Archer Croft, "long wig, down to the knees, sitting. Father *(recte,* brother) of the handsome Mrs. Dyer. In yellow with a blue mantle"; Mrs. Dyer. "In yellow with a blue mantle";

Robert Dyer

Mrs. Philips of Coedgain, mother of George Philipps, M.P. for Carmarthen 1780-84 "bad"; and one portrait "unknown". Later, the owner, William Herbert Dyer, sold the estate, mansion, with some of the furniture to Thomas Phillips, but the fate of the portraits is unknown.

After the house had been bought for Thomas Phillips, considerable repairs and improvements were made during the years 1803-05, "as it had been left to run greatly out of repair" – so the purchaser's father wrote at the time. During those years it was completely re-roofed, and interior changes made. Since a belief has arisen in recent times that the ground-floor kitchen is the location of the former chapel, we should recall Gulston's words showing it to have been on an upper storey, which is supported by references to the stripping and taking down "of the roof of the chapel" in 1804. The first reference to the modern view known to me, occurs in 1906, when the resident, Colonel Mayhew wrote: "The chapel, which is now the kitchen with the laundry over it, is easily traceable. The walls are of considerable thickness . . . The length is 46 feet, breadth 24 feet. It would accommodate about 150 persons. This apartment lies strictly east and west, and there is little doubt that it represents the site of the bishop's domestic chapel, but it retains not a single trace of its ecclesiastical origin" *(Trans. Carms. Antiq. Soc.* ii, p. 157). This was honest speculation, but not evidence.

The heraldic achievement placed in the window lighting the staircase and hall, was the work of John Walters Philipps who inherited the property in 1824, and in the following year received a patent authorising him to bear the arms, and he was the probable builder of the *porte cochere* of the main entrance. The sorry fate of the armorial window is set forth below. Several photographs have survived of the three-storied house, with a range of nine windows on the upper floor, the ranges on the two lower storeys being broken by the pedimented pillared porch. One was taken in 1871 by C. S. Allen of Tenby (in possession of Lieut.-Col. W. H. Buckley, D.L., of Castell Gorfod), another appears on page 42 of D. Morgan's *Story of Carmarthenshire,* 1909, and a third in *The Destruction of the Country House,* 1975, no. 123, where the caption incorrectly states that it was "altered in the early 19th century for John Walters Philipps".

However detailed the description of a country house may be, the picture is incomplete without knowledge of the people who dwelt within its walls, for it is they who gave "life" and "atmosphere" to the building, and by construction, alterations and additions, impressed on it their personalities and the fashions of different periods. In the following pages we shall meet some of the men and women who walked through the portals of Aberglasney, note how they comported themselves, and judge of their contributions to the times in which they lived.

Thomas of Aberglasney

The earliest known owners of Aberglasney were descendants of Elystan Glodrudd, the 11th century ruler of the territory between Wye and Severn, represented in modern times by the county of Radnor. The first of his descendants to have associations with Carmarthenshire, Sir Gruffydd ab Elidir, Knight of Rhodes, married Gwenllian daughter of Rhys Gryg (d. 1234) son of Yr Arglwydd Rhys, Prince of Deheubarth, and doubtless the marriage led to Gruffydd settling in his wife's ancestral district. From this time onwards the menfolk espoused wives from leading families in west Wales, were intimately concerned with local affairs, and held Crown appointments which indicate the status of the family and the trust im-posed in its members by successive monarchs.

Gruffydd's son, Owain, described in genealogies as "Esquire of the Body" to Edward III, married Joyce daughter of Rhydderch ap Maredudd ap Rhydderch ap Rhys ap Dinawal. He was followed by his son Llywelyn Ddu, who married Elen daughter of Rhydderch ap Rhys ap Bledri of Cilsant. Llywelyn Ddu was succeeded by his son who bore his father's Christian name and became known as Llywelyn Foethus (the Luxurious) of Llangathen, to whom armorists have assigned the coat-of-arms, *argent* on a cross *sable* five crescents *or*, and in dexter chief a spear head *gules*. His son, Gruffydd ap Llywelyn Foethus, is described by such style in contemporary Ministers' Accounts as Constable of Maenordeilo during the years 1355-58. By his wife Lleucu daughter of Ievan Llwyd ap Gruffydd Foel of Glynaeron, he had two sons, Rhys and Ievan, and three daughters, Janet who, about 1356, married Rhys ap David Fongam, Jonet who married Nicholas ap Philip, from whom descended Sir Rhys ap Thomas of Dinefwr, and Alice who married Morgan ap Maredudd, Escheator of the county of Carmarthen in 1377-80, from whom stemmed the Morgan family of Tredegar.

The two sons, Rhys and Ieuan, led a life of some ambiguity, being royal officers at one stage, outlawed rebels at another, but despite voyaging in troubled seas, both contrived to survive. Rhys held numerous appointments under the Crown; in 1386 he held the post of Constable of Catheiniog and Maenordeilo, in the years 1392-1400 Beedle of Catheiniog, in 1398-1400, deputy-farmer of Llanllwch, and in 1400 the important office of Sheriff of the royal county of Carmarthen. During the rising of Owain Glyndwr, the younger brother Ieuan joined the insurgents, with the result that he was declared an outlaw, and his confiscated lands (together with those of his confederate Llywelyn ap Gruffydd Fychan of Caeo who was hanged in 1401) were granted to Rhys who had remained loyal to the Crown. Rhys was further rewarded in 1402 by being made Forester of Glyn Cothi and Pennant, and Constable of Dryslwyn Castle. However, by the following year, Rhys had transferred his allegiance to Glyndwr to whom he opened the gates of Dryslwyn on 4 July 1403. The King lost no time in stripping Rhys of his appointments, declaring him rebel and outlaw, and granting all his lands to Thomas Dyer of Carmarthen who had been despoiled by Glyndwr's troops.

After anxious years in the wilderness, Rhys made his peace with the King, and in October 1409 received a pardon and restoration of the confiscated property. Some offices were also restored to him, and in 1411 we find him holding once again the post of Constable of Catheiniog and Maenordeilo.

Rhys ap Gruffydd ap Llywelyn Foethus married Maud daughter of Sir William Clement, Lord of Tregaron, Cardiganshire, whose family held a leading position in south-west Wales. He left a son, Rhydderch ap Rhys.

It is certain that Rhydderch lived in the family house in Llangathen, and there can be little doubt that this was Aberglasney. An ode addressed to him by Lewis Glyn Cothi (fl. 1447-86) extols his ample wealth, wide learning, knowledge of the Scriptures, he was "Pope of the land of Cetheiniawg" who owned several mansions, and extolled his main residence as a fair court *(llys wen)* set amid leafy groves in Llangathen, built of dressed stone, white-washed, environed by gardens, orchards, and vineyards, and young oaks reaching to the skies:

> *Iddo ef mae neuadd falch*
> *Ac un wengaer gam wyngalch*
> *Ac o gylch ogylch i hon*
> *Naw o arddau yn wyrddion*
> *Perllanwydd a gwinwydd gwyr*
> *Derw ieuainc hyd yr awyr.*
>
> *(Lewis Glyn Cothi,* ed. E. D. Jones, *p.* 185)

Rhydderch was followed by his son Thomas who married Maud daughter of Jenkin Llwyd ap Jenkin ap Ieuan Llwyd ap Ieuan Fychan who traced his lineage to Cynfrig Efell of Powys. Thomas does not seem to have achieved any position or to have impressed contemporaries, but his son became an eminent man known beyond the confines of his native Carmarthenshire.

He was William ap Thomas, also known as William Thomas, described by Tudor genealogists as of Aberglasney, doubtless the "fair house" extolled by Lewis Glyn Cothi in the ode to William's grandfather. Like earlier forebears he took an active part in public life, held several of the most influential appointments in west Wales, and received the honour of knighthood. In 1509 he was Constable of Carmarthen Castle, Sheriff of the royal counties of Carmarthen and Cardigan, Steward of Cantref Mawr, Carmarthenshire, and of the county of Cardigan, and twelve years later Constable of Llanbadarn Castle (Aberystwyth). In 1541-2 he became the first High Sheriff of the newly constituted shire of Carmarthen.

Sir William Thomas's wife belonged to an extremely wealthy and important family, high in the Royal favour, holding offices both in the Principality and in the councils of the realm. She was Jane daughter of Sir William Herbert of Coldbrook (Mon.) by Jane daughter of Sir William Griffith of Penrhyn, Chamberlain of Gwynedd.

Sir William Thomas of Aberglasney died soon after serving the office of High Sheriff, and his will, dated 26 January 1541-2, was proved in London on 15 March 1542-3. He desired to be buried in the "new chancel" of the church of Llangathen, and left 100 shillings to a priest "to pray for my soul"; he bequeathed 12 pence to the cathedral church of St. David's; £30 a year to his wife Jane, £30 to his daughter Mary, and £20 to each of his daughters Winefrede and Mawde, all of which were to be charged on testator's lease of the suppressed Carmarthen Priory and the farm of Llanfihangel yscorne (Rhos y Corn) and Llanllwni included in that lease; £10 to each of his sons John, Bartholomew, and George; plate to "the Lady my bedfellow"; all household stuff at Ocle Park to his daughter Elizabeth; mentions his son Rice William; and left 8 yards of cloth and a quarter's wages to "Sir Roger my chaplain"; and refers to his lease of the suppressed house of "Olde Kayrmarthen" (Priory). Among witnesses was Master Lewis David "my ghostly father". He had fifteen children, and was succeeded by his eldest surviving son, Rhys.

Rhys Thomas (called Rice William in his father's will) succeeded to Aberglasney. He was a Justice of the Peace in 1552, High Sheriff of Carmarthenshire in 1565. His forebears had been associated with north Wales for a long time – Lewis Glyn Cothi mentions the family's "courts" at Llandecwyn in Gwynedd – and Rhys's maternal grandmother was a Griffith of Penrhyn. His own marriage to Jane daughter of Sir John Puleston of Caernarvon, brought him into closer touch with the north, where he had a residence at his manor of Aber, and in 1563 was High Sheriff of Anglesey, and ten years later, of Caernarvonshire. He died in 1577, and was followed by his young son William Thomas, born in 1551.

William Thomas's marriage to Elen daughter of William Griffith of Caernarvon son of Sir William Griffith, Chamberlain of north Wales by Margaret daughter of John Wynn of Gwydir, increased his commitments in Gwynedd. He was elected member of parliament for Caernarvonshire in 1585. Aberglasney remained his chief residence, and he continued the family's participation in Carmarthenshire affairs, serving as High Sheriff in 1576 and again in 1582. He also took part in England's continental wars, and in 1586 commanded a force of 200 Welshmen at the battle of Zutphen where he was killed, and where his brother-officer, Sir Philip Sidney was mortally wounded. William Thomas was only 35 years of age when he fell. He was followed by his son, also named William, born in 1572, who remained a ward of the Queen until he came of age, and is described as owning estates in the shires of Carmarthen, Caernarvon, and Anglesey. He seems to have lived entirely in Caernarvonshire, and is probably the man who sold Aberglasney to Bishop Rudd, between 1594 and 1614. He was knighted, became a Justice of the Peace and Deputy Lieutenant of Caernarvonshire, and High Sheriff of that county in 1607. Although his principal residence was always in the town of Caernarfon, he built, about 1600, a new residence at Aber, near the site of an older house (probably the work of his father or grandfather). Sir William's house, later called Penybryn, still stands. His successors moved to yet another mansion near the county town, which remained the family's principal seat until alienated during the present century. Sir William was the last of the descendants of Llywelyn Foethus to have owned Aberglasney.

Rudd of Aberglasney

From early times the Church had made advancement to high position possible for men even of the most modest background, provided they possessed ability and character, and the Church's association with the country's governors ("nobility, clergy, and gentry", a normal stratification in bygone days) gave status to its clergy, some of whom were enabled not only to attain to positions of eminence in their own calling, but to establish families of consequence in secular life. It was to a Churchman that the next family at Aberglasney owed its entry into the ranks of Carmarthenshire landowners.

Little is known of the origins of Anthony Rudd. His father, Robert Rudd, a Yorkshireman, possessed sufficient means to provide his son with a university education. Born about 1549, Anthony entered Trinity College, Cambridge, where he graduated B.A., proceeded M.A., became a Fellow of his college, and later a doctorate of divinity was bestowed on him. Having taken Holy Orders, his superior intellect soon drew the recognition and admiration of contemporaries. In 1584 he became Dean of Gloucester, and in 1594 Bishop of St. Davids. He might have achieved further advancement – he was in line to the Archbishopric of Canterbury – and greatly favoured by the Queen herself, but whose smiles he unhappily forfeited after delivering, in 1596, a sermon containing opinions to which she was distinctly unsympathetic. His published sermons reveal a grasp of theological and philosophical propositions, and skill in presenting doctrines in attractive form; of a conciliatory and humane nature, we are told that at the Hampton Court conference held in 1603 he "spoke in favour of compromising with the Puritans" (Joseph Lord's manuscript account of the Rudds, 29 September 1739). From another source we learn that "he wrought much on the Welsh by his wisdom, and won their affection", and "by thrift and by leases of ecclesiastical property, built up an estate for his children" (Fuller, *Church History,* bk x). Among these leases was one granted to him by the Crown on 27 December 1597, of the rectory and church of St. Peter, Carmarthen, and the chapels of Manorgain, Newchurch, and Llanllwch (late possessions of the dissolved Priory of Carmarthen) together with tithes and profits, for the lives of the Bishop, his wife, and son Rice, at a yearly rent of £48. He improved Llangathen church and "continued the south aisle eastwards flush with the east wall of the chancel, designing it to contain his own remains, as well, doubtless, as the fine characteristically huge monument of the times which was erected to the bishop's memory by his wife in 1616" *(Report. Anc. Mon. Carms,* 1917, pp. 157-8). I have quoted earlier Archdeacon Yardley's statement that he purchased a good estate and built a handsome seat with a chapel, in Llangathen parish. In addition to building this residence, he paid attention to his official residence, spending considerable sums in restoring the episcopal palaces at Abergwili and St. David's.

The mansion he built at Aberglasney, probably stood on or near the site of the older house of the Thomases, which was demolished. The extent of the estate in Llangathen, and from whom it was purchased, is not known, but the vendor may have been a member of the Thomas family which by then had settled permanently in north Wales. Of his additional purchases, we know more. On 10 March 1608-9, Sir John Lewes and Dame Bridget his wife, of Abernantbychan, Cards., George Philipps, esquire, and Anne his wife, of Cardigan (the said Anne being formerly wife of James Lewes, esquire), and Richard Lewes of Abernantbychan, gentleman, conveyed the following Carmarthenshire properties to the Bishop in fee simple:

Langunnor parish – Ty Gwyn, Allt Ddu, Carreg Lwyd, Morva Towarchen (3 acres), five 'rudges' of arable called Llain pen y Morfa, a meadow called Park y lland Vawr (4 acres), and a yearly rent of 3s. 5d. "out of Towy".

St. Ishmaels parish – Sythyn alias Tythyn John Lawrence.

Abergwili parish – a water grist mill called Tythyn Clyne y velin.

County Borough of Carmarthen – Eleven messuages and gardens, a close of pasture, two closes or parks, a tan house, all in Priory Street; one messuage in King Street; a messuage and backhouses in Key Street; six messuages in Lower Water Street; a messuage in St. Mary Street; and one more messuage.

Pencarreg parish – the rectory and church of Pencarreg "late parcell of the possession of the dissolved monastery of 'Estar-de Cleres' (Ystrad Fflur), and all its profits"; a house, messuage or tenement annexed to the rectory, part of the said dissolved monastery, with all tithes etc., and manorial court leets, dues, renders etc, in the town, village, parish, hamlets or fields of Pencarreg in that parish.

The covenant to enable the purchase to be completed, included seven messuages, a mill, a dove-house, seven gardens, seven orchards, and 2,500 acres in Llangunnor, Llangain, St. Ishmaels, Abergwili, and Pencarreg; the rectory of Pencarreg; 3s. 4d. yearly rent in Llangunnor; twenty-six messuages, thirty gardens, ten orchards, and eighteen acres in the county borough of Carmarthen. These properties, in addition to unspecified properties in Llangathen, purchased earlier, indicate that the total acreage must have been considerable.

Having provided for his family, the good bishop extended his humanity to the less favoured members of his flock. By will, dated 25 January 1614, he granted the messuage and lands called Tir Ffynnon Deilo in Llandeilofawr (purchased from David William Griffith) and six acres intermixed with the said messuage (purchased from John Thomas ap Rhydderch), to his wife Anne and son Rice Rudd (whom he appointed executors) directing that within two or three years following testator's death, they should purchase a place in Abergwili or in the town of Carmarthen, "for the seating of a House convenient for four poor men" (to be nominated by the executors) and "sett up the said house divided into partitions for a convenient habitacon of the said foure men severally", and to ensure payment of £20 6s. 0d. yearly, whereof £5 was to be given to each of the four poor men, and 16 shillings for the repair "of the said Hospital House"; the charity to be advised by learned counsel to ensure its perpetuity.

Such was the founder of the new line at Aberglasney. The Bishop died on 7 March 1614-15, and was buried in Llangathen church, where a fine monument, decorated with his coat of arms *(azure* a chevron *ermine* between three bells *argent),* perpetuates his memory. By his wife Anne *(née* Anne Dalton of Thurnham, Lancs.), he had three children – Anthony, said to have married "a lady of considerable fortune in the county of Gloucester, and died without issue", and administration of his goods was granted in PCC on 5 May 1620 to the widow, Margaret; Robert who died without issue; and Rice who became sole heir to the estate.

Having succeeded to Aberglasney, Rice Rudd's estate was enhanced on 12 March 1616-17 by a patent from King James, granting him free warren in the capital messuage of Aberglasney, Abersannan, Bryn Melin in Talachlayan, Nant y Mabe, Llanylais Yr Ynis, Altygaer, Tyr y Crongaer, Nantywellan, in the parishes of Llangathen, Llanegwad, Llanfynydd, Llandeilofawr, and Abergwili; and also in the lordships of Kathinocke, Droslwyn, Altigaer, Widigada, Kilsaen, Manordilo, Llan y Hernin, and Tyr yr Escob.

A further expression of Royal favour came on 8 December 1628 when Rice was created a Baronet of the United Kingdom. He took an active part in public life. In 1619, and again in 1636, he served as High Sheriff of Carmarthenshire; and during the Civil War supported the Royal cause, and for his loyalty suffered the heavy fine of £581 12s. 7d.

Shortly after the Bishop's death, the widow and her son Rice, put the charitable bequest in force. They bought a site in Carmarthen town, erected a hospital house, with five partitions, as the widow wished to add one more almsman to the four provided for by her late husband, and she now allocated the sum of £100 to maintain the additional charge. Many years later, on 29 June 1640, Sir Rice Rudd, "for per-petuating the pious and charitable works" of his parents, executed a deed of feoffment to Richard, Earl of Carbery, Morgan (Owen) Bishop of Llandaff, Sir William Vaughan of Torycoed, Henry Vaughan of Derwydd, Rowland Philipps and Lodwick Lewis, mayor and recorder of Carmarthen, respectively, and the Revd. William Nicholson of Llandeilofawr, clerk, of "all that Hospitall or Almshouse scituat and being in the said towne and county Borough of Carmarthen in a streete there called St. Peter's Streete otherwise The Priory Street . . . with appurtenances heretofore purchased of and from Sir John Lewes, knight, and John Price, gentle-man, and situate lying between the messuage late of Sir Fulke Conwey, knight, now of Sir John Bankes, knight, being the Priory Land, of the one part, and the messuage late of John Bowen, gentleman, deceased, of the other part, and all the premises in the will of the late Bishop contained . . . and also that tenement in occupation of John Rees David Harry called Tir y Clynne, and another messuage in occupation of John Hugh Parrey called Cadare Veinac, for ever". The five poor men were to be known as "the Brethren of Bishop Rudd's Hospitall and Almes-house", and Sir Rice and his heirs and assigns, being owners of Aberglasney, were to have the visitation and correction of all defaults in the said Hospitall or Almeshouse, and power of removal of any of the poor men for any crime, or who should die or be removed; and that Sir Rice and his heirs, owners of Aberglasney for the time being, were to take rents and profits of the said premises for so long as he or they should repair the said Hospitall and pay £5 apiece to the five poor men, and to have power to grant leases of the said Lands (the Hospital excepted) for 21 years or 3 lives at £26 yearly at the least, to be used for the repair of the Hospital; and should a chamber or chambers become vacant or that Sir Rice or his heirs allow it to become a ruin, then it would be lawful for the Earl of Carbery or the owner for the time being of the capital messuage or mansion place called Golden Grove to elect any poor man to the vacancy, such man to be single, without a wife, and to be an inhabitant of Carmarthenshire or of the county borough, and so poor, aged, or decrepit that he has no other means of support, and that they can demand 20 shillings yearly for repair from Sir Rice and his heirs.

Sir Rice Rudd married, firstly, Jane (her portion, £600) daughter of Thomas ap Rhys of Rickeston in Brawdy, Pembs., who died in 1626; and, secondly, Elizabeth daughter of Sir Thomas Aubrey of Llantrithyd, Glam., who died without issue. He made his will on 3 April 1662, and died in May 1664, leaving the following children by his first wife – Anthony, see later; Urien, died without issue; Thomas to whom I shall return later; Anne, married firstly her cousin-german James ap Rhys of Rickeston (will proved 1660), secondly James Lewes of Coedmore, Cards., and thirdly James Philipps of Cardigan Priory; Constance, who bequeathed a picture of Mary Magdalene, the portraits of Sir Rice the first baronet, and his lady, the patent of baronetcy, the grant of the family arms, and other family muniments, to her nephew Rice Rudd who had great difficulty in obtaining possession of them.

The eldest son, Anthony Rudd, matriculated at Oxford on 4 December 1635, aged 16. In 1640 he married Judith daughter of Thomas Rudd of Higham Ferrers, Northants. He inherited neither the title nor the estate, for he died during his father's lifetime. His widow (who afterwards married Goddard Pemberton) survived him by about fifty years. He left two children – (Sir) Rice Rudd, see below; and Mary who married [—] Pemberton; she died soon after her brother, and her only child, Thomas Pemberton became M.P. for Higham Ferrers in 1702, and by his wife, Martha, left an only child Mary who died without issue before 1705. By his will, the said Thomas Pemberton charged his estate with the payment of his own debts and those of his uncle Sir Rice Rudd, and appointed as trustees his wife Martha, Thomas Hanbury, Storey Barker, and Roger Pemberton of Peterborough.

Rice Rudd, born *circa* 1643, succeeded his grandfather, as second baronet. About 1661 he married a lady with a portion of £1,000, namely Dorothy the 18-year-old daughter of Charles Cornwallis of High Holborn (whose ward Rice had been during his minority), sister of Sir Francis Cornwallis of Abermarlais. On 27 October 1682, he conveyed all his Carmarthenshire estate to Owen Brigstocke, William Wogan, and Roger Mainwaring, on trust, to the use of grantor for life, and for payment of all debts, with remainder to grantor's heirs of the body, remainder to his cousin, Anthony Rudd and his heirs male, remainder to grantor's nephew, Thomas Pemberton and his heirs male, with remainder to grantor's right heirs. Later, Sir Rice mortgaged the Aberglasney and Northamptonshire estates, which were accordingly vested in Storey Barker of the Middle Temple and the Hon. Thomas Wentworth of Wentworth Woodhouse, esquires, by way of security. Just before he died he directed that his estate in Higham Ferrers was to be sold to pay debts, and should the money thus realised prove insufficient, then the Aberglasney estate was to be sold as well. He was a Justice of the Peace and a Deputy Lieutenant for Carmarthenshire, and a Commissioner of Assessment in 1664-80 and again 1689-90.

Sir Rice, sat in the House of Commons for many years, as member for Higham Ferrers for the years 1679-81, and for Carmarthenshire from 1689 until his death, intestate, in London in July 1701. He was buried in Llangathen church, and the administration of his estate granted to his sister, Mrs. Mary Pemberton. He had no issue, and the title passed to his cousin-german, Anthony Rudd.

We now return to Thomas Rudd, youngest son of the first baronet. He married Anne daughter of Thomas Newsham of Abersannan in Llanfynydd parish, by whom he had a son, Anthony, and four daughters, Clarinda, Jane, Dorothy, and Anne. He predeceased his wife who afterwards married John Edwardes of Rhydygors near Carmarthen.

Thomas's only son, Anthony Rudd lived at Capel Evan (then in Llanelli parish, but now in that of Pontyberem) which he held under a lease from his cousin, the second baronet, on whose death in 1701 he succeeded as third baronet. Sir Anthony married firstly, Magdalene daughter of Sir Henry Jones Bt., of Abermarlais, but she died without issue; and secondly Beatrice daughter of Sir John Barlow, Bt., of Slebech, Pembs., heiress of her mother Beatrice elder daughter and heiress of Sir John Lloyd of Forest Brechfa. The pre- and post-nuptial settlements of Sir Anthony and Beatrice, were dated 7 September 1699 and 29 August 1704, and after the marriage they were mainly associated with Forest.

After succeeding to the title, Sir Anthony experienced difficulty in obtaining both the personalty and realty of his cousin Sir Rice who had died festooned in debt. To recover possession, he instituted an action on 5 February 3 Anne (1705) in the High Court of Chancery against Storey Barker, Hon. Thomas Wentworth, Sir William Wogan, Thomas Hanbury of the Middle Temple, Roger Pemberton, Thomas Lloyd of Berllandywyll, Miss Mary Davies of Ty Llwyd, Edward Davies of Pentre (Carms.), the Revd. Richard Willis of Higham Ferrers, and others. The result of the suit is not recorded, but it is clear that he did not recover the fee simple of Aberglasney, which, together with other parts of the Carmarthenshire estate, was sold in June 1710 by the Hon. Thomas Wentworth (a mortgagee) to Robert Dyer, to pay the long-standing debts of the second baronet. This marked the end of the association of the Rudd family with Aberglasney.

Sir Anthony was buried at St. Peter's Carmarthen on 27 June 1706. The widowed Beatrice married on 27 September 1709 Griffith Lloyd, barrister, of Cwmgwili (d. 1713), and died February 1735–36. By her, Sir Anthony had three children, namely:

1. Sir John Rudd, who succeeded as fourth baronet, and married Mary daughter and co-heiress of Sir Thomas Powell, Bt., of Broadway, near Laugharne. He was the last in the male line of the Rudds of Aberglasney, and on his death without surviving issue on 15 July 1739, the baronetcy became extinct. His wife outlived him by very many years, and her will was proved in 1802.

2. Anthony Rudd, a clergyman and unmarried, was buried at St. Peter's Carmarthen on 26 December 1738.

3. Anne married Richard Jones of Taliaris, who, about 1721-22, took the additional name of Gwynne; they had issue.

Dyer of Aberglasney

The origins of the next owners of Aberglasney differed radically from those of the previous occupants. The Dyers were townsfolk, well-to-do tradesmen, who in the fifteenth and sixteenth centuries appear as burgesses of Carmarthen, two of the family serving as mayors of that town in 1503 and 1504, and from the early 17th century as burgesses of Kidwelly. Like several other families they entered the ranks of the country landowners through the medium of the law. This profession has often provided advancement to a lawyer sufficiently competent, diligent, and astute, for in addition to the prospect of a flourishing practice, there were opportunities of obtaining official posts, both local and national, that were prestigious and influential as well as lucrative. Success in this profession enabled the Dyers to exchange the description of "gentleman" for that of "esquire".

In 1918 a history of the Dyers appeared from the pen of the late Mr. Francis Green in volume VII of *West Wales Historical Records,* and although by no means complete, it remains an instructive contribution, rendering it unnecessary for me to do more than to provide a précis, and to include additional information that has come to light since Mr. Green published his essay.

We start with Robert Dyer, baptised at Kidwelly on 30 March 1634, son of Robert and Elinor Dyer of that town. Practically nothing is known of him, but a pedigree compiled by Hugh Thomas, Deputy-Herald of Arms, states that he married "Mary the daughter of David Williams of Brynhafod by Anne Prinker" *(recte,* Bryncir). Now, the family papers of Williams of Brynhafod, preserved at Lovesgrove, Cards., among the Aberglasney muniments in Carmarthen Record Office, reveal that David Williams of Brynhafod, did indeed marry Mary daughter of John Bryncir ap Robert Wynn Bryncir, of Bryncir in Caernarvonshire, but no reference is contained to a daughter named Mary Williams, or intermarriage with anyone surnamed Dyer, and neither is anything found in sources like parish registers and probate wills. It is possible that another David Williams existed, for such nomenclature was by no means uncommon, and that it was his daughter who became wife of Robert Dyer. Nothing further has been discovered about Robert Dyer and Mary (Williams) his wife, except that they had a son, Robert, who became an attorney at law.

According to Hugh Thomas, Robert Dyer the attorney married Catherine daughter and co-heiress of Robert Cocks, but the Aberglasney papers state, with greater credibility, that her maiden name was Benet. After marrying he left Kidwelly and settled in Llanfynydd, and it was in that parish church that his children were baptised. The house in which he lived has not been identified. His office was in Carmarthen town where he continued to practise, and prospered sufficiently to enable him in June 1710 to buy the mansion house of Aberglasney, the manor of the Priory of Kidwelly, and properties in Llangathen, Llanddarog, and Llanfihangel Rhosycorn, from the Hon. Thomas Wentworth who held a mortgage on the estate of the financially embarrassed Rudds. Soon after 1714 he took up residence at Aberglasney, and there died some eight years afterwards.

Robert Dyer of Aberglasney was buried at Llangathen on 12 July 1720, and his will dated 16 May was proved in London on 22 November following. Catherine survived him, and is described as widow in 1723. They had six children:

1. John Dyer, baptised 2 February 1696–7, buried Llanfynydd on 20 March 1697-8.

2. Robert Dyer, baptised on 17 March 1698 – see later.

3. Thomas Dyer, baptised on 28 October 1700, educated at Westminster School, matriculated at Christ Church College, Oxford, on 18 June 1723. He became a parson, and is described in the will of his brother John, as rector of Bedhampton, Flints., in 1754. He was also Yeoman of the Almonry. He died in 1780 leaving no issue by his wife Dorothy *(née* De La Place).

4. John Dyer, baptised on 28 October 1701, educated at Westminster School, and afterwards entered his father's office in Carmarthen. Finding legal work distasteful, he turned

to the arts and became an accomplished artist and poet. In middle age he took Holy Orders, and after ordination by the Bishop of Lincoln, was presented in 1740 to the rectory of Calthorpe, Leics., and later held various livings in Leicestershire and Lincolnshire. Among his better known poems are "Grongar Hill" (part of the family estate, near Aberglasney), "The Ruins of Rome", and "The Fleece". Wordsworth addressed a sonnet "To the poet John Dyer". He died in December 1757, and was buried at Coningsby, Lincolnshire. His will was proved in London on 1 March 1758. By his wife Sarah (*née* Ensor) he had a son and three daughters, all of whom died without issue.

5. Benet Dyer, baptised on 22 August 1704, educated at Westminster School, married Grace widow of Thomas Lloyd of Berllandywyll, Llangathen, daughter and heiress of David Lloyd of Crynfryn, Cards. He was High Sheriff of Cardiganshire in 1736, and died without issue.

6. Francesca, baptised on 22 June, and buried on 16 September, 1703.

Robert Dyer, heir to Aberglasney, matriculated at Balliol College, Oxford, on 22 October 1714 as son of "R. Dyer of Llanvynny". He read law, and in 1718 became a barrister at the Inner Temple. He married Frances a daughter of Sir Herbert Croft, Bt., of Croft Castle, M.P. for Hereford, a descendant of Owain Glyndwr. She brought with her a fortune of £2,000, the pre- and post-nuptial settlements being executed on 25 August 1720 and 15 August 1723. Joseph Gulston saw the portraits of Mr. and Mrs. Dyer hanging in Aberglasney in 1783, and of the latter he observes, "This beautiful woman was very flighty, almost insane – the generation have suffered from this connexion". Robert Dyer died intestate on 2 October 1752, aged 55 and was buried at Llangathen, where his wife had been buried on 28 April 1740, aged 45. Administration of goods was granted many years later, on 13 August 1770, to his second son Francis. He had four children:

1. Robert Archer Dyer see later.

2. Francis Dyer, baptised at Llangathen in 1722, married in 1749 Anna Maria daughter and co-heiress of John Herbert of Court Henry, by Sarah (Jones) his wife. He settled at his wife's home. Their only child, Sarah Dyer, married William Phillips of Lincoln's Inn, barrister, and they, too, had an only child, Frances Maria Phillips who married firstly, Sir Charles Napier, G.C.B., (d. 1852), and secondly, Richard Alcock.

3. William Dyer, according to an abstract of title among the Aberglasney documents, "for many years before he became of age and till his death was out of his mind". Nevertheless, he was sufficiently capable of making a will on 18 February 1746-7, duly proved at Carmarthen by his eldest brother on 5 September of that year. Probably, he was somewhat eccentric.

4. John Dyer, died when very young.

Robert Archer Dyer, the eldest son was admitted at the Middle Temple on 27 April 1743. He succeeded to Aberglasney, and married a lady with a fortune of £1,000, namely Elizabeth daughter and co-heiress of John Herbert of Court Henry by Sarah (Jones) his wife. The wedding took place shortly after the pre-nuptial settlement had been executed on 13 September 1746.

Despite marriages to well-to-do wives, some of them heiresses, the family ran into financial difficulties, for on 25 August 1742, and again on 19 April 1743, Robert Dyer, the father, and his son R. A. Dyer, mortgaged the Aberglasney estate in the sum of £1,000, to Thomas Corbett of St. Margaret's, Westminster. After marrying, R. A. Dyer mortgaged parts of his property in Llangathen and Llanegwad in the sum of £500 to his father-in-law of Court Henry, on 27 January 1746-7. His difficulties increased as the years passed, and by August 1768 his debts and encumbrances amounted to £2,456. 14s. 6d., which his eldest son engaged to discharge in due course.

The harassed R. A. Dyer left Aberglasney and settled at the Herefordshire village of Bosbury where he was living in 1770. He was obliged to alienate some Carmarthenshire properties, and on 3 March 1785, R. A. Dyer, esquire, "late of Aberglasney but now of Bosbury", sold Cross Inn and Treginning, and the field called Cae Canol, in Llangathen parish, to William Jones of Cilsaen, tanner. His wife died in 1764, and he died between 1785 and 1788.

R. A. Dyer left behind him at Aberglasney a commonplace book which has survived among the muniments of the Phillips family which acquired the estate from the last of the Dyers. A veritable pot-pourri, as so many such compilations are, it contains jottings relating to estate and personal affairs, medical recipes, extracts from law books, matters concerning the poor law, precepts for magistrates and lawyers, verses, philosophical reflections, and so on. A few examples that may provide readers with the flavour of the contents, are given in an appendix to this essay. Robert Archer Dyer left two children:

1. William Herbert Dyer, born 22 June 1747, heir to Aberglasney.

2. Robert Herbert Dyer, born 3 August 1748. He entered the Royal Navy as a midshipman. At 10 of the clock of the night on 29 November 1768, he was walking on the deck of HMS *Boreas* then lying off Lisbon, when "a block fell on his head and kill'd him on ye spot", he was "decently interr'd at Lisbon" – so wrote his brother-officer Francis Parry who was with him at the time of the distressful event. Administration of goods was granted to his brother on 14 October 1769.

William Herbert Dyer, the last of the family, was a magistrate, and in 1776 served as High Sheriff of Carmarthenshire. Shortly he was staggering among the thornbushes of debt. On 24 May 1770 he conveyed, by way of security, the mansion and demesne of Aberglasney, and other properties, to his uncle Francis Dyer of Court Henry; and on 2 August of the same year mortgaged the estate in £3,000 to Peter Holford of Lincoln's Inn Fields. On 17 June 1776 Dyer gave a bond for a further loan of £500 to Holford. These debts were eventually redeemed, and on 3 March 1785, Aberglasney and the other mortgaged properties were reconveyed to him. But he was far from being out of the wood, and on 9 November 1788 was obliged to mortgage the estate in the sum of £2,350 to Herbert Lloyd the Carmarthen attorney. In that year too, the Court Henry estate was partitioned between the three daughters and co-heiresses of John Herbert, and a one-third share passed to W. H. Dyer as representative of his late mother Elizabeth, one of the co-heiresses. Although this proved a temporary relief to his troubles, affairs continued to deteriorate. A flood of debts, large and small, now lapped at his threshold.

Finally, in 1798, Aberglasney and other properties were offered for sale. After a good deal of haggling, the estate, consisting of the mansion and sixteen other properties, all in Llangathen parish, were sold in 1803 to Thomas Phillips, for £10,500. Details of the transaction, which proved protracted and difficult, not to say devious, are set forth in the next section of this essay.

Having lost his ancestral home, W. H. Dyer lived for some time in London, and afterwards in Shropshire. Just before the high tide of his misfortunes, he had married Mary Oakley sister of John Oakley of Firgrove, Shropshire, esquire, the post-nuptial settlement being executed on 3 November 1797. He died without issue in 1821. Mrs. Dyer died about the year 1838, and was buried at Bishop's Castle.

Phillips (Philipps) of Aberglasney

Unable to withstand creditors' cannonades any longer, the harassed W. H. Dyer instructed Herbert Lloyd the Carmarthen attorney, in 1798, to advertise the Aberglasney estate for sale. The property was described as a mansion and farms com-prising 584 acres, let (except the mansion and adjoining farm) on leases producing a clear yearly rental of £311: "the Mansion is Large and Handsome, consists of four Good Rooms on the Ground Floor, with suitable bedrooms and convenient offices fit for the reception of a large Family, extensive outbuildings, a good Garden, and Excellent Water at Command . . . the premises in good repair . . . in the vale of Towy near the Celebrated Grongar Hill (which is part of the Estate) and Commands a beautiful Prospect of Dynevor Castle and Park and other attractive Views." Such was the notice that Mr. Lloyd placed in the newspapers. Although Dyer was living there at the time, the house, as we shall see, was certainly not "in good repair". The asking price was £15,000, but no prospective buyer seemed prepared to offer anything like that sum, and at the beginning of June 1801, a crestfallen Dyer wrote to inform the attorney that he would accept £10,000 guineas "in ready money" for the property.

At this juncture a new name appears in the chronicle of Aberglasney, that of Phillips. Of modest antecedents, the family emerged from the haze in the late 17th century, and we find them living at Penhill in Llangathen. Theophilus Phillips of that place married Anne, daughter of Thomas Lewes of Crugmor near Cardigan and his wife Anne Middleton of Middleton Hall. Their only son, Thomas Phillips, born on 7 December 1725, became a tanner, and conducted a profitable business in Pembroke town. On 24 December 1747 he married a Jane Morgan of Llandovery (died in 1766) and secondly, in 1770, a Miss Lloyd (died in 1803). By the first wife, he had three children, all of whom in their different ways became involved with the purchase of Aberglasney, namely:

1. Thomas Phillips, junior, surgeon, of India.

2. John Phillips of Llandeilo, attorney at law, who changed the spelling of his name to Philipps, and married Florentia Mary Bridget Lloyd of Glansevin, by whom he had an only daughter.

3. Bridget Phillips who married on 1 February 1780 Abel Walters of Perthcereint, Cards., (who had started life as a tanner) and had a son John Walters of Newcastle Emlyn, attorney, and two daughters Frances and Jane Walters.

Thomas Phillips, junior, studied medicine, and after qualifying went to India as a surgeon in the Honourable East India Company. He arrived there about 1768-70, and during thirty-two years of service, rose to be Head Surgeon, and by 1800 had £25,000 invested in the Company's funds, and could look forward to enjoying a reasonable pension on retirement. One matter to note here, since later it was to provide a few complications, was that during his India service he had fallen in love with the wife of a common soldier, one Mrs. Jane Moore, who came to live with him.

On 1 May 1799 the surgeon wrote to his father informing him that he proposed to return to his native land within five or six years, and wished to buy an estate in Carmarthenshire where he could make his home. He also wrote to his sister Bridget, stating that the property he wished to acquire should produce a yearly rental of £600 or £700, and asked her to instruct her husband Abel Walters to move in the matter. On receiving this letter, Abel and Bridget wrote to the latter's brother John Phillips, the Llandeilo attorney, asking him to look for a suitable estate, and the father wrote in similar terms to his lawyer son.

The attorney made enquiries, and considered that Aberglasney, then in the market, might be suitable, but felt that £15,000 was an excessive price. However, as soon as the figure had been lowered to 10,000 guineas, Herbert Lloyd, acting for Dyer, immediately sent a note to John Philipps acquainting him of the turn of events. Losing no time Philipps went on 4 June 1801 to see Lloyd who told him of the condition that the purchase money was to be paid in full at the following Michaelmas. They discussed the situation amicably

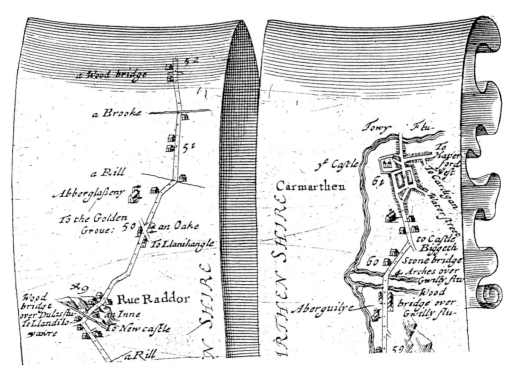

Ogilvy's map of Aberglasney

enough, but Philipps could not engage to pay by that date as he feared the money could not be transferred from India in sufficient time to satisfy Mr. Dyer. Although acting for Dyer, Herbert Lloyd was friendly with Philipps, and as we shall see, showed him favour in course of the transaction.

About the same time, Mrs. Bridget Walters wrote to the surgeon that the Allt y Cadno estate with its "handsome mansion", and producing about £1,300 p.a., was to be sold for about £32,000, but that another estate in the market was "Aberglasney near the broad oak . . . a sweet place, the situation is delightful. I fancy you must remember it. It belongs to the family of the Dyers, and there is a very hansom mansion on this place, the house co'd not (have been) built for less than £4,000", and the estate, worth nearly £500 yearly, "will be sold for about near £11,000. This is worth buying".

On 29 June Sir John Philipps wrote a long, interesting letter to his brother, which shows that there had been a misunderstanding between them in the past. Advising him that Aberglasney had "everything to commend it for the price that is required, 10,000 guineas", he goes on to say, 'The particulars I sent to my father which he has forwarded to you . . . Mr. Dyer will not dispose of Aberglasney without immediate payment. I wish I could on my own security procure the money for you. I should not hesitate in doing it. When Paxton comes down I will see him, and if he has any friend that will advance the money on ample security, I will buy it and pay for it until your money arrives. It's so desirable a thing that I am anxious you should have it. It will be an immediate residence for any gentleman. My dear brother, if it was possible you could look into my heart you would find it was made of material that would entitle me to your forgiveness. It never intentionally gave you offence, but has ever been warm for your prosperity and happiness. At this place we are surrounded by great folks. Perhaps there is not a neighbourhood in England superior to it. I sometimes feel the pride of my family which is inferior to none of them. It's as ancient as the best. One pedigree which I have extracted from the Herald Office, comes down regularly and lineally from the Tribes as far as Sir John Lewes of Abernant Vychan who was Ranger in Hyde Park in the reign of Charles the 2nd (now held by Lord Grenville). He was my father's great grandfather. I have his picture now in my house, when Ranger. More of this when we meet. I observe the seal you used with your arms on your letter to my father, to be very poorly and imperfectly done. I shall by the con-veyance that brings you this, send you another which I beg your acceptance. It will be consigned to the case of Messers Paxton in London to be forwarded to you. The motto is Welsh, in English it signifies 'My God and my Country (Chymru is Wales) . . .'." He ends, "Your sincere and affectionate brother John Philipps".

The attorney was not without pride of ancestry or without attachment to the indicia of gentility. Although the Phillips ancestors were no great shakes, marriages had allied them to the powerful houses of Lewes, Vaughan, and Middleton, and the descent, by the distaff from the Ranger of Hyde Park is wholly true. But changing the spelling of his name, which implied paternal descent from the aristocratic stock of Cilsant, Cwmgwili, Coedgain, and Picton Castle whose members exclusively spelled their name as Philipps, was not justified, and his father and brother continued to use the homely spelling of their inherited name.

But present concerns were more pressing than genealogical rambles, and Philipps proceeded with the prosaic task of raising money. On 30 October 1801 he wrote to William Paxton in London, asking whether he could find someone to advance the purchase money for two years at 5 per cent, to be repaid as soon as the surgeon's money was transferred from India, adding that he would be willing to convey his own estate, worth £500 p.a., as additional security if required. Paxton, not very favourable to the proposal, demurred, but agreed to consider it.

Before long, a darker cloud cast its shadow over negotiations. Mr. Ablett a wealthy businessman from Manchester, seeking a country estate in Wales, arrived in Carmarthenshire, and on 16 April 1802, accompanied by his friend Dr. Parr of Pentre Parr near Llandeilo, called on John Philipps. Ablett was considering buying some properties from Lord Cawdor, for which he was prepared to pay £30,000. During this exploratory talk, Aberglasney was not mentioned. Two days later, Philipps had to attend the assizes at Carmarthen, where he met Ablett and Parr, who told him they had heard that Aberglasney was for sale, and Ablett added he had already seen Mr. Dyer who had referred him to Herbert Lloyd. Philipps answered that he himself had been negotiating for that estate "for a friend", that he intended consulting Lloyd on the following morning and would acquaint Ablett of the outcome. What Ablett did not disclose to Philipps, was that he was prepared to pay an extra £2,000 to Mr. Dyer.

Early on 19 April the thoroughly alarmed Philipps called on Lloyd, who clearly favoured the application of his fellow attorney, and said that the estate would be lost unless Philipps contracted at once to buy the property and guarantee to produce the purchase money by Michaelmas. Tomorrow would be too late. Philipps signed there and then, and rode immediately to Pentre Parr to inform Mr. Ablett that he had contracted to buy Aberglasney, and "Mr. Ablett appeared satisfied, as it was for my brother, and I had long before been in treaty for it". He returned to Carmarthen in the evening, and on the following morning attended on Lloyd who prepared the articles of agreement, and sent an express letter to his father at Pembroke (who was acting in *loco parentis* for his surgeon son) requesting him to come to Carmarthen without delay to sign the document. Answering by return the father said he was too unwell to make the journey (he was gone 76 years of age) but was prepared to meet him at Tavernspite. This was agreed, and on 24 April, Philipps and Lloyd made the journey and the preliminary formalities were completed. One more formality remained before the conveyance deeds could be prepared, namely Dyer's signature to the agreement. On 26 April, Lloyd journeyed to Aberglasney and placed the document before the vendor.

But a new complication had arisen. Not only did Dyer know of Ablett's interest, but more important, that he was prepared to pay £2,000 over and above the 10,000 guineas that the property had been advertised for. This was sweet music in the ears of the straitened vendor. He flatly refused to sign. Lloyd, as his legal adviser, warned that refusal might result in a bill being exhibited against him in the High Court of Chancery to enforce the contract. He still refused.

Finding it impossible to withdraw, but still averse, Dyer wrote to Lloyd on 28 April that he would sign provided £1,050 was paid immediately by Philipps as deposit, to Messrs. Morris, the Carmarthen bankers. Frantic by being faced with the necessity of finding such a sum at short notice, Philipps called on Messrs. Marten's bank in the county town on 4 May, and happily for him, they arranged for the money to be paid straight away to Messrs. Morris. The purchase was now firm – provided that the remainder of the money was raised by Michaelmas. Although acting for the vendor, Herbert Lloyd had been sympathetic towards Philipps throughout, and without his warnings and advice the latter would have been out-manoeuvred by the impecunious Dyer and the aspiring Mr. Ablett.

In high feather, Thomas Phillips wrote from Pembroke on 10 May to his son at Cawnpore, telling him, "your brother and I have at last purchased the Aberglasney estate for you. Your brother has been indefatigable in the business through-out, and saved it by one single day only from being sold to people that came down from Manchester who would have given £2,000 more for it that what we contracted for, which is £10,500 . . . Don't leave sixpence in India behind you". As we shall see, the optimism displayed in the father's letter proved somewhat premature. True, they had made a firm contract, but the money still remained to be raised. It is certain that the surgeon advanced the bulk of the money, for on 14 June 1802, Messrs. Cockerell, Trail, & Co., of Calcutta, gave him a receipt for 78,000 secca rupees to be lodged towards the purchase (the rupee being worth 2s. 6d. in English currency). However, owing to distances and the uncertainty of shipping movements, the money remained overseas – when it was most urgently needed at Carmarthen.

To raise the money in so short a time proved a stiff fence. And Mr. Ablett was by no means finished. On 3 June Philipps had received a sharp letter from the Manchester firm of solicitors, Milne, Serjeant, & Milne, contending that the purchase contract for Aberglasney had in fact been made in favour of their client Mr. Ablett! Philipps ignored this, and on 23 June received another letter couched in similar terms. After some further correspondence, threats and counter threats, it was agreed that the matter be submitted to the arbitration of Lord Robert Seymour of Taliaris and Mr. Lewes of Llysnewydd. Early in August, the arbitrators pronounced in favour of Philipps. Nevertheless, further efforts were made to persuade him to surrender the agreement, and an offer of £2,000 for so doing, was declined.

Dyer, too, continued to be obstructive. Philipps now found difficulty in obtaining an abstract of title from him, and on 25 August prepared a case for counsel's opinion in respect of the vendor's refusal. Dyer found further excuses for ignoring repeated applications, for until the abstract was delivered, the purchase could not proceed nor could the conveyance deeds be drawn up. At last, on 24 September, he capitulated. Although he did not suspect it, Dyer's recalcitrancy proved a godsend for the purchaser, as the delays resulting from his lack of co-operation, enabled Philipps to procure an extension of the time for the production of the remainder of the purchase money. The business could not have come at a more inopportune time for a buyer, as Thomas Phillips wrote on 8 October to his son in India, "the late war has drain'd this country of all its cash".

It never rains but it pours. Philipps' cousin, John Morgan of Carmarthen, who had promised to advance £6,000 towards the sum needed, suddenly died of a paralytic stroke, and the executors could do nothing in the matter, so that now Philipps had to search for further likely sources – and quickly – for time was running out. Accordingly, on 3 October, accompanied by his father, he called on Paxton at Middleton Hall, and asked whether he would assist in raising the money. Paxton declined, as no money had been forthcoming from India, saying that he could have nothing more to do in the matter.

Paxton's attitude may have been influenced by the fact that John Philipps had supported Hamlyn Williams of Edwinsford in the contest for the seat of the county, against Paxton in 1802. On 5 November, Philipps wrote to his brother about the election, saying that Paxton "had no right to expect that I should have supported him for the county. He knew eight months before that I could not, and if his behaviour towards you is actuated by motives of resentment to me, he is unworthy of the confidence of any man".

But all was not lost, and in a letter written on 9 November, Philipps informed his brother that although "Messrs. Paxton's conduct has been unhandsome in the extreme", Messrs. Lubbock, the London bankers, "good friends", had agreed to accommodate him. Early in December he completed arrangements with Lubbock's house, who advanced him the sum of £9,450, which was paid to Dyer's bankers on 11 December 1802.

The rain clouds had not quite blown over even yet. Messrs. Lubbock and their lawyers requested later that the Aberglasney estate be conveyed to them by way of additional security. Philipps went to London to see them, refused their request, and the matter dropped.

All that remained was execution of the deeds, first obtaining counsel's opinion on the question of trustees and other legal points. This took several months, including Chancery proceedings. Finally, the deeds were drawn, and on 4 May 1803 were brought to Aberglasney for Dyer's signature. Dyer refused. But it was his last, and unavailing stand. After further discussion with lawyers, Dyer and his wife signed the deeds on 16 May 1803. Philipps secured the attornment of tenants, and the property was in full possession of the new owner. The news was sent to India, and on 20 August 1803, Thomas Phillips wrote to his father from Dinapore, to say he was glad that the purchase of the Aberglasney estate had been completed – "nor shall it again ever quit your family".

For the purchasers it had been a walk over very hot coals – difficulties in obtaining money, great distances by land and sea, the intervention of other prospective buyers, the efforts of Dyer to obtain a better bargain – as John Philipps afterwards said to his brother, "Dyer tried every way to get off the Contract, but failed". The bill of costs, for the work done on behalf of his brother amounted to £307 5s. 11d.

The property is described in "A particular of the Aberglasney Estate purchased by John Philipps in Trust for his Brother Thomas Phillips and since conveyed to him", together with the yearly rents of each lot, as follows:

1. Mansion and demesne, part of the demesne let at £65.
2. Cottage on Tyrland (   ).
3. Grey House, with cottage £126.
4. Cottage on Tyrland, £1 11s. 6d.
5. Llanlais, £100.
6. Broad Oak, £10. 10s. 0d.

7.   East (or Upper) Grongar, £36 15s. 0d.
8.   West (or Lower) Grongar, £21.
9.   Penyrheol, £8.
10.   Llangathen Public House, £2 10s. 0d.
11.   Cottage and garden, £1 17s. 0d.
12.   A house, 1d.
13.   House and garden, £3.
14.   House and garden, £1 11s. 6d.
15.   A house, 10s.
16.   Part of a field. 3d.
17.   Part of Pigeons field, £2 2s 0d.

As the mansion had deteriorated during the latter years of Dyer occupancy, one of John Philipps's first concerns was to render it suitable for the reception of the new owner. Between 1803 and 1805 he paid particular attention to the fabric; a great deal of glazing and mending of windows was carried out, new doors and grates put in; a carpenter was paid £4 19s. 11d. for mending the roof and leading and windows; a tiler received £21 11s. 0d. for newly tiling and painting the mansion; timbers were bought for rafters, and 4,000 slates; an ironmonger received £20 12s. 11d. for further lead for the roof; a smith received £6 6s. 0d. for putting bells in the tile house; another tiler was paid 12 shillings for "stripping the chapel", and a carpenter 15s. 6d. for taking down "the roof" of the said chapel. Attention was paid to the demesne, the fishpond repaired, the pigeon house tiled and repaired and a cupola made for it surmounted by "a vane and eagle" for £7 15s. 0d., frames for hotbeds put in the garden, and young trees bought from Miller and Sweet the Bristol nurserymen. The sum of £125 19s. 0d. was paid to Dyer for furniture left in the house, and further furniture was bought at the sale of Lord George Murray, Bishop of St. Davids, for £128 4s. 0d., and mahogany articles at Mr. de Lambert's sale for £9 9s. 0d. Bedroom furniture was bought in Swansea, Irish linen, Welsh and English blankets, carpets, rugs, chairs, and other household goods including a large mahogany side-table "for the Great Hall' for £6 6s. 0d. He engaged a gardener, with his wife as housekeeper, at the combined wages of 20 guineas per annum, and a maid at £5. By the time Thomas Phillips arrived, the mansion would be ready to receive him.

Thomas Phillips, accompanied by Mrs. Jane Moore, and his friend Elliot Voyle, left India in January 1805 and after arriving in London, took lodgings at 22 Bury Street. His father, who had retired from the tannery to live with his daughter Bridget Walters at Perthcereint, wrote to Thomas on 7 September 1805 telling him that although Aberglasney had been "left to run greatly out of repair, your brother has new-roofed it"; he has great plans for his son – "you will be in the Commission of the Peace", and, more ominously, "I shall be looking out for a *wife* for you that will make you happy in the enjoyment of your long laboured service in India, but your sister who has been at Aberglasney this week was informed that you were married at St. Helena, which I can hardly believe". Knowledge of the liaison with Mrs. Moore had been kept from him, and it would appear that Bridget was going to break the news gently. After all, he was now an octogenarian.

Some coolness developed between the father and his son John, and between the latter and his brother Thomas. The reason for this is not apparent, and it must be recalled that had it not been for the exceptional efforts of John, the estate would not have been acquired for the family. On 15 October 1805 the father wrote to John Lubbock, M.P., asking him to visit Thomas who was still in London, and unwell, and advising him to get "some honest man, who is a stranger, to settle his affairs, that is in no ways interested, and *not his brother* who would wish to grasp the whole to himself, rob his sister and her children of all". About the same time the new owner began to resent the actions of his father and brother, considering they were interfering too much in his affairs and taking too many decisions upon themselves. Further letters sent by the father and his lawyer son, to Thomas, contained requests for the recipient not to reveal the censorious contents of the missives to the other.

These warnings determined the new owner to instruct a London lawyer, Mr. Turner of Fetherston Buildings, Holborn, to handle all further business concerning Aberglasney. On 2 November 1805 an aggrieved John Philipps wrote from Llandeilo, to tell Thomas "I have been cutt to my soul . . . By God I have not slept three hours in these two nights", which he followed up with another letter despatched on the next day, to say "I am sure length of days will not fall to my lott; the Aberglasney wrinkles which appear in my face, and other tokens, assure me of it", and requests him to come soon to Aberglasney. In November, too, misunderstanding arose concerning the deeds which John Philipps wished to retain until his brother came to the county.

After arriving in London, Thomas Phillips had been unwell, being partly the reason for his prolonged stay there. His father, somewhat peeved and disappointed when he learnt at last of the association with Mrs. Moore, wrote on 5 March 1806 advising him that when he came to Aberglasney, he should esconce his "female companion" there, otherwise, "she will be ill-used after being your companion so many years and after bringing her so many thousand miles with you into a strange country. After you have placed her at Aberglasney, and not before, we shall all of us here greatly rejoice and heartily embrace you at Perthcereint". By April 1807 Thomas Phillips had arrived at the mansion. Later in the year he received a letter from the East India Company's house in London confirming that the Company had agreed he could retire and that his pension of £300 a year would be payable from Midsummer last. Equally acceptable, was a conveyance of the tanyard and premises at Pembroke, made to him by his father. Thomas and Mrs. Moore (known locally by the courtesy title of "Mrs. Phillips") settled in at the mansion, welcomed by all his relations who were frequent guests there. The old father died at Perthcereint on 25 November 1812.

The father's prediction that Thomas would become a Justice of the Peace, was fulfilled, and in 1813 he served as High Sheriff of Carmarthenshire, his nephew John Walters of Newcastle Emlyn acting as deputy.

The family dovecots were fluttered in 1823 when Thomas Phillips proclaimed his intention of marrying Jane Moore, by then a widow, and on 3 June of that year, the pre-nuptial settlement was executed, which, as well as providing for Jane, contained detailed clauses relating to the disposal of his property. The Aberglasney estate, together with a sum of £25,000 and a lac of rupees invested in the Treasury of the Honourable East India

Company, were to be enjoyed by Jane for life, with remainder to his nephew John Walters and his issue male and female, in default to Mrs. Florentia Jane Wood, only child of John Philipps of Llandeilo; provision was to be made for his sister Mrs. Bridget Walters, and an annuity for Richard Garland of Taunton (Jane Moore's brother); and he stipulated that whosoever inherited Aberglasney was to take the surname of Philipps, either together with his own, or solely, and to quarter the arms of Philipps with his own family arms. It will be noted that John Philipps was passed over, and that the chances of his daughter, Mrs. Wood, inheriting were remote. John died on 29 October 1833, aged 79.

The union legalised after so many years of companionship proved brief, for Thomas Phillips died on 25 June 1824 and was buried at Llangathen. The widow moved to Pentre Parr, where she died on 3 July 1845, having enjoyed an annuity of £600 charged on her husband's estate. John Oxenham of Taunton proved her will in London in January 1846.

On his uncle's death, John Walters, attorney at law, of Newcastle Emlyn, succeeded to the estate (subject to the widow's interest) and came to reside at the mansion. In March 1825 he obtained a Royal Licence enabling him to be known in future as John Walters Philipps, and to bear the arms of Walters and Philipps, quarterly, for which the following bill was presented to him by Sir George Naylor, Garter King of Arms – for Royal Licence £44 12s. 0d., Duty Stamp £50, Patents of Arms for Walters and for Philipps £65 10s. 0d. each, making a total sum of £225 12s. 0d.

John Walters Philipps caused the arms to be displayed in painted glass and placed in the large window lighting the fine staircase leading upwards from the great hall. I saw the window on several occasions, greatly admired the colours and workman-ship, and fortunately I copied the blazon in February 1965. I have a special reason for giving the description in full here, as follows: shield, quarterly, 1 & 4 *or* a lion rampant *sable,* between in chief two fleur de lys, and in base a stag's head erased *gules* (Philipps). 2 & 3 *gules* three snakes nowed *vert,* between in chief two spear heads *argent,* and in base a rose *argent:* crests on a wreath *or* and *sable* a lion rampant *sable* holding in forepaws an escutcheon *or* charged with three snakes nowed *vert,* the dexter hind paw resting on a fleur de lys *or.* 2, on a wreath *or* and *gules* an eagle displayed *or,* its body entwined with two snakes, and holding in each claw a rose *gules* slipped *vert:* motto – FY NEW A CHYMRU; the whole embellished with mantling. (The word NEW should read NUW.)

Alas, when I called there three years later, accompanied by my friend Mr. David Lloyd of Coedmore, I found that the house had been entered by hooligans, and the heraldic window smashed to smithereens. Mr. Lloyd and I spent considerable time collecting the glass fragments, which we placed on a table in the hall, in the hope that someone might try to reassemble the pieces to their former pattern, so far as was possible. I reported it to the owner, but do not know what resulted. It would appear that the description I made of this colourful window is now the sole memorial of its former existence.

The attorney turned squire added to his property by the purchase of the mansion and demesne of Hafod Neddyn, Bryn Hafod Fach, Gwern Fawr, and Crug y Whil. He became a magistrate, and in 1841 served as High Sheriff of Carmarthenshire, and among his expenses for that year was £10 for a new pair of armorial banners with bullion lace, cord, and tassels, all of silk, made by the well-known antiquary George Grant Francis at his Carriage and Harness Manufactory, Swansea.

By his wife Anne, fourth daughter of Thomas Bowen of Waun Ifor, Cards., whom he married in 1817, he had a son and three daughters. He died on 14 May 1867, his wife having predeceased him on 5 February 1848, and both lie buried in the Aberglasney chapel in Llangathen church. Their children were:

1. Thomas Philipps Walters Philipps, died in infancy.

2. Bridget Jane Walters Philipps, married in 1853 Cecil Anson Harries of Llanunwas, Pembs. She died on 8 July 1881 and was buried at Llangathen. Her husband died in Canada on 23 April 1908. There was no issue.

3. Mary Anne Walters Philipps – see later.

4. Elizabeth Frances Walters Philipps, married in 1851, Frederick Lewis Lloyd Philipps of Pentypark, Pembs. She died without issue on 24 February 1900.

Mary Anne Walters Phillipps married in 1844 John Pugh Vaughan Pryse of Bwlchbychan, Cards., and died on 21 June 1851, leaving an only child. Her husband married, secondly, Decima Dorothea Rice of Llwynybrain.

Mrs. Mary Anne Pryse was the only one of her generation to leave issue, namely Mary Anne Emily Jane Pryse born on 7 May 1849. She married Colonel Charles George Adams Mayhew (sometime of the 23rd Foot) who later came to live at Aberglasney. Both were dedicated to the rigours of Temperance which they advocated with zeal and diligence, and were responsible for building a Temperance Hall near Aberglasney. She died without issue on 19 December 1939, the last of the line of Phillips (Philipps) who had acquired the estate some one-hundred-and-thirty-six years previously. The last of the gentry to reside at Aberglasney was Mr. G. Eric C. V. Evans, son of General L. P. Evans, V.C, of Lovesgrove near Aberystwyth, and great-grandson of J. P. V. Pryse of Bwlchbychan by his second wife Decima Dorothea (Rice). After Mr. Eric Evans's untimely death in 1950, the mansion and demesne were sold.

This essay is based mainly on the Aberglasney Collection preserved in the Dyfed Record Office at Carmarthen, and on family muniments at Lovesgrove in possession of Mr. Christopher Evans who kindly allowed me to consult them, and also on the various sources noticed in the text. I am grateful to my friends Mr. D. Emrys Williams of the National Library of Wales, and Mr. Roland Thorne of London, for certain information relating to the Rudd and Dyer families.

APPENDIX

Extracts from the Commonplace Book of Robert Archer Dyer of Aberglasney, mentioned above.

In the Spring of 1743 he visited London and his accounts show that he bought a variety of goods – clothes, wigs, snuff box, knee buckles, a sword, books and tickets for the theatre.

On 12 May he writes, ruefully, "It cost in 6 weeks time £47.6.10, which tells me I must wear plain clothes and not study to be in ye fashion. When a man is flush he has no contrivance, but lays out his money foolishly to gratify an idle appetite of being in ye fashion and is sure to buy things at ye dearest rate. From this day I intend to allow myself 1s. per diem, ne plus ultra".

1745   June 1. "I propose for the future that Husbandry shall take up the main of my thoughts, and to take a pleasure in walking over ye ground and observing what is wanted to be done, and to see what methods my tenants take to make up their rents, who is the best farmer, the most active and industrious and most capable to improve the tenement, to censure ye lazy and unstriving tenant, and to encourage ye industrious one, and in general to search into ye customs, practices, and different methods of farming, that I may make up ye most of my estate".

c. 1745. "Memorandum. To build a Summer House on ye rising twmp on ye right-hand on Grongar; to plant ye sides with firr."

1745   May 20. "Caught a violent scarlet feaver which came upon me attended with a Quinzy, by frequent taking of ye river in fishing ye months of April and May – 4 guineas to Dr. Foy. N.B. I hope ye remembrance of this Distemper will check the too ardent desire of any sport whatsoever, as no sport, the most easy or gentle, if too violently pursued but will certainly hurt ye faculties of ye Body or Mind in ye end."

1745   September 16. "Assisted in taking depositions of witnesses in order to discover a felony charg'd upon one who made his escape after he was taken; and found my ignorance in swearing Constables to pursue; found I did not know how [to] deliver the charge which put me to great confusion, and which made me then resolve to take down Precedents in writing, of oaths, mittimuses and other common forms, that I may not be at a loss for the future to transact common business without ye help and ye immediate perusal of books – to these ends to keep a Common Place Book and to carry it with me upon all occasions of going from home".

"Memorandam. I intend making a collection of reflections or thoughts upon various subjects as they occur in my mind. For instance, one, a moral reflection – Though a countrey Gentleman is a stranger to honours, fame and riches, of civil or military employments, yet he ought to be well satisfy'd that he has more leisure than either ye Statesman or ye Soldier to serve a noble king, ye king of righteousness, and thereby to reap to himself a far more glorious and eternal reward in Heaven."

1746   August 28. "Account of my cloathes – a green plush coat, silver buttons, a brown flowered silk waistcoat, a red knap waistcoat, a brown fustian breeches, a red alapeen breeches, a black velvet breeches, two white Holland waistcoats, two white waistcoats with Jacks, two merry derry waistcoats."

"Ale bottled in July 1746 (brew'd in March before) – 20 dozen quart bottles, 23 large bottles (14 quarts)."

"Memorandum. A very good method to sit every morning at your scrutore an hour to study your affairs."

"Scheme for studying for 3 months, Decr., Jany, Feby 1747. 1 hour every morning, Office *of Justice* etc. 2 hours every morning, Scot's *Christian Life*. Evening casual reading. Night – 2 hours *Virgil."*

"Memorandum of schemes – To make a collection of subjects upon every letter in ye Alphabet, for instance, what may be said of Cheerfulness, Melancholy, etc."

"Memorandum. Never to put gold and silver in ye same Pocket loose, by which means I once lost half a guinea."

"Memorandum. Lost a mare which cost me £15 15.0. by pampering her up in ye stable and giving her no exercise. She was taken ill of a Tuesday noon and died a Wednesday night – as I esteem of an apoplexy. Let this teach young Jockeys that ye best way of keeping a horse is out by day and in at night."

1746 November 4. "Agreed with Josy to serve ye year 1746 for three Pounds, a new pair of strong shoes, my cast off shores, boots, etc. Remains of last year's wages £1 15.8."

1747 June 22. "My wife was brought to bed of her first child, 5 o'clock evening, (named) William Herbert Dyer."

1748 August 3. "My second son Robert Herbert Dyer was born 11 o'clock forenoon."

On 12 July 1752 he complains he has pains in the head, etc., and listlessness, "the whole mass of blood being reumatiz'd. Dr. Foy whom I consulted, told me the distemper is brought on by fishing and a sedentary life, and by my experience I am convinced of the truth of it."

Amongst the entries are "Verses to a young lady in the Country", composed probably before his marriage (unless of course it is a copy)

> *"Dear lover of domestick life*
> *Foe to ambition, noise and strife*
> *By no vain Fancys drawn aside*
> *To the false glittering paths of Pride*
> *Thy passions all compos'd, thy mien*
> *Easy and free, thy looks serene,*
> *Thus formed to give those joys refin'd*
> *Which spring from love and friendship joyn'd*
> *Keep me no longer from thy arms*
> *But give me up, O give me all thy charms".*

Aberglasney, front restoration

CWMGWILI AND ITS FAMILIES

LITTLE IS KNOWN of the administration of the Cwmgwili estate during the incumbency of John George Philipps, M.P. (1761-1816), but he does not seem to have alienated any part of it. Indeed, in 1790, he added to it by buying several slangs adjoining his farm of Pante from the Revd David Scurlock of Blaencorse, near St. Clears, for £80. His wife wrote on 21 February 1785, that Mr. R. Morgan had asked her to remind him about the "stragglin wood" which should be cut as the tenants ("so far from Cumgwilly and from your sight") felled "ever so fine trees", and Morgan had discovered that a great many fine trees had been cut down "and the roots of them covered with grass that they might not be discovered". According to Morgan the wood could be sold for over £200. On 10 May 1785, John George Philipps agreed to sell to David Lewis of Carmarthen, tanner, all timber, trees, saplings. underwoods, etc, growing upon the farms of Trefynis, Rwythfawr, Cwmhowell, and Tir Terrant Elias, in Abergwili parish, for the sum of £240.[1]

Mr. Philipps entered into partnership with some of his neighbours to work a mine at Capel Dewi, and on 9 February 1785 Richard Lewis wrote from Abergwili Palace to enquire whether he could take up a one-sixth share which Mr. Philipps had promised him. If Mr. Philipps agreed to this, he would pay the money to Mr. Stewart, the treasurer. Lewis informed him that "some favourable discovery had this week been made at the mine".[2]

Apart from the affairs of the Borough, he was busy in county concerns, especially as a magistrate. He was a member of Llandeilo'r Ynys Turnpike Trust, and took a special interest in road communications and their effect upon agriculture. A letter from Richard Jones Llwyd written on 3 May 1790 to J. G. Philipps at the Somerset Coffee House in the Strand indicates the attitude of Carmarthenshire landowners towards taxes and tolls – "A double toll upon turnpikes will materially prejudice this county. Most of the Turnpikes in this county were made originally to facilitate the carriage of coal, lime, and manure, and they depended upon the conveyance of those articles for their existence. Lime has of late years advanced in price from 6s. 6d. the horse-load to 14 shillings, so that farmers can now scarcely afford to buy it. Lay another tax upon it, it puts that article beyond their reach and they have no substitute. Farm yards and composition dunghills being in their infancy, I will venture to say that if lime and manure and coal are not exempted from double toll, it will nearly ruin the agriculture in this county"; he further hopes that tax on transfers of real property will be confined to Bonds and Mortgages. "As to the tax upon deeds, it may induce the gentlemen

of the law to curtail the enormous prolixity of modern conveyances and reduce them to their former conciseness and simplicity. Laymen may then have some guess at their meaning and content".[3]

Despite long absences from Cwmgwili during his parliamentary career, his domestic life was harmonious. There is no doubt that he and his wife Anne (Ball) were deeply in love, and it is from her numerous letters to him that we obtain glimpses of their family life. He, on the other hand, does not appear to have been a good correspondent, a fact commented upon in letters from his wife and friends.

Anne kept him posted not only with domestic news but with news of various friends and acquaintances. It is clear that she missed his company, and ends one letter (10 February 1785) with the words, "Adieu my dear, Cumgwilly is very dull without my JGP". Both were attached to the children, and Anne's letter to him on 12 February 1785 contains an account of her two small sons, "Little Griffith talks of you every day; he says that his papa is gone to London to buy him a new hat and a fine sash, so you can see the little rogue begins to grow coxcomical already as he talks of nothing but his dress. Little John is no less proud of his smart greatcoat that came home today; he would not take it off till he went to sleep . . . I don't know when to leave off when I begin to write to you. I am sure that I scribble a vast deal of nonsense for the sake of prolonging the time. Believe me my Dear that nothing can give me greater pleasure than writing to you. May you enjoy every happyness is the ardent prayer and sincere wish of your ever faithful and affectionate wife, Anne Philipps. P.S. – I would give the world to be with my ever Dear JGP, believe me there can be no happyness or pleasure for me without you. Pray write every post my Dear Mr. Philipps." On 7 April 1787 she wrote that she had read that the House of Commons had been adjourned till 23 April – "Pray what will you do with yourself all that time? I wish to God it was in my power to make a pair of wings for you to fly home with. Since you have left Cwmgwilly I live here the world forgetting, by the world forgot. Your happiness is the chief study of my life".

Shortly after his return to London in February 1784, Anne says that Griffith "has been searching for you in the parlour, the study and in our rooms, crying all the way 'Papa, papa'. . . I love you far too much to do anything contrary to your desire". Later in the month she chides him – "Why have you not written the last two posts? Hearing from you is my only pleasure." In a letter dated 28 February 1785 she again chides him for not writing oftener, for she wrote to him by every post, "Don't forget to be a Welshman tomorrow, and let little Griffith have the leek when you come home". Being a member of parliament was an expensive business and Anne was often busy getting in the rents, and raising money by other means to meet his occasions, often pressing, in the Metropolis.

Anne kept him informed of domestic and estate affairs, the farm at Cwmgwili and sale of commodities, and particularly about local political moves. She often urged him to take steps that would advance his interests. In 1784 she told him he should pay his compliments to Mr. Powell (Nanteos), who was to be High Sheriff of Cardiganshire – "You know there is nothing lost by civility".

She found her husband's aunt, the masterful Mrs. Jane Davies of Penylan, somewhat of a trial. Anne had been unwell in the early part of 1785 (she was often ailing), and had allowed herself to be persuaded, against her real inclination, to accompany Mrs. Davies to a dance at Kidwelly – "I should not have gone had it not been for Mrs. Davies of Penylan who pestered me to death two days before about it. She sent to tell me it would be so ungenteel and very odd of me if I did not go as Mr. Lloyd was so kind as to come to fetch me, and Mr. Billy her son was affronted with me at Kidwelly because I did not choose to dance with him. I hope I shall never see Mrs. Davies at Cumgwilly again. You have always told me I behaved too well to her and I now see it myself, but I was always happy to do every thing in my power to oblige any of your family". In April 1785 she was quite ill, and everyone was most kind to her except "Mrs. Davies of Penylan, and she has behaved like a Brute". But this was a passing pique, Mrs. Davies was often at Cwmgwili, and took the elder boys to Penylan when Mrs. Philipps was brought to bed of her other children and when she was ill. It is not unlikely that Mrs. Philipps was inclined to brood over her illnesses. In 1790 Mrs. Jane Davies wrote a bantering letter to her brother, John George Philipps, "I remember you have often laughed at the idle chit-chat of the female pen, but nevertheless I have ventured your giving me a place in the list of such laughable beings, from the hope that even insignificant subjects, may for a minute or two divert my sisters' attention from thinking of her complaints, which, I hope, will every day become less and less, and that very soon we may have the pleasure to see her return in perfect health".

After her husband's death Mrs. Jane Davies lived at a house in Carmarthen belonging to her brother, whom she badgered continually about repairs and improvements. "Some time past notices were given to every house to erect troughs under the tiles. It has not been done here and the cornice being rotten, part of it fell down nearly on Miss B. Lloyd's head, which might have killed her. Now the rain soaks into part of the front wall. I have sent to Evans the carpenter to do it, and hope you agree. I have sent to Jas George to get lime for the brewing kitchen which was stript by wind this last week all the southerly side. I wish for your sake and my own comfort that the outside was not in so poor a state, I'll take care to keep the inside comfortable without damage done to it."

This house proved troublesome and its later tenant, Mrs. Jane Davies' unmarried daughter Anne, proved as vigorous as her mother; for instance – "Dear Uncle, I have received a letter from my brother William in consequence of yours to me last Wednesday. He tells he had receipts for everything in the house. The shelf & dresser with several other things, my mother bought of Mr. Hoskins who had bought them of the tenant before him; the dog-wheel she bought of old Mrs. Rice and James Evans the carpenter. We have not sold the locks as you have been told. William also has the receipt for the marble slab in the parlour, which my mother put down but that we left there. The shelf, dresser & dog wheel the man who has taken the house bought by auction at £1 2s. 6d., but on being told at Cwmgwilly they belonged to the house has refused to pay for them. Do you wish to buy them? if not they will be taken down tomorrow and sold. To whom shall I deliver the key of the street door on Michaelmas day. We then leave Carmarthen for Penylan and to make some visits we have promised before we leave Wales. I hope should your Daughters be left without father or mother (which is certainly not impossible) that they may not find a Landlord or uncle as tenacious about such a trifle as we have found. Wishing you and my cousins health & happiness, I am dear Uncle, your affectionate Anne Davies."

Anne Philipps's life was not made pleasanter by the fact that her brother, Herbert Ball, and others of the family, proved difficult about paying her marriage portion and other monies due. On 28 March 1789 she wrote to her husband that she had heard from brother Herbert, who said he had been cheated of half his fortune, but promised he would send "your money this term". She adds that "a Mob has destroyed and layd waste all the enclosures of the commons about the town this last week. I am afraid it will end seriously if there is not a stop put to it soon; the first Rebellion that ever happened in Carmarthen was about enclosing the Commons. I hope it will not end as it did then".

In 1791 (?2) another child, Grismond, was born. She wrote to her husband on 25 March 1792, "Old Mr. Rogers and Mr. John Lloyd called on me last Friday, the old gentleman said he was anxious to see another Grismond Philipps before he died; you cannot imagine how many old people has come here to see the child on account of his name", adding that the boys are constant at their books, and ending on a more mundane note, "I assure you I will sell fresh butter every week and have a shilling a pound for it."

John George Philipps had considerable commitments: the expenses of living in London and maintaining the household at Cwmgwili were heavy, and in addition he had to pay an annuity to his mother (who did not die until 1810), while the education of the children, and, in due course, the portions of the daughters, added to his liabilities. Elections and petitions had proved burdensome, and in 1800 he was becoming financially embarrassed. His somewhat offhand attitude to business did not help. On 14 June 1800, his solicitor, John Lloyd of Carmarthen, implored him, "If you intend coming down, do bring the money to pay off the mortgage, if not there is no object in coming. I know your indolence in your concerns and I would wish you could get any friend of yours in Town to be active in the business and the money would soon be got. . . . I know you will excuse the liberties I have taken of digging you out of your indolence".[4]

To meet his occasions he sold farms in the parishes of Abergwili, Newchurch, Llanllawddog, Llanarthney, and Llandeilofawr, of the estimated capital value of £12,000 – £13,000. This was done mainly to enable him to pay off the inherited £4,000 mortgage and other debts. The purchase money for those farms amounted to £9,000.[5] In 1805 he sold part of the woodlands for £1,800.

Despite indolence in some matters, he was active enough in others. He took a prominent part in raising and training the militia, served in the Royal Carmarthenshire Fusiliers, first as Captain and then as Major and second-in-command to the commanding officer, Lord Cawdor, and accompanied the regiment when it did duty, for instance, in 1798 at Wrexham, Liverpool, Pewsey (Wiltshire), and elsewhere in England, and for some time at Dublin.

Anne had endured many spells of ill-health, and was ailing for most of 1804 and 1805. Her condition worsened, and on

Cause and effect

2 April 1806 she was buried at Abergwili, aged about 45 years. She had been a good, affectionate wife, and J. G. Philipps felt her loss grievously. However, he soon took a second partner, "On the rebound" so the late Sir Grismond Philipps informed me. Apparently he had proclaimed his intention to marry the first woman he met on his return to Cwmgwili from his wife's funeral. She turned out to be his servant-maid Anne Thomas, whose father kept the Black Horse Inn in Water Street, Carmarthen. The marriage settlement was made on 2 December 1807, and they married at Abergwili Church on the 10th of that month.

He had always been plump – in January 1796 a friend wrote to him, "Nash says you are grown fat and indolent" – and in later years grew excessively corpulent, suffering bouts of ill-health, particularly from that popular squirarchical complaint, gout. He died on 26 May 1816, aged 54, and was buried in the family vault in Abergwili church. His will, dated 19 May 1816, was proved in PCC on 11 May 1822. The widow Anne afterwards married, in 1823 at Llangain, Captain Henry Harding, Adjutant of the Royal Carmarthen Fusiliers, who died on 14 September 1830 in his 64th year; on 11 August 1831 the widow married, at St. George Hanover Square, her third husband, Captain John Bankes Davies of Myrtle Hill, near Carmarthen.

After saying that Mr. Philipps had been a Member of Parliament for nearly twenty years, the obituary notice in The Cambrian for 1 June 1816, went on – "during which time zealously devoted to the principles of Mr. Fox, and warmly attached to his person, he almost invariably supported the politics of that distinguished statesman. Well-versed in the laws and history of the country, he was on all occasions an able and upright magistrate. His memory was very retentive, and possessing a fund of anecdote, his presence always enlivened the circle in which he moved. As a landlord he was most indulgent.

By his first wife Anne (Ball) he had seven children:

1. Griffith Philipps, born in July 1782, educated at Ystrad Meurig School (Cardiganshire) and at Mr. James Edwards's school in Fairford. When twelve years of age he wrote to his father (14 April 1794) ". . . my sister Eliza completes her seventh year today. Eliza and Anne are constantly in school, and merry little Grismond tells everybody 'Papa gon to Lanon, buy pitty sing for Gtsi';" the writer says he would be pleased and obliged for a present, "Not for a pretty thing but for an useful book", and ends, "Mama desires me to

ask your opinion of that great, very great man, Danton as you used to call him". On 15 December 1800 he matriculated at Jesus College, Oxford, graduated B.A. in 1806, and proceeded M.A. in the following year. The payments his father had to make for his bills at Jesus College suggest that he was in no way extravagant. He did not enjoy robust health, and died unmarried at Cwmgwili, aged 25 years and was buried at Abergwili on 23 December 1807.

2. John George Philipps, born in September 1783 – see later.

3. Elizabeth ("Eliza") Catherine Philipps, born on 14 April 1787, married Peatre Garland of Lincoln's Inn, barrister-at-law (her portion, £2,000). They lived in London and Michaelston, Essex, and had issue.

4. Anna Martha Philipps ("Tiddy"), born in August 1788; married on 3 November 1807 at Abergwili, William Edwardes Tucker,[6] of Sealyham, Pembrokeshire. A man of bewildering nomenclature, he was born William Tucker Edwardes but in compliance with the request of his uncle, Admiral Tucker, assumed the name of William Edwardes Tucker but afterwards transposed his name into William Tucker Edwardes. He was High Sheriff of Pembrokeshire in 1829, and died on 8 May 1858, aged 74. His widow died in 1876. They had nine children.

5. Grismond Philipps, born on 5 February 1792 – see later.

6. Georgianna Jeannetta, born in April 1796, died in December 1799.

7. Emma Louisa Mary, born in 1802, married at Abergwili on 7 September 1824 Dr. Robert Williams, M.D., of Bedford Place, London, and had issue.

By his second wife Anne (Thomas), he had an only child, Frederic Philipps, born in October 1808, and baptised at Abergwili on 24 March 1818, being then nine years old. When a youth, he lost the sight of one eye after it had been pierced by an arrow accidentally discharged by Dr. Henry Lawrence. As a result he wore a black patch over the eye in the manner of a pirate, and became known as "Patch" Philipps. He was a Justice of the Peace and lived for a time at Llwyndu. His path was not wholly smooth; he amassed large debts for which he was thrown into gaol. The poor fellow eventually died of apoplexy in Bristol on 30 August 1838, at the early age of 31, and his remains were brought back for burial at Abergwili. His wife, whom he had married on 28 June 1831, was Elizabeth daughter of Lewis Pugh, publican, of the Castle Inn, Haverfordwest. After her husband's death she returned to live at the inn, and was buried at Uzmaston on 23 May 1841. They had at least three children.

John George Philipps the Younger, 1783-1869

John George Philipps received his early education at Ystrad Meurig school, and on 12 March 1796 the master reported that John's "diligent application, his open behaviour, and the fair progress he has made, entitle him to my warmest recommendation". Later in that year he entered the Royal Navy, being thirteen years of age, and went to sea with his father's friend, Admiral John Macbride. John Nash wrote to the young sailor's father on 23 September 1796. ". . . I have the highest accounts of poor little John – he crawls up the ropes like a young monkey, and there is not a masthead that he had not been at the top. He is extremely liked by everybody in the ship and will make a thorough sailor; he is now on his way to the *Minotaur* where the admiral is about to hoist his flag . . . none of you ever write to little John. I cannot wonder that you are so bad a correspondent with your friends when you neglect even your son. It will be necessary to assign John an allowance, say £30 a year." Soon, he was to experience what was, mercifully, an unusual occurrence in the Navy, mutiny, and on 1 May 1797 wrote to his father that he could not have done so sooner as "the men would not let any letter out of the ship without reading, till lately"; and on 11 May tells him that everything will be settled as soon as the King's pardon comes down, that a great many officers had been turned out of different ships by the mutineers, especially *Mars* and *Duke* who have no officer at all on board, and that Lord Howe was expected to arrive. By firmness, moderation, and tact, Howe soon brought the sailors back to their allegiance.

Scaling the mast

He saw active service within two years of joining his ship. In 1798 he was present at the Battle of the Nile, at the capture of Naples, Cittce (Malta), and Rome, and at Barcelona and Egypt. In 1804 he received his first promotion; on 5 March 1806 was appointed Lieutenant of the *Lavina*; on 8 December of the following year appointed to the sloop *Pilot,* and on 24 March 1808 to the sloop *Speedy*. On 2 February 1809 he was serving on the *Shirley* at Spithead where he had just arrived from Newfoundland after a passage of 21 days, and told his father, "A great bustle prevails here at this moment occasioned by sending the Troops from Spain. I assure you it is very distressing to see the poor fellows almost the whole of them, both Men and Officers, being half naked. All the hospitals here are quite full of the sick and wounded. The mortality is very great amongst them. You can't walk the street without meeting the funeral of some gallant fellow going to his last home, about thirty die daily. Regiments that mustered a thousand strong have only brought home three hundred. Sir John Moore's retreat is supposed to be one of the first that ever was made, the Country has suffered a severe loss in him as he was the only person in our army that Buonaparte would allow to be a General. It is rumoured here that another expedition of sixty thousand men is to be sent off immediately . . . for some part of Spain. I fear they will be served in the same manner as the last as it is impossible that we can fight against so great a superiority in numbers. If a sufficient force could be sent I have no doubt but we should thrash them. All the Officers that I have seen who have come from Spain agree in saying that the French are not equal to our troops in personal bravery as they could never stand against our charge."[7] He added he had received a letter from Mr. Morris (the banker) that he (i.e. J.G.P.) had been admitted a burgess of Carmarthen.

This was the "other end" of the retreat from Corunna and the evacuation of the British troops from Spain.

Between 1809 and 1813 he served as a Lieutenant in HM ships *Majestic* and *Redpole,* and on 6 May 1814 was appointed in the same rank to the *Monmouth* or any ship where the flag of Admiral Foley might be flying. Promotion came on 22 October 1814 when he was made Commander of the *Reliance,* and in the following year he became a Captain in which rank he was to retire later.

The few letters that have survived offer some glimpses of naval affairs during the latter part of his service. On 5 February 1812 he wrote from HMS *Monmouth,* off the Downs, about "the melancholy fate of the *St. George,* and the *Defence,* only eighteen members of their crews having been saved after they had foundered in a storm. The body of Captain Atkins of the *Defence* had been washed ashore, which was to be buried, "by order of the King with the honours of War", and about seventy more bodies were also recovered, but the bodies of Admiral Reynolds and Captain [?Ginon] had not been found. The bodies of two females were washed ashore, and, from her dress, one was believed to be the Admiral's daughter. The *St. George* went down in deep water at Boston on 24 December. He noted that his father had been appointed High Sheriff, which would mean a great deal of work should parliament be dissolved in course of the year.[8] Later in the month he wrote to tell his father that "the fleet at this anchorage have subscribed two days pay for the benefit of the relations of those that were lost in the *St. George* and the *Defence,* and it is expected that such a subscription will be made throughout the Navy; heavy gales have damaged several ships; the Admiral, a heavy man, fell from his horse the other day, but is much better"; "smuggling is carried on to a great extent at this place, several of them of late have been taken"; he expects that Grismond who was home at Cwmgwili is as good a sportsman as he is a soldier particularly after the daily practice he takes, but he (the writer) has "knocked down a few snipe this winter"; adding, "I don't think his Royal Highness the Prince Regent so determined a man as what was thought he would be when the restrictions were taken off; it is generally thought here that if the Catholics are not emancipated there will be disturbance in Ireland, such a business would be very unfortunate at the present moment".[9]

The *Monmouth* was still off the Downs when he wrote to his father on 15 May 1812. He has learned that Grismond is still at home, but supposes that the affair at Badajos will soon occasion his departure to join the first battalion; when he does go it would be a good thing to get him recommended if possible to General Picton "who appears to be a rising character in the Army and might be of great service to him"; he was sorry to see Mr. Thomas Tucker's name in the list of severely wounded, who, he has been informed, is to be one of Picton's aides-de-camp; it is said promotions will take place on the Prince Regent's birthday, and "I should like very much to be included, pray have you any interest as High Sheriff?

I shall be much obliged to you if you will have the goodness to speak to Lord Cawdor about it when you see him; everybody is quite in a gloom about the assassination of Mr. Perceval."[10]

The last surviving letter from him was sent to his father from the Admiral's Office, Deal, on 8 June 1814. He tells him of "the landing of the allied Sovereigns in England the day before yesterday, and certainly was a most gratifying sight"; the Admiral received them at Dover, taking the writer with him as aide de camp; "before our arrival there we could see the *Impregnable* with the Royal standards of Russia and Prussia flying at her mastheads, standing over from Boulogne under a press of sail with the squadron following. Dover was then filling very fast besides 3,000 troops that had marched in under the Earl of Rosslyn from all quarters were flocking in so that by five in the evening the crowd was immense. The tide having ebbed too much in the harbour for the Monarchs to land there, it was set that they should land on the beach directly under one of the forts called Archcliff; a stage provided for the occasion was accordingly placed there, and the troops were stationed in two lines from thence to Mr. Hector's house which was prepared for the Emperor, and again from thence to the York Hotel where the King took up his residence. At six the *Impregnable* with the whole Squadron anchored in the road, at 6 the Sovereigns shoved off in the barge accompanied by His Royal Highness and followed by all the boats under two Royal salutes from the ships. The yards were manned and three cheers given at the same time. When they were about half way on shore a general cheer from the immense crowd welcomed them to the British shore, and upon landing they were received, under two Royal salutes from all the batteries, by Lords Rosslyn and Yarmouth, the Russian and Prussian ambassadors, General Barlow and a great many military officers, Admiral Foley and a great many naval officers. The Sovereigns appeared much pleased at the attention shewn them. They conversed and shook hands with a great many people very cordially. The Emperor is a very fine looking fellow about 5 foot 11 in height, very square about the shoulders, well made, and pleasing in his manner. He looks younger than he is, and struck me at first sight to be in his countenance not unlike what Mr. Davies of Penylan was 20 years ago. The King is taller but thinner in his person than the Emperor. He looks about 40, was dressed in his uniform and has very much the appearance of a soldier. I was also gratified with the sight of Blucher and Platoff the Hetman of the Cossacks. They are both fine looking old men. Blucher was particularly well received by the soldiers as he passed between the lines. They all cheered him and as many shook hands with him as could get near him. They stopped at Dover that night, and set off for London early next morning."[11]

After leaving the Navy he returned to Carmarthen. Like all his family he was a Whig, and made a brief incursion into politics, when in the Reform election of 1831 he contested the Borough against the Tory, John Jones of Ystrad. Feelings ran high, and as a result of the rioting that broke out soon after the poll was opened, the borough sheriffs declined to make a return, and on 30 April certified they had been unable to execute the writ "from the uproar, tumult and violence which prevailed", whereupon the House of Commons directed that a new election be held. As a precaution, a large force of constables was drafted to maintain order, and a force of dragoons quartered in Llandeilo. Nevertheless violence continued during the polling but not to the extent at the former poll, and on 25 August, Jones was returned with 274 votes to Philipps's 203.

On 1 February 1808 J. G. Philipps had married Frances Eliza Hawford, his address being then given as Furnace House, Carmarthen, and it was there that they were still living in 1835. Later they settled at Ystradwrallt near Nantgaredig. He was appointed a Deputy Lieutenant in 1821, was a Justice of the Peace, and served the office of Mayor of Carmarthen in 1817 and again in 1836.

A list of the farms and lands of the Cwmgwili estate, made in 1821, shows its extent to be as follows:

Abergwili parish. Cwmgwili demesne, Cwmgwili Mill, Danyrhiw, stable at Abergwili, Rhydwyalchen, Rhydyrhaw, Trefynis, Pentre fynis fields, Machroes, Tir y Graig, Grug House, Baily glas, Glantowy, Cwmhowell, Rwythfawr, Fald fields and Parkcapel, Capel bach, Foes Mawr.

Newchurch parish. Blaenige, Falefach, fields in Folefawr, Llech-igon, Pistillgwyon and Godrewene, Waunilane issa, Clynmelyn slangs, Ewich Tomlid, Pantau, Henallt (part), Ffynnon Wiber, Penllwvncrwn.

Merthyr parish. Place y parke, Cwmdyhen, Nantypair, Park y berllan, Tir y banal.

County of the Borough of Carmarthen. Henallt. House in town (Mr. Tardrew), Welt and fields (Dr. Morgan), Cots and fields.

Llanegwad parish. Ddolwyrdd.

Llanpumpsaint parish. Bedw bach, Derimisk, Derwen groes.

Captain J. G. Philipps died in April 1869. He had the following children:

1. John George Hawford Philipps, born 19 February 1809, entered the army, served in the 61st Foot, and attained the rank of Captain. He lived sometime at Sarnau, Meydrim parish, and at Ystradwrallt, and was a magistrate; married Elizabeth only child of Edmond James, R.N.; he died on 15 November 1864, aged 55, and was survived by his wife who died on 23 May 1886, aged 71. They had five children:

    i. John George Philipps, born on 31 August 1846, died on 22 March 1854.

    ii. Vaughan Lloyd Philipps born at Sarnau on 14 April 1848, admitted to the Middle Temple on 18 April 1868, became a magistrate, and a lieutenant in the Carmarthenshire Artillery Militia: he died on 26 January 1885.

    iii. Elizabeth Philipps, died an infant in 1849.

    iv. Emma Ellen Philipps, baptised at Abergwili on 19 August 1850, married in 1879, Antony William John Stokes of St. Botolphs, Pembrokeshire, lived for some time at Ystradwrallt, and had issue.

    v. Elizabeth Frances ("Lilla") Philipps, baptised at Abergwili on 5 January 1851, died on 11 July 1883.

2. Griffith Grismond Philipps, born 28 November 1811, entered the Royal Navy, served as a Lieutenant in the *Royal William*, the *Cornwallis* (1838), *Seringapatam* (1839), *Hecate* (1845), *Acheron* (1847), Merlin (1855), and on 26 May 1856 was appointed Commander of HM sloop *Scout*, and later retired in that rank.

When in Carmarthen he lived at Ferryside.[12] By his wife, Georgina Wilkinson of Barbadoes, whom he married in 1852, he had five children:

    i.   Fanny Philipps, married on 18 January 1877, J. H. Sandwith, R.N.

    ii. Georgina Elizabeth Emma Philipps, married on 20 August 1879, R. Manning Driver of Cromwell Road, London.

    iii. Magdalen Philipps.

    iv. Griffith Grismond Philipps, Lieut. R.N., married on 30 April 1895, the youngest daughter of William Arthur of Wellesburn, Compton Clifford, near Plymouth.

    v. John George Philipps.

3. Grismond Frederic Philipps, baptised at Abergwili on 22 November 1815.

4. Emma Eliza Philipps, born 1814, married John Jeffreys de Winton of Maesderwen, Breconshire, and had issue.

5. Lloyd Price Philipps, Captain in E.I.C.S. He married a daughter of Thomas Tardrew, druggist, of Guildhall Square, Carmarthen.

6. George Vaughan Philipps, entered the Royal Navy, and on 3 May 1853 was appointed Lieutenant in HMS *Royal William*. He married, firstly, a Miss Galley, and secondly, a daughter of Nicholas Brabyn of Llanelli.

7. Herbert Folkes Philipps, baptised at Abergwili on 11 July 1817, buried on 2 June 1843.

8. Cecil Elizabeth Philipps, eldest daughter, unmarried in 1850.

9. Georgina Catherine Philipps, baptised at Abergwili on 2 August 1820.

10. Mary Anne Philipps, privately baptised in London on 19 October 1831, publicly at Abergwili on 12 August 1832.

11. William Thomas Philipps, baptised at Abergwili on 20 February 1822.

12. Charles Henry Philipps, baptised at Abergwili on 16 January 1824.

13. Edmund Garland Philipps, baptised at Abergwili on 7 July 1825.

14. Lloyd Rice Philipps, baptised at Abergwili on 5 March 1827. He lived in Abergwili village, married Maria Anne . . . , and their daughter Augusta Louisa was baptised on 26 October 1866.

15. George Vaughan Philipps, baptised at Abergwili on 30 November 1829.

16. Elizabeth Grace Philipps, baptised at Abergwili on 5 August 1834.

Grismond Philipps, 1792-1850

Grismond Philipps, younger son of John George Philipps and Anne (Ball) his wife, was baptised at Abergwili on 12 February 1792, and educated at Lewis Tumor's school at Bradmore House, Hammersmith. A letter he wrote to his father on 7 June 1806 is interesting for its account of the school curriculum. He tells his father that he pays attention to arithmetic, geometry, composition, and versification, and "Latin I am of course required to study every day. The authors I read are Ovid's Metamophoses and Terence to which my attention has been regularly directed during this half-year. I therefore, flatter myself that I have not laboured without deriving very considerable benefit. And to French I have not been less attentive, conscious that I cannot, with any degree of credit to myself, leave a school where I have had

A Regimental tailor

opportunities of acquiring a thorough knowledge of it, without having availed myself of them. And since I constantly read French into English, and write French exercises every afternoon, I do not think that you will hereafter find that I have neglected the advantages I have. And since I daily read French, I have some hope that I shall acquire a good accent and proper pronunciation. The French master is very particular with us in this respect".

At first his father had intended to send him to Oxford, but it was decided later that he should take up a military career. In July 1809 he was gazetted a 2nd Lieutenant in the 23rd Regiment, the purchase money being £450. In August he reported to Horsham Barracks, and was briskly engaged in buying uniform and other necessaries of an officer's life. These included a bed £14 14s. 0d., boots and shoes £4, pantaloons £1 14s. 0d., mess fees £3 3s. 0d., great-coat £4 14s. 0d., feather 2s. 6d., gorget 10s. 6d., furnishing his room £4, and jacket and trousers for his servant £1. He found that mess cost a good deal of money – £2 4s. 0d. every week, 14 shillings for dinner, 1s. 6d. every afternoon for wine, and 1s. for breakfast. On 12 September he wrote to his father that they had received very bad news from Flushing, all the soldiers were sick except 40, and that he expected to be sent to join the regiment. On 11 October the regiment was ordered to march in a few days' time from Horsham to Colchester, and Grismond asked his father for money to help to pay a mess bill and marching expenses, but on 29 October he wrote that as so many officers were sick the regiment would not march till the following spring.

Like many young subalterns he found his pay inadequate to support his inclinations, and had to apply to his father on numerous occasions for assistance. On 29 August 1810, Lieut. Col. William Wyatt, commanding the 2nd Battalion 23rd Regiment, wrote to John George Philipps saying that he trusted there would be no further necessity for Lieut. Philipps to make demands on him, for "he has promised to be more cautious in the future. I consider £80 for the first year is adequate for a young gentleman entering the army, but after the first year I do not think a subaltern can do with less than £100 . . . Lieut. Philipps's debts have arisen from imprudence and not vice".

In 1810 he was posted to the 1st Battalion, then due for overseas service in Wellington's army. In the following year he was fighting in the Peninsula, and on 19 May 1811 wrote from "Field of Battle near Albuaria".[13] "Dear Father, I have only just time to inform you that the army under the command of General Beresford (to which our Regiment was attached) had had a severe engagement with the French under the command of Soult in which they were entirely defeated with the loss of about 8,000 men killed and wounded having left the latter in our hands. I have escaped unhurt thank God for it, as it is Wonderfull to me how I did. Our Brigade consisting of the 1 & 2 Batt of the 7th Reg and our own was ordered to charge a column of the enemy which we did in a most Gallant manner. We advanced to within about twenty paces of them without firing a shot when our men gave three cheeres, and fired, the enemy broke in great confusion. We followed them, but were obliged to retreat as their cavalry were going to make a charge on us. The Brigade entered the Field two thousand five hundred strong and we can now only muster 700 men, the strength of our . . . may . . . a slaughter . . . been. The British Tre . . . amounted 7,000, and . . . killed and wounded . . . will then the baseness of the . . . as I am obliged to enter the . . . and write on my knees . . . every time to say that from the fatigue I have undergone I have been obliged to borrow 50 Dollars to buy a horse and have . . . a bill upon for the money with I trust you will have the goodness to accept . . . give . . . remember . . . Mrs. Evans . . . I am / Dear Father / your dutiful son / G. Philipps."

At the end of the Peninsular War the Regiment returned to England, and the young lieutenant enjoyed some well deserved leave at Cwmgwili until the re-emergence of Napoleon brought an abrupt halt to his enjoyments. On 19 March 1815, the adjutant Captain John Enoch, wrote informing him that orders had been received to hold the 23rd in readiness for embarkation for foreign service, and that Lieut. Philipps was to proceed immediately to join battalion headquarters at Gosport. In the event, the battalion was engaged at Waterloo, suffering 100 casualties, including the Colonel killed, but Grismond escaped unscathed. After the peace, the regiment returned to England and in 1820 was stationed at Horsham and Lewes, and we find Grismond writing to his brother, John George Philipps, for money to meet his pressing occasions. He retired with the rank of captain and came to live at Cwmgwili.

When he married, on 11 July 1822, at Llansaint church, he was living at Croft Cottage, Llanllwch, within the parish of St. Peter's, Carmarthen. His wife Catherine was daughter of John Warlow, a well-to-do wine and brandy merchant of Haverfordwest, and Catherine Picton daughter of John Picton of Poyston near Haverfordwest and Cecil daughter and heiress of the Revd. John Powell of Llandough, Glamorgan. Mrs. Catherine Warlow's brother was the renowned General Sir Thomas Picton who fell at Waterloo. Grismond's father-in-law eventually bought Castle Hall near Milford, to which he retired.

By the pre-nuptial settlement dated the day before the wedding, Grismond settled Glantowy, Ffosymaen, Tir y Graig in Abergwili parish to the uses of the marriage, and assured £300 per annum for his bride in lieu of dower during widowhood. The trustees were the Revd. Edward Picton of Iscoed (brother of the General), David John Edwardes and Henry Lewis Edwardes Gwynne both of Rhydygors, and the bridegroom's brother, John George Philipps.

Later they moved to Cwmgwili. Grismond Philipps kept diaries, and those for the years 1833-1849 have survived, providing interesting glimpses of the life of a country gentleman of that period. Although brief, often terse, the entries are sufficient to reveal the writer as kindly, humane, and conscientious, devoted to his wife and children, and enjoying a happy domestic life. Fond of the open air, he was a tremendous walker and often went on foot to Carmarthen and back, to Abergwili church, and to see tenants and friends in the district.

As a county and a borough magistrate he was closely concerned with administration of justice and county affairs that came within the ambit of Quarter Sessions held alternatively at Carmarthen and Llandeilo. There was as much civil as criminal business at the Sessions in those days. He attended often as a Grand Juror at the Assizes, and waited on the judge. On 3 March 1833 he attended the judge to St. Peter's church, and afterwards dined with him at Mr. Jones's house, Ystrad; on the following day he gave evidence against "the rioters", George Thomas and Woolcock, but the jury acquitted them; and on the day after, he dined with the borough Grand Jury. Complaints about "judge's lodgings" are by no means new. On 16 July 1834 we are informed that the Quarter Sessions engaged new lodgings for the judge, "he having complained of the old". Some alarm must have been caused in court on 11 July 1837, when Grismond was a Grand Juror, and he reported in the diary that "the Judge had a fit". On these occasions the Grand Jurors dined together at some hostelry, the "Bush" for instance (1840).

Like all his forebears he was closely associated with Carmarthen, and served as Mayor in 1827 and again in 1833. He was already a county magistrate, and on 4 November 1833 qualified as Borough magistrate. He sat on the Borough bench on 2 January 1834 when Mr. Price the saddler was fined £8 and costs for buying hides from the wreck of the *Brothers of Liverpool;* and on 11 February Grismond and the Revd. Edward Picton of Iscoed, rode to inspect the *Brothers,* where they "took up some of the wreck". The magistrates scrutinised very carefully all administrative matters and appointments brought before them, and on 25 April 1834 for instance refused to confirm the appointment of the general overseers for St. Peter's parish because they considered them unsuitable,

It was a time of agricultural distress in west Wales, which culminated in the Rebecca Riots, aimed principally at turnpike gates and tolls which were particularly burdensome for the farmers. Grismond Philipps felt the impact of the economic difficulties and there are several references to the rents being "slow coming in". He was on the Bench at Carmarthen on 2 November 1833 when two men were fined for refusing to pay tolls. He had been closely associated with road improvements, and the diaries record his attendances at Turnpike Trust meetings between 1836 and 1846, held at Carmarthen, Pensarn, Llangyndeyrn, Llanelli and elsewhere in the county. Matters did not improve, the grimalkin Rebecca raised her viper-wreathed head, and riots broke out. On 19 June 1843 Grismond noted that there was "a tremendous row" in Carmarthen and "the military sent for a troop of the 4th Light Dragoons". Matters were not improved by the slowness of the authorities in trying to resolve grievances, and when the magistrates met in Carmarthen on 22 and 23 June to discuss "the state of the country", Grismond noted "nothing done". These words also follow several meetings of the Trusts which he attended. An example of the attitude of the dis-affected appeared in a Welsh notice affixed to some buildings in Felin Wen near Abergwili, which read, in translation: "Notice. We as children from our childhood have heard our respected mother give her opinion on several things, and it is Justice she wants and will have. The notice is given to any person or persons that takes any farm before asking and getting leave from the present holder, that his life and property will be in danger. For that, let all persons after this notice take care that they do not take Ty Llwyd, Abergwilly, &c. Furthermore be it known to the Landlord that he must lower his rents as other respected great men do if not we shall see him according to our promise. [signed] Charlotte and Lidia. Castle Newidd. Awst 5/43".

On 16 March 1846 he walked to Carmarthen to attend a Board Road Meeting "respecting moving the gates. Nothing done", but when he went to a similar meeting on 1 July following he was able to note "the gates were removed on Monday".

The liaison between the gentry and the forces of law and order is reflected in Grismond's diaries. Time and again he dined at the messes of the military units that had arrived to quell disorders, and often entertained officers to dinner at Cwmgwili and invited them to sporting pastimes – shooting, hunting, fishing, horse-racing, etc. Thus, on 1 July 1843, Colonel Love and the officers of the 4th Dragoons called at Cwmgwili where "the haymakers were alarmed at their appearance". On the following day he returned the call, and two days later "went to see the cavalry exercise". On 22 February 1844 Lieut. Keightley of the 76th Regiment called, on 27 September Lieuts Holding and Deacon of the 13th Dragoons dined with him, and on 16 October 1845 Captain Hamilton and Lieut. Clutterbuck of the 37th Regiment; on 29 August, accompanied by his two daughters he drove to a picnic at Kidwelly given by the officers of the 6th Dragoons; and on 12 November he walked to Carmarthen to dine with the officers of the 37th. On 10 August 1846 he and his son, young Grismond, dined at the mess of the 37th, and on 12 September he called on the dragoons. On 14 June 1847 he noted that Capt. Hammersley's troop of the 1st Dragoon Guards marched into Carmarthen, and on 16 October following he called on the officers of the 43rd then stationed in the town.

Such attachment was natural in a former regular officer, and whose son had entered his father's former regiment. He entertained several old comrades at his home. On 3 November 1841 he recorded that "Morden an old brother officer" had dined at Cwmgwili, and on 18 December 1844 he "heard from my old friend Dean of the 23rd"; on 18 October 1849, Major Enoch of the 23rd arrived and stayed a couple of days, and on Monday 19 November he recorded, "The Colours of the 23rd Regt. in which I served [were] placed in Carmarthen church, escorted by the 14th Regt. and 5th Dragoon Guards", and when he went to that church on the following Sunday he tells us that he "sat under the Colours of my dear old Regiment the 23 RWF". The authorities had been extremely slow in sending him medals to which he was entitled, but on 12 February 1849 he noted that he "received my Peninsular medals", and on the following evening proudly "went to the Ball [at Carmarthen] with my Peninsular medals on".

Voluntary work took up much of his time. He attended numerous parish and vestry meetings at Abergwili. He had reason to regret his attendance on 4 April 1833 to appoint overseers – "Dined there, and smoked a pipe which made me very ill." He was an active member of the Board of Guardians and took part in improving the poorhouse, and on 4 July 1836 attended the first meeting of the Board at Carmarthen. His humane feelings are reflected in his conduct in April 1847, when he attended meetings at Abergwili to discuss ways to "assist the poor to set potatoes", and personally went around the parish "to collect for the poor".

A good churchman, he attended both Abergwili and St. Peter's churches. Accompanied by his wife and children, he sometimes walked, sometimes rode in the carriage, and when a sermon was particularly good, noted the text in his diary. On 3 February when the Revd. Mr. Jones "read himself into Abergwilly church", he noted "an excellent sermon". He was particularly impressed with the Revd. Mr. Bevan who preached at St. Peter's from Timothy 16. 15. on 7 April 1833. When the weather proved forbidding he sensibly stayed at home, but by no means neglected religious observances – "dyletswydd teulu" as old Welsh folk called it. When obliged to stay at home on Sunday 1 December 1833, he "read prayers to my children and wife"; on Sunday 24 January 1847, the weather con-fined the family to the house, and "I read prayers at home to the children"; and Sunday 10 September 1849 was a "wet day, no church, read prayers at home". He was conversant with Welsh, and recorded being present with his family in Abergwili church on 9 November 1834, when the service was conducted in that language. An old custom is recalled by the entry for Wednesday 10 October 1849, when, together with his children, he walked to St. Peter's church, being "a fast day and humiliation for the cholera" (known in the days of my youth as *cyfarfod ymostyngiad*). The Bishop of St. Davids and other clergymen, were frequent callers at Cwmgwili.

Like all Welsh gentry of that period, Grismond Philipps farmed. Accordingly, he could sympathise with his tenants during difficult times, knowing from personal experience the results of bad harvests, low prices, the costs of feeding stuffs and other necessaries. Neither could a tenant impose upon one who "know it at first hand". He conducted mixed farming, grew crops of wheat, oats, barley, and hay; kept sheep, pigs, and calves for the market and for home consumption; grew fine crops of potatoes and turnips; but the main emphasis was on cattle. The entries in the diaries indicate the scope of his activities and are particularly valuable to students of economic history since he often includes prices. Thus, on 21 May 1833 he bought a cow and calf at a sale at Towy Castle, but "on coming home a stallion kicked the calf, which was killed by a butcher on the spot", and adds feelingly, "I got 5 shillings for it"; on Sunday, 14 July 1833, "the bull broke out of the field and alarmed Davies", and in September wisely sold the lively animal for £5; he attended the pig fair at Carmarthen on 13 August 1833, and at the Alltygog sale on 4 September bought ten mows of wheat at 19 shillings each, on 17 January 1834 he bought 20 sheep at 13s. 4d. each; his fondness for attending fairs took him regularly to Abergwili, Carmarthen, and Mydrim. The entry for 15 April 1842 contains this interesting piece of information – "John Brown's fair held at Abergwilly, the Corporation of Carmarthen (where this fair was usually held) having raised the tolls". He made a careful note of happenings to his cows – "Nancy and Deborah took the bull", "Polly calved a she-calf", "Margaretta calved a female", and so on. In 1835-6 he bought a cow at Goode's sale for £8 15s. 0d., a "bait horse" for £16 15s. 0d., and a chestnut mare for £21. He attended Agricultural Meetings at Carmarthen, and competed in cattle shows; on 2 October 1846 he took cattle to Abergwili fair, but as prices were so low, brought them home again; on 9 June 1846 he "ringed the bull's nose"; and on 2 August of the following year thatched a haystack, but a week later had to open it because it had "heated too much", a hazard of old-time farming.

He was interested in afforestation, and planted numerous trees in hedgerows and around Cwmgwili to provide shelter for man and beast in wintry weather, as well as several plantations which in due course would have commercial value. In 1835 he sold trees in Cwm wood for £40, and four years later sold a quantity of bark to a tanner. He was particularly fond of flowers and flowering bushes which he planted around the house and in the garden. In February 1833 he was busily engaged in pruning the rosebushes and in January 1836 planted rhododendrons and lilac in the shrubbery. He produced a home made weed deterrent, and in 1833 noted in his diary, "Grass or weeds springing up amongst gravel or in courtyards may be destroyed for years by mixing a pound of sulphur and a pound of lime in a couple of gallons of water, and pouring this liquor over the weeds".

His recreations consisted mainly of field sports – fox and otter hunting, beagling, shooting, and fishing. The Carmarthenshire packs with which he hunted met at Maesycrigie, Bronwydd Arms, Pantycendy (Capt. Evans' hounds), Glangwili, and other places. He notes on 13 February 1833, hounds found near New Inn and "ran him into Cardiganshire", and on 27 March 1846 hounds met at Glangwili gate and killed a bag fox after a fast run of twenty-five minutes. In Pembrokeshire he hunted with Edwardes of Sealyham and with Mr. Roch of Butter Hill's hounds (1835). On 22 February 1833 after dining with Mr. Rees of White House they went coursing together and killed two hares, but Grismond found it "bad sport", and "Mr. Rees very dull"; in October and November he hunted with Howell's beagles and saw fourteen hares killed. On 1 October 1833 he went shooting and killed a pheasant; and in December 1844 he went rabbit shooting at Iscoed where "little Bean the spaniel bit me when taking a jay from him". Most of his fishing was done on the Gwili, Towy, and Teifi, and his best catch seems to have been 19 sewin taken in a weir on the Gwili on 20 August 1845. He attended race meetings at Carmarthen, Haverfordwest, and Newgale, and in April 1833 attended the steeplechase at Cheltenham when he happened to be there on legal business. Occasionally he was present at a private match, such as that on 20 January 1847 when his son Grismond's horse ran unsuccessfully against Mr. Davies of Penallt's mare.

To ward off indoor tedium he played at cards, and when in Haverfordwest, at billiards. The sums he won or lost at these diversions were very small, ranging from one to six shillings. I suppose we can include bets in this category. Making bets on all sorts of matters was then a popular pastime, usually made after dinner, sometimes in order to settle an argument. On two occasions in 1833, when dining at Cwmgwili, Mr. Goode (the estate agent) bet £5 with Mr. B. Davies of Maesycrigie, that the rental of the Glanbran estate in 1807 or 1808 was £5,000: at another dinner there, Mr. Goode bet Mr. B. Davies that Mr. Llewellyn's glasshouse was longer than his garden; on 9 November 1834, the inveterate Mr. B. Davies bet Mr. Philipps six bottles of champagne that Mrs. (?Hitton) had not had a child by her present husband; on 28 April 1835 Mr. Saunders of Glanrhydw bet Mr. Philipps a dinner "for the present party" that there would be rooks fit to shoot on 29 April.

He was loyal to friends, and whenever death or other mishap befell them, was genuinely upset. He felt some responsibility for their actions, and became apprehensive when they took a step which he himself felt to be unwise. When his old friend John Davies decided to take a partner, he entered in his diary on 27 July 1843, "John Davies married this day to Mrs. Jones widow of old Jones the Banker of Llandovery – God help him".

His home life was harmonious. He suffered much from gout, and as he was a bon viveur there is little doubt of the cause of that painful affliction. Mrs. Philipps does not seem to have enjoyed robust health, and spent longish spells with her kinsfolk in Pembrokeshire. They were very fond of each other, and although there were occasional tiffs they were soon patched up. When confined to the house on a rainy Sunday in February 1844, he admits being "Out of temper with my wife; she threatened to cut my throat; in bed early my throat not cut"; but within a few days he was referring to her as "my dear wife". On 23 October 1846, she was out of humour with him, and he recorded "Catherine my wife calls me a fat . . . (the last word defies interpretation, mercifully perhaps). He was extremely indulgent to his children, their illnesses caused him much unease, and any death in the family much anguish. The little girls were sent to a boarding school at Haverfordwest. The boys were educated in a private school at Llanstephan, and he often drove them in a carriage to Iscoed, then to the Ferry whence they crossed the estuary by boat. He took his wife and children to picnics at Dynevor and Llanarthney, to circuses and concerts at Carmarthen, on trips into Pembrokeshire, and his sons accompanied him on hunting, shooting and fishing expeditions. Occasionally some trips were made by water, as on 14 August 1847 when he took his wife and three daughters in a carriage to the bend in the river below Green Castle, "where the steamer stops", whence they sailed down the Towy to the open sea and so on to Tenby.

The family enjoyed holidays at Haverfordwest, Little Haven, Tenby, and Ferryside. During the years 1833-49, he only ventured far afield on three occasions – to Gloucester 1833 on legal business, to London in January 1840 when his son Grismond entered King's College, and in December 1847 when he accompanied his son Jack to buy the latter's uniform to go to Madras as a Cadet in the H.E.I.C. The speed with which post coaches took him may be judged from the fact that on 22 January 1840 he left Carmarthen at 5 a.m., arrived in Cheltenham at 9 p.m. and got to London in the evening of the 23rd. After seeing the Zoological Gardens and visiting the theatre, he started his homeward journey at 8 p.m. on 28 January, and arrived at Cwmgwili at 9 p.m. the following day. The travelling in December 1840 was equally fast; leaving London on the 24th, and arriving in Cwmgwili at 4 p.m. on Christmas Day.

On 10 November 1842 Philipps's friend John Jones of Ystrad (the political hatchet had long been buried) died. When the sale of Jones's effects took place on 9 August of the following year, Grismond Philipps turned up early with a purseful of guineas in his pocket. The main reason for his attendance was because a fine portrait of the celebrated General Sir Thomas Picton was listed in the catalogue. This, with some other things, he bought and proudly bore away to Cwmgwili much to the delight of Mrs. Philipps, the General's niece. The portrait required cleaning and on 11 January 1847 he took it to Mr. Francis, a portrait painter at Carmarthen, who had agreed to undertake the work. At the same time he commissioned the artist to paint portraits of his sons Grismond and John. After several sittings in January and February the sons' portraits were completed, and the father pronounced them " a good likeness So far, so good". But Mr. Francis fell behind hand with the rent, whereupon the owner of the house, Thomas Joseph, seized the General's portrait saying he intended to impound it until the tenant had cleared the arrears. When Grismond Philipps heard of the turn of events, he was furious and demanded the portrait as his property. Joseph refused to hand it over, and in April the aggrieved owner brought an action in the courts. The trial took place on 20 October, and a verdict was given for the plaintiff. He recorded in his diary – "In town about my picture and the trial. Sir Thomas Picton returned to me."

The diaries tell us little about the management of the estate, and contain no hint of financial difficulties. However, the deeds convey a different impression. On 21 November 1833 Grismond mortgaged Ffoesymaen, Tyngraig, and Llechigon, to William Evans of Haverfordwest, solicitor, for £1,000, and by way of additional security assigned his life insurance policy for the like sum. In 1840 Evans assigned mortgage and policy to the widow Mary Lewis of Walton, Pembrokeshire, and four years later she assigned them to two farmers, William Lewis of New Moat and James Lewis of Walton East. The mortgages were redeemed in 1846.

On 3 November 1838 he mortgaged Blaenige to the widow Eliza Jones of Quay Street, Carmarthen, for £1,000, which he redeemed on 6 July 1846; on 18 May 1839 he gave a bond for the payment of £200 to David Evans of Clyngwyn, Newchurch parish, and on 31 March 1840 a bond for £150 to George Williams of Ffoesymaen; on 25 April 1842 he mortgaged Vole-vach, Cwmgwili Mill, Porthdwy otherwise Cwmduhen, and Nantypair, for £700 to the widow Anne Mapleton of Carmarthen executrix of Elizabeth Cow of Carmarthen, deceased; on 3 January 1843 he mortgaged Cwmgwili Mill for £200 to David Cozens of Carmarthen, which he redeemed three years later; on 8 February 1844 he mortgaged Glantowy, Rwythfawr, Tirygraig, Maebrosfach, Ffald, Cwm, Cwmcastell fach, Penlan cwm, and Nantypair, to Thomas Parry of Carmarthen for £500, and on 28 December in the same year gave a bond for payment of £253 and interest to David Price, tailor, of Cork Street, Westminster; on 14 June 1847 he mortgaged the capital messuage and demesne lands of Henallt to Thomas Eaton of Haverfordwest, land-agent, for the considerable sum of £5,500, and on 15 December of the same year Henallt farm to the widow Mary Berry of Tenby, for £200.

Although these incumbrances may seem considerable, the capital value of the properties far exceeded the sums in which they were mortgaged and so long as interest was paid, the mortgages could stand or be assigned until the mortgagor found it convenient to pay them off. His main income came from the estate rental, augmented by farming activities, sale of timber, and royalties from quarries, such as the one at Blaenige.

His stepmother, Anne, continued to enjoy a life interest in the estate, and on 3 August 1841 joined with her then husband John Bankes Davies of Myrtle Hill, and her stepson Grismond Philipps, to grant a lease for lives of a parcel of land at Plasyparke (Merthyr parish) to William Jones of Dover Hill, Merthyr parish, tailor, who agreed to erect a dwelling house thereon.

Grismond Philipps died at Cwmgwili on 28 April 1850, in his fifty-ninth year. By his will, made at Croft Cottage, Llanllwch, on 22 July 1828, proved in London on 27 May 1850, he left everything to his wife Catherine. She died on 20 May 1854.

They had the following children:

1. Grismond Philipps, born 4 October 1824 – see later.

2. Edmund Garland Philipps, died on 10 March 1826, aged 8 months.

3. Edward Philipps, born in 1828, died at Haverfordwest and was buried at 8 of the clock in the morning of 8 December 1837 at St. Mary's church in that town.

4. George Henry John ("Jack") Philipps, received a cadetship in the E.I.C. Service in the 1840s, and sailed to Madras. He became a Lieutenant in the 41st Madras Native Infantry, and obtained his company in 1862. He married and had three children:

> i.   Grismond Philipps.
> ii. Alice Philipps, and
> iii. Blanche Elizabeth ("By") Philipps who married Colonel James FitzGerald of the Berar Commission and had a son, James FitzGerald and a daughter Cecil Blanche FitzGerald, who married George Lyon Woodham-Smith, solicitor in 1928. Mrs. Cecil Woodham-Smith is the well-known historian of our day.

5. William Philipps, born on 22 June 1832 – the "dear little William" of his father's diary – was placed in school at Llanstephan in July 1838. He settled at Llandeilo. On 18 September 1861 married Ellen Mary Powell Watkins only child of Hugh Powell Watkins of Merton, Bishopston, Glamorgan. He died on 19 May 1908, his wife having predeceased him on 19 August 1901. They had the following children:

> i.   Charles Henry Philipps of El Tab, Pessara, Ceylon, tea planter, who died unmarried in London on 1 October 1916.
> ii. Charlotte Augusta Philipps, died unmarried on 11 August 1950.
> iii. Arthur Edward Philipps of Fulham died unmarried, 15 November 1935.
> iv. John Vaughan Philipps of Bath, Chief Constable, died unmarried 1 May 1950.
> v.   Hugh Grismond Philipps of Llandeilo, solicitor, married Elizabeth, and died on 26 September 1936.
> vi. William Picton Philipps of Rhosmaen, Llandeilo, Chief Constable of Carmarthenshire, married, firstly Ruth daughter of Sir Brodrick Hartwell, Bart., by whom he had three daughters; and secondly, Mrs. Valentine by whom he had John William Picton Philipps, solicitor.

6. Cecil Elizabeth Philipps, born 14 February 1826, married on 14 February 1860 James Baillie of Enniskillen, captain 82nd Foot. He became a Major-General and died on 7 January 1901, aged 84. His wife died on 15 November 1892, aged 66. Both were buried at Abergwili. They had issue.

7. Catherine Anne Prudence Philipps, born 15 April 1830, married on 14 March 1851, as his second wife, Walter Rice Howell Powell of Maesgwynne, landowner, progressive farmer, Master of Fox Hounds, in 1849 High Sheriff, and from 1880 to 1885 Member of Parliament (Liberal) for Carmarthenshire. Owing to his low stature he was affectionately known as "Y Dyn Bach" he died on 25 June 1889. Their 2nd daughter and co-heiress

married in 1874 William Francis Roch of Butter Hill (1849-1889), by whom she had Mary Catherine Roch, ultimate heiress of Maesgwynne, who in 1907 married Wilmot Vaughan, by whom she had issue.

8.   Charlotte Maria Philipps, baptised at Abergwili on 10 October 1833, married before 1860, Frederick Augustus Edwardes of Pilroath, Llangain parish.

9.   Frances Philipps, married on 31 March 1860 Arthur Henry Saunders-Davies of Pentre, Pembrokeshire, who served as High Sheriff in 1861. They had issue.

10.   Anne Philipps, baptised at Abergwili on 30 January 1838, married Professor J. Brandt, M.A., on 25 April 1882 at Holy Trinity private chapel, at Pentre, Pembrokeshire.

11.   Mary Anne Philipps, baptised at Abergwili on 8 March 1836.

The later Grismonds

Grismond Phillips, b. 1824

Grismond Philipps the eldest son, was born at Croft Cottage, Llanllwch, on 4 October 1824, entered King's College, London, in January 1840, and from there was commissioned into the family regiment, the 23rd, Royal Welsh Fusiliers. On 12 July 1842, his father noted in his diary – "My dear son Gris left his home to join his regt, the 23rd. God bless him. Went off in good spirits". In 1844-49 (and later) he served with the regiment in Canada. He retired before 1854 as a Captain and returned to live in Cwmgwili. He was a Justice of the Peace, and in 1865 was appointed a Deputy Lieutenant for the county.

On 28 February 1854 he married Mary Anne daughter of Captain Thomas Bowen of Pantyderi, north Pembrokeshire, a former officer in the 10th Hussars. By the marriage settlement, dated three days before the wedding, Grismond Philipps settled the Cwmgwili estate in the parishes of Abergwili, Abernant, Llanegwad, Merthyr, Newchurch, and St. Peter's, Carmarthen, to the uses of the marriage. The two most important of the properties were the capital messuages of Cwmgwili and Wythfawr. The bride's dower was £1,000 and she was assured a jointure of £300 a year for life from her husband's estate. During the years 1858-60 he sold a large number of farms in order to pay off incumbrances on the estate, which amounted to over £20,000.

He died at Cwmgwili on 11 September 1891, and his widow in 1902. By his will dated 16 December 1871 he bequeathed wines, liquors, fuel and other consumable household stores and provisions, linen, china, and glass, to his wife absolutely, and bequeathed his other furniture and utensils, books, pictures, prints, and plate (including "the plate left me by Colonel Chester") to trustees to hold to the use of his wife for life and afterwards to be enjoyed by those entitled to the Cwmgwili demesne estate, and directed that Colonel Chester's plate "be kept and retained in my family as an heirloom".

They had the following children:

1. Grismond Philipps, born November 1867 – see later.

2. John Picton Philipps, born October 1870.

3. Catherine Elizabeth Philipps, baptised at Abergwili on 22 May, 1855, married on 10 July 1877, Colonel Edward Hugh Bearcroft, C.B., of Mere Hall, Droitwich, Worcestershire. Their pre-nuptial settlement was dated 9 July 1877, her portion being £2,000. Col. Bearcroft died on 27 January 1932, his wife in December 1933. They had no issue.

When he succeeded to the Cwmgwili estate in 1891, Grismond Philipps was twenty-four years of age. Like his forebears

Edith Margarette,
wife of Major Grismond Philipps, d. 1927

he was particularly fond of horses and field sports of all kinds, and was a familiar figure at hunt and race meetings and agricultural shows. He served for some years in the Carmarthenshire Artillery Militia, and afterwards in the Pembroke Imperial Yeomanry from which he eventually retired with the rank of major. Although he lived for some years in Cheltenham he remained deeply interested in local affairs and was a Justice of the Peace for his native county. In May 1897 he married Edith Margarette daughter of William Picton Evans of Treforgan near Cardigan, who, like her husband, descended from the family of General Picton. Major Philipps died on 7 October 1927, and his widow survived him for nearly twenty years, dying on 29 May 1947. They had an only son, Grismond Picton Philipps.

Grismond Picton Philipps was born on 20 May 1898, and educated at the Royal Military Academy, Sandhurst. At the outbreak of the First World War he was sixteen years of age, and three years later, in 1917, was gazetted to the Grenadier Guards with whom he served in France. He was promoted to the rank of captain in 1925, and retired from the regiment in 1933. While serving with the Grenadiers he had been seconded for a tour of duty as adjutant to his county Territorial unit, the 4th Battalion The Welch Regiment, and in 1934 was promoted to the rank of major, and from 1938, lieutenant-colonel commanding the battalion. Sometime after the outbreak of the second World War he returned to the Brigade of Guards, and in 1941 became a brevet-major. His duties kept him in England, mainly at Windsor, and in 1945 he was appointed Commander of the Royal Victorian Order for personal services to the Royal Family. Thirteen years later he received the honour of Knighthood. After the war he continued to take a personal interest in the reconstituted Volunteer Force, and from 1960 to 1964 was Honorary Colonel of his old Territorial battalion.

On 4 November 1925 he married Lady Marjorie Joan Mary Wentworth-FitzWilliam, second daughter of the seventh Earl Fitz-William. They had an only son. The marriage was dissolved in 1949.

Sir Grismond's record of voluntary service is impressive. In 1935 he was appointed a Deputy Lieutenant, in 1938 a Justice of the Peace, and later served as chairman of the Carmarthen County Bench. He was Vice-Lieutenant from 1936 until 1954, when he was appointed Lord Lieutenant and *Custos Rotulorum* for Carmarthenshire, offices he held until his death thirteen years later. His associations with the government and administration of the county had always been close, he having been a county councillor for the Abergwili division from 1945 to 1952. Before becoming Lord Lieutenant, he took a brisk part in political life, and for twenty-five years was chairman of the Carmarthen Division Conservative Association, and was a former President of the Council of Conservative and Unionist Associations of Wales and Monmouthshire.

Sir Grismond Phillips, d. 1967

In outlook, Sir Grismond was an Elizabethan, interested in most aspects of life, proficient in everything that engaged his attention – in fact an all-rounder. He read widely, particularly biography and history, and had a special affection for the 15th century on which he was an acknowledged master. He was fond of drama, music, portraiture, and the arts generally, and looked forward with delight to attending hymn-singing festivals in Carmarthen. As a founder member, and for some years chairman of Television Wales and the West, he was able to influence and direct the cultural activities of that broadcasting body during the period of its existence. Equally, his highly successful chairmanship of the Historic Buildings Council for Wales afforded him ample opportunity for preserving some outstanding examples of our country's architectural heritage. In addition, he served as a Governor and Council Member of the National Library of Wales, and a Council Member of the National Museum of Wales, and was elected a member of the gorsedd of bards of the Royal National Eisteddfod. Both as president and chairman of the Carmarthenshire Antiquarian Society and of the Carmarthenshire Community Council, he stimulated and advanced local interest in historical studies; he took an active part in the formation of the County Record Office, and his continued support was an assurance of its success. He largely administered the Cwmgwili estate himself, possessed a sound knowledge of farming, afforestation, and gardening, and did much to beautify the demesne lands around his historic home. To his presidency, too, the Carmarthenshire Federation of Young Farmers Clubs (his special concern) and the Carmarthen Chamber of Agriculture, were deeply indebted for advice and guidance. In every field that he entered he became a good shepherd.

Mr. and Mrs. Griffith William Grismond Philipps

Providence had endowed him with many gifts, but the quality for which he will be mainly remembered, was his humanity. Modest, courteous, good-natured, generous, Sir Grismond attracted the loyalty and friendship of people in all walks of life, and the Bishop of St. David's statement at his memorial service that "he had walked with kings but retained the common touch" was no more than an affirmation of literal truth.

Sir Grismond Picton Philipps died on 8 May 1967, aged 69, and was buried in Abergwili churchyard. A memorial tablet, raised by public subscription, was placed above the family pew in the parish church where he had been a faithful worshipper for many years.

He was followed at Cwmgwili by his only son, Griffith William Grismond Philipps, born on 19 May 1935. Educated at Eton, he served as a 2nd Lieutenant in the Grenadier Guards. On 17 May 1964 he married Ingrid Matilda, daughter of Med. Dr. von Sydow of Sweden, and has the following children:

1. John George Grismond Philipps, b. 30 July 1965.
2. Marianne Sioned Philipps, b. 13 Feb. 1967.
3. Charlotte Ingrid Philipps, b. 24 Aug. 1969.
4. Ebba Serena Philipps, b. 4 March 1971.
5. Eva Gotilda Joan Philipps, b. 27 December 1979.

The significance of the survival of this ancient family through many generations of change, vicissitudes, even dangers, does not rest alone on its capacity to surmount the challenges it was called upon to face, but rather on its steadfast adherence to the ideal of voluntary public service, which remains the hallmark of excellence and the imprimatur of all goodness.

REFERENCES

1 N.L.W. Cwmgwili DD, No. 113.
2 *ibid.,* No. 178.
3 CRO. Cwmgwili MSS, No. 450. The attitude of R. J. Llwyd is of particular interest when we recall that he was a member of the Llandeilo'r Ynys Trust in which he had invested £100, that he was a landowner, and a barrister-at-law.
4 See Cwmgwili MSS, Nos. 472A, 427, 488, 490.
5 *ibid.,* No. 702.
6 His brother Thomas Edwardes Tucker, Captain in the 23rd Regiment, became ADC to General Picton, and was wounded at Badajos.
7 CRO, Cwmgwili Collection, No. 606.
8 CRO, *ibid.,* No. 651.
9 *ibid.,* No. 652.
10 *ibid.,* No. 656. Spencer Perceval, Prime Minister 1809-12.
11 *ibid.,* No. 688.
12 On 2 May 1854 it was reported, "Griffith Philipps has been appointed to the Transport Service and has left the Ferryside" – CRO, *Plas Llanstephan Documents,* No. 878; and N.L.W. *Cwmgwili DD,* No. 482.
13 Albuera, perhaps the bloodiest battle of the Peninsular War.

Trefenty, the House by the Marsh

MY INTRODUCTION to Trefenty came in an unusual way. After the first World War, a kinsman of my father's, whose family had been engaged for several generations in the coastal seaborne trade, replaced his sailing vessel with a small steamship which would have to place less reliance on the uncertain element that so often had determined the course of her predecessors. At the time of which I write the vessel called at numerous ports and wharves between Liverpool and Bristol carrying mixed cargoes, but mainly flour for a well-known firm dealing in that commodity. I was fortunate to be able to spend part of my summer holidays on board, and those voyages – the greatest thrill of my boyhood days – remain among my most fragrant memories of those distant times. To the captain and his mariners such voyaging was but a means of subsistence, to me it was adventure, discovery, romance.

On this particular occasion I came aboard from the quayside at Haverfordwest. We then sailed on the ebb along the broad Cleddau and put in at Milford Haven for the night. On the following day we reached Tenby. Our next port of call was to be St. Clears. It was a beautiful day, the elements friendly, we reached Laugharne ahead of the estimated time, and there rode quietly for an hour or so in order to gain full advantage of the flow, for the river Tâf is tidal, and St. Clears could not be reached unless the waters were in our favour. As we cruised up river the captain drew my attention to various landmarks, navigational guides that ensured our safe progression along the comparatively narrow waterway. While the craft was negotiating a slight bend I pointed across marshland on the opposite bank to a knoll on which a tall weather-tiled double-gabled house stood within a coppice, a smiling statue in a green cloak. I was intrigued by the delectable cameo. What is it called? Trefenty, I was told. We chugged on for some further two miles until we came safely alongside the wharf at Lower St. Clears.

Late on the following day we were outward bound, borne leisurely on the calm bosom of the Tâf. As we rounded the final bend I looked inland and saw again the tall house, the roof and chimneys, and the uppermost branches of the guardian trees, bathed in the light of the evening sun – pure poetry, a Welsh *englyn* come to life. Over fifty years were to roll by before I saw Trefenty again.

Childhood memories

During the subsequent years I devoted my energies to antiquarian research, involving among others such topics as ancient families, historic houses, heraldry, customs and traditions, and in so doing inevitably made the acquaintance of Trefenty, but in an academic sense. Before discussing my findings, perhaps it will be convenient if I include first a prècis of the history of the parish of Llanfihangel Abercywyn, so that Trefenty may be placed in its tenurial and topographical setting.

Topographical
Comprising 6,149 acres, the ecclesiastical parish of Llanfihangel Abercywyn lies six-and-a-half miles to the west of the county town of Carmarthen. Shaped like the capital letter Y, it is bounded by the rivers Cywyn, Gynin, and Tâf, and occupies the western part of the headland known in ancient times as Penrhyn Dyfed. On the east, beyond the Cywyn, are the parishes of Llandeilo Abercywyn and Llangynog, on the north are Meidrim and Llangynin, on the west St. Clears. Devoted wholly to the pursuit of agriculture, the land rises gradually northwards to reach its highest point of 450 feet just to the south east of Castell Gorfod, Among the main farms in this river-nourished parish are Trefenty, Pentowyn, Rushmoor, Glasfryn, Wenallt, Foxhole, Lower Court, Pant Dwfwn, Asgood, Trecadwgan, Plas y Gwer, Wern and Esgair. Of these, the five first named were former gentry residences, centres of modest estates once characteristic of the rural scene in Wales.

Near the southern tip of the headland, on a knoll, 142 feet above the estuary, and about 500 yards from the bank, stands Trefenty, well placed among the 350 acres of attached farmland. Generally the fields are large and on gently sloping ground, so that we need not be surprised to learn that in 1870 "the popular sport of hare coursing at Trefenty gave exercise and recreation of a very enjoyable description". To the south-east, just below the buildings, are the remains of the original parish church, which ceased its ministrations in 1848 when a new and more central church was built through the generosity of Mr. K Richards of Trecadwgan, near the Carmarthen-St. Clears road.

To recognise the oldest parts of the ruined church is difficult, owing to extensive additions and repairs that have been made to it in course of the centuries. More intriguing are the sepulchral slabs in the graveyard, carved and ornamented with human figures and designs, memorials to members of a family of consequence of the late 12th or early 13th centuries, who had probably lived at Trefenty or at the mound-and-bailey castle on the west side of that house. In quite recent times these monuments are said to mark the graves of "pilgrims" who died on their way to, or from, the shrine of Dewi Sant, which has led some romantics to refer to them as "pilgrims' graves", and the church as the "pilgrim church". But it must be emphasised that no reference whatsoever to pilgrims being associated with this church occurs in any record, document, or tradition, and the authors of tours, topographical and antiquarian works prior to 1860 are wholly silent on the matter. The observation about the "pilgrims' graves" made in the Carmarthenshire volume of the Royal Commission on Ancient Monuments, "It is to the revival of interest in Welsh antiquities, and the publication of guide books to Welsh districts, that we probably owe the birth of the legend", is as accurate as it is shrewd. The church has been abandoned for over a century and a quarter, and the local prophecy that should the graveyard ever be neglected the parish would be visited by a plague of snakes, remains unfulfilled. During the later period few worshippers came to the church of Llanfihangel, mainly because of remoteness, particularly during wintry weather. On one occasion, the congregation consisting of only the vicar, and pious old Mr. Evans of Llandeilo (his own church being then in disrepair), who always attended accompanied by a faithful sheepdog to whom he was devoted, the vicar is said to have introduced into the prayers this extempore distich –

> Dduw, maddeu i ni ein tri
> Ifans Llandeilo a finne a'r ci,

which I have ventured to translate as "Lord, may forgiveness for us three be found Evans Llandeilo, myself, and the hound".

We might note here some points of similarity between the old churches of Llanfihangel and Llandeilo, just over a quarter of a mile apart – both are situated near the river bank at the southernmost tip of their parishes, both are built alongside important manor houses, and both are in complete ruin.

Historical Sketch

The district surrounding Trefenty has a long and interesting history. From early days the territory that now includes the parish, formed a comote known as Ystlwyf (later, Oysterlow) in the large cantref of Gwarthaf in the kingdom of Dyfed which remained under its own rulers until the 10th century when it was absorbed into the kingdom of Deheubarth ruled by Hywel Dda and his descendants.

It must be remembered that Dyfed included, not only what became Pembrokeshire, but west Carmarthenshire so far as the Dark Gate (Perth Tywyll) in the town of Carmarthen.

Evidences of early settlement in Llanfihangel Abercywyn are provided by remains of earthen fortifications in a field belonging to Penycoed farm on the banks of the Gynin, while the name of the farm Castell y Waun in the east of the parish suggests the former existence of a similar outpost. A maenhir in one of Trefenty's fields probably marks the resting place of a bygone worthy, as does another in a field called Cae Maenllwyd on Lower Court farm.

Of all these remains the most significant is the large mound-and-bailey castle immediately west of Trefenty house, a site of tactical importance for it dominated the river valleys embracing the headland as well as the seaward approaches. An early record calls it Castell Aber Cavwy, but the last word is considered to be a scribal error for the word Taf-wy, that is, 'the castle at the estuary of the river Tâf'. The mound is about 25 feet high, with summit diameter of 75 feet. As the surrounding land has been under cultivation for many centuries, the fosse has partially disappeared. The bailey, extending towards the curtilage of Trefenty, measures 150 feet long by 90 feet wide. The fortification was built by the Normans in the beginning of the 12th century, possibly on the site of an earlier Welsh castell. In the year 1116 Bledri ap Cadifor of Cilsant, interpreter between Welsh and Norman, was entrusted with the defence of the castle for Robert Courtemain.

Undoubtedly the most important area of the parish was around Trefenty. Here stood the castell, alongside it the homestead of Trefenty, and a few hundred yards away the parish church. Such churches were often built in the vicinity of the most important dwelling in a parish, and may explain the situation of the church of Llanfihangel in this remote spot. Incidentally, the formation of ecclesiastical parishes in south-west Wales was the work of Bernard, Norman bishop of St. Davids from 1115 to 1148, and in all probability it was during those years that the boundaries of Llanfihangel Abercywyn were defined.

The Normans maintained the bounds and identity of the comote of Ystlwyf (Oysterlow), so that its boundaries remained unchanged, for more often than not, the conquerors did little more than change the overlordship and system of tenure. As we shall see, the comote continued to be known as such, while its tenurial jurisdiction was that of a feudal manor or lordship.

Despite Norman penetration, the comote was often held by Welsh princes. In 1171 King Henry confirmed The Lord Rhys in possession of Ystlwyf, and some time after 1188 Rhys granted certain lands within the comote as an endowment to Whitland Abbey. During the 13th century it continued to be held by the princes from time to time, and also by the Earls of Pembroke. After the year of 1282 the comote formed part of the county of Pembroke under the jurisdiction of the earls. In 1390 John Joce was appointed steward of "the lordship of Oysterlow": six years later the king granted "the comote of Oystrelowe" to his consort, Queen Isabel as part of her dower; in 1415 eight archers from the comote fought at Agincourt; in 1462 extensive lands which included "the lordships and manors of Osterlowe, Trayne Clynton, and St. Clears" were granted by the Crown to William Herbert, later Earl of Pembroke. Eventually it reverted to the Crown, and in 1520 the King appointed John Thomas ap Philip one of the "dapifers" of the King's Chamber (son of Sir Thomas ap Philip of Picton Castle) and John Lloyd one of the pages of the Chamber, to be Stewards and Receivers of "the manors or lordships" of Llanstephan and Oisterlowe, with a salary of 100 shillings per annum out of the issues of the said lordships.

In all medieval records Oysterlow continued to be described variously as comote, or lordship, or manor, lying in the county of Pembroke, that is within the Earldom. Part of the comote was held by the monks of Whitland Abbey, but at the Dissolution reverted to the Crown, and thereafter was leased to various people. In 1587 it was described as the "manor or grange called Usterlowe alias Escloigh [Ystlwyf] late parcel of the dissolved monastery of Whitland".

Wales was radically restructured in 1536 when the jurisdictions of the marcher lordships were abolished and the land divided into shires on the English pattern. Cantref Gwarthaf and all lands included in that area, were adjudged to be a part of the newly-formed shire of Pembroke, but strong objections were made to this arrangement, with the result that six years later the cantref was transferred to the shire of Carmarthen. The parish of Llanfihangel Abercywyn was then placed in the administrative Hundred of Derllys, and so continued to our times.

Subsequent owners of Trefenty

In 1590 the lordship of Oysterlow was granted by Letters Patent to Sir John Perrot. This included the woodland of Cardiff Forest (also called Cardeeth) lying between Whitland and Pont y Fenni, where a farm called Forest still exists. Sir John Perrot of Haroldston near Haverfordwest, born in 1530 belonged to a well established and influential family in west Wales. He took a prominent part in public affairs and became well known at Court. Edward VI created him a Knight of the Bath, and he was one of the four gentlemen who bore the canopy at the coronation of Queen Elizabeth. High appointments followed – member of the Council of Wales and the Marches in 1571-73, Lord President of Ireland 1584-88, Privy Councillor in 1589. However, he was rash and impetuous, finally, unwise conduct led to his arrest, and in April 1592 he was tried, found guilty of treason, and sent to the Tower where he died later in that year before sentence could be carried out. As we learn from the trial, he had been given to somewhat picturesque utterances, and Dean Swift tells us, "Sir John Perrot was the first man of quality to have sworn *by God's wounds* . . . The oath still continues and is a stock oath to this day". It is amusing to reflect that the hall of remote Trefenty once resounded to this verbal confection. It became contracted to *Zounds!*

By his first wife, Anne daughter of Sir Thomas Cheyney of Shurland, Kent, Sir John Perrot had a son and heir, Thomas. Fortunately he had powerful friends, and soon after his father's death, the forfeited estates were restored to him, and later he was knighted. During his younger days he was very much the Elizabethan beau, and Nichols in *Progresses of Elizabeth,* volume II, page 319, describes his extravagant appearance at the Tilt yard in 1581, as follows – "Sir T. Perrot and Master Cooke were both in like armour, beset with apples and fruit, the one signifying Adam, the other Eve, who had hair hung all down his helmet."

Some unusual features attended Sir Thomas Perrot's marriage in July 1583 at Broxbourne, Hertfordshire, to Dorothy Devereux daughter of Walter, Earl of Essex, by Lettice Knollys his wife. One source states that he married "under extraordinary and mysterious circumstances," an account of which will be found in Strype's *Life of Bishop Aylmer.* His father-in-law, who had been created first Earl of Essex in 1572, owned large estates in Wales, with a seat at Lamphey in south Pembrokeshire, and when he died in Ireland in 1576, his body was brought to Carmarthen and buried at St. Peter's church on 26 November when the Bishop of St. Davids preached the funeral sermon from Apocalypse XIV, 13.

By Dorothy his wife, Sir Thomas Perrot had an only surviving child, Penelope. The exact date of his death is not known, but it took place shortly before 1595, for in that year the widowed Dorothy married Henry (Percy) 9th Earl of Northumberland, known as the "Wizard Earl" because of his involvement with astrology and alchemy, and according to one observer he was "passionately addicted to tobacco smoking". For some years she lived an "unquiet life" with this capricious nobleman, but, reconciled, became his "most untiring petitioner and advocate". Happily, Dorothy enjoyed the friendship and support of the Queen, and in May 1605 was godmother to the Princess Mary. She died in August 1619, the Earl in 1632.

Penelope Perrot sole heiress to the paternal possessions, married a member of an old Cornish family, namely Sir William Lower of St. Wynnow's, M.P. for Bodmin in 1602, and for Lostwithiel in 1603, in which year he was knighted. He settled at his wife's residence, Trefenty. At this time the estate in Carmarthenshire consisted of the grange of Oysterlow and thirty properties, comprising 2,600 acres. In a lawsuit of 1605 one Edward Yates of Buckland contested the right of Sir William Lower of Trefenty and Penelope his wife to "the herbage of the wood called Cardiff Forest in the grange and farm of Usterlo".

A distinguished scholar and astronomer, Sir William Lower carried out many observations and experiments at Trefenty. He co-operated with Thomas Harriott, another noted astronomer and an expert mathematician who brought out the first English telescope in 1609, about a year after Galileo. During that year Lower made careful observations of the moon and drew a rough map of its surface, fortunate in having assistance from a neighbouring landowner, John Protheroe of Nantyrhebog, who, as well as being an enthusiastic student of the heavens, had established a small glass factory near London and so could produce lenses for telescopes and like instruments. Furthermore, Protheroe was blessed with remarkable eyesight which proved a valuable asset in the astronomical studies that engaged much of his time.

Early in 1610 Lower and Protheroe made a further study of the moon's features, greatly helped by a small Dutch telescope that Harriott had sent to them. In a letter to Harriott, Lower wrote that he had detected certain lineaments of the moon, adding "I must confess I can see none of this without my cylinder: yet an ingenious younge man that accompanies me here often and loves you and these studies much, sees manie of these things even without the helpe of the instrument, but with it sees them most plainielie, I mean the younge Mr. Protheroe".

On 12 April 1615 Sir William Lower died at Trefenty. Not many years later his friends died, Harriott in 1621 and Protheroe (who had been one of Harriott's executors) in the latter part of 1624.

As dower the widowed Penelope received £400 per annum charged on "the grange of Oysterlow in Abercowyn Llanfihangel". She did not remain a widow for long, and in 1619 married Sir Robert Naunton of Letherington, Suffolk, Secretary of State to King James, and Master of the Court of Wards. Sir Robert, knighted at Windsor in 1614, a favourite of the first two Stuart kings, had a distinguished career as author, scholar, courtier, diplomat, and Member of Parliament. He died on 27 March 1635. By Penelope he had an only surviving child, a daughter.

It is nor known whether the twice-widowed Penelope returned to Trefenty. As the result of her Royalist sympathies during the Civil War, she was invited by Parliament in 1645 to compound for her estate assessed at worth £800 per annum. She died some time after this, and was buried with her first husband Sir William Lower. By him she had two children, Thomas and Dorothy.

The son Thomas Lower had been posthumously born on December 1615, some eight months after his father's death. He seems to have spent part of his life at the family's Cornish home, St. Wynnow's. On 1 May 1637 he mortgaged the grange of Oysterlow to the Earl of Pembroke and the Earl of Carbery. A survey made of the grange in 1650 shows that it was then held by Lord Carbery at a yearly rent of £28 1s. 6d. It later reverted to the Trefenty family. During the Civil War Thomas Lower was a Royalist, and in February 1647 obliged to compound for the grange of Oysterlow and for lands in Cornwall. He died unmarried on 5 February 1661, and the estates passed to his sister, Lady Dorothy Drummond.

The sister, Dorothy Lower, was born in 1607, and before she was ten years old she had married Maurice Drummond, Gentleman Usher of the King's Chamber. He was knighted at Hampton Court on 10 July 1625. Dorothy also held a Court appointment, and in 1627 was a Lady of the Queen's Privy Chamber. Sir Maurice died in 1642. Dorothy spent a widowhood of some 35 years. In 1661 she inherited from her brother the Trefenty estate then consisting of the messuages and lands of Trefenty, Lower Court, Pant Dwfwn, Asgood, Astis, Park yr Abbot, Park Newydd, a tenement and a mill, a house and shop, and four unnamed tenements and lands, with a rental of £386.

Although she had spent most of her life in London, Dorothy did not forget her Carmarthenshire patrimony, and of all the owners of Trefenty is the only one whose name is still invoked in the parish of Llanfihangel Abercywyn, at least once a year. By indenture executed on 20 May 1673. Dame Dorothy granted to Piers Butler and Richard Caryll an annuity of £10 charged on her properties called Asgood, Aestis, and Park yr Abbot, to be distributed among the poor of the parish after her decease. Several years after she had died, the two said trustees discussed the charity with her daughters and co-heiresses, and by a deed made on 30 May 1695 they confirmed the charity as a perpetual rent charge to be paid by "such person or persons as from time to time should be farmers or tenants of Treventy and St. Clears, both in the said parish, by and with the advice and approbation, nevertheless, of the parson of the said parish". The tenants responsible for producing the money at that time were Daniel Evans of Trefenty, and John Halford of Pentre (the "St. Cleare" of the deed). The Lady Drummond Charity, as it is known, continues to operate.

Some leases granted by Lady Dorothy included the yearly duties and services that figured prominently in similar transactions of the 17th and 18th centuries. Thus, in £670 she leased four farms comprising 630 acres in the parish of Llanfihangel Abercywyn, to

Edmund Thurlow at a rent of £73, and rendering to lessor 4 capons at Christmas, 4 horseloads of lime of 2 shillings in lieu, a day's reaping at Trefenty by 4 men or 2 shillings in lieu, and the best beast or £5 by way of a heriot when due. Another lease was granted in the same year to Morris William, of a tenement of about 50 acres at a rent of £80, and rendering one day's ploughing at Trefenty or one shilling in lieu, one day's harrowing or six pence, a man for one day to reap corn or six pence in lieu, a couple of capons at Christmas or 2 shillings in lieu, the best beast or 30 shillings as a heriot when due and furthermore to bestow two hundred of lime in stone, being six barrels to the hundred, upon land on the tenement first broken or ploughed up.

Lady Dorothy Drummond died about 1677, in which year her will was proved. She had four daughters among whom the family estates were divided. Only the eldest need concern us here, Penelope Drummond, who married Edmund Plowden of Plowden Hall, near Lydbury, head of a long-descended Roman Catholic family in Shropshire; he also owned an estate at Aston-le-Walls in Northamptonshire. His younger brother, Francis was Comptroller of the Household to King James II. Edmund Plowden died in 1677 at the comparatively early age of 37, and Penelope, who lived latterly in London, died in 1699. They had five sons and a daughter. Of the sons, four became Jesuits, and only one, William Plowden, remained "in the world" and served as a Colonel in the Life Guards of King James II, thus inheriting the estates, although a younger son. The only daughter, Dorothy Plowden, noted for her luxurious hair which measured five cascading feet, married firstly Philip Draycott, secondly Sir William Goring.

From this time onwards the Trefenty estate remained in possession of the Plowdens who resided wholly at their English residences, and Trefenty continued to be let to substantial farming tenants. They also continued to be lords of the manor and grange of Oysterlow, of which Trefenty was the capital messuage, and to appoint stewards and other manorial officials from among local people. The acreage of the Trefenty estate had remained fairly constant, and in the Land-owners' Return, printed in 1873, William Henry Francis Plowden (died in July 1870) is recorded as owning 1,285 acres in Carmarthenshire, yielding an estimated rental of £5,746. About that time Trefenty was sold to the Ecclesiastical Commissioners and remained in their possession until 1920 when, in accordance with the Welsh Church Acts following the Disestablishment, the ownership was transferred to the University of Wales, the present landlord. The Plowdens, descendants of the earliest known owners of Trefenty, still reside at their attractive Shropshire seat.

The House, Environs, and some tenants of Trefenty
The house of Trefenty occupies a small plateau-like elevation, 142 feet above sea-level, commanding a splendid prospect of the surrounding countryside. It is flanked by lawns on the north and west sides, with traces of a former ha-ha separating them from the meadow beyond. The outer perimeter of the lawn on the south side had been enclosed by a wall which was removed in the period 1888-1906. Immediately to the east is a large walled garden, and beyond that, modern outbuildings.

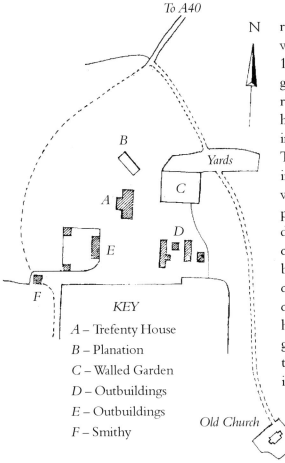

To A40

N

B

Yards

C

A

D

E

F

KEY

A – Trefenty House
B – Planation
C – Walled Garden
D – Outbuildings
E – Outbuildings
F – Smithy

Old Church

Trefenty as shown on the Tithe Map of 1841
(not to scale)

The stone-built, three-storeyed residence, with the main entrance on the west front, probably dates from the early 17th century. Until recently the southern gable-end was weather-tiled, and the removal of the tiling revealed windows that had been blocked, doubtless to reduce the incidence of window tax of earlier days. The wall has now been cemented, alas. An imposing structure, with walls of great width and strength, the house possesses a puzzling feature. As it now stands it is a double-pile house with 17th century characteristics, except that the roof valley between the piles is broad, with four chimney stacks grouped together in the centre, whereas in the usual double-pile house the chimneys are placed in the gable-ends. Unfortunately, in the 1936s the interior was remodelled and modernised so radically (it is now divided into three houses) as to render it impossible to determine with certainty the original plan and arrangements.

For the accompanying drawing of the house as it is today I am grateful to the artistry of Mrs. E. M. Lodwick which has contributed so notably over the years to our appreciation of the landscape as well as preserving a pictorial record of the ancient buildings of Carmarthenshire.

No early plans exist to guide us, and the earliest known map, at least which provides the outline ground plan, is the tithe map of the parish, surveyed and drawn in 1841. This delineates the mansion, and a short distance immediately to the south of it, two groups of outbuildings. Those at the south-western end consisted of one fairly large building (still existing with a ground and upper floor, two dormer windows, and fireplaces) once used as a dwelling probably for servants; and three smaller structures, one of which is described as "smith's shop". The group at the south-eastern end, below the walled garden, also consisted of four buildings, two being fairly large. Flanking the mansion beyond the lawn on the north, grew a plantation.

Between 1841 and 1888 radical changes had taken place. All, save one, of the buildings on the south-western side were taken down, their foundations today being overgrown with grass. Traces of the smithy remain. The group on the south-eastern side was wholly demolished, the site now covered with rough grass and rushes. Following the demolition, a

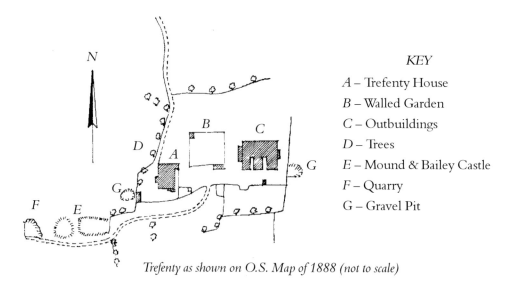

KEY

A – Trefenty House
B – Walled Garden
C – Outbuildings
D – Trees
E – Mound & Bailey Castle
F – Quarry
G – Gravel Pit

Trefenty as shown on O.S. Map of 1888 (not to scale)

large and imposing range of outbuildings was erected on a virgin site immediately to the east of the walled garden, and continue to fulfil the purpose for which they were built, and, indeed can claim to be among the best in the country. I am indebted to Mr. K. T. Lenny of John Francis, Thomas Jones, and Sons for the outline ground plans of Trefenty and its buildings in 1841 and 1888.

On the 1841 map the Plowden properties in the parish are listed as Trefenty (301 acres), Foxhole (179 acres), Dole Wirion (9 acres), Gwanfy (8 acres), Pant Dwfwn (371 acres), all in the tenancy of John Waters, and Lower Court (401 acres) in the tenancy of William Thomas, the whole amounting to some 1,269 acres at that time.

Trefenty and neighbouring farms were fortunate inasmuch as their lime kilns could be supplied by coastal vessels. The tithe map shows a lime kiln at Pont ddu on the Cywyn, and another to the north of Foxhole on the Tâf. And there may have been others, for one of Trefenty's fields is still called Parc yr Odin. The marshlands along the river banks had to be protected from erosion and inundation particularly from high tides. Canon Conrad Evans has quoted a record of 1675-6 among the Plowden archives, which states that numerous boatloads of stone were brought "to the severall causeways at Treventy made for the preservation of the marsh from the sea".

Generally, the tenants of Trefenty were men of substance. On 20 August 1661 Dame Dorothy Drummond, widow, granted a lease of 21 years of Trefenty to John Evans of Talybont in the neigh-bouring parish of Llandeilo Abercywyn, and William Smith of Llanfihangel Abercywyn, gentlemen. This John Evans was one of the three sons of David Evans of Llechwedd Deri in Cardiganshire, High Sheriff of that county in 1641. David's two younger sons settled in Carmarthenshire, Rees (who married Anne Lloyd of Plas Llanstephan) at Talybont where he died in 1697, and John who lived at Talybont before coming to Trefenty in 1661. John Evans paid £1 14s. 0d. in respect of a subsidy in 1673, being the highest payment in the parish, and in 1688 was High Sheriff of Carmarthenshire – the only time that the appointment was held by a resident of Trefenty. His will was proved in 1691.

Much later, on 5 November 1745, William Plowden esquire, granted a lease of 21 years of Trefenty (then 256 acres) to John Jenkins of the same parish, yeoman, at a yearly rent of £87.

In 1778, Trefenty and Foxhole tenanted by John Jenkins and Lewis Evan respectively, were advertised to let as good farmhouses with convenient outhouses in good and tenantable repair, with upwards of 450 acres in excellent heart. On each farm there was a lime kiln situated within 20 yards from the river banks where coal and limestone could be landed for their use. The Waters family took the farms, and continued the tenancy of Trefenty in John Jenkins for a few more years. Prior to this advertisement the house seems to have required repair, for on 5 July 1778, John Philipps of Carmarthen, agent for Plowden, wrote to the owner that Trefenty had been "repaired since you were there, excepting a few yards of the tyling which is to be done". This suggests that Plowden had visited the house, perhaps staying there on short visits off and on.

Llandeilo Abercywyn

Llandeilo Abercywyn window detail

The Waters family came into local prominence in the latter part of the 18th century. Members of the family farmed some of the largest farms in the district – Gardde, Rushmoor, Pant Dwfwn, Fox-hole, Trefenty, and in the first part of the 19th century, Sarnau, where they built a small attractive residence. They came to Trefenty about 1778, and on 20 August 1816, Edmund Plowden gave a lease (probably a renewal) of Trefenty, Foxhole, and Pant Dwfwn, for 62 years to Thomas Waters, and in 1798 he obtained a lease of Llandeilo Abercywyn farm from Philip Protheroe of Bristol, so that he had become one of the largest farmers in the county. He prospered sufficiently to establish a private bank, "Thomas Waters and Sons", at Carmarthen. When Thomas died in 1819 at the age of 70, the bank passed to his sons, one of whom, John, lived at Trefenty, becoming a burgess of Carmarthen in 1818 and later a Justice of the Peace for the county. Alas, as a result of the depression from about 1828 onwards, the bank foundered, in 1832 had to suspend payment and the firm was declared bankrupt. After this, John Waters lived wholly at Trefenty where he died on 6 February 1852 at the age of 64. He was the last to be buried in the old churchyard of Llanfihangel Abercywyn.

Some episodes in Trefenty history

In the *Antiquities of Laugharne* (1880) Mary Curtis has this to say about "the farmhouse called Treventy which occupies the site of a monastery. I visited this house which is large and substantially built, the walls enormously thick, bearing marks of great age . . . I have been told that the dairy only is part of it [monastery]; that the kitchen before it was altered was a curious place. It is divided into two, and appears more ancient than the rest of the house. There was, a while ago, in front of the house, a passage with a roof to it, along which funerals had a right to pass to the church; out of it they have formed two rooms. At the back of the house I observed some walls looking very old. About ten minutes' walk from this farm, on the St. Clears side of it, is a small cottage very ancient, the walls exceedingly thick; it is called 'Treventy Gate'." She adds this about Trefenty mansion – "Opposite the front of the house, the river way, are earth works; here tradition says a battle was fought" – this is the castell of which I have spoken earlier.

Reference to the funeral practice is contained also in D. E. Jenkins's *Life of the Rev. Thomas Charles, B.A., of Bala,* published in 1908. He wrote, "Another custom of the parish is the old passage in the farmhouse of Treventy . . . Funerals weddings, and the ordinary congregation had to pass through on their way to Church, and each individual had to present his (or her) name to the tenant of Treventy on passing through. There was no public way passing the Church, and the owner of the Manor of Oysterlow Grange had no desire to forfeit his right and allow the public to claim a right of way; and this, probably was an ingenious contrivance whereby each person might be kept conscious of the private ownership of the path down to the Church. Even the horses and their litter had to pass with the body through the limits fixed by the old thick walls and the whitewash". In 1841 the path to the church is shown well eastwards of the house and outbuildings, and in all likelihood the custom had been discontinued before that time, and Miss Curtis tells us that the passage had existed "a while ago". Memory of it still lingers, but Mrs. Thomas the present occupier tells me no traces whatsoever remain.

Another tradition refers to an underground passage once leading from the house to the church, and thence to Llangynog church several miles away. But this class of talk is "common form", and similar tales are told of numerous mansions in Great Britain and on the Continent.

Perhaps most beguiling of all, is the local memory concerning an unconventional circumstance attending cheese making at Trefenty. About the years 1860-64, Mr. Plowden permitted a shepherd to keep two cows on the demesne. Their milk enabled him to make cheese which he sold to augment his scanty wages. As he could not afford to buy a cheese-press *(peis)* the enterprising fellow went to the deserted churchyard and took a few of the fallen headstones, and with deftness and ingenuity fashioned the necessary article, which despite its homely construction proved, thoroughly efficient. Farmhouse cheeses in those days were large and circular, often well over a foot, even two feet, in diameter, as delicious to the taste as nutritious for the system. Now, one of the stones used by the adroit shepherd bore the inscription "In memory of David Thomas", and those words came out clearly etched on the cheeses. He carried them to St. Clears and was not long before he attracted customers, one of whom having read the inscription on his purchase, observed "You have resurrected this cheese from Llanfihangel churchyard!" This caused much mirth, and thereafter the succulent produce of Trefenty became known throughout the district as "the Resurrection Cheese" – *caws yr Atgyfodiad.*

Indeed, Trefenty must be unique among Welsh mansions inasmuch as it has given a metaphor to the language. In olden days of gentry and farmer occupation, the households at Trefenty were particularly numerous, a circumstance advertised in striking manner on washing-day when the hedgerows and bushes around the house were bonneted with garments of many colours and varieties. And so, when a housewife has an unusually large "washing", she is said to have a *golch Trefenty.* As families are now much smaller, and as mechanical inventions have reduced dramatically the number of servants required on farms, washing day is no longer burdensome, often hardly noticeable, but the saying *golch Trefenty* is still heard, when for some reason the "washing" reaches formidable proportions.

My chronicle is ended. Castle, manor house, knights, courtiers, astronomers, gentry, farmers, bankers, passage, tunnel, Resurrection Cheese, wash-tub and all, I bid you adieu. Over the centuries there have been many transformations. On several occasions the ownership of Trefenty has changed hands, finally to become the fee simple of the University of Wales, an institution dedicated to the educational and intellectual progress of our people. But the land, that indestructible asset, continues unchanged. Trefenty's husbandmen still plough the fields and scatter the seed and garner the grain, still rear cattle and sheep, whose increase is devoted to human sustenance. Outwardly, the old mansion preserves in large measure its traditional appearance, adorning an environment of hill, woodland, meadow, and stream, canopied *azure* and vested *vert*, a vignette of loveliness. My visit was, in a way, a fulfilment. As I gazed seaward from the sward below the buildings, a scene from the past suddenly came alight, and I fancied I could see a vessel gliding on the placid flow, on her deck an ancient mariner, and at his side a bare-headed youth pointing excitedly towards the grey pile on the distant knoll.

SOURCES

 Archaelogia Cambrensis. 3rd Ser. Vols. XI, XII.
 Burke's *Landed Gentry.*
 Carlisle, T. *Topographical Dictionary of Wales,* 1808.
 Charity Commissioners Report, 1898.
 Complete Peerage, The.
 Cowley, F. G. *The Monastic Orders of South Wales* 1066-1349. 1977.
 Curtis, M. *The Antiquities of Laugharne,* 1880.
 Dictionary of National Biography.
 Dictionary of Welsh Biography.
 Dwnn, L. *Heraldic Visitations of Wales,* 1848. Vol. I, pp 89-90.
 Edwards, I ap O. *Star Chamber Proceedings concerning Wales.*
 Evans, Revd. Canon Conrad. *The Story of a Parish,* 1975.
 Green, F. "Early Banks in West Wales," *West Wales Historical Records,* VI.
 Jenkins, D. E. *Life and Times of Rev. Thos. Charles of Bala,* 1908.
 Jones, E. G. *Exchequer Proceedings concerning Wales.* 1939.
 Jones, Francis. "The Squires of Hawksbrook," *Trans. Hon. Soc. Cymmr.* 1938.

Jones, T. I. Jeffreys. *Exchequer Proceedings concerning Wales, temp James I.* 1955.

Landowners, Return of. 1873.

Lewis, E. A. & J. C. Davies, *Court of Augmentations concerning Wales. 1954.*

Lewis, S. *Topographical Dictionary of Wales.* 1840 edn.

Lloyd, Sir J. E. (ed). *History of Carmarthenshire.* 2 vols.

Owen's *Description of Pembrokeshire.* Vol. I (1892), 45, 213.

Nicholas, T. *County Families of Wales.* 1872.

Nichols, J. *Progresses of Queen Elizabeth.*

Royal Commissioners Ancient Monuuents Report, Carmarthenshire. 1917.

Transactions Carmarthenshire Antiquarian Society.

MAPS

Tithe Map 81 Schedule, Llanfihangel Abercywyn 1841 (in N.L.W.).

Colby, T. O.S. Map Carmarthenshire, 1830-.

Kitchin, T. Map of Carmarthenshire, 1754.

O.S. Maps of Llanfihangel Abercywyn. 6 inch and 25 inch scale 1886-1906.

Rees, W., South Wales in the 14th century.

Manuscripts

Church in Wales Records (in N.L.W.).

Francis Green, MSS (in Haverfordwest County Library).

Parish Registers, Llanfihangel Abercywyn (in Carmarthenshire Rec. Office).

Slebech Deeds (in N.L.W.).

I am grateful to the following for useful local information:

Mr. & Mrs. A. E. Thomas of Trefenty;

The Revd. Canon Conrad Evans, vicar of Llanfihangel Abercywyn;

Mr. R. T. Lenny of Messrs. John Francis, Thomas Jones & Sons, Carmarthen;

Major W. K. Buckley, M.B.E., for his comments on this essay in manuscript form.

Photo: Grenville Barrett, L.R.P.S.

Geese at Hendre Farm, Llanybri, owned by Mrs. S. Hutchinson

NASH AND DOLAU COTHI

VERY LITTLE research has been made on the architecture of country houses in Wales. We know a fair deal about the abode of farmers and cottagers since few fundamental alterations have been made in them from quite early time. However we cannot say the same of our "stately homes", since they represent period fashion in no uncertain manner, and as the occupants possessed the wherewithal they could afford to alter their houses as taste, fashion, and comfort demanded. Thus it is that today few of our country houses give us a true picture of what they looked like in olden times. Some have been altered, others added to, and many have been entirely rebuilt from time to time.

John Nash (1752-1835), who became architect to King George IV, was responsible for several of the stately houses of South Wales, and an admirable work by John Summerson, entitled "John Nash" (published 1935) gives an account of his activities in south Wales and elsewhere. Since its publication I have been fortunate enough to find additional material relating to the activities of this eminent architect in Wales. John Nash was associated with at least five other well known houses not mentioned by Mr. Summerson. These include (1) Dolau Cothi, Carmarthenshire, (2) Witston, Monmouthshire, (3) Llanaeron, Cardiganshire, (4) Foley House, Haverfordwest, and (5) Temple Druid, north Pembrokeshire.

Much architectural knowledge may be gleaned from the private papers of our ancient families, and the Dolau Cothi Manuscripts deposited in the National Library of Wales by the Revd. H. Lloyd-Johnes, give some interesting details of the house of Dolau Cothi in earlier times. The ravages of age, weather and vermin had then to be combated as in our own days.

On 28 July, 1780, J. Davies of Glyn Maes, writes to John Johnes – "I have been this morning and Tuesday before at Dolau Cothi, and all things there are at present pretty well, and William of Bryn Eglwys has, to last Tuesday, Taken and Destroyed above 80 rats, and he went off that Evening; But there are a great many of them remaining still . . .". He adds that rats have entered the barley chest near the Dairy and also the malt chest.

On 24 December, 1780, Mrs. B. Johnes, Croft Castle, writes to Mrs. Johnes of Dolau Cothi ". . . I can't help thinking Dolau Cothi an unhealthy Place from the Dampness wch always prevails even in the higth of Summer and In spightlt of large Fires, wch I was an Eye witness to . . .".

Ensign John Johnes of the 64th Regiment of Foot (afterwards squire of Dolau Cothi and father of Judge Johnes), came home on furlough from Ireland in 1787. In his diary, on 12 October, 1787, we find the entry, "Came safe to Dolecothy by two, poor old place is going to decay".

Two years later, on 15 March 1789, Mrs. Jane Johnes of Havod, writes to her brother, John Johnes of Dolau Cothi – "the Builder shall also be sent but let me beg of you to enter into no agreement with him till I see you. He can give you a plan, but I wish you would not think of any addition to the Old House. I am sure if you do, you will repent it. The situation is horrid, quite in a pool. If you were to have a new House built near where the old Pigeon House stands it would be very pretty. The old Garden would not be too great a distance from it, but I shall say no more, you must be the proper judge . . .".

On 28 March following she writes to her brother again – "I hope the builder and Brick-maker have been with you er this. Tell Mary Anne to have the shrubs and violets moved to the Garden or they will all be destroyed, and tell her to send [me] some of the violets . . .". It is not known who the "Builder" mentioned in the letters was, but in 1792 Nash was definitely on the scene. The same Mrs. Jane Johnes writes to her brother on 22 March 1792 – "I am glad Nash can make you a comfortable house by an addition to the old, for if one can save two or three hundred pound tis certainly a thing to be considered . . .".

On 17 June 1792, John Nash writes from Carmarthen to John Johnes, enclosing designs for the proposed alterations, and regrets that he did not have an opportunity, when he called at Dolau Cothi, of consulting him about the Inn and farm house mentioned by the squire in a previous letter. After his return from London, about 16 July next, he will be happy to wait on Mr. Johnes. An estimate of the alterations, exclusive of carriage and timber and lathes is £436. Chimney pieces and glass for the greenhouse, having been purchased by Colonel Johnes [of Havod] are not included in this figure.

A bill for materials bought for Captain Johnes of Dolau Cothi by John Nash, dated 22 September 1794, gives the following particulars – Two marble chimney pieces with carving and woodwork complete, £42. Two packing cases for ditto, with cartage, porterage, wharfage, sufferance, etc. £2 12s. 6d. Total, £44 12s. 6d. Received of Mrs. Johnes, £20. Balance due, £24 12s. 6d.

Nash writes again from Carmarthen on 16 October, 1794, saying that he has ordered the doors as Mr. Johnes desired. The man he bought them of will send the bill to Mr. Johnes. It will be very hard if he himself should have to pay for them. As the doors have been at Carmarthen for the last three months, there was no necessity at all for doors to have been made at Dolecothy, knowing that doors were ordered of this man.

There was evidently a hitch in the business, and on 25 November following Nash writes again to say that Mr. George has informed him that there is nothing more to be done at Dolau Cothi at present. He will be ready to wait upon him at all times, and will be in the country till the 9th December next. "Your two Chimney pieces have been here many months and may suffer from lying, besides the expense of cellar room. One of them, Mrs. Johnes paid for - the other I have paid for, when you have received and fixed them I will send you the receipt for both of them. What is to be done with the doors?"

The Mr. George referred to in the letter was Nash's Clerk of the works who was helped by one F. Compton. On 3 December 1794, John Johnes paid R. George the sum of five guineas subsistence money for F. Compton and his wife. An undated letter from Nash to Mr. Johnes may relate to this payment; he writes – "The Bearer I send to put up the steam kitchen - when it is fixed I will beg the favour of you to let the carpenter board it up and keep the rain from it," and the writer asks him to pay the man five guineas when he has finished the job as the man has to return to London from Dolau Cothi. In this year, too,

Nash at work

John Johnes acquired a billiard table, and, in his diary, on 5 September 1794, he writes – "Put up ye Billiard table, and play'd the first game on it with my eldest sister."

On 31 March 1795, some furniture came to Dolau Cothi from Carmarthen, and on 21 November following John Johnes writes – "Sent Thomas Thomas ye carpenter from ye barn, he having had possession of it 2 years 5 months and 3 weeks. Began my home Saturday June ye 15th 1793" (sic). He paid 10s. 10½d. for bricks in 1795.

On 5 January 1796 John Nash writes from Carmarthen that Mr. George is about "to leave my employment and I shall be under the necessity of assigning the care of the rest of your work to another clerk". He wishes to know whether this will be agreeable to Mr. Johnes. There is also some money owing for the bricks, "and you will please recollect that the Chimney piece is not paid for." Three weeks later, 23 January 1796, Nash writes again, enclosing his receipt and bill for the work – "The whole of the Glass ordered for Col. Johnes was sent to Hafod except some which I used (with the leave of Mr. Johnes) for my hothouse, the dimensions of which will be taken by Mr. George and for which I shall give credit to Col. Johnes – the glass therefore, which he promised you, must be had from Hafod."

On 8 February 1796, he writes from 30 Duke Street, St. James's, saying that he has drawn the bills upon Mr. Johnes as requested.

This, as far as I know, completed Nash's association with the architecture of Dolau Cothi. However repairs and alterations went on, and certain entries in John Johnes' diaries give an idea of the changes and worries of a country house over a century ago, e.g.

1797   December 17 – Paid Danl Williams ye Mason in full for building ye wall of the billiard room, £2. 10s. 1d.

1807   February 7 – ". . . one bed in ye Blue room without a blanket . . ."

1808   September 28 – Plumber here from Llandovery about ye leaden gutters.
       December 5 – Made ye Drains below ye spout trough.

1813   October 12 – David Davies begun yesterday to make a stairs from the servants hall to the room above.

1813   October 14 – Two carpenters, one copper (cooper?) here.

1814   February 11 – Barker's brother, for sweeping ye flues, 7s,

        June 15 – David Davies here yesterday and today making a frame for my room window.

        June 30 – David Davies painting my bedroom.

        July 11 – David Davies here about a cupboard for our bedroom.

        September 28 - Daniel the slater and his workmen came here about twelve. They are lathing over ye servants' hall.

        October 8 – Masons and carpenters here about the room above ye servants's hall.

        John Johnes of Dolau Cothi, whose latter years were never free from painful visitations of the gout, died in 1815. An obituary notice published on 4 November of that year says "compelled by severe paroxysms of the gout to retire from the army, he rebuilt the mansion-house of his ancestors, cultivated and improved the family estate . . .".

MIDDLETON HALL, LLANARTHNE
Now the site of the National Botanic Garden of Wales

ONE AND A HALF MILES south of the village, near the road leading southwards to Porthyrhyd. Nothing is known of this house until the advent of the Middletons who built the first mansion on which they bestowed the name Middleton Hall. Dwnn recorded several pedigrees of the North Wales Middletons, and one of the Carmarthenshire family, but no connection between these is shown, and equally, the antecedents of Henry Middleton the first of the Carmarthenshire line, remain unknown. Henry, builder of the original mansion, and High Sheriff in 1644, was succeeded by his son Christopher, High Sheriff in 1668. As the house contained 17 hearths in 1670 it would appear that it was amongst the larger residences in the county. His son Richard followed, High Sheriff in 1701, died in or about 1733, leaving a son Henry and daughter Elizabeth. Henry died without issue, and Middleton Hall and the estate passed to his only sister and heir Elizabeth Middleton. She married Thomas Gwyn of Gwempa.

        By a deed of 14 August 1745 Thomas Gwyn, Elizabeth his wife, and their eldest son and heir apparent Richard, assigned their mortgage of £2,000, of the capital messuage and demesnes of Middleton Hall, Gwempa, and other messuages, to the brothers

Thomas and William Corbett of London. The mortgage was later redeemed. Thomas Gwyn died in 1752, his wife in 1756, and their eldest son, Richard Gwyn, then settled at Middleton Hall, and became High Sheriff in 1761. On the death of his parents he received the Middleton and Gwempa estates with annual rentals of £592 and £783 respectively; and about 1746, married, against parental wishes, Elizabeth daughter of Major General Francis Fuller of Gregories, Bucks. But Richard was to set Middleton and Gwempa on the downward path. As a result of personal debts and mortgages he owed £10,000 by 1767, and was sent to the King's Bench prison where he languished until 27 May 1771 when he was discharged under the Insolvent Debtors Act of 9 George III. He was succeeded by his eldest son and heir Francis Edward Gwyn (b. 1748) who received the parental estates 'which, despite the mortgages they carried, were still extensive'. Also, he added to the mortgages and debts, which amounted to £36,909 by 12 March 1776, and was obliged to convey the estates to Messrs Froggat and Smith to sell so that the debts could be discharged. Francis Edward Gwyn was last of the family to own the Middleton Hall estate. Despite all this he lived in a blaze of glory. It commenced in 1765 when he borrowed £2,000 from his brother-in-law, George Collier (later Vice-Admiral Sir George Collier) to help him to find £3,000 to buy a commission in the army. He became a captain in Hale's Regiment of Horse, and later Lieut. Colonel of 15th Dragoons. He served as a major in North America under Generals Howe, Clinton, and Cornwallis. On 19 October 1765 he was appointed A.D.C. to King George III. In March 1794 he became Colonel of the 25th Light Dragoons, and later was appointed Governor of Sheerness. He was promoted Major General on 19 April 1794, and Lieut. General on 16 June 1799. On 30 December 1779 he had married Mary daughter of Lieut. General Charles Horneck, a lady with a portion of £3,000. She was the 'Jessamy Bride' socalled by Oliver Goldsmith who was in love with her, and had her portrait painted by Sir Joshua Reynolds. She survived her husband who died in London 'of exhaustion from age' on 13 January 1821. And so departed the former squire of Middleton Hall and Gwempa. In 1789 Middleton Hall was sold to William Paxton (later knighted) who had acquired a fortune in India. As he had political ambitions, he decided to establish a home in the County, and it was for Paxton that the celebrated architect S. P. Cockrell designed the grand mansion that was built during the years 1793-95. The verdict of contemporaries on the result seems unanimous. Lipscomb in 1802 calls it 'one of the best built and most magnificent houses in Wales'; Skrine speaks of 'the splendid modern seat of Sir William Paxton, which far eclipses the proudest of the Cambrian mansions in Asiatic pomp and splendour; this house may justly be admired for the exterior beauty of its figure, as well as for its internal elegance and decoration . . . a vast pile of Portland stone curiously chiselled and finished in the highest style of the Grecian taste . . .'; Carlisle in 1811 proclaims, 'The splendid mansion of Myddleton Hall yields to none in the Principality in its architecture and internal elegance of decoration'; and Rees in 1815 reveals that 'The present mansion of Middleton Hall is built near an old family residence bearing the same name but now converted into a farm house', and that the tower on a hilltop a little to the north of the mansion, to commemorate Nelson's victories, 'The tower (known as Paxton's folly) lately erected here after an elegant design by Mr. Cockerell'. But change was soon to be made in ownership. A sale catalogue advertised the sale of Middleton Hall on 19 August 1824. It was bought by Edward Hamlyn Adams a Jamaica merchant, whose eldest son Edward adopted the surname Abadam thereafter borne by the family. Like his predecessor, the new owner of Middleton Hall had made his fortune abroad, and like him too became a Member of Parliament for the county (in 1833), and in 1831 was High Sheriff. The family remained in possession until the opening of the 20th century. It remained empty for some years and became dilapidated. However, on 10 November 1931 the mansion was completely destroyed by fire. *Sic transit gloria mundi.*

Sources: Carms. R.O., John Francis s.c.; Carlisle, *T.D.W.;* Barber, *Tour;* Rees, *Beauties;* Lipscomb, *Journey into S. Wales;* Skrine, *Tours;* Buckley, *Sheriffs:* Burke, *Visitations,* 1855, III; Vaughan, *South Wales Squires;* Jenkins, *Llanarthney, The Destruction of the Country House;* Lloyd, *Lost Houses of Wales.*

Middleton Hall Sale Catalogue, 1824

A VALUABLE FREEHOLD ESTATE, nearly Two Thousand Six Hundred & Fifty Acres, mansion, park, residence, and lands, beautifully ornamented with wood and water, abounding with game, pheasants, and wild fowl; the waters stored with trout, tench, carp, &c.

Particulars and Conditions of Sale, of the valuable and important Freehold Estate. An highly advantageous Property for Residence and Investment, Comprising The Magnificent Mansion, Middleton Hall, adapted for the accommodation of a nobleman, or family of the first distinction, erected within a few years by an architect of the first eminence. Seated in a park, beautifully diversified in hill and dale, ornamented by fine grown timber and plantations. An extensive lake, and stream of water flowing through the lands, with waterfalls, shady groves and walks by the water side, woods, carriage drives and rides, hot and cold chalybeate and vapour baths; Capital & Extensive Range of Attached & Detached Offices of all denominations, Coach Houses, Stables, and other Out buildings, farm yard, and farming buildings, a excellent and extensive Walled Garden, well planted, Hot House, Conservatory, Green House, Grapery, Orchards, &c.

At a short distance, a pleasant Desirable Residence, or Home Farm, with all requisite buildings, Farm Houses, and Buildings, Cottages, &c, and nearly Two Thousand Six Hundred & Fifty Acres of meadow, pasture, arable, and wood land, all compact, with a beautiful tower. Erected to the Memory of the Noble Hero the late LORD NELSON, forming a grand and prominent feature in the Property, and a Land Mark in the County, opposite to which are The Ruins of Dryslwyn Castle, and the Grongar Hills, With the Towy winding to a great extent, presenting a scenery that may vie with any County, situate in the Parishes of Llanarthney and Landarrog.

About Seven Miles from Carmarthen, on the high Mail Coach Road to Haverfordwest, late the residence & property of Sir W. Paxton, Deceased: which, by direction of the trustees and executors, will be sold by Auction, By Mr. Robins, (of Warwick House, Regent Street,) at Garraway's Coffee House, Change Alley, Cornhill, London, on Thursday, 19th of August, 1824, at Twelve o'clock.

In One Lot

The Mail Coach passes from London to Carmarthen at Two o' Clock, and returns at Ten o'Clock in the Evening; the Roads are excellent, a good Neighbourhood, and Country abounding with highly Picturesque Scenery.

To be viewed by applying on the Premises, where Particulars may be had; at the Bear, Llandilo; the Inns, Carmarthen; Cold Blow Inn Narberth; the Baths, and Library, at Tenby; Blue Boar, Haverfordwest; Ship and Castle, Swansea; King's Head, Gloucester; Hotel, Hereford; Star, and Hop Pole, and Mr. Bentley, Worcester; Angel, and Star, and of Mr. Adams, Oxford; Hen and Chickens, Birmingham; Bush, Bristol; Hotel, Bath; of Messrs. Hall and Brownley Solicitors, New Boswell Court, Carey Street; at Garraway and of Mr. Robins, No. 170, Regent Street, where Tickets for viewing may be had, and Plans of the Estate seen. Tickets for viewing may be also had of Thomas Morris, Esq., Carmarthen; and of Thomas Lewis, Esq., Llandilo.

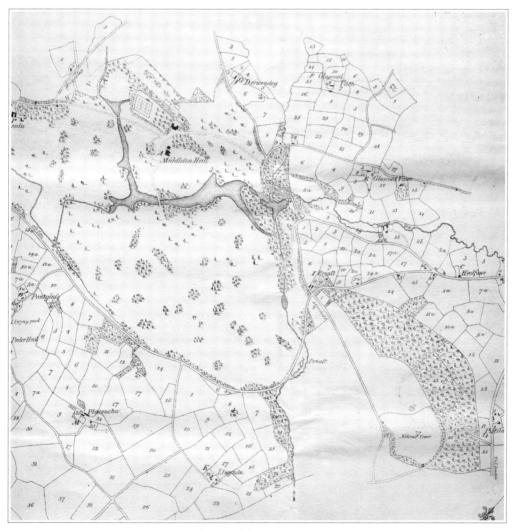

Detail from Middleton Hall Estate map

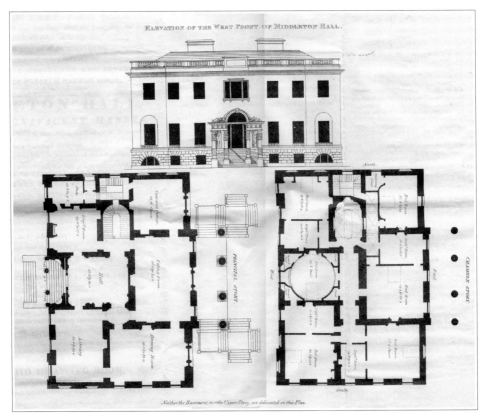

Middleton Hall floor plan

Particulars of The Valuable Freehold Estate, Abounding with Pheasants, Game, and Wild Fowl, with Waters stored with Trout, Carp and Tench, &c. Situate In the County Of Carmarthen, (Land-Tax Redeemed, except a small Part), Most Desirable for a Residence and Invest-ment, Late the Property of Sir William Paxton, deceased, comprising:

Middleton Hall – A truly Magnificent Mansion, Adapted for the Accommo-dation of a Nobleman, or Family of Distinction. Erected on a handsome Elevation, within a few years, by a very eminent Architect of the Metropolis. Seated on an elevated Spot, in the midst of a beautiful Valley, branching off to the Eastward of the River Towey, between a Chain of Hills to Llandilo and the Sea, forming A Grand and Highly Picturesque Scenery, With Lodges at the East and Western Extremities of the Estate.

The Approach on the West is from Swansea, By a long Carriage Drive, and Bridge over a Part of an extensive Lake of clear Water, considerably enlarged, and rendered highly Ornamental by the late Possessor, nearly encompassing the Lawn, on which the Mansion is seated:

On the West front there is

An Elegant Portico, with two flights of stone steps, niches on each side and figures, a Sashed Door, with sliding Shutters, leading to:

An Entrance Hall, Twenty-Six Feet by Twenty Feet, paved with Stone, ornamented by Pilasters and Recesses, the Walls Stuccoed and painted Grey, handsome Cornice, and Stone Chimneypiece;

A Library, Thirty Feet by Twenty-One Feet, finished in an elegant Style, with open Bookcases and Presses under, painted White, Walls Stuccoed and Coloured, elegant Statuary Marble Chimneypiece; communicating to

A Splendid Drawing Room, fronting the South, Commanding the most grand and extensive Views of Wood, Water, Hill, and Dale, Thirty-Three Feet by Twenty-Two Feet, walls hung with white-ground India Paper, enriched with Trees and Birds, costly Statuary Marble Chimneypiece, Venetian Windows and Columns, and Sashes to the Base, opening to Balconies; adjoining thereto,

A Noble Dining Parlour, Thirty-Six Feet by Twenty-Four Feet, with double Doors, Walls Stuccoed in Panels, Recesses and Plasters, rich Cornice and Ornaments, costly Statuary Marble Chimneypiece, Walls enriched with Entablatures of Druidical and Historical Paintings, entwined with Vine Ornaments, sashes to the base, opening to

A Grand Portico, with double Flight of

Stone Steps, and Balustre, leading to a charming Lawn, with the Lake in Front, which is overhung with beautiful Woods and Plantations, and embraces a most delightful rich scenery, scarcely to be surpassed, and forming

A Grand Amphitheatre, encompassed by the distant Hills, the Scenery of which is enlivened by a magnificent Tower;

A Breakfast Parlour, Twenty-Two Feet Square, adjoining the Dining Room, Walls Stuccoed in Panels, neat Cornice, Coved Ceiling, Venetian Windows with Columns;

A Study, Nineteen Feet by Seventeen Feet-Six, halls Stuccoed, near Cornice, Coved Ceiling, Marble and Wood Chimney-piece, folding Doors, opening to the Hall;

A Dressing Room, adjoining, Walls Stuccoed, Marble Chimneypiece, and Wood Dressings; Water Closet, &c. &c,

A Vestibule, or Inner Hall, with A handsome Principal Oak Staircase, Iron Balustre, and Mahogany Handrail, lighted by a Dome; a Secondary Brown Oak Staircase.

On the first floor, On the North Side,

A Spacious Bed Chamber, neatly Papered, Black & White Marble Chimneypiece a water closet adjoining; Lobby leading to

A Capital Bed Chamber, Twenty-Four-Feet-Four by Twenty-Two-Feet-Four, with a large *Dressing Room* adjoining, Walls handsomely Papered, near Cornice, Marble and Wood Chimneypieces in both;

Another Spacious Bed Chamber, Adjoining Twenty-Two-Feet-Four Square, and a *Dressing Room,* Walls hung with Green Paper, Marble Chimneypieces in both.

And on the South Front, *Another Bed Chamber,* Twenty-One-Feet-Two by Eighteen-Feet-Eight, Walls coloured Green; a *Dressing Room* adjoining, Walls Papered, Wood Chimneypieces in each;

A Circular Boudoir, or Ladies' Morning Room, Over the Hall, Handsomely finished with Pilasters, Circular Recesses, Walls hung with Trellis Paper, Marble and Wood Chimneypiece, Closet &c: *Lobby,* leading to

Another Bed Chamber, Nineteen-Feet-Six by Eighteen-Feet-Four, and a Dressing Room adjoining, Walls handsomely Papered, Marble and Wood Chimneypiece in each.

On the Upper Floor,

A Large Secondary Bed Chamber, Housemaid's Closet, Lobby, and *Staircase* to the Leads; and *Eight Sleeping Rooms* for Servants, with *Lobby* between; Cistern, Closet, &c.

On the Roof of the House,

A Large Reservoir for Water, which is supplied from a Spring in the Park, conveyed by Pipes, and affords a never-failing Supply to the House and Offices, Garden and Bath; On the Secondary Staircase a large Closet; Housemaid's Closet; and a Cistern to supply the Water Closets.

Basement, two large Cellars under the Drawing Room and Library; a Pantry; Porter Cellar;

A Capital Wine Cellar, Twenty-Two-Feet by Twenty, fitted up with Catacombs;

Housekeepers Room, Still Room, with Sink, and Water laid on, Dresser, Closet, and Shelves; a large Hall, for Servants, Four Closets; Men's Dressing Room; Shoe and Knife Room, paved with Stone;

An Excellent Butler's Pantry, With Range of Presses at one End, Dresser and Shelves, Sink, and Water laid on, boarded floor.

Detached Offices, Communicating by a Paved Corridore, Consisting of A Housekeeper's Store Room, with Dresser and Closet; a capital Kitchen adjoining, fitted up with Dresser and Shelves, and Paved with Stone, Lobby, leading to a Staircase, and four rooms for servants over; Adjoining the Kitchen, a Scullery, with Dresser and Sink, well supplied with good Water; a Laundry and Wash House; a Brew House, Paved; and large Cistern;

An Enclosed Yard, A Capital Dairy, paved with Stone, Wood Dressers; a Scullery adjoining; a Cheese Room, paved, and raised boarded Floor;

A Bake House, and Drying Ground, Pheasantry, Walled in; Coal and Wood Houses outside;

A Substantial Building, Erected of Brick and Stone, Rough-Cast, on an hand-some Elevation, with a Copula and Archway, containing Stables for twenty-two horses, and a box Stable, Two large Coach Houses, and Harness Room, two Staircases, four Lodging Rooms for Men, and Lofts; In Front of the Stables, in this Yard, a covered ride; A Slaughter House; a Stack Yard, with a Cottage, Boiling House, and Dog Kennel; Two Dog Kennels near the above; an enclosed Farm yard, with long range of Cow Stalls, Calf Pens, &c; near the Mansion, screened by a lofty plantation of firs, &c.

A handsome Conservatory, About Thirty-Six Feet long, stored with fine productive Vines; A flower Garden Round, and Lawn in Front, With dry gravelled Walls, and folding Gates at the Entrance; Walks through the Plantation to

Edward Adams of Middleton Hall

A Capital Kitchen Garden, Walled round, and Clothed with choice well-selected Fruit Trees, Stocked, Cropped and Planted, Containing about Three Acres;

Capital Hot House, Peachery, and Grape House, &c;

A Gardener's House, with Seed;

A Good Orchard, well Planted with Young Trees;

An Ice House, etc.

Melon Ground, Pine Pits, &c; Around the Mansion, on the East and West Sides, are Gravelled Walks, which branch in various Directions through the Park, Woods, Plantations, &c some of which lead to A beautiful Lake of fine, clear Water, of considerable Extent, serving Aquatic purposes; by the side of which there are other umbrageous walks, presenting fresh views; and lead, by a bridge, to

An Enchanting Dell, with a Flower Garden; A Rustic Building, with a Chalybeate, and vapour bath, with dressing rooms, &c; A Grotto, and a Chalybeate Spring, which has Pipes, conducting the overflow to the outside of the Park.

The Pleasure Grounds Are laid out with exquisite Taste, with delightful shady diversified Walks, (richly ornamented by Nature, and greatly improved by Art), by the Lake and Streams of Water, with

A Majestic Waterfall, Enlivened by Flower Gardens, and the interesting Scenery that alternately presents itself to the Eye. Another Ornamental Building, or Bath House, By the Side of the lake, secluded by a Grove; the interior is adapted as A Plunging Bath; and also a Hot Bath With Furnace Room; and a Dressing Room.

The Park Abounds with a Variety of other Walks and Drives, presenting a fresh and varied Scenery at almost every point; around it is the beautiful Vale, through which the Towey

Paxton's Tower

winds in grandeur; and at a distance, Dynevor Castle, the Ruins of Dryslwyn Castle, and the Grongar Hills, are seen; And on the North Side of the Park, upon the Summit of a hill, which is adorned by fine thriving Plantations (through which there is a Variety of Drives) stands

A Gothic Tower, Erected by the late liberal-minded Possessor, in Commemoration of our Noble Hero, Lord Nelson; A grand Ornament and Land Mark in the County. On the Ground Floor, Three Spacious Lofty Arches for the Admission of Carriages, On the Principal Story, *A Banqueting Room,* with Gothic Ceiling; *A Boudoir and Closet,* over which *A Prospect Room or Observatory,* with Turrets, Three of the Windows are fitted with Stained Glass, One Window representing his Lordship, the others emblematical of his Fate, From which there is a Panoramic View, of a grandeur and extent that may justly be said to stand unrivalled. On the upper Part a Lead Flat, and *Two Entrance Lodges.*

At a distance from the Mansion, within the Park, *A Pleasant and Desirable Residence,* or Home Farm, Seated on a Lawn, nearly surrounded by Plantations, containing on the Upper Story, Two Spacious Bed Chambers, and Two Dressing Rooms, neatly Papered; *A Lobby,* and *Two Bed Rooms* opposite.

On Ground Story,

A Trellis Portico Entrance to a Neat Hall;

A Drawing Room, With Circular Bowed End, Walls hung with glazed Paper, Marble and Wood Chimneypiece.

A Dining Parlour About Eighteen Feet by Sixteen Feet, Walls hung with glazed Paper, Dado black Marble Chimneypiece. A neat Study, correspondently fitted up.

Offices, Butler's Pantry, a good Kitchen, with Dresser, Shelves, &c; and Bed Room over the Larder; Store Room, &c, A Cool Dairy; Scullery; a Bake House and Brew House in one; A Yard, and Coal Hole.

Large Farm Yard. A Coach House; Stalls for Four Horses, with Loft over a Large open Cart Shed, with Granary; and Bins over; Poultry House; a Dove Cote; Yard, with Pond of Water; Cart Stable for Eight Horses; Cart House; and Nag Stable.

An enclosed fold Yard, with Barn; Straw House; Cow House; Cart Shed; Piggery; Stock Yard; Carpenter's Shop; and Saw Pit; all with Slated Roofs.

The Park contains upwards of Five Hundred and Seventy-Four Acres, in a Ring Fence, in Hand, with the Following Farms and Lands, forming a Domain of nearly 2,650 acres, viz. Middleton Hall Mansion, Park, Pleasure Grounds, Gardens, Offices, Plantations, Woods, &c. &c. 574a, 3r, 19p.

Porthyrhyd Chapel, and Burial Ground, On Lease for a Term of Nine Hundred and Ninety-Nine Years from Michaelmas 1823, at the Yearly Rent of 6s.

Porthyrhyd Chapel House, consisting of A Parlour; Kitchen; and two bed rooms over; Dairy, Back Kitchen; and School Room; Garden; Cow House, &c. In the occupation of the Rev William Williams, Tenant at Will. Admeasurement included in Wernfraidd.

Porthyrhyd Shop, consisting of A Parlour; Kitchen; Chandlers Shop; Wash-house; Two Bed Rooms over; Yard; Coal House; Garden, with Court in Front; In the Occupation of Mary Morgan, Tenant at Will.

The Lord Nelson Public House; situate On the Road Side from Carmarthen to Swansea, consisting of A Stone-Built House; With Entrance; Parlour; Kitchen; Back Kitchen; Pantries; Wash-House; Brew-House; Bed Rooms over; Stables for four Horses; Coal House; Piggeries; Garden, and Out-Buildings; containing 0a 3r 12p In the Occupation of Richard Powel, Tenant at Will.

Recapitulation – Middleton Hall Estate

	Quantity		
Description	*Acres*	*Roods*	*Perches*
Middleton Hall Mansion, Park, Pleasure Ground Plantations, Woods, Cottages &c in Hand	574	3	19
Pisteldewwy Farm	187	1	12
Heolfawr	69	2	7
Penalt Farm	46	0	9
Glascoed Vawr	103	0	25
Glascoed Vach	37	1	8
Hendrewnin	68	3	29
Derwendeg	30	3	32
Llwyndu and Reidheig	180	0	3
Placeucha	201	3	1
Weinwen	100	2	36
Gettyddiefawr	87	3	26
Gettydiefach	38	1	8
Llywynjenkin	62	1	11
Llan	112	1	15
Peder Heol	16	1	1
Pantglass	46	1	14
Twiling	35	1	4
Gorsdu	27	1	13
Llwynbach	58	3	9
Wernfraid	84	1	38
Porthyrhyd Mill	18	2	34

Description	Quantity		
	Acres	Roods	Perches
Porthyrhyd Farm	55	3	14
Lord Nelson Inn	0	3	12
Maesmynys	42	0	25
Wick	153	0	15
Brynhir	68	0	0
Lake Allotment	124	0	20
Total Freehold	2,632	3	4
Leasehold			
Penaltfach	6	1	0
Holywell	6	0	0
Total Leasehold	12	1	0
Total			
Middleton Hall Estate	2,645	0	4

There are sundry Chief Rents upon this Estate, amounting to £1 16s. 11d. of which, £1 8s. 7d. is paid by the Tenants.

There is a small modus, in lieu of Vicarial Tithes, in both Parishes.

"Going, going . . . gone!"

SNIPPET FROM EDWINSFORD

Educational Costs

Sir Rice Williams of Rhydodyn – An account of disbursements made by Rice in 1664-65, shows that he received part of his education in London, probably at an inn of court. The account includes £2 5s. 0d. for horse hire and charge from Gloucester to London, £22 for two suits of clothes, £1 to the "officers of the House" at coming to London, £14 for diet "in and out of commons during the term", £4 for lodging, £3 for three month's fencing, £1 15s. 0d. for five month's dancing; making (with other items) a total of £73. Towards this he received £69 from home, and noted "so that there remains to be paid £2 to my uncle Thomas Williams and £2 to my cousin Charles Powel", who had accommodated him pending the receipt of the allowance." According to his mother in 1676, he had spent over two years abroad, probably touring, for he never followed any calling apart from undertaking unpaid public duties in the manner of landed gentlemen of those days.

THE GWYNS OF GWEMPA

GWEMPA in Llangyndeirne (Llangyndeyrn) parish is set in a pleasant hollow in a re-entrant through which a rivulet runs westwards to join the Gwendraeth Fach about a third of a mile away. The present dwelling is of late 16th or early 17th century construction, with a massive Jacobean chimney stack rising to the full height of the house which consists of two main storeys and an attic storey, with traces of former dormer windows. In plan it was a three-unit house, with subsequent additions, for houses invariably increase in size and amenities with the growing affluence of their owners. Gwempa became one of the larger residences in the county and in 1670 was assessed at nine hearths for taxation purposes which compares favourably with its neighbours in the parish – Alltycadno, Frood, (Ffrwd), Glyn (Abbey), five hearths apiece, and the larger Torycoed with twelve. After it ceased to be a gentry residence about the beginning of the nineteenth century, the house was reduced in size and the interior rearranged to suit farming requirements. Indeed several changes were made in much later times, as, for example, the new window inserted in one pine-end a few years ago. Nevertheless it remains an impressive pile, and inclines the mind of the onlooker to the days of squirearchy when the owners set forth to attend to shrieval duties, dispensed justice in their parlours attended by Javelin men, and when ladies in patches and silks glided leisurely along the green lawns.

The stone bridge built by former owners over the stream and leading to the old drive to the house is noteworthy, also the ambitious range of outbuildings on the slope above, an usual concomitant of these ancient residences. One of the earliest owners of Gwempa was Cadwgan Fychan son of Ievan Glyn Cadwgan Fawr of Kidwelly. Cadwgan Fychan married Gwyrfil, and from their descendants come the Vaughans of Trimsaran.

In medieval times Gwempa had been the home of freeholders. About 1450 Morgan ap Morgan lived there, and his daughter and sole heiress, Margaret, brought the property to her husband, of whom nothing is known beyond his Christian name, Lewis, who came to live at Gwempa. Their son and heir, Owen ap Lewis of "Wempant alias Wempa", married Elizabeth, daughter of a neighbour, David ap Robert. They too had an only child, the heiress Margaret. She married David Gwyn son of John Gwyn of Ystlys y Coed in the parish of

Llannon. This marriage established the Gwyn family at Gwempa where it was to remain for a further seven generations. Originally the name was spelled Gwyn, but it occasionally took the forms Gwynn and Gwynne, but in this essay I shall retain the shorter spelling, for that is the form that it more usually took.

The ancestor of the Gwyns, Meredith Bwl Mawr was son of Walter ap Gwilym who traced his lineage to Cadwgan Fawr, a Breconshire magnate seated at Talgarth, (C of A Protheroe ms iv (2) fo. 194). Meredith first settled at Llandovery, and finally at Cilyrychen in Llandybie parish, and was employed locally as a trusted servant of the Crown. "Meredith Boule ap Walter", (Meredydd Bwl Mawr) was the Collector of the Royal Lordship of Mallaen in north Carmarthenshire, and in 1417 he collected the subsidy there for King Henry V's expedition to France; and as "Maurice" Boule was Beadle of Cantref Mawr in 1432/33, of Cethinog in 1435, and Eschaetor of Carmarthen in 1435/6.

Meredith Bwl Mawr had a son David, one of the men of Carmarthenshire who fought at the battle of Agincourt. The *Exchequer Accounts* (46/20) contain a list of men selected from the lordship of Iscennen to accompany Henry V's army to France in 1415, among whom the name "David ap Meredith Boule" is included. Fifth in descent from this warrior was the David Gwyn who married Margaret, heiress of Gwempa.

David Gwyn was followed at Gwempa by his eldest son John Gwyn who served as High Sheriff of the county in 1622. He married Martha daughter of Charles Vaughan of Cwmgwili by his wife Katherine Jones. His will was proved at Carmarthen in 1642, in which he mentions his son Charles and his grandson Richard. He left two children, Charles Gwyn and Catherine who married John Powell of Pentre Meurig in Llanwrda, and was mother of judge Sir John Powell.

Charles Gwyn married Jane daughter of David Evans of the Gnoll, Neath by Elinor daughter of Sir Walter Rice of Newton now called Dynevor Castle. He was High Sheriff of the county in 1646. In the Hearth Tax of 1670, Gwempa was taxed for nine hearths which shows that it was then a substantial residence. He had two sons, Richard, and Anthony Gwyn who remained at Gwempa where he made his will on 4 September 1694 which was proved on 9 March 1694/5. As he died during his father's lifetime Charles never succeeded to Gwempa. He had married Mary daughter of Leonard Bilson of Maple Durham, Hampshire by whom he had seven children, After his death Mary remarried, as his third wife in 1703, Rawleigh Mansel of Muddlescombe, (Mudlescwm), and died in June 1716. Charles's children were as follows:

1. Richard Gwyn, who succeeded his grandfather to the Gwempa estate. According to Alcwyn Evans mss, he was "an idiot, who for love and affection to his brother Thomas, and in order to enable him to marry the heiress of Middleton Hall by deed dated 1709 settled Gwempa estate, valued then at £783. 19 6 p.a., in trust on Thomas, subject to provision for himself for life, and to raising sums of money for his younger brothers Leonard, Charles and Bilson Gwyn". The deed was executed on 31 March 1709, whereby Richard "in consideration of the great love and affection" he bore to his next brother Thomas, and so that he could make a marriage settlement on Thomas should he marry, conveyed all his estates in Carmarthen, Brecon and Pembrokeshire

to him, on condition that money would he raised to provide for his other three younger brothers.

2. Thomas Gwyn, see later.

3. Leonard Gwyn who matriculated at Jesus College, Oxford, on 28 June 1710 aged 17, and was entered at Lincolns Inn in the following year. Little is known of him apart from the fact that he embarked on a military career which he ended as a Colonel. His wife, Frances, whose identity has not been established, died in 1776. They had an only son, William Gwyn who is described as of Landgnard Fort, Kent, who we learn had an only son, named after his father.

4. & 5 Charles and George Gwyn left no issue.

5. Bilson Gwyn, still living in 1768 and unmarried.

6. Mary Gwyn, only daughter, married Rowland Lewis of Torycoed, (High Sheriff 1719), son of George Lewis, vicar of Abergwili, Rowland died in 1731.

In 1709, Thomas Gwyn succeeded to Gwempa, under the terms of the deed executed by his elder brother. As the years passed one of the trustees died, and another had declined to act, and so in 1721 an Act of Parliament was obtained to rectify any defects in the deed, and by the Act conveyed two mansions and demesnes, (Gwempa and Pont Antwn), 56 farms, 3 corn mills and 2 smith-forges in south-east Carmarthenshire alone. When Thomas Gwyn inherited Middleton Hall through his wife in 1738, that estate comprised the mansion and demesne of Middleton Hall, 40 farms and 3 corn mills in four parishes. In addition there were properties in Breconshire, part of the Hay Castle estate. The annual rentals of the Gwempa and Middleton estates at this time amounted to £783 and £592 respectively. All the Carmarthenshire properties (except the capital messuage called Pont Antwn), were to be held by Thomas Brigstocke and John Howell for 1,000 (one thousand!) years, upon trust, to the use of the said Thomas Gwyn in tail male, with remainder to the right heirs of Richard Gwyn for ever, and to pay Richard Gwyn £70 p.a. for life, and £5 p.a. to Anthony Morgan for life; and upon further trust that if the money arising by sale of estates in Breconshire should prove deficient; with power to raise £2,000 for a younger son or children of the said Thomas Gwyn; with power to Thomas Gwyn to grant leases for three lives; and to make jointure for his life.

Thomas Gwyn served as High Sheriff in 1731. According to some pedigrees he married Martha, daughter of Edward Mansel of Henllys in Gower but she died without issue, however I have seen no confirmation of this; but of his marriage which took place before 1720 to Elizabeth daughter of Richard Middleton of Middleton Hall by Elizabeth Rice of Newton there can be no doubt. In 1733 Elizabeth's only brother Henry married Elizabeth daughter of Henry Price, post-master of Carmarthen and provided they had no children, Elizabeth Gwyn would be heiress to the Middleton Hall estate. Henry duly died without issue on 18 May 1738 and the estate passed to Thomas and Elizabeth Gwyn.

On 10 March 1740 their eldest son Richard placed part of the estate in the hands of Gabriel Powell and Mary his wife, George Meares, Hugh Meares, Thomas Meares and Richard Cuny, trustees in order to secure the portion of their four younger children. To raise the money for the portions Thomas Gwyn mortgaged part of his estates. Thus on

2 April 1748 Thomas Corbett loaned him £300, secured on the estate, the money to be used "towards placing out" the third son, Leonard Gwyn. Thomas Gwyn of Gwempa made his will on 20 January 1752 and died in the following June. His widow died on 31 March 1756. They had three sons and two daughters, namely:

1. Richard Gwyn inherited Gwempa and Middleton Hall. He matriculated at St. Johns College, Oxford on 17 May 1737 aged 17. He was High Sheriff in 1761. He married Elizabeth daughter of Major-General Francis Fuller of Gregories, Bucks, and his wife Christiana. Their prenuptial settlement dated 27 March 1746 states that her portion was £6000. By her he had three children, Francis Edward Gwyn, Thomas George Gwyn and Christiana who married the distinguished Vice-Admiral Sir George Collier from whom she was later divorced.

Richard Gwyn became heavily indebted to several persons and several judgements were obtained in the courts against him and he was imprisoned for some time in the Kings Bench Prison, and on 27 May 1771 was discharged under the Insolvency Act of George III. By 1767 he owed £10,000 and had to agree to sell parts of the Gwempa estates to pay the debts, and agreed that the remainder of the estates should be settled to the uses of the family. He had found difficulty in paying the £3,000 portion of his daughter Mrs. Collier, and on 22 December 1765 he borrowed the money, secured on the estate; however he failed to satisfy his daughter, and on 13 June 1769 he became bound to Sir George Collier in the penal sum of £4,000. secured to pay £2,000 and interest at 4½ per cent. In November 1767 he had to assign his estates to Mr. Inman and Mr. Lister, (who had backed him on several court actions) for 99 years if he so lived. On 17 December 1772 he was obliged to convey the capital messuage of Gwempa and other lands to William Parry, to secure the sum of £250. Things went from bad to worse, and by 1775 he owed at least £10,700. The sins of the father were visited on his eldest son and heir apparent. This was Francis Edward Gwyn who had entered on a military career. On 7 June 1765, Sir George Collier lent £2,000 being part of £3,000 to F.E. Gwyn to obtain a commission in the army.

On 13 June 1769 Francis Gwyn became 21 years of age, and as the estates were no longer in his father's hands, he inherited what was left of them. Debts still remained unpaid, and in 1773 Major Gwyn, (as he then was), decided to sell outright parts of the Gwempa estates. Things continued to deteriorate, and in 1775 he conveyed all his remaining estates to Messrs Froggett & Smith to sell and undertook to pay their costs and expenses, and to pay the following sums: £1,000 (to Sir William Mansel), £5,700 to Mrs Place, £2,000 to Sir George Collier, £1,000 to Thomas Gwyn and £1,000 to John Woodhouse, and to receive any surplus money to his own uses. The estate to be sold were expected to amount to about £3,500 while the total debts amounted to the considerable figure of £22,000. What was left of the Gwempa estate was expected to raise about £11,176 and the Middleton Hall estate about £16,500 and a further £5,325 for properties already contracted to be sold. In this way the sun set on the Gwyns of Gwempa.

Francis Edward Gwyn was the last of the family to own Gwempa. He spent most of his life away from Wales. His military career was a distinguished one. He served as a Major in the American Revolutionary War under the generals Howe, Clinton and Cornwallis, and on 9 March 1794 became Colonel of the 22nd Dragoons, Governor of Sheerness and was appointed A.D.C. to King George III. On 30 December 1779 he married at Great Barton, Staffs, Mary daughter of General Horneck, a lady of striking beauty. She was 'the Jessamy Bride', so called by Oliver Goldsmith who was in love with her, and her portrait was painted by Sir Joshua Reynolds. The prenuptial settlement is dated 6 March 1776, her portion £3000. Francis Gwyn died 'of exhaustion of age' on 13 January 1821 in Marylebone parish, City of Westminster. His wife by whom he had no issue survived him.

2. Thomas Gwyn died without issue in 1765 or 6.

3. Leonard Bilson Gwyn, baptised at Llangyndeyrn on 5 April 1728. On 2 April 1748 Thomas Corbet loaned £300 to Thomas and Elizabeth Gwyn 'towards placing out' their third son Leonard. According to his father's will (1752) £500 had been paid to settle him in partnership with Christopher Noble in the wine trade. How long he remained in the wine trade is not known, but he became Receiver of Taxes for Carmarthenshire. He took part in public life, was a JP, High Sheriff in 1769, and Mayor of Kidwelly in 1778. His wife, whom he married in 1762 was Mary Bridget daughter of Anthony Rogers of Carmarthen, heiress of her brother Lewis Rogers, (died 1776). He bought the Glyn Abbey estate, and it was there he died in 1798, leaving Glyn to his unmarried daughter Catherine. He had four children, Thomas and Leonard who both died without issue, Catherine Middleton Gwyn, Rachel who died without issue and Elizabeth Maria, born 3 March 1763, who married John Wigley of Carmarthen by whom she had John Gwyn Wigley born about 1783; she predeceased John Wigley who about 1790-1 married a second wife, Cordelia Price of Llanddewi Aberarth, Cardiganshire.

4. Mary Gwyn, married in 1740 Gabriel Powell (1710-1788) attorney, Recorder of Swansea, and Steward of the Duke of Beaufort. Their eldest son was Sir Gabriel Powell who married and had issue.

5. Elizabeth Gwyn, married Edward Brown of Plas Newydd, Llandefaelog, son of Francis Browne of Frood. He was living in 1768.

Catherine Middleton Gwyn baptised on 24 January 1771 inheritrix and last owner of the Glyn Abbey estate, seems to have been a lady of somewhat uncertain temperament. The estate at that time was large, with extensive woodlands and mines of coal and culm, yielding a considerable rental. When she was in France in 1815 she invited a Swiss, one John Henry Bodmer to become her agent and steward He accepted, and had acted in that capacity for four years when disagreements arose between them, with the result that he was dismissed by Miss Gwyn, who instigated a suit against him in the Chancery of the Great Sessions. From the papers in the case we are enabled to see the state of the property and of affairs at Glyn Abbey at this time.

The complainant stated that she owned large estates in the county, personally occupied the mansion house and demesne of Glyn Abbey, and in 1815 employed Bodmer as her agent, receiver and farm bailiff, and continued in her employment until July 1819 when she dismissed him for bad management and misconduct. During that period Bodmer resided at the mansion house and cultivated the demesne and other lands for his own use and benefit, contrary to her express instructions, cut down considerable timber and retained rents and profits of the estate and collieries without accounting for them. On dismissal he delivered an account claiming £4,246 for monies expended by him, and charged her with £568 for disbursements and expenses in connection with the cultivation of the demesne and farm, but without rendering an account of profits thereupon, and further charged her £925 for improvements made by him. Miss Gwyn said that she took him into service' in compassion when he was very poor and in indigent circumstances, having expressed his willingness to render services for a very small and trifling reward beyond his maintenance. But he also charges her in the account with £1000 as compensation for services from 15 July 1815 to 15 July 1819, whereas if the accounts were truly made it would show that a great sum was due to her. He now protests that she employed him at £150 p.a., and lately commenced an action in the Great Sessions claiming £1,038 from her'.

Bodmer had a different and more detailed tale; he belonged to a most respectable family in Switzerland, and in 1799 obtained a commission in the British army and continued in service until 1814, having been a prisoner for some years at Verdun. After the peace of 1814 he was placed on half-pay. In March 1815 he met Miss Gwyn at the house of a friend in Paris. Bonaparte landed from Elba and was expected daily in Paris, and the whole of France was in great agitation. Miss Gwyn who had no friends, attendants or servants, was extremely terrified, and finding that Bodmer intended to go to Brussels, solicited him to take a seat in her carriage to protect her. After arriving in Brussels, Bodmer procured the appointment of Military Secretary to His Serene Highness the Duke of Bouillon, and Senior Captain to the Duke's own Regiment of Foot. Miss Gwyn stayed in Brussels, and Mr. B. "paid her that attention which an unprotected female stranger, and the native of a country for which he felt every gratitude, was entitled at his hands". She told him that she owned a large property in Wales and complained of a combination by her late father's executors assisted and instigated by some of the neighbouring gentry, to deprive her or injure her property. She made advantageous offers to him if he would manage her affairs at home, and assured him that as soon as she could, by his help, terminate a most expensive Chancery Suit instituted against her by her father's executors, which had obliged her to leave the country, she would erect iron works on her estates, and place them under Bodmer's management and control, and that he would share a minority of the profits, and she also asked him to be her general and confidential agent. Until the furnace was erected he was to have more than an equivalent for the appointment he held with the Duke of Bouillon. Accordingly on 15 July 1815 he resigned his commissions, worth £300 p.a. and accompanied Miss Gwyn to England, and arrived at Glyn Abbey on the night before Kidwelly fair in October. She engaged him at £250 p.a.

They discovered that her father's executors were 'on the eve' of having a receiver appointed for the estate by the Court of Chancery. Mr. B. made up accounts and collected voluminous papers on Miss Gwyn's behalf, and went to London on her behalf, with the result that she was successful, and in undisputed possession of the estate. No trouble occurred between them until 1819. However Miss Gwyn 'has been celebrated for litigation, with no conciliatory qualities'. By her negligence and extravagance Miss Gwyn had become involved in considerable difficulties, from which she was extracted through Mr. B.'s assiduity. She was continually from home, and no sooner were her embarrassments removed by the activity of Mr. B. and while he was still harassed by creditors then, Miss Gwyn 'tormented him with applications which were out of his power to satisfy'. The erection of the proposed iron forge was delayed, and she paid no attention to his advice. Accordingly when she was away in July 1819, he wrote to her to say he could no longer stay in her house. She arrived back at Glyn Abbey on 14 July, and he left on the same day.

He denied mismanagement, and to the accusation that he had cut down valuable timber, said that those he had cut were "small and crooked", and done in order to thin out the woodland, and the timber and bark had been sold to Mr. Nevill and Mr. Pemberton for the coal pits for £43 and £38 respectively; bark to Mr. Williams and Roger Price of Carmarthen for £84 and £141 respectively, and some other timber for £53, all of which sums he delivered to his mistress. His accounts mention repairs and improvements, such as 'erecting a wing adjoining Glyn Abbey mansion with several other additional buildings, making a complete new roof thereto, and taking down the old one, taking down the entire inside of the house and completely building anew and altering the whole thereof". He built a new cart house and storehouse in the farmyard adjoining the mansion, a new roof was put on a large building containing entirely new stables, a new hay-loft, several room for servants, outhouses for the farm, making large quantities of stone culverts for conveying water to and from the farmyard, weeding extensive woods surrounding the demesne, new building a large mill with immense drains, draining boggy fields near the mansion, embanking about a mile of the river in order to protect crops from floods, new fences and hedges on almost the whole of the demesne and on the two adjoining farms, Tanerdy and Tynycoed. He claimed that £1038. 10 4½ was due to him for these works. He insisted that he had been promised a yearly salary, and produced a servant from Glyn Abbey, one Mary Rees who was in the parlour one day "putting balls on the fire" when she heard her mistress tell her great friend Miss Bassett that she allowed Mr. Bodmer £250 p.a. The outcome of the case is not known.

Her experience with foreigners had not been particularly happy, but soon after Bodmer's departure another came on the scene – Caesar Adam Marcus, Count de Witts, whom she married. The marriage took place before 26 February 1835 when further probate of her father's will was granted to her, which describes her by her married name. She died in November 1840, without issue leaving Gwempa to her nephew T. G. L. C. Powell of Swansea who took the surname Gwyn in 1841.

After the departure of the Gwyns, Gwempa was let to tenants. The coat of arms of the family above the porch and other indices of gentility, were removed, the house being adapted to farming requirements, this is the house that greets our eyes today, and despite all the changes that have taken place, continues to retain a stateliness to remind us of former days of affluence. Two large adjacent walled gardens, the upper one for flowers, strawberries, etc. the lower used as an orchard are to the rear of the house, and said to be haunted. Gwempa later became part of the Glanrhydw estate and is now owned by Mr. Thomas Lloyd, of Freestone Hall, Pembrokeshire and Court Henry, Carmarthenshire and tenented by Mr. and Mrs. Phillips.

CARMARTHENSHIRE CAMEOS

Photographs by Grenville Barrett, L.R.P.S.

Harmony in Carmarthenshire where ancient arches span tranquil waters

Carmarthenshire personality, farmer Keith Beynon with pictures of old Gellideg in its heyday

Historic Rhydarwen House in a golden valley. Owain Glyndwr once crossed the nearby ford.
On the distant hill stands Dryslwyn Castle

A wing of Glyn Abbey, once a home of culture and gracious living

BIBLIOGRAPHICAL ABBREVIATIONS

Anc Mon Pembs	Ancient Monuments Commissioners Pembrokeshire
Arch Cam	Archaeologia Cambrensis
B.B. St. Davids	Black Book of St. Davids 1326
B.G. Charles NCPN	Non-Celtic Place Names, Dr. B.G. Charles, 1938, Ldn. Medieval Studies
Burkes's L. G. 1850	Burke's Landed Gentry, 1850 edn
C of A	College of Arms, London
Carms RO	Carmarthenshire Record Office
Carms Studies 1974	Carmarthenshire Studies, presented to Major Francis Jones, ed. T. Barnes and N. Yates, Carmarthen, 1974
Chancery Proc	Chancery Proceedings Ser. II 420/40
DNB	Dictionary of National Biography, 63 vols., Ldn. 1885-1900, reprinted Oxford 1921-22
DWB	Dictionary of Welsh Biography down to 1940, London 1959
Dwnn	Heraldic Visitations see Meyrick, Samuel Rush
Fenton Tour Pembs	An Historical Tour through Pembrokeshire, Richard Fenton. 1811
Fo	Folio
G. G. MSS	Golden Grove Manuscripts
ibid	See last reference
J.B.A.A.	Journal of British Architectural Association
L.T.	Land Tax lists
Laws Little England	Laws, Little England beyond Wales, edn. 1888
Lewis TDW	Lewis Samuel, A Topographical Dictionary of Wales. Vols. 1 & 2, London 1833, 4th Edn
MS	Manuscripts
NLW	National Library of Wales
PRO	Public Record Office
Papers of G.S.	Great Sessions
Pembs RO	Pembrokeshire Record Office
Pembs Arch Svy	Pembrokeshire Archaeological Survey
Pembs Hist	The Pembrokeshire Historian
Protheroe	Protheroe Beynon Collection
R.Comm on Land in Wales	Royal Commission on Land in Wales
RCAM	Royal Commission for Ancient and Historical Monuments in Wales, An Inventory of the Ancient Monuments in Wales and Monmouthshire, London 1917
Rees, *Beauties of S. Wales*	Rees Thomas, The Beauties of England and Wales, South Wales, Vol. XVIII, London 1815
S.C. (JF) 1988	John Francis Sale Catalogues
Steegman Portraits	A Survey of Portraits in Welsh Houses, Vol. II, J. Steegman, Cardiff 1962
Taylor's Cussion	George Owen, the Taylor's Cussion, London
Thos. Lloyd, *Lost Houses*	T. Lloyd, The Lost Houses of Wales, SAVE London 1986
Timmins Nooks Pembs	Nooks & Corners of Pembrokeshire 1895. Timmins
Trans Cymmrodor	Transactions of the Honourable Society of Cymmrodorion
V.L.	Voter's Lists
W.W.H.R.	West Wales Historical Records

INDEX

Peacock at Rhydarwen

WELSH HISTORICAL SOCIETIES

Notice to all researchers of Welsh history

The National Library of Wales is a vast treasure house of Welsh records.

We highly recommend their efficient and supremely helpful staff and up-to-date facilities for any imaginable facet of past Welsh historical records.

The National Library of Wales

Aberystwyth, Ceredigion, Wales SY23 3BU

Telephone: 01970 632800   Fax: 01970 615709

www.llgc.org.uk   e-mail: holi@llgc.org.uk

Carmarthenshire Antiquarian Society

Membership Secretary: Mrs E. Dale Jones
Telephone: 01267 232085

The London Pembrokeshire Society

Hon. Secretary: David Morris
Telephone: 0208 6731767

Ceredigion Antiquarian Society

Membership Secretary: Gwyn Davies
Telephone: 01970 625818

Pembrokeshire Historical Society

Hon. Secretary: Mrs A. Eastham
Telephone: 01348 873316

THE WELSH HISTORIC GARDENS TRUST

This charitable trust was formed ten years ago to raise the profile of the historic parks and gardens of Wales and to play a role in their preservation and restoration. At that time the future for gardens in Wales looked all too bleak. Many had fallen victim to insensitive planning, lack of money or sheer indifference. Things are rather different today. There is a great deal of interest in visiting gardens of all descriptions and learning about their history. But the dangers have not gone away. If the gardens that people love to visit are to be preserved for their children and their children's children, an organisation dedicated to fostering knowledge and an informed understanding of this great national heritage is still essential.

If you would like to join the Welsh Historic Gardens Trust, please contact:

The Membership Secretary,
Peter Williams,
Llangunnor House, Crickadarn,
Builth Wells,
Powys LD8 3PJ
Telephone / Fax: 01982 560 288